CW00953850

EARLY GREEK PHILOSOPHY

VI

LCL 529

EARLY GREEK PHILOSOPHY

VOLUME VI

LATER IONIAN AND ATHENIAN THINKERS

PART 1

EDITED AND TRANSLATED BY

ANDRÉ LAKS AND GLENN W. MOST

IN COLLABORATION WITH
GÉRARD JOURNÉE

AND ASSISTED BY
LEOPOLDO IRIBARREN

HARVARD UNIVERSITY PRESS
CAMBRIDGE, MASSACHUSETTS
LONDON, ENGLAND
2016

Library of Congress Control Number 2015957358
CIP data available from the Library of Congress

ISBN 978-0-674-99707-3

Composed in ZephGreek and ZephText by
Technologies 'N Typography, Merrimac, Massachusetts.
Printed on acid-free paper and bound by
The Maple-Vail Book Manufacturing Group

CONTENTS

LATER IONIAN AND
ATHENIAN THINKERS
PART 1

25. ANAXAGORAS [ANAXAG.]

According to what seems our most reliable information, Anaxagoras was born in 500 BC and died in 428, making him an older contemporary of Empedocles. The chronology of his stay in Athens, which he visited, doubtless attracted by Pericles' cultural politics, and where he seems to have remained for thirty years, is documented but is difficult to reconstruct. It is with Anaxagoras that philosophy, which earlier had been Ionian and Italian, definitively gains a foothold in Athens—the echo can clearly be heard in the theater, especially in Euripides' tragedies (see **DRAM. T75–T80**). This development was evidently not uncontroversial; Anaxagoras was tried on a charge of impiety, the first of its kind, on the basis of a decree passed in 438/7 that made the teaching of theories regarding celestial phenomena a crime (cf. especially **P23**). From his book, which Plato tells us could be bought in the marketplace at Athens, there remain about twenty fragments; the great majority are preserved by Simplicius in his commentary on Aristotle's *Physics*. Most of these fragments come from the beginning of his book, where the indications bearing on the principles of his doctrine were concentrated: the statements that every thing contains a part of every other thing and the ones regarding the infinitely small and the organization of the world by Mind (*Nous*).

2

ANAXAGORAS

But numerous doxographical reports also provide rather precise information about his specific cosmological and physiological theories. In the interpretative tradition founded by Plato, Anaxagoras' importance derives from the role he assigned to *Nous,* but also from the distance existing between this potentially teleological principle and particular explanations, in which it was not directly applied; although this same problematic is also present in Aristotle, the latter concentrates essentially on the implications of Anaxagoras' infinitism, of which the implications remain uncertain to this day. It seems certain in any case that Anaxagoras had no qualms about paradoxes, as is suggested by his assertion that snow is black since water is too, according to Homer (**D7**).

BIBLIOGRAPHY

Editions

P. Curd. *Anaxagoras of Clazomenae. Fragments and Testimonia* (Toronto-Buffalo-London, 2007).
D. Lanza. *Anassagora. Testimonianze e frammenti* (Florence, 1966).
D. Sider. *The Fragments of Anaxagoras,* 2nd ed. (Sankt Augustin, 2005).

Studies

D. J. Furley. "Anaxagoras in Response to Parmenides" (1976), in *Cosmic Problems* (Cambridge, 1989), pp. 47–65.
J. Mansfeld. "The Chronology of Anaxagoras' Athenian

Period and the Date of his Trial," *Mnemosyne* 32
(1979): 39–69, and 33 (1980): 17–95.

M. Schofield. *An Essay on Anaxagoras* (Cambridge 1980).

OUTLINE OF THE CHAPTER

P

D

ANAXAGORAS

ANAXAGORAS [59 DK]

P

Chronology (P1–P5)

P1 (< A1) Diog. Laert. 2.6–7

Ἀναξαγόρας Ἡγησιβούλου ἢ Εὐβούλου, Κλαζομένιος. οὗτος ἤκουσεν Ἀναξιμένους [. . .] [7] λέγεται δὲ
κατὰ τὴν Ξέρξου διάβασιν εἴκοσιν ἐτῶν εἶναι, βεβι-
ωκέναι δὲ ἑβδομήκοντα δύο. φησὶ δ' Ἀπολλόδωρος ἐν
τοῖς Χρονικοῖς [*FGrHist* 244 F31] γεγενῆσθαι αὐτὸν τῇ
ἑβδομηκοστῇ Ὀλυμπιάδι, τεθνηκέναι δὲ τῷ πρώτῳ
ἔτει τῆς ὀγδοηκοστῆς[1] ὀγδόης.

---

[1] ὀγδοηκοστῆς F[3] et Meursius: ἑβδομηκοστῆς BP

P2 (< A43) Arist. *Metaph.* A3 984a11

Ἀναξαγόρας δὲ ὁ Κλαζομένιος τῇ μὲν ἡλικίᾳ πρότε-
ρος ὢν τούτου [. . . cf. **R8**].

P3 (< A5) Diog. Laert. 9.41

γέγονε δὲ τοῖς χρόνοις, ὡς αὐτός φησιν ἐν τῷ Μικρῷ

ANAXAGORAS

Chronology (P1–P5)

P1 (< A1) Diogenes Laertius

Anaxagoras, son of Hegesiboulus or Euboulus, from Clazomenae. He studied with Anaximenes [. . .]. He is said to
have been twenty years old when Xerxes crossed over
[= 480/79 BC] and to have lived seventy-two years. Apollodorus in his *Chronology* says that he was born in the 70th
Olympiad [= 500/496] and died in the first year of the
88th [= 428].

P2 (< A43) Aristotle, *Metaphysics*

Anaxagoras of Clazomenae, who was earlier than him [i.e.
Empedocles] in age [. . .].

P3 (< A5) Diogenes Laertius

As he himself [i.e. Democritus] says in his *Small Ordering*

διακόσμῳ, νέος κατὰ πρεσβύτην Ἀναξαγόραν, ἔτεσιν
αὐτοῦ νεώτερος τετταράκοντα. [. . . = **ATOM. P9**]

P4 (< A4) Cyrill. Alex. *Jul.* 1.15

ἑβδομηκοστῇ Ὀλυμπιάδι φασὶ γενέσθαι Δημόκριτον
καὶ Ἀναξαγόραν, φιλοσόφους φυσικοὺς [. . .].

P5 (A4) Eus. *Chron.*

[Ol. 80.1] Anaxagoras moritur.

The Meteorite at Aegospotami (P6–P7)

P6 (< A11) Plin. *Nat. hist.* 2.149–150

celebrant Graeci Anaxagoran Clazomenium Olympiadis
LXXVIII secundo anno praedixisse caelestium litterarum
scientia quibus diebus saxum casurum esset e sole, idque
factum interdiu in Thraciae parte ad Aegos flumen, qui
lapis etiam nunc ostenditur magnitudine vehis, colore
adusto, comete quoque illis noctibus flagrante. [. . .] [150]
in Abydi gymnasio ex ea causa colitur hodieque modicus
quidem, sed quem in media terrarum casurum idem
Anaxagoras praedixisse narretur.

of the World, he was young when Anaxagoras was old, as he was forty years younger.

P4 (< A4) Cyril of Alexandria, *Against Julian*

They say that Democritus and Anaxagoras, natural philosophers, were born in the 70th Olympiad [= 500/496] [. . .].

P5 (A4) Eusebius, *Chronicle*

[Ol. 80.1 = 460 BC] Anaxagoras dies.[1]

   [1] Perhaps this notice results from confusion between Anaxagoras' *akmê* (conventionally forty years of age) and his death.

The Meteorite at Aegospotami (P6–P7)

P6 (< A11) Pliny, *Natural History*

The Greeks record that during the second year of the 78th Olympiad [467/66][1] Anaxagoras of Clazomenae predicted, on the basis of his knowledge of the science of astronomy, the days on which a stone would fall from the sun, and that this occurred during the daytime in a region of Thrace near Aegospotami; the stone is still displayed, a wagonload in size, of a scorched color; during those nights there was also a comet that blazed. [. . .] For this reason, in the gymnasium of Abydos even today one [scil. stone] is venerated, of middling size to be sure, but one of which they say that the same Anaxagoras foretold that it would fall onto the earth.

   [1] According to the inscription on the Parian Chronicle (A11 DK), the event occurred in 468/67. The *Chronicle* of Eusebius (A11 DK) dates the event to 466.

P7 (< A12) Plut. *Lys.* 12

οἱ δὲ καὶ τὴν τοῦ λίθου πτῶσιν ἐπὶ τῷ πάθει τούτῳ
σημεῖόν φασι γενέσθαι· κατηνέχθη γάρ, ὡς ἡ δόξα
τῶν πολλῶν, ἐξ οὐρανοῦ παμμεγέθης λίθος εἰς Αἰγὸς
ποταμούς. καὶ δείκνυται μὲν ἔτι[1] νῦν, σεβομένων αὐτὸν τῶν Χερρονησιτῶν. λέγεται δ' Ἀναξαγόραν προ-
ειπεῖν ὡς τῶν κατὰ τὸν οὐρανὸν ἐνδεδεμένων[2] σωμάτων γενομένου τινὸς ὀλισθήματος ἢ σάλου ῥῖψις
ἔσται καὶ πτῶσις ἑνὸς ἀπορραγέντος· [. . . = **D46**]. τῷ
δ' Ἀναξαγόρᾳ μαρτυρεῖ καὶ Δαίμαχος ἐν τοῖς Περὶ
εὐσεβείας ἱστορῶν [*FGrHist* 239 A57] ὅτι πρὸ τοῦ πεσεῖν τὸν λίθον ἐφ' ἡμέρας ἑβδομήκοντα πέντε συνεχῶς κατὰ τὸν οὐρανὸν ἑωρᾶτο πύρινον σῶμα παμ-
μέγεθες, ὥσπερ νέφος φλογοειδὲς [. . .].

[1] ἔτι ⟨καὶ⟩ Koraïs   [2] ἐνδεδεμένων A[2] ed. Ald.: ἐνδεδυ-
μένων GL: ἐνδινουμένων Koraïs

Other Predictions (P8–P9)

P8 (A6) Philostr. *V. Ap.* 1.2 (p. 3.6–12 Kayser)

τίς οὐκ οἶδε τὸν Ἀναξαγόραν Ὀλυμπίασι μὲν, ὁπότε
ἥκιστα ὗε, παρελθόντα ὑπὸ κωδίῳ ἐς τὸ στάδιον ἐπὶ
προρρήσει ὄμβρου οἰκίαν τε ὡς πεσεῖται, προειπόντα
μὴ ψεύσασθαι, πεσεῖν γάρ, νύκτα τε ὡς ἐξ ἡμέρας
ἔσται καὶ ὡς λίθοι περὶ Αἰγὸς ποταμοὺς τοῦ οὐρανοῦ
ἐκδοθήσονται, προαναφωνήσαντα ἀληθεῦσαι;

P7 (< A12) Plutarch, *Lysander*

Others say that the fall of the stone occurred as a sign of this disaster [scil the defeat of the Athenian fleet at Aegospotami in 405]. For, according to the opinion of most people, an enormous stone fell from the sky at Aegospotami. And it is displayed now, and the inhabitants of the Chersonese venerate it. Anaxagoras is said to have foretold that there would be a slippage or shaking of the bodies fastened onto the heavens and that one of them, becoming detached, would be propelled away and would fall down. [. . .] Daemachus too bears witness in favor of Anaxagoras in his *On Piety:* he reports that for seventy-five days before the stone fell, an enormous fiery body like a flaming cloud was continuously seen in the sky [. . .].

Other Predictions (P8–P9)

P8 (A6) Philostratus, *Life of Apollonius of Tyana*

Who does not know that Anaxagoras was not mistaken when, although it was not at all raining at Olympia, he appeared at the stadium under a sheepskin, predicting rain in this way, and also when he foretold that a house would fall down (for it did), and that he turned out to be right when he predicted that the day would turn to night, and that stones would be set loose from the sky near Aegospotami?

P9 (A10) Amm. Marc. 22.16.22

hinc Anaxagoras lapides e caelo lapsuros et putealem limum contrectans tremores futuros praedixerat terrae.

His Hostility to Democritus (P10)

P10 (< A1) Diog. Laert. 2.14

ἔδοξε δέ πως καὶ Δημοκρίτῳ ἀπεχθῶς ἐσχηκέναι ἀποτυχὼν τῆς πρὸς αὐτὸν κοινολογίας.

Anaxagoras at Athens (P11–P26)
His Move from Ionia to Athens (P11–P13)

P11 (< A1) Diog. Laert. 2.7

ἤρξατο δὲ φιλοσοφεῖν Ἀθήνησιν ἐπὶ Καλλίου,[1] ἐτῶν εἴκοσιν ὤν,[2] ὥς φησι Δημήτριος ὁ Φαληρεὺς [Frag. 150 Wehrli] ἐν τῇ τῶν Ἀρχόντων ἀναγραφῇ, ἔνθα καί φασιν αὐτὸν ἐτῶν διατρῖψαι τριάκοντα.[3]

[1] Καλλι<άδ>ου Meursius   [2] ἐτῶν εἴκοσιν ὤν del. Diano: ἐτῶν εἴκοσιν <ἐκεῖ διατρίβ>ων Mansfeld   [3] τριάκοντα B: λ′ P: πεντήκοντα (i.e. ν′) Marcovich

P12 (< A7) Ps.-Galen. *Hist. phil.* 3

οὗτος δὲ τὴν Μίλητον ἀπολελοιπὼς ἦκεν εἰς τὰς Ἀθήνας [. . . = **P16**].

P9 (A10) Ammianus Marcellinus, *Histories*

It is from these [i.e. the secret writings of the Egyptians] that Anaxagoras foretold that stones would fall from the sky, and, by examining the mud in wells, that there would be earthquakes.

His Hostility to Democritus (P10)

P10 (< A1) Diogenes Laertius

He seemed in some way to feel hostile toward Democritus, since he had failed to enter into contact with him [= **ATOM. R10;** cf. **R1**].

Anaxagoras at Athens (P11–P26)
His Move from Ionia to Athens (P11–P13)

P11 (< A1) Diogenes Laertius

He began to do philosophy at Athens while Callias [scil. was archon = 456], at the age of twenty,[1] as Demetrius of Phaleron says in his *List of Archons;* they also say that he spent thirty years there.

[1] According to this chronology, Anaxagoras was born in 476. Perhaps "Calliades" (archon in 480) should be read.

P12 (< A7) Ps.-Galen, *Philosophical History*

He [i.e. Anaxagoras], having left Miletus, came to Athens [. . .].

P13 (< A7) Clem. Alex. *Strom.* 1.63

οὗτος μετήγαγεν ἀπὸ τῆς Ἰωνίας Ἀθήναζε τὴν δια-
τριβήν [. . . = **P17**].

Anaxagoras' Students in Athens (P14–P22)
Euripides (P14)

P14

a (< A21) Alex. Aet. Frag. 7.1

ὁ δ᾽ Ἀναξαγόρου τρόφις[1] ἀρχαίου[2] [. . .].

[1] τρόφιμος mss., corr. Bergk   [2] αρχαιου mss. (αρχι-
διον X): χαιοῦ Valckenaer

b (< A20c) Satyr. *Vit. Eur.* (Frag. 37 Col. 1.22–25 Schorn)

ἐ[τίμ]α[1] δὲ τὸν Ἀναξαγόραν δαιμονίως . . .

[1] suppl. West

c (< A1) Diog. Laert. 2.10

[. . .] Εὐριπίδην, μαθητὴν ὄντα αὐτοῦ [. . .].

d (< A33) Gal. *Plac. Hipp. Plat.* 4.7

[. . . = **P38b**] τοῦτο λαβὼν Εὐριπίδης τὸ νόημα [. . . =
DRAM. T80].

P13 (< A7) Clement of Alexandria, *Stromata*

He brought the practice [scil. of philosophy] from Ionia to Athens [. . .].

Anaxagoras' Students in Athens (P14–P22)
Euripides (P14)

P14

a (< A21) Alexander of Aetolia

The nursling of old Anaxagoras [scil. Euripides] [. . .].

b (< A20c) Satyrus, *Life of Euripides*

He [i.e. Euripides] honored Anaxagoras extraordinarily
. . .

c (< A1) Diogenes Laertius

[. . .] Euripides, who was his student [. . .].

d (< A33) Galen, *On the Opinions of Hippocrates and Plato*

[. . .] Euripides took this idea [i.e., "I knew when I begot him that he was mortal," from Anaxagoras; cf. **P38**].

e (< A20a) Schol. in Pind. *Ol.* 1.91 (p. 38.11–12 Drach-
mann)

[. . .] Ἀναξαγόρου δὲ γενόμενον τὸν Εὐριπίδην μαθητὴν [. . . = **DRAM. T75a**].

Thucydides (P15)

P15 (≠ DK) Marcell. *Thuc.* 22

ἤκουσε δὲ διδασκάλων Ἀναξαγόρου μὲν ἐν φιλοσόφοις,[1] ὅθεν, φησὶν ὁ Ἄντυλλος, καὶ ἄθεος ἠρέμα ἐνομίσθη, τῆς ἐκεῖθεν θεωρίας ἐμφορηθείς [. . .].

---

[1] ἤκουσε . . . φιλοσόφοις post ἐμφορηθείς hab. mss., transp.
Casaubon

Archelaus (P16–P17)

P16 (< A7) Ps.-Galen. *Hist. phil.* 3

οὗτος [. . . = **P12**] καὶ Ἀρχέλαον τὸν Ἀθηναῖον πρῶτον
εἰς φιλοσοφίαν παρώρμησεν.

P17 (< A7) Clem. Alex. *Strom.* 1.63

[. . . = **P13**] τοῦτον διαδέχεται Ἀρχέλαος, οὗ Σωκράτης
διήκουσεν.

e (< A20a) Scholia on Pindar's *Olympians*

[. . .] Euripides, who was Anaxagoras' student [. . .].

Cf. also **DRAM. T76–T81**

Thucydides (P15)

P15 (≠ DK) Marcellinus, *Life of Thucydides*

Regarding his teachers, he [scil. Thucydides] studied with Anaxagoras among philosophers, because of which, Antyllus says, he was considered to be a little bit atheistic, since he had filled himself up with theory coming from that source [. . .].

Archelaus (P16–P17)

P16 (< A7) Ps.-Galen, *Philosophical History*

[. . .] and it was this man [i.e. Anaxagoras] who was the first to stimulate Archelaus the Athenian to practice philosophy.

P17 (< A7) Clement of Alexandria, *Stromata*

[. . .] He [i.e. Anaxagoras] was succeeded by Archelaus, with whom Socrates studied.

See also **ARCH. P1–P6; SOC. P8**

Pericles (P18–P22)

P18 (A15) Isocr. *Ant.* 15.235

Περικλῆς δὲ δυοῖν ἐγένετο μαθητής, Ἀναξαγόρου τε τοῦ Κλαζομενίου καὶ Δάμωνος [. . .].

P19 (A15* Lanza) Plat. *Alc.* 118c

[ΑΛ.] λέγεταί γέ τοι, ὦ Σώκρατες, οὐκ ἀπὸ τοῦ αὐτομάτου σοφὸς γεγονέναι, ἀλλὰ πολλοῖς καὶ σοφοῖς συγγεγονέναι, καὶ Πυθοκλείδῃ καὶ Ἀναξαγόρᾳ [. . .].

P20 (< A15) Plat. *Phaedr.* 269e–270a

[ΣΩ.] κινδυνεύει, ὦ ἄριστε, εἰκότως ὁ Περικλῆς πάντων τελεώτατος εἰς τὴν ῥητορικὴν γενέσθαι. [. . .] πᾶσαι ὅσαι μεγάλαι τῶν τεχνῶν προσδέονται ἀδολεσχίας καὶ μετεωρολογίας φύσεως πέρι· τὸ γὰρ ὑψηλόνουν τοῦτο καὶ πάντῃ τελεσιουργὸν ἔοικεν ἐντεῦθέν ποθεν εἰσιέναι. ὃ καὶ Περικλῆς πρὸς τῷ εὐφυὴς εἶναι ἐκτήσατο· προσπεσὼν γὰρ οἶμαι τοιούτῳ ὄντι Ἀναξαγόρᾳ, μετεωρολογίας ἐμπλησθεὶς καὶ ἐπὶ φύσιν νοῦ τε καὶ ἀνοίας ἀφικόμενος, ὧν δὴ πέρι τὸν πολὺν λόγον ἐποιεῖτο Ἀναξαγόρας, ἐντεῦθεν εἵλκυσεν ἐπὶ τὴν τῶν λόγων τέχνην τὸ πρόσφορον αὐτῇ.

Pericles (P18–P22)

P18 (A15) Isocrates, *Antidosis*

Pericles was the student of two teachers, Anaxagoras of Clazomenae, and Damon [. . .].

P19 (≠ DK) Plato, *First Alcibiades*

[Alcibiades:] They say, Socrates, that he [i.e. Pericles] did not become wise on his own, but that he associated with many wise men, like Pythocleides and Anaxagoras [. . .].

P20 (< A15) Plato, *Phaedrus*

[Socrates:] No doubt, dear friend, it is for good reason that Pericles became the most perfect of all with regard to oratory. [. . .] All the arts that are most important need to chatter idly and to explain celestial phenomena regarding nature: for that is where this sublime intelligence and effectiveness in all matters seems to come from. This is exactly what Pericles acquired, in addition to his natural capacity. For I think that when he encountered Anaxagoras, who was this kind of man, he became filled with explanations about celestial phenomena and arrived at the nature of intelligence and its contrary, matters about which Anaxagoras spoke a lot, and derived from there, so as to apply it to the art of speeches, what is useful for this.

P21 (A16) Plut. *Per.* 6

λέγεται δέ ποτε κριοῦ μονοκέρω κεφαλὴν ἐξ ἀγροῦ τῷ
Περικλεῖ κομισθῆναι καὶ Λάμπωνα μὲν τὸν μάντιν,
ὡς εἶδε τὸ κέρας ἰσχυρὸν καὶ στερεὸν ἐκ μέσου τοῦ
μετώπου πεφυκός, εἰπεῖν ὅτι δυεῖν οὐσῶν ἐν τῇ πόλει
δυναστειῶν τῆς Θουκυδίδου καὶ Περικλέους εἰς ἕνα
περιστήσεται τὸ κράτος παρ' ᾧ γένοιτο τὸ σημεῖον·
τὸν δ ' Ἀναξαγόραν τοῦ κρανίου διακοπέντος ἐπιδεῖ-
ξαι τὸν ἐγκέφαλον οὐ πεπληρωκότα τὴν βάσιν, ἀλλ'
ὀξὺν ὥσπερ ᾠὸν ἐκ τοῦ παντὸς ἀγγείου συνωλισθη-
κότα κατὰ τὸν τόπον ἐκεῖνον, ὅθεν ἡ ῥίζα τοῦ κέρατος
εἶχε τὴν ἀρχήν. καὶ τότε μὲν θαυμασθῆναι τὸν Ἀναξαγόραν ὑπὸ τῶν παρόντων, ὀλίγῳ δ' ὕστερον τὸν
Λάμπωνα τοῦ μὲν Θουκυδίδου καταλυθέντος τῶν δὲ
τοῦ δήμου πραγμάτων ὁμαλῶς ἁπάντων ὑπὸ τῷ Περικλεῖ γενομένων.

P22 (A32) Plut. *Per.* 16

καὶ μέντοι γε τὸν Ἀναξαγόραν αὐτὸν λέγουσιν ἀσχο-
λουμένου Περικλέους ἀμελούμενον κεῖσθαι συγκεκα-
λυμμένον ἤδη γηραιὸν ἀποκαρτεροῦντα, προσπεσόν-
τος δὲ τῷ Περικλεῖ τοῦ πράγματος ἐκπλαγέντα θεῖν
εὐθὺς ἐπὶ τὸν ἄνδρα καὶ δεῖσθαι πᾶσαν δέησιν, ὀλο-
φυρόμενον οὐκ ἐκεῖνον ἀλλ' ἑαυτόν, εἰ τοιοῦτον ἀπο-
λεῖ τῆς πολιτείας σύμβουλον. ἐκκαλυψάμενον οὖν τὸν
Ἀναξαγόραν εἰπεῖν πρὸς αὐτόν· "ὦ Περίκλεις, καὶ οἱ
τοῦ λύχνου χρείαν ἔχοντες ἔλαιον ἐπιχέουσιν."

P21 (A16) Plutarch, *Pericles*

They say that one day the head of a ram with only one horn was brought to Pericles from the countryside, and that the prophet Lampon, when he saw that the horn was strong and solid and had grown from the middle of the forehead, said that, of the two forces in the city, Thucydides' and Pericles', the power would pass over to one man, the one to whom this sign had appeared. But Anaxagoras demonstrated, when the skull had been cut in half, that the brain had not occupied the whole of its place, but had become elongated like an egg and had slipped out of the whole of the cavity toward the place where the root of the horn began. At the time, those present admired Anaxagoras, but a little later it was Lampon, when Thucydides was dismissed and absolutely all of the political power passed over to Pericles.

P22 (A32) Plutarch, *Pericles*

They say that Anaxagoras himself, while Pericles was busy, lay neglected, an old man, his face already covered by a veil [i.e. ready to die], and that he was starving himself to death; but when this matter was brought to Pericles' attention, he was dismayed, ran to the man immediately, and entreated him as forcefully as he could, lamenting not Anaxagoras, but himself, if he lost such a political advisor. Then Anaxagoras uncovered his face and said to him, "Pericles, those too who have need of a lamp pour oil into it."

See also **MEL. P4**

Anaxagoras' Trial (P23–P26)

P23 (< A1) Diog. Laert. 2.12, 13–14

[12] περὶ δὲ τῆς δίκης αὐτοῦ διάφορα λέγεται. Σωτίων μὲν γάρ φησιν ἐν τῇ Διαδοχῇ τῶν φιλοσόφων [Frag. 3 Wehrli] ὑπὸ Κλέωνος αὐτὸν ἀσεβείας κριθῆναι διότι τὸν ἥλιον μύδρον ἔλεγε διάπυρον· ἀπολογησαμένου δὲ ὑπὲρ αὐτοῦ Περικλέους τοῦ μαθητοῦ, πέντε ταλάντοις ζημιωθῆναι καὶ φυγαδευθῆναι. Σάτυρος δ᾽ ἐν τοῖς Βίοις ὑπὸ Θουκυδίδου φησὶν [Frag. 16 Schorn] εἰσαχθῆναι τὴν δίκην ἀντιπολιτευομένου[1] τῷ Περι- κλεῖ· καὶ οὐ μόνον ἀσεβείας, ἀλλὰ καὶ μηδισμοῦ· καὶ ἀπόντα καταδικασθῆναι θανάτῳ. [13] [. . . cf. **P40**] Ἕρμιππος δ᾽ ἐν τοῖς Βίοις φησὶν [Frag. 30 Wehrli] ὅτι καθείρχθη ἐν τῷ δεσμωτηρίῳ τεθνηξόμενος. Περι- κλῆς δὲ παρελθὼν εἶπεν[2] εἴ τι ἔχουσιν ἐγκαλεῖν αὐτῷ[3] κατὰ τὸν βίον· οὐδὲν δὲ εἰπόντων "καὶ μὴν ἐγώ," ἔφη, "τούτου μαθητής εἰμι· μὴ οὖν διαβολαῖς ἐπαρθέντες ἀποκτείνητε τὸν ἄνθρωπον, ἀλλ᾽ ἐμοὶ πεισθέντες ἄφετε." καὶ ἀφείθη· οὐκ ἐνεγκὼν δὲ τὴν ὕβριν ἑαυτὸν ἐξήγαγεν. [14] Ἱερώνυμος δ᾽ ἐν τῷ δευτέρῳ Τῶν σπο- ράδην ὑπομνημάτων [Frag. 41 Wehrli] φησὶν ὅτι ὁ Περικλῆς παρήγαγεν αὐτὸν ἐπὶ τὸ δικαστήριον διερ- ρυηκότα καὶ λεπτὸν ὑπὸ νόσου, ὥστε ἐλέῳ μᾶλλον ἢ κρίσει ἀφεθῆναι.

[1] ἀντιπολιτευομένου] <τοῦ> ἀντιπολιτευσαμένου Bergk
[2] εἶπεν mss.: εἰπεῖν <ἐκέλευσεν> Croenert
[3] αὐτῷ mss.: corr. Stephanus

Anaxagoras' Trial (P23–P26)

P23 (< A1) Diogenes Laertius

[12] Reports vary about his trial. For Sotion says in his *Succession of the Philosophers* that he was accused of impiety by Cleon because he said that the sun is a mass of red-hot metal; he was defended by Pericles himself, his student, and was fined five talents and exiled. Satyrus in his *Lives* says that he was brought to trial by Thucydides (who opposed Pericles politically) [cf. **P21**], and not only for impiety but also for supporting the Persians; and that he was condemned to death in absentia. [13] [...] Hermippus says in his *Lives* that he was imprisoned to await execution; but Pericles delivered a speech, asking the people whether they had anything to accuse him [i.e. Pericles] of in his life, and when they said they did not, he said, "And yet I am this man's student; do not allow yourselves to be carried away by slanders and do not kill the man, but listen to me and set him free." And he was set free; but he could not endure the affront, and so he killed himself. [14] Hieronymus says in Book 2 of his *Scattered Notes* that Pericles brought him into the courtroom, feeble and emaciated by illness, so that he was released, more out of pity than because of a verdict.

P24 (A17) Diod. Sic. 12.39.2

πρὸς δὲ τούτοις Ἀναξαγόραν τὸν σοφιστήν, διδάσκαλον ὄντα Περικλέους, ὡς ἀσεβοῦντα εἰς τοὺς θεοὺς
ἐσυκοφάντουν.

P25

a (A17) Plut. *Per.* 32

περὶ δὲ τοῦτον τὸν χρόνον [. . .] ψήφισμα Διοπείθης
ἔγραψεν εἰσαγγέλλεσθαι τοὺς τὰ θεῖα μὴ νομίζοντας
ἢ λόγους περὶ τῶν μεταρσίων διδάσκοντας, ἀπερει-
δόμενος εἰς Περικλέα δι' Ἀναξαγόρου τὴν ὑπόνοιαν
[. . .] Ἀναξαγόραν δὲ φοβηθεὶς ἐξέκλεψεν[1] καὶ πρού-
πεμψεν ἐκ τῆς πόλεως.

[1] ἐξέκλεψεν Emperius: ἐξέπεμψεν mss.

b (< A18) Plut. *Nic.* 23

[. . .] ἀλλ' ἀπόρρητος ἔτι καὶ δι' ὀλίγων καὶ μετ' εὐλα-
βείας τινὸς ἢ πίστεως βαδίζων. οὐ γὰρ ἠνείχοντο
τοὺς φυσικοὺς καὶ μετεωρολέσχας τότε καλουμένους,
ὡς εἰς αἰτίας ἀλόγους καὶ δυνάμεις ἀπρονοήτους καὶ
κατηναγκασμένα πάθη διατρίβοντας τὸ θεῖον, ἀλλὰ
καὶ Πρωταγόρας ἔφυγε καὶ Ἀναξαγόραν εἰρχθέντα
μόλις περιεποιήσατο Περικλῆς.

P24 (A17) Diodorus Siculus

And besides these [i.e. Phidias and Pericles, who had ordered a statue], they [scil. Pericles' enemies] falsely accused Anaxagoras the 'sophist' (*sophistês*), who was Pericles' teacher, of committing impiety with regard to the gods.

P25

a (A17) Plutarch, *Pericles*

About this time [scil. at the beginning of the Peloponnesian War] [. . .] Diopeithes proposed a law according to which those who did not acknowledge divine matters or who taught theories about celestial phenomena would be prosecuted, making use of Anaxagoras in order to direct suspicion against Pericles. [. . .] In fear he [i.e. Pericles] seized Anaxagoras in secret and sent him away from the city.

b (< A18) Plutarch, *Nicias*

[. . .] but it [i.e. Anaxagoras' theory about the light of the moon, cf. **D38**] was still secret and circulated only among a small number of people, demanding some degree of precaution or trust. For people did not tolerate the natural philosophers, who were called at that time "talkative airheads" because they reduced divinity to irrational causes, nonprovidential powers, and necessitated processes: so that Protagoras was exiled [cf. **PROT. P19**] and Pericles only barely managed to rescue Anaxagoras from imprisonment.

P26

a (A38) Plut. *Exil.* 17 607F

ἀλλ' Ἀναξαγόρας μὲν ἐν τῷ δεσμωτηρίῳ τὸν τοῦ κύ-
κλου τετραγωνισμὸν ἔγραφε [. . .].

b (< A3) *Suda* A.1981

ἔφυγε δὲ ἐξ Ἀθηνῶν Περικλέους αὐτῷ συνειπόντος.

Another Student: Metrodorus of Lampsacus (P27)

P27 (< 59 A1, < 61.2) Diog. Laert. 2.11

[. . .] Μητρόδωρον τὸν Λαμψακηνόν, γνώριμον ὄντα
αὐτοῦ [. . .] [cf. **D98**].

Character (P28–P32)

P28 (A13) Plat. *Hipp. mai.* 283a

[ΣΩ.] καταλειφθέντων γὰρ αὐτῷ πολλῶν χρημάτων
καταμελῆσαι καὶ ἀπολέσαι πάντα· οὕτως αὐτὸν
ἀνόητα σοφίζεσθαι.

P29 (< A30) Arist. *EN* 6.7 1141b3–8

διὸ Ἀναξαγόραν [. . . = **THAL. P13**] καὶ τοὺς τοιούτους
σοφοὺς μέν, φρονίμους δ' οὔ φασιν εἶναι, ὅταν ἴδωσιν

P26

a (A38) Plutarch, *On Exile*

But while Anaxagoras was in prison he was drawing [or: writing about] the squaring of the circle [. . .].

b (< A3) *Suda*

He was exiled from Athens, Pericles having spoken in his favor.

Another Student: Metrodorus of Lampsacus (P27)

P27 (< 59 A1, < 61.2) Diogenes Laertius

[. . .] Metrodorus of Lampsacus, who was his pupil [. . .].

Character (P28–P32)

P28 (A13) Plato, *Greater Hippias*

[Socrates:] He neglected the great wealth that he had inherited and lost everything—so stupid was the wisdom he practiced.

P29 (A30) Aristotle, *Nicomachean Ethics*

That is why they say that Anaxagoras [. . .] and men of this sort are wise, but not prudent, when they see that these

ἀγνοοῦντας τὰ συμφέροντα ἑαυτοῖς, καὶ περιττὰ μὲν
καὶ θαυμαστὰ καὶ χαλεπὰ καὶ δαιμόνια εἰδέναι αὐ-
τούς φασιν, ἄχρηστα δ᾽, ὅτι οὐ τὰ ἀνθρώπινα ἀγαθὰ
ζητοῦσιν.

P30 (< A13) Plut. *Per.* 16

ἀπάδοντα[1] μὲν οὖν ταῦτα τῆς Ἀναξαγόρου σοφίας,
εἴγε καὶ τὴν οἰκίαν ἐκεῖνος ἐξέλιπε καὶ τὴν χώραν
ἀνῆκεν[2] ἀργὴν καὶ μηλόβοτον ὑπ᾽ ἐνθουσιασμοῦ καὶ
μεγαλοφροσύνης.

   [1] ἅπαντα mss., corr. Valckenaer, alii alia
   [2] ἀνῆκεν Bryan: ἀφῆκεν mss.

P31 (< A1) Diog. Laert. 2.6

οὗτος εὐγενείᾳ καὶ πλούτῳ διαφέρων ἦν, ἀλλὰ καὶ
μεγαλοφροσύνῃ, ὅς γε τὰ πατρῷα τοῖς οἰκείοις παρ-
εχώρησεν [. . .].

P32 (A21) Ael. *Var. hist.* 8.13

Ἀναξαγόραν τὸν Κλαζομένιόν φασι μήτε γελῶντά
ποτε ὀφθῆναι μήτε[1] μειδιῶντα τὴν ἀρχήν.

   [1] μή mss., corr. Hercher

men do not know what is useful for themselves, and they say that these people know what is extraordinary, marvelous, difficult, and divine—but useless, since their studies are not directed toward human goods.

P30 (< A13) Plutarch, *Pericles*

This [i.e. the careful management of Pericles' household by his slave Euangelus] is in disaccord with the wisdom of Anaxagoras, if it is true that, because of his enthusiasm and nobility of spirit, he abandoned his household and left his land fallow and as pasture.

P31 (< A1) Diogenes Laertius

He was distinguished for high birth and wealth, but also for nobility of spirit, for he ceded his patrimony to his relatives [. . .].

P32 (A21) Aelian, *Historical Miscellany*

They say that Anaxagoras of Clazomenae was never seen laughing nor smiling at all.

Apothegms (P33–P41)

P33 (A28) Arist. *Metaph.* Γ5 1009b25–28

Ἀναξαγόρου δὲ καὶ ἀπόφθεγμα μνημονεύεται πρὸς τῶν ἑταίρων τινός,[1] ὅτι τοιαῦτ᾽ αὐτοῖς ἔσται τὰ ὄντα οἷα ἂν ὑπολάβωσιν.

  [1] τινός EJA[b]: τινάς recc.

P34 (cf. A48) Iambl. *Protr.* 8 (p. 48.16–18 Pistelli)

"ὁ νοῦς γὰρ ἡμῶν ὁ θεός," εἴτε Ἑρμότιμος εἴτε Ἀναξ-αγόρας εἶπε τοῦτο, καὶ ὅτι "ὁ θνητὸς αἰὼν μέρος ἔχει θεοῦ τινος."

P35 (A30) Arist. *EE* 1.5 1216a10–14

τὸν μὲν οὖν Ἀναξαγόραν φασὶν ἀποκρίνασθαι πρός τινα διαπορoῦντα τοιαῦτ᾽ ἄττα καὶ διερωτῶντα τίνος ἕνεκ᾽ ἄν τις ἕλοιτο γενέσθαι μᾶλλον ἢ μὴ γενέσθαι, "τοῦ" φάναι "θεωρῆσαι τὸν οὐρανὸν καὶ τὴν περὶ τὸν ὅλον τάξιν."

P36 (A29) Clem. Alex. *Strom.* 2.130

Ἀναξαγόραν μὲν γὰρ τὸν Κλαζομένιον τὴν θεωρίαν φάναι τοῦ βίου τέλος εἶναι καὶ τὴν ἀπὸ ταύτης ἐλευ-θερίαν λέγουσιν [. . .].

Apothegms (P33–P41)

P33 (A28) Aristotle, *Metaphysics*

A saying of Anaxagoras' is also reported by one of his companions: that beings would be for them such as they supposed them to be.

P34 (cf. A48) Iamblichus, *Protreptic* (from Aristotle, *Protreptic*)

"Our mind is god": either Hermotimus or Anaxagoras said this, and that "a mortal life has a share in a god" [cf. **R9**].

P35 (A30) Aristotle, *Eudemian Ethics*

They say that Anaxagoras said to someone who had difficulties of this sort and kept asking why one might prefer to be born rather than not to be born, "To observe the sky and the order in the universe."

P36 (A29) Clement of Alexandria, *Stromata*

For they say that Anaxagoras of Clazomenae said that the goal of life is observation and the freedom that comes from this [. . .].

P37 (A30) Arist. *EN* 10.9 1179a13–15

ἔοικε δὲ καὶ Ἀναξαγόρας οὐ πλούσιον οὐδὲ δυνάστην
ὑπολαβεῖν τὸν εὐδαίμονα, εἰπὼν ὅτι οὐκ ἂν θαυμά-
σειεν εἴ τις ἄτοπος φανείη τοῖς πολλοῖς.

P38

a (A7* Lanza) Cic. *Tusc.* 3.30

[. . .] Anaxagorae, quem ferunt nuntiata morte filii dixisse:
"sciebam me genuisse mortalem."

b (< A33) Gal. *Plac. Hipp. Plat.* 4.7

διὸ καὶ τὸ τοῦ Ἀναξαγόρου παρείληφεν ἐνταῦθα, ὡς
ἄρα τινὸς ἀναγγείλαντος αὐτῷ τεθνάναι τὸν υἱὸν εὖ
μάλα καθεστηκότως εἶπεν "ᾔδειν θνητὸν γεννήσας"
[. . . **P14d**].

P39 (A31) Val. Max. 8.7 ext. 6

quali porro studio Anaxagoran flagrasse credimus? qui
cum e diutina peregrinatione patriam repetisset posses-
sionesque desertas vidisset, "non essem," inquit, "ego sal-
vus, nisi istae perissent."

P40 (< A1) Diog. Laert. 2.7, 10–11, 13

[7] αἰτιαθεὶς γὰρ ὑπ᾽ αὐτῶν ὡς ἀμελῶν· "τί οὖν," ἔφη,
"οὐχ ὑμεῖς ἐπιμελεῖσθε;" καὶ τέλος ἀπέστη καὶ περὶ

P37 (A30) Aristotle, *Nicomachean Ethics*

Anaxagoras too seems not to have supposed that the happy man is wealthy or powerful, for he said that he would not be surprised if he seemed someone strange to most people.

P38

a (≠ DK) Cicero, *Tusculan Disputations*

[. . .] they say that when the death of his son was reported to him Anaxagoras said, "I knew that I had begotten a mortal."

b (< A33) Galen, *On the Opinions of Hippocrates and Plato*

For this reason he [i.e. Posidonius] has cited in this connection Anaxagoras' saying: when someone reported to him that his son had died, he retained his composure and said, "I knew that I had begotten a mortal."

P39 (A31) Valerius Maximus, *Memorable Deeds and Sayings*

What kind of zeal should we believe it was that set Anaxagoras aflame? When he returned to his country after a long stay abroad and saw his estates in a state of abandon, he said, "I myself would not be safe, if these had not perished."

P40 (< A1) Diogenes Laertius

[7] When he was accused by them [i.e. his relatives] of neglecting it [i.e. his patrimony], he said, "Why then don't

35

τὴν τῶν φυσικῶν θεωρίαν ἦν, οὐ φροντίζων τῶν πο-
λιτικῶν. ὅτε καὶ πρὸς τὸν εἰπόντα "οὐδέν σοι μέλει
τῆς πατρίδος"; "εὐφήμει," ἔφη, "ἐμοὶ γὰρ καὶ σφόδρα
μέλει τῆς πατρίδος," δείξας τὸν οὐρανόν [. . .] [10]
[. . .] πρός τε τὸν εἰπόντα εἰ τὰ ἐν Λαμψάκῳ ὄρη ἔσται
ποτὲ θάλαττα, φασὶν εἰπεῖν· "ἐάν γε ὁ χρόνος μὴ ἐπι-
λίπῃ." ἐρωτηθείς ποτε εἰς τί γεγέννηται, "εἰς θεωρίαν," ἔφη, "ἡλίου καὶ σελήνης καὶ οὐρανοῦ." πρὸς
τὸν εἰπόντα· "ἐστερήθης Ἀθηναίων," "οὐ μὲν οὖν,"
ἔφη, "ἀλλ' ἐκεῖνοι ἐμοῦ." ἰδὼν τὸν Μαυσώλου τάφον
ἔφη· "τάφος πολυτελὴς λελιθωμένης ἐστὶν οὐσίας εἴ-
δωλον." [11] πρὸς τὸν δυσφοροῦντα ὅτι ἐπὶ ξένης τελευτᾷ, "πανταχόθεν," ἔφη, "ὁμοία ἐστὶν ἡ εἰς Ἅιδου
κατάβασις." [. . .] [. . . = **P23**] [13] ὅτε καὶ ἀμφοτέρων
αὐτῷ προσαγγελέντων, τῆς τε καταδίκης καὶ τῆς τῶν
παίδων τελευτῆς, εἰπεῖν περὶ μὲν τῆς καταδίκης, ὅτι
ἄρα[1] "κἀκείνων κἀμοῦ πάλαι ἡ φύσις κατεψηφίσατο,"
περὶ δὲ τῶν παίδων, ὅτι "ᾔδειν αὐτοὺς θνητοὺς γεννήσας." (οἱ δ' εἰς Σόλωνα τοῦτο ἀναφέρουσιν, ἄλλοι εἰς
Ξενοφῶντα.)

[1] ἄρα mss.: "ἀλλὰ Richards

P41 (A34) Stob. 4.52b

Ἀναξαγόρας δύο ἔλεγε διδασκαλίας εἶναι θανάτου,
τόν τε πρὸ τοῦ γενέσθαι χρόνον καὶ τὸν ὕπνον.

you take care of it yourselves?"; and in the end he withdrew and devoted himself to the observation of natural phenomena, not paying any attention to political matters. And when someone said to him one day, "Do you have no care for your fatherland?" he replied, "Don't be blasphemous: for I do care for my fatherland, and indeed very much"—and pointed to the sky. [. . .] [10] [. . .] To someone who asked him whether the mountains in Lampsacus would someday become sea, they say he replied, "Yes, if time is not lacking." Asked one day for what purpose he had been born, he answered, "To observe the sun, the moon, and the sky." To someone who said, "You have been deprived of the Athenians," he replied, "Not at all, but they have been, of me." When he saw the tomb of Mausolus he said, "An expensive tomb is the image of a petrified wealth." [11] To someone who complained that he was dying abroad he said, "From every place the descent to Hades is the same." [. . .] [13] And once when both pieces of news were reported to him, one about his condemnation and the other about the death of his children, he said about the condemnation, "Nature has long since condemned both them and me," and about his children, "I knew that I begot them as mortals." (Some people attribute this saying to Solon, and others to Xenophon.)

P41 (A34) Stobaeus, *Anthology*

Anaxagoras said that there are two things that teach us about death: the time before our birth, and sleep.

Nickname (P42–P43)

P42 (< A1) Diog. Laert. 2.6

[. . . cf. **R33**] παρὸ καὶ Νοῦς ἐπεκλήθη· καί φησι περὶ
αὐτοῦ Τίμων ἐν τοῖς Σίλλοις [Frag. 24 Di Marco] οὕτω·

καί που Ἀναξαγόρην φάσ' ἔμμεναι, ἄλκιμον ἥρω
Νοῦν, ὅτι δὴ νόος αὐτῷ, ὃς ἐξαπίνης ἐπεγείρας
πάντα συνεσφήκωσεν ὁμοῦ τεταραγμένα
πρόσθεν.

P43 (A15) Plut. *Per.* 4

[. . .] Ἀναξαγόρας [. . .] ὃν οἱ τότ' ἄνθρωποι Νοῦν
προσηγόρευον, εἴτε τὴν σύνεσιν αὐτοῦ μεγάλην εἰς
φυσιολογίαν καὶ περιττὴν διαφανεῖσαν θαυμάσαντες,
εἴθ' ὅτι τοῖς ὅλοις πρῶτος οὐ τύχην οὐδ' ἀνάγκην
διακοσμήσεως ἀρχήν, ἀλλὰ νοῦν ἐπέστησε καθαρὸν
καὶ ἄκρατον ἐν μεμιγμένοις πᾶσι τοῖς ἄλλοις ἀποκρίνοντα τὰς ὁμοιομερείας.

ANAXAGORAS

Nickname (P42–P43)

P42 (< A1) Diogenes Laertius

[. . .] For this reason [i.e., the cosmogonic role of mind; cf. **D27**[1]] he was nicknamed 'Mind.' And Timon says about him in his *Mockeries* (*Silloi*):

> And they say that Anaxagoras is somewhere, valorous hero,
> 'Mind,' because he has a mind that, having suddenly awakened
> All things that were jumbled beforehand, pinched them together.

[1] Diogenes Laertius locates this episode at the beginning of the treatise, like Aëtius (cf. **ANAXAG. D3,** n. 2).

P43 (< A15) Plutarch, *Pericles*

[. . .] Anaxagoras [. . .] whom the men of that time called 'Mind,' either because they admired the great understanding, manifestly superior, that he had for natural philosophy (*phusiologia*), or because he was the first to establish as the principle for ordering the whole world not chance or necessity but pure and unmixed mind, which separates the homoeomeries[1] in all the other things, which are mixed [cf. **D27**].

[1] On the meaning of this term, see **D3,** n. 1.

Cf. also **P48**

A Doubtful Anecdote (P44)

P44 (A40) Cod. Monac. 490, f. 483v

τὸν Ἀναξαγόραν δέ φασίν τινες λόγον περὶ ἀπόρων
ζητημάτων γράψαντα τοῦτον Ἱμάντα καλέσαι διὰ τὸ
ταῖς δυσπορίαις ἐνδεσμεῖν, ὡς ᾤετο, τοὺς ἀναγινώ-
σκοντας.

Last Years and Honors (P45–P48)

P45 (< A3) Suda A.1981

καὶ ἐλθὼν ἐν Λαμψάκῳ ἐκεῖσε καταστρέφει τὸν βίον
ἀποκαρτερήσας. ἐξήγαγε δὲ τοῦ ζῆν ἑαυτὸν ἐτῶν ο΄,
διότι ὑπ' Ἀθηναίων ἐνεβλήθη ἐν δεσμωτηρίῳ οἷά τινα
καινὴν δόξαν τοῦ θεοῦ παρεισφέρων.

P46 (< A1) Diog. Laert. 2.14–15

καὶ τέλος ἀποχωρήσας εἰς Λάμψακον αὐτόθι κατ-
έστρεψεν. ὅτε καὶ τῶν ἀρχόντων τῆς πόλεως ἀξιούν-
των τί βούλεται αὐτῷ γενέσθαι, φάναι· "τοὺς παῖδας
ἐν ᾧ ἂν ἀποθάνῃ μηνὶ κατὰ ἔτος παίζειν συγχωρεῖν."
καὶ φυλάττεται τὸ ἔθος καὶ νῦν.[1] τελευτήσαντα δὴ αὐτὸν ἔθαψαν ἐντίμως οἱ Λαμψακηνοὶ καὶ ἐπέγραψαν·

ἐνθάδε, πλεῖστον ἀληθείας ἐπὶ τέρμα περήσας
οὐρανίου κόσμου, κεῖται Ἀναξαγόρας. [Anth.
Gr. 7.94]

---

[1] ⟨ἔτι⟩ καὶ νῦν Cobet

ANAXAGORAS

A Doubtful Anecdote (P44)

P44 (A40) From a miscellaneous manuscript in Munich

Some people say that Anaxagoras wrote a treatise about unsolvable problems and called it *Thong,* because he expected readers to be trussed up by its difficulties.

Last Years and Honors (P45–P48)

P45 (< A3) *Suda*

And after he reached Lampsacus he ended his life there by starving himself to death. He killed himself at the age of seventy because he had been imprisoned by the Athenians for introducing a new doctrine about god.

P46 (< A1) Diogenes Laertius

And in the end he retired to Lampsacus and died there. And when the magistrates of the city asked him what he wished to be done regarding himself, he asked that children be allowed to play every year in the month in which he had died; and this custom is preserved to the present day. When he died, the citizens of Lampsacus buried him with great honor and inscribed an epitaph:

> Here, having arrived at the farthest limit of the truth
> About the celestial world, Anaxagoras reposes.

P47 (A23) Alcid. in Arist. *Rhet.* 2.23 1398b15

καὶ Λαμψακηνοὶ Ἀναξαγόραν ξένον ὄντα ἔθαψαν καὶ τιμῶσιν ἔτι καὶ νῦν.

P48 (A24) Ael. *Var. hist.* 8.19

[. . .] καὶ βωμὸς αὐτῷ ἵσταται καὶ ἐπιγέγραπται—ὁ[1] μὲν Νοῦ ὁ[2] δὲ Ἀληθείας.

---

[1] οἱ Koraïs   [2] οἱ Koraïs

P47 (A23) Alcidamas in Aristotle's *Rhetoric*

The citizens of Lampsacus buried Anaxagoras, who was a foreigner, and they honor him to the present day.

P48 (A24) Aelian, *Historical Miscellany*

An altar has been erected for him too [i.e. besides the epitaph in his honor, cf. **P46**] and it bears an inscription, one [scil. says] that it is dedicated to Mind, another to Truth.

Iconography (P49)

P49 (A27) Richter I, p. 108 and Figures 574–75; Richter-Smith, p. 86 and Figure 49; Koch, "Ikonographie," in Flashar, Bremer, Rechenauer (2013), I.1, pp. 223, 225.

ANAXAGORAS [59 DK]

D

Only One Book (D1)

D1 Diog. Laert.

a (< A37) 1.16

οἱ δὲ ἀνὰ ἓν συγγράψαντες·[1] [. . .] Ἀναξαγόρας.

> [1] συγγράψαντες BP, γρ. F[2]: σύγγραμμα F[1]

b (< A1) 2.11

πρῶτος δὲ Ἀναξαγόρας καὶ βιβλίον[1] ἐξέδωκε συγ-
γραφῆς.[2]

> [1] βιβλίον ‹ἕν› Gigante
> [2] σὺν γραφαῖς Ruestow, alii alia

Three Summaries Going Back Ultimately to
Theophrastus (D2–D4)

D2 (< A41) Simpl. *In Phys.*, pp. 26.31–27.17

τῶν δὲ ἀπείρους τῷ πλήθει λεγόντων οἱ μὲν ἁπλᾶς

ANAXAGORAS

D

Only One Book (D1)

D1 Diogenes Laertius

a (< A37)

[...] others, who wrote only one treatise: [...] Anaxagoras.

b (< A1)

Anaxagoras was also the first person to publish a book in the form of a treatise.[1]

[1] Text and meaning uncertain.

Three Summaries Going Back Ultimately to Theophrastus (D2–D4)

D2 (< A41) Simplicius, *Commentary on Aristotle's* Physics

Among those who say that they [i.e. the principles] are infinite in number, some said that they are simple and

ἔλεγον καὶ ὁμογενεῖς οἱ δὲ συνθέτους καὶ ἀνομογενεῖς
καὶ ἐναντίας, κατὰ δὲ τὸ ἐπικρατοῦν χαρακτηριζομέ-
νας. Ἀναξαγόρας [. . .] κοινωνήσας τῆς Ἀναξιμένους
φιλοσοφίας, πρῶτος μετέστησε τὰς περὶ τῶν ἀρχῶν
δόξας καὶ τὴν ἐλλείπουσαν αἰτίαν ἀνεπλήρωσε, τὰς
μὲν σωματικὰς ἀπείρους ποιήσας· πάντα γὰρ τὰ
ὁμοιομερῆ, οἷον ὕδωρ ἢ πῦρ ἢ χρυσόν, ἀγένητα μὲν
εἶναι καὶ ἄφθαρτα, φαίνεσθαι δὲ γινόμενα καὶ ἀπολ-
λύμενα συγκρίσει καὶ διακρίσει μόνον, πάντων μὲν
ἐν πᾶσιν ἐνόντων, ἑκάστου δὲ κατὰ τὸ ἐπικρατοῦν ἐν
αὐτῷ χαρακτηριζομένου. χρυσὸς γὰρ φαίνεται ἐκεῖνο,
ἐν ᾧ πολὺ χρυσίον ἐστὶ καίτοι πάντων ἐνόντων. λέγει
γοῦν Ἀναξαγόρας ὅτι "ἐν παντὶ παντὸς μοῖρα ἔνεστι" καὶ "ὅτῳ πλεῖστα ἔνι, ταῦτα ἐνδηλότατα ἓν
ἕκαστόν ἐστι καὶ ἦν" [cf. **D26, D27**]. καὶ ταῦτά φησιν
ὁ Θεόφραστος [Frag. 228A FSH&G] παραπλησίως τῷ
Ἀναξιμάνδρῳ λέγειν τὸν Ἀναξαγόραν· ἐκεῖνος γάρ
φησιν ἐν τῇ διακρίσει τοῦ ἀπείρου τὰ συγγενῆ φέρεσθαι πρὸς ἄλληλα, καὶ ὅτι μὲν ἐν τῷ παντὶ χρυσὸς
ἦν, γίνεσθαι χρυσόν, ὅτι δὲ γῆ, γῆν· ὁμοίως δὲ καὶ
τῶν ἄλλων ἕκαστον, ὡς οὐ γινομένων ἀλλ᾽ ἐνυπαρχόντων[1] πρότερον. τῆς δὲ κινήσεως καὶ τῆς γενέσεως
αἴτιον ἐπέστησε τὸν νοῦν ὁ Ἀναξαγόρας, ὑφ᾽ οὗ διακρινόμενα τούς τε κόσμους καὶ τὴν τῶν ἄλλων φύσιν
ἐγέννησαν.

---

[1] ἐνυπαρχόντων Eᵃ· ὑπαρχόντων DEF

homogeneous, others that they are composite, nonhomogeneous, and contrary, but characterized by what dominates. Anaxagoras [. . .], after having shared in the philosophy of Anaximenes, was the first person to transform the doctrines about the principles and to supply the missing [scil. final] cause. As for the corporeal principles, he posited that they are infinite. For all the homeomers like water, fire, or gold, are ungenerated and indestructible, and they only appear to be generated and destroyed by virtue of combination and separation, since every thing is in every thing, and each thing is characterized by what dominates in it. For that thing appears as gold in which there is much that is golden, even if every thing is in it. At least, Anaxagoras says that **"in every thing there is a portion of every thing"** and **"that of which each thing contains the most, this is what it is and was most manifestly"** [cf. **D26, D27**]. And Theophrastus says that Anaxagoras speaks in a way similar to Anaximander, for the latter says that at the time of the separation of the unlimited, related things move toward each other, and that everything that was gold in the whole becomes gold, and whatever earth, earth, and similarly for each of the other things, on the idea that they are not generated but were already present within earlier [cf. **ANAXIMAND. R7–R9**].[1] As for motion and generation, Anaxagoras assigned as their cause mind, by the action of which things, in separating, generated the worlds and the nature of everything else.

[1] Theophrastus is summarizing Anaximander's theory in Anaxagorean terms.

D3 (A46) Aët. 1.3.5 (Ps.-Plut.) [περὶ ἀρχῶν τί εἰσιν]

Ἀναξαγόρας [. . .] ἀρχὰς τῶν ὄντων τὰς ὁμοιομερείας
ἀπεφήνατο· ἐδόκει γὰρ αὐτῷ ἀπορώτατον εἶναι, πῶς
ἐκ τοῦ μὴ ὄντος δύναταί τι γίνεσθαι ἢ φθείρεσθαι εἰς
τὸ μὴ ὄν· τροφὴν γοῦν προσφερόμεθα ἁπλῆν καὶ μο-
νοειδῆ (οἷον τὸν Δημήτριον ἄρτον,[1] τὸ ὕδωρ πίνοντες)
καὶ ἐκ ταύτης τρέφεται θρὶξ φλὲψ ἀρτηρία σὰρξ
νεῦρα ὀστᾶ καὶ τὰ λοιπὰ μόρια· τούτων οὖν γιγνομένων ὁμολογητέον ὅτι ἐν τῇ τροφῇ τῇ προσφερο-
μένῃ πάντα ἐστὶ τὰ ὄντα, καὶ ἐκ τῶν ὄντων πάντα
αὔξεται· καὶ ἐν ἐκείνῃ ἐστὶ τῇ τροφῇ μόρια αἵματος
γεννητικὰ καὶ νεύρων καὶ ὀστέων καὶ τῶν ἄλλων· ἃ
ἦν λόγῳ θεωρητὰ μόρια· οὐ γὰρ δεῖ πάντα ἐπὶ τὴν
αἴσθησιν ἀνάγειν, ὅτι ἄρτος καὶ τὸ ὕδωρ ταῦτα κατα-
σκευάζει, ἀλλ' ἐν τούτοις ἐστὶ λόγῳ θεωρητὰ μόρια·
ἀπὸ τοῦ οὖν ὅμοια τὰ μέρη εἶναι ἐν τῇ τροφῇ τοῖς
γεννωμένοις ὁμοιομερείας αὐτὰς ἐκάλεσε καὶ ἀρχὰς
τῶν ὄντων ἀπεφήνατο, καὶ τὰς μὲν ὁμοιομερείας
ὕλην, τὸ δὲ ποιοῦν αἴτιον νοῦν τὸν πάντα διαταξάμε-
νον. ἄρχεται δὲ οὕτως· "ὁμοῦ πάντα χρήματα ἦν" [cf.
D9], νοῦς δὲ αὐτὰ διήρηκε[2] καὶ διεκόσμησε [. . .].

---

[1] ἄρτον ⟨ἔδοντες⟩ prop. Mau   [2] διήρηκε Lachenaud:
διῆρε mss.

D3 (A46) Aëtius

Anaxagoras [. . .] asserted that the principles of the things
that are are the homeomeries.[1] For it seemed to him to be
very difficult to explain how something can come about
out of what is not, or be destroyed into what is not. In any
case the food that we ingest is simple and of a single species (like the bread of Demeter and water when we drink
it), and out of this are nourished the hair, veins, arteries,
flesh, sinews, bones, and all the other parts. But since this
happens, it must be recognized that everything that exists
is present in the food ingested and that everything grows
from out of the things that are; and that in that food there
are parts that generate blood, sinews, bones, and everything else—parts that are observed by reason. For one
should not refer everything to sensation, because bread
and water produce these things, but they contain parts
visible by reason. Given, then, that the parts (*merê*) in food
are similar (*homoia*) to the things that are generated, he
called them 'homeomeries' (*homoiomereiai*) and asserted
that they are the principles of the things that are, and that
the homeomeries are the matter, and the efficient cause is
mind, which organized everything. He begins as follows:
"All things were together" [cf. **D9**], and mind has separated them and put them in order[2] [. . .].

[1] 'Homeomeries' (or 'homeomers') is the Aristotelian term for
homogeneous substances. These terms do not go back to Anaxagoras. Cf. **R14–R15.** [2] Aëtius' formulation suggests that
the action of mind was mentioned from the very beginning of the
treatise, but this was not the case (cf. also **P42**).

D4 (< A42) (Ps.-?) Hippol. *Ref.* 1.8.1–12

[1] μετὰ τοῦτον γίνεται Ἀναξαγόρας [. . .]. οὗτος ἔφη τὴν τοῦ παντὸς ἀρχὴν νοῦν καὶ ὕλην· τὸν μὲν νοῦν ποιοῦντα, τὴν δὲ ὕλην γινομένην· ὄντων γὰρ πάντων ὁμοῦ, νοῦς ἐπελθὼν διεκόσμησεν. τὰς δὲ ὑλικὰς ἀρχὰς ἀπείρους ὑπάρχειν καὶ τὰς σμικροτέρας[1] αὐτῶν ἄπειρα[2] λέγει.[3] [2] κινήσεως δὲ μετέχειν τὰ πάντα ὑπὸ τοῦ νοῦ κινούμενα συνελθεῖν τε τὰ ὅμοια. καὶ τὰ μὲν κατὰ τὸν οὐρανὸν κεκοσμῆσθαι ὑπὸ τῆς ἐγκυκλίου κινήσεως· τὸ μὲν οὖν πυκνὸν καὶ ὑγρὸν καὶ τὸ σκοτεινὸν καὶ ψυχρὸν καὶ πάντα[4] τὰ βαρέα συνελθεῖν ἐπὶ τὸ μέσον, ἐξ ὧν παγέντων τὴν γῆν ὑποστῆναι· τὰ δ' ἀντικείμενα τούτοις, <τὸ ἀραιὸν καὶ>[5] τὸ θερμὸν καὶ τὸ λαμπρὸν καὶ τὸ ξηρὸν καὶ τὸ κοῦφον, εἰς τὸ πρόσω τοῦ αἰθέρος ὁρμῆσαι.

---

[1] σμικροτέρας mss.: σμικροτάτας Marcovich
[2] an ἀπείρους?   [3] καὶ τὰς σμικροτέρας . . . λέγει: κατὰ τὴν σμικρότητα αὐτῶν τὸ ἄπειρον λέγων Diels
[4] πάντως Diels   [5] <τὸ ἀραιὸν καὶ> C. W. Mueller

---

[3] τὴν δὲ γῆν τῷ σχήματι πλατεῖαν εἶναι καὶ μένειν μετέωρον διὰ τὸ μέγεθος καὶ διὰ τὸ μηδὲν εἶναι κενὸν καὶ διὰ τὸ[1] τὸν ἀέρα ἰσχυρότατον ὄντα φέρειν ἐποχουμένην τὴν γῆν. [4] τῶν δὲ ἐπὶ γῆς ὑγρῶν τὴν μὲν θάλασσαν ὑπάρξαι <ἐκ> τε τῶν ἐν αὐτῇ ὑδάτων, <ὧν> ἐξατμισθέν<των> τὰ ὑποστάντα[2] οὕτως γεγονέναι, καὶ ἀπὸ τῶν καταρρευσάντων ποταμῶν. [5] τοὺς δὲ ποταμοὺς καὶ ἀπὸ τῶν ὄμβρων λαμβάνειν τὴν ὑπόστασιν,

D4 (< A42) Ps.-Hippolytus, *Refutation of All Heresies*

[1] After him [i.e. Anaximenes] comes Anaxagoras [. . .]. He said that the principle of the whole is mind and matter, mind that makes, and matter that becomes. For when all things were together, mind supervened and separated and organized them. He says that the material principles are unlimited [scil. in number] and that the smaller ones among them are unlimited.[1] [2] All things participate in motion because they are moved by mind, and similar things are combined. What is in the heavens has been ordered by the circular motion: the dense, the moist, the dark, the cold, and everything heavy has combined toward the center, and the earth was formed from their solidification; what is opposed to them, ⟨the rarefied,⟩ the warm, the bright, the dry, and the light, rushed outward toward the farthest part of the aether.

[1] Text uncertain.

[3] The earth is flat in shape and remains floating because of its size and because there is no void and because the air, which possesses a very great force, bears the earth which rides upon it. [4] As for what on the earth is liquid, the sea is composed both from the waters that it contains (after evaporation, what remained was this) and from the rivers that pour into it. [5] The rivers derive their existence both from rains and from the waters that are under the earth.

---

[1] τοῦτο Usener   [2] ⟨ἐκ⟩ τε τῶν . . . τὰ ὑποστάντα Diels: τά τε ἐν αὐτῇ ὕδατα ἐξατμισθέντα ὑποστάντα mss.

καὶ ἐξ ὑδάτων[3] τῶν ἐν τῇ γῇ· εἶναι γὰρ αὐτὴν κοίλην
καὶ ἔχειν ὕδωρ ἐν τοῖς κοιλώμασιν. τὸν δὲ Νεῖλον
αὔξεσθαι κατὰ τὸ θέρος καταφερομένων εἰς αὐτὸν
ὑδάτων ἀπὸ τῶν ἐν τοῖς ἀρκτοῖς[4] χιόνων. [6] ἥλιον δὲ
καὶ σελήνην καὶ πάντα τὰ ἄστρα λίθους εἶναι ἐμ-
πύρους, συμπεριληφθέντας ὑπὸ τῆς ‹τοῦ›[5] αἰθέρος
περιφορᾶς. εἶναι δ᾽ ὑποκάτω τῶν ἄστρων ἡλίῳ καὶ
σελήνῃ[6] σώματά τινα συμπεριφερόμενα, ἡμῖν ἀόρατα.

   [3] ὑδάτων L in marg.: αὐτῶν cett.   [4] ἀνταρκτικοῖς
Roeper   [5] ‹τοῦ› Brandis   [6] ἥλιον καὶ σελήνην mss.,
corr. Roeper

[7] τῆς δὲ θερμότητος μὴ αἰσθάνεσθαι τῶν ἄστρων
διὰ τὸ μακρὰν εἶναι[1] τὴν ἀπόστασιν τῆς γῆς· ἔτι δὲ
οὐχ ὁμοίως θερμὰ τῷ ἡλίῳ διὰ τὸ χώραν ἔχειν ψυ-
χροτέραν. εἶναι δὲ τὴν σελήνην κατωτέρω τοῦ ἡλίου,
πλησιώτερον ἡμῶν. [8] ὑπερέχειν δὲ τὸν ἥλιον μεγέθει
τὴν Πελοπόννησον. τὸ δὲ φῶς τὴν σελήνην μὴ ἴδιον
ἔχειν, ἀλλὰ ἀπὸ τοῦ ἡλίου. τὴν δὲ τῶν ἄστρων περιφορὰν ὑπὸ γῆν γίνεσθαι. [9] ἐκλείπειν δὲ τὴν σελήνην
γῆς ἀντιφραττούσης, ἐνίοτε δὲ καὶ τῶν ὑποκάτω τῆς
σελήνης, τὸν δὲ ἥλιον ταῖς νουμηνίαις σελήνης ἀντιφραττούσης. τροπὰς δὲ ποιεῖσθαι καὶ ἥλιον καὶ
σελήνην ἀπωθουμένους[2] ὑπὸ τοῦ ἀέρος. σελήνην δὲ
πολλάκις τρέπεσθαι διὰ τὸ μὴ δύνασθαι κρατεῖν τοῦ
ψυχροῦ. [10] οὗτος ἀφώρισε πρῶτος τὰ[3] περὶ τὰς
ἐκλείψεις καὶ φωτισμούς. ἔφη δὲ γηίνην εἶναι τὴν
σελήνην ἔχειν τε[4] ἐν αὐτῇ πεδία καὶ φάραγγας. τόν

For this latter is hollow and contains water in its cavities. The Nile rises in the summer when waters coming from snows to the north[1] flow down into it. [6] The sun, the moon and all the heavenly bodies are fiery stones which are carried along by the rotation of the aether. There exist below the heavenly bodies certain bodies that are borne along together with the sun and moon and that are invisible to us.

[1] But cf. **D66.**

[7] The heat of the heavenly bodies is not perceived because of the earth's considerable distance from them. Moreover, they are not hot as the sun is because they occupy a colder region. The moon is below the sun, closer to us. [8] The sun surpasses the Peloponnese in size. The moon does not possess its own light but receives it from the sun. The revolution of the heavenly bodies occurs under the earth. [9] The eclipse of the moon occurs when the earth stands in the way, and sometimes the bodies below the moon, and that of the sun, when the moon stands in the way at the time of the new moon. The returns [i.e. solstices] of both the sun and the moon occur when they are repelled by the air. But the moon turns frequently because it is not able to overcome the cold. [10] He was the first person to determine what is involved in eclipses and illuminations [i.e. the lunar phases]. He said that the moon is like the earth and possesses plains and precipices.

---

[1] καὶ διὰ post εἶναι del. Gomperz   [2] ἀπωθουμένους T: -μένης LOB   [3] τὰ Gronovius: τὰς mss.   [4] τε LB: δὲ O

τε⁵ γαλαξίαν ἀνάκλασιν εἶναι τοῦ φωτὸς τῶν ἄστρων
τῶν μὴ καταλαμπομένων⁶ ὑπὸ τοῦ ἡλίου. τοὺς δὲ
μεταβαίνοντας ἀστέρας ὡσεὶ σπινθῆρας ἀφαλλομέ-
νους γίνεσθαι ἐκ τῆς κινήσεως τοῦ πόλου.

⁵ δὲ Roeper
⁶ καταλαμβανομένων mss., corr. Menagius

[11] ἀνέμους δὲ γίνεσθαι λεπτυνομένου τοῦ ἀέρος ὑπὸ
τοῦ ἡλίου καὶ τῶν ἐκκαιομένων πρὸς τὸν πόλον
ὑποχωρούντων καὶ ἀποφερομένων.¹ βροντὰς δὲ καὶ
ἀστραπὰς ἀπὸ θερμοῦ γίνεσθαι, ἐμπίπτοντος² εἰς τὰ
νέφη. [12] σεισμοὺς δὲ γίνεσθαι τοῦ ἄνωθεν ἀέρος εἰς
τὸν ὑπὸ γῆν ἐμπίπτοντος· τούτου γὰρ κινουμένου καὶ
τὴν ὀχουμένην γῆν ὑπ᾽ αὐτοῦ σαλεύεσθαι. ζῷα δὲ τὴν
μὲν ἀρχὴν ἐν ὑγρῷ γενέσθαι,³ μετὰ ταῦτα δὲ ἐξ ἀλ-
λήλων· καὶ ἄρρενας μὲν γίνεσθαι, ὅταν ἀπὸ τῶν δεξιῶν μερῶν ἀποκριθὲν τὸ σπέρμα τοῖς δεξιοῖς μέρεσι
τῆς μήτρας κολληθῇ, τὰ δὲ θήλεα κατὰ τοὐναντίον.

¹ ἀποφερομένων LB: ἀποφαινομένων O: ἀνταποφερομένων
Usener   ² ἐμπίπτοντος B: ἐκπίπτοντος LO   ³ γενέσθαι LO: γεννᾶσθαι B

Epistemology (D5–D8)

D5 (B21) Sext. *Adv. Math.* 7.90

ὁ μὲν φυσικώτατος Ἀναξαγόρας ὡς ἀσθενεῖς διαβάλ-
λων τὰς αἰσθήσεις "ὑπ᾽ ἀφαυρότητος¹ αὐτῶν, φησίν,

The Milky Way is the reflection of the light of the heavenly bodies that are not illuminated by the sun. The shooting stars come, like sparks leaping down, from the movement of the pole.

[11] Winds occur when the air becomes thin because of the sun and what is completely burned recedes toward the pole and withdraws from it. Thunder and lightning occur because of heat, when it falls onto clouds. [12] Earthquakes occur when the upper air falls onto the air that is located under the earth; for when this latter moves, the earth, which rides upon it, is shaken too. Living beings were born at the beginning in what was moist, and after this from one another; and males are born when the seed, having been separated out from the parts on the right, becomes fastened onto the parts of the womb on the right, females when the opposite occurs.

Epistemology (D5–D8)

D5 (B21) Sextus Empiricus, *Against the Logicians*

Anaxagoras, the natural philosopher *par excellence,* reproaches the senses with their weakness, saying, **"because of their feebleness, we are not able to dis-**

---

¹ ἀμαυρότητος Ritter

οὐ δυνατοί ἐσμεν κρίνειν τἀληθές," τίθησί τε πίστιν
αὐτῶν τῆς ἀπιστίας τὴν παρὰ μικρὸν τῶν χρωμάτων
ἐξαλλαγήν· εἰ γὰρ δύο λάβοιμεν χρώματα, μέλαν καὶ
λευκόν, εἶτα ἐκ θατέρου εἰς θάτερον κατὰ σταγόνα
παρεκχέοιμεν, οὐ δυνήσεται ἡ ὄψις διακρίνειν τὰς
παρὰ μικρὸν μεταβολὰς καίπερ πρὸς τὴν φύσιν ὑπο-
κειμένας.

D6 (< B21a) Sext. Emp. *Adv. Math.* 7.140

ὄψις τῶν ἀδήλων τὰ φαινόμενα.

D7

a (< A97) Sext. Emp. *Pyrrh. Hyp.* 1. 33

[. . .] ὁ Ἀναξαγόρας τῶ¹ λευκὴν εἶναι τὴν χιόνα ἀντε-
τίθει, ὅτι ἡ χιὼν ὕδωρ ἐστὶ πεπηγός, τὸ δὲ ὕδωρ ἐστὶ
μέλαν, καὶ ἡ χιὼν ἄρα μέλαινά ἐστιν.

¹ τῶ <κατασκευάζοντι> Mutschmann

b (A98) Schol. A in *Il.* 16.161

μέλαν ὕδωρ] Ἀναξαγόρας ἐπεὶ φύσει μέλαν· καὶ γοῦν
ὁ καπνὸς μέλας ἐστὶν ἐκ τοῦ ὕδατος τῶν ξύλων ἀνιέ-
μενος.

D8 (< A96) Aët. 4.9.1 (Stob.) [εἰ ἀληθεῖς αἱ αἰσθήσεις]

[. . .] Ἀναξαγόρας [. . .] ψευδεῖς εἶναι τὰς αἰσθήσεις.

tinguish what is true," and cites as proof of their untrustworthiness the gradual change of colors. For if we took two colors, black and white, and we poured drop by drop the one into the other, our sight would not be able to distinguish the gradual changes, although they exist in the nature of things.

D6 (< B21a) Sextus Empiricus, *Against the Logicians*

Appearances: vision of things that are invisible.

D7

a (< A97) Sextus Empiricus, *Outlines of Pyrrhonism*

[. . .] Anaxagoras opposed to snow being white [scil. the argument] that snow is frozen water, that water is black, and hence that snow is black.

b (A98) Scholia on Homer's *Iliad*

"black water": Anaxagoras, since it is by nature black: indeed, smoke is black because it ascends from the water present in logs.[1]

> [1] It is uncertain whether the last part of the sentence belongs to Anaxagoras.

D8 (< A96) Aëtius

Anaxagoras [. . .]: sensations are deceptive.

*From the Opening of Anaxagoras' Book: Principles
and the Primordial State of the World (D9–D14)*

D9 (B1) Simpl. *In Phys.*, p. 155.26–30 [διὰ τοῦ πρώτου
τῶν Φυσικῶν λέγων ἀπ᾽ ἀρχῆς]

ὁμοῦ χρήματα πάντα ἦν ἄπειρα καὶ πλῆθος καὶ
σμικρότητα· καὶ γὰρ τὸ σμικρὸν ἄπειρον ἦν. καὶ
πάντων ὁμοῦ ἐόντων οὐδὲν ἔνδηλον[1] ἦν ὑπὸ σμι-
κρότητος· πάντα γὰρ ἀήρ τε καὶ αἰθὴρ κατεῖχεν
ἀμφότερα ἄπειρα ἐόντα· ταῦτα γὰρ μέγιστα ἔνεστιν
ἐν τοῖς σύμπασι καὶ πλήθει καὶ μεγέθει.[2]

[1] ἔνδηλον EF: εὔδηλον D   [2] ταῦτα . . . μεγέθει abiudic.
Anaxag. Sider

D10 (B2) Simpl. *In Phys.*, pp. 155.31–156.1 [μετ᾽ ὀλί-
γον]

καὶ γὰρ ἀήρ τε καὶ αἰθὴρ ἀποκρίνονται ἀπὸ τοῦ
πολλοῦ τοῦ περιέχοντος, καὶ τό γε περιέχον ἄπειρόν
ἐστι τὸ πλῆθος.

D11 (A70) Theophr. *Sens.* 59

τὸ μὲν μανὸν καὶ λεπτὸν θερμόν, τὸ δὲ πυκνὸν καὶ
παχὺ ψυχρόν, ὥσπερ Ἀναξαγόρας διαιρεῖ τὸν ἀέρα
καὶ τὸν αἰθέρα.

*From the Opening of Anaxagoras' Book: Principles
and the Primordial State of the World (D9–14)*

D9 (B1) Simplicius, *Commentary on Aristotle's* Physics
["through Book 1 of his *Physics,* saying at the beginning"]

**All things were together, unlimited both in quantity
and in smallness; for what was small too was unlimited. And as all things were together, nothing was
manifest on account of the smallness. For air** (*aêr*)
and aether (*aithêr*)**, both of them being unlimited,
covered them all. For these are the greatest things
present in the totality of things, both in quantity and
in magnitude.**

D10 (B2) Simplicius, *Commentary on Aristotle's* Physics
["shortly after" **D9**]

**For both the air and the aether separate out from
the surrounding mass, and what surrounds is itself
unlimited in quantity.**

D11 (A70) Theophrastus, *On Sensations*

What is rarefied and thin is warm, what is dense and thick
is cold, as Anaxagoras distinguishes air and aether.

D12 (< B4) Simpl. *In Phys.*, p. 34.21–26 (et al.)

πρὶν δὲ ἀποκριθῆναι ταῦτα¹ πάντων ὁμοῦ ἐόντων
οὐδὲ χροιὴ ἔνδηλος ἦν οὐδεμία· ἀπεκώλυε γὰρ ἡ
σύμμιξις ἁπάντων χρημάτων, τοῦ τε διεροῦ καὶ τοῦ
ξηροῦ καὶ τοῦ θερμοῦ καὶ τοῦ ψυχροῦ καὶ τοῦ λαμπροῦ καὶ τοῦ ζοφεροῦ, καὶ γῆς² πολλῆς ἐνεούσης
καὶ σπερμάτων ἀπείρων πλῆθος³ οὐδὲν ἐοικότων ἀλλήλοις. οὐδὲ γὰρ τῶν ἄλλων οὐδὲν ἔοικε τὸ ἕτερον
τῷ ἑτέρῳ.⁴ τούτων δὲ οὕτως ἐχόντων ἐν τῷ σύμπαντι
χρὴ δοκεῖν ἐνεῖναι⁵ πάντα χρήματα.

¹ ταῦτα om. Simpl. p. 156.4, del. Sider: πάντα Wendt
² γῆς Simpl. p. 156.7: τῆς mss.   ³ πλήθους mss., corr.
Schorn   ⁴ οὐδὲ . . . τῷ ἑτέρῳ hab. Simpl. p. 156.8, om.
Simpl. p. 34.25, post ἑτέρῳ lac. susp. Sider   ⁵ ἐν εἶναι mss.,
corr. Bessarion

D13 (< B4) Simpl. *In Phys.*, pp. 34.29–35.9 (et al.) [μετ'
ὀλίγα τῆς ἀρχῆς τοῦ πρώτου Περὶ φύσεως p. 34.25–
26, μετ' ὀλίγα p. 156.1]

τούτων δὲ οὕτως ἐχόντων χρὴ δοκεῖν ἐνεῖναι¹ πολλά
τε καὶ παντοῖα ἐν πᾶσι τοῖς συγκρινομένοις καὶ
σπέρματα πάντων χρημάτων καὶ ἰδέας παντοίας
ἔχοντα καὶ χροιὰς καὶ ἡδονάς, καὶ ἀνθρώπους γε
συμπαγῆναι καὶ τὰ ἄλλα ζῷα ὅσα ψυχὴν ἔχει, καὶ
τοῖς γε ἀνθρώποισιν εἶναι καὶ πόλεις συνῳκημένας²
καὶ ἔργα κατεσκευασμένα, ὥσπερ παρ' ἡμῖν, καὶ

D12 (< B4) Simplicius, *Commentary on Aristotle's* Physics [probably shortly after **D10,** perhaps after **D13**]

Before these things [i.e. probably air and aether] **separated out, all things being together, there was not any manifest color either; for it was prevented by the mixture of all things, of the moist and the dry, of the warm and the cold, of the bright and the dim, with much earth present within, and seeds unlimited in quantity not at all resembling one another. For none of the other things either was similar to each other. These things being so, one must think that all things are present in the totality of the whole.**

D13 (< B4) Simplicius, *Commentary on Aristotle's* Physics ["shortly after the beginning of the first book *On Nature*"; "shortly after" **D10,** probably shortly after **D12**[1]]

These things being so, one must think that many things and of all kinds are present in all the aggregates and [or: i.e.] **seeds of all things, possessing all kinds of shapes, colors, and flavors; and that in particular human beings were formed** [literally: solidified] **as well as all the other animated beings** (*zôa*) **that possess life** (*psukhê*); **and that these human beings possess inhabited cities and cultivated fields, just as among us, and that they have a sun and a**

---

[1] The last sentence of **D12** is almost identical with the first sentence of **D13.**

---

[1] ἐν εἶναι mss., corr. Diels
[2] συνημμένας Simpl. p. 157.12

ἠέλιόν τε αὐτοῖσιν εἶναι καὶ σελήνην καὶ τὰ ἄλλα,
ὥσπερ παρ' ἡμῖν, καὶ τὴν γῆν αὐτοῖσι φύειν πολλά
τε καὶ παντοῖα, ὧν ἐκεῖνοι τὰ ὀνήιστα[3] συνενεικάμενοι εἰς τὴν οἴκησιν χρῶνται. ταῦτα μὲν οὖν μοι
λέλεκται περὶ τῆς ἀποκρίσιος, ὅτι οὐκ ἂν παρ' ἡμῖν
μόνον ἀποκριθείη, ἀλλὰ καὶ ἄλλῃ.

[3] τὰ ὀνήιστα Simpl. p. 157.15, alia leviter discrepantia p. 35.7

D14 (B9) Simpl. *In Phys.*, p. 35.14–18 [μετ' ὀλίγον]

[. . .] οὕτω τούτων περιχωρούντων τε καὶ ἀποκρινομένων ὑπὸ βίης τε καὶ ταχυτῆτος· βίην δὲ ἡ ταχυτὴς ποιεῖ, ἡ δὲ ταχυτὴς αὐτῶν οὐδενὶ ἔοικε χρήματι
τὴν ταχυτῆτα τῶν νῦν ἐόντων χρημάτων ἐν ἀνθρώποις, ἀλλὰ πάντως πολλαπλασίως ταχύ ἐστι.

Nothing Comes from Nothing (D15–21)

D15 (B17) Simpl. *In Phys.*, p. 163.20–24 [ἐν τῷ πρώτῳ
τῶν Φυσικῶν]

τὸ δὲ γίνεσθαι καὶ ἀπόλλυσθαι οὐκ ὀρθῶς νομίζου-
σιν οἱ Ἕλληνες· οὐδὲν γὰρ χρῆμα γίνεται οὐδὲ
ἀπόλλυται, ἀλλ' ἀπὸ ἐόντων χρημάτων συμμίσγε-
ταί τε καὶ διακρίνεται. καὶ οὕτως ἂν ὀρθῶς καλοῖεν
τό τε γίνεσθαι συμμίσγεσθαι καὶ τὸ ἀπόλλυσθαι
διακρίνεσθαι.

moon and the other [scil. heavenly bodies], **just as among us, and that the earth produces for them many things and of all kinds, of which they gather the most useful ones into their household and make use of them. This then is what I had to say about the separation, that there will not have been separation among us alone, but elsewhere too.**[2]

[2] Some scholars think that Simplicius' quotation comprises two fragments, the first having a general bearing, the second (starting with "and that these human beings") bearing on other worlds than ours. But this passage may also refer to other regions of the world we inhabit.

D14 (B9) Simplicius, *Commentary on Aristotle's* Physics ["shortly after" **D13**]

[. . .] **while these things revolve and separate out under the effect of the force and rapidity. As for the force, it is the rapidity that causes it, and their rapidity does not resemble anything, as far as rapidity is concerned, among the things that exist now among humans, but it is certainly many times more rapid.**

Nothing Comes from Nothing (D15–D21)

D15 (B17) Simplicius, *Commentary on Aristotle's* Physics ["in the first book of the *Physics*"]

The Greeks do not conceive correctly either what it is to come to be or what it is to be destroyed. For no thing comes to be or is destroyed; but rather, out of things that are, there is mixing and separation. And so, to speak correctly, they would have to call coming to be 'mixing' and being destroyed 'separating.'

D16 (B5) Simpl. *In Phys.*, p. 156.10–12

τούτων δὲ οὕτω διακεκριμένων γινώσκειν χρὴ ὅτι
τὰ¹ πάντα οὐδὲν ἐλάσσω ἐστὶν οὐδὲ πλείω. οὐ γὰρ
ἀνυστὸν πάντων πλείω εἶναι, ἀλλὰ πάντα ἴσα ἀεί.

¹ τὰ DE, om. F

D17 (< A50) Arist. *Phys.* 3.5 205b 1–5

Ἀναξαγόρας [. . . = **R20**] στηρίζειν γὰρ αὐτὸ αὐτό
φησι τὸ ἄπειρον· τοῦτο δέ, ὅτι ἐν αὑτῷ (ἄλλο γὰρ
οὐδὲν περιέχειν) [. . .].

D18 (< A43) Arist. *Metaph.* A3 984a11–16

Ἀναξαγόρας δὲ [. . . = **R8**] ἀπείρους εἶναί φησι τὰς
ἀρχάς· σχεδὸν γὰρ ἅπαντα τὰ ὁμοιομερῆ καθάπερ
ὕδωρ ἢ πῦρ οὕτω γίνεσθαι καὶ ἀπόλλυσθαί φησι, συγκρίσει καὶ διακρίσει μόνον, ἄλλως δ' οὔτε γίγνεσθαι
οὔτ' ἀπόλλυσθαι ἀλλὰ διαμένειν ἀΐδια.

D19 (cf. A54) Aët. 1.17.2 (Ps.-Plut.) [περὶ μίξεως καὶ
κράσεως]

οἱ περὶ Ἀναξαγόραν [. . .] τὰς κράσεις κατὰ παράθε-
σιν.

D16 (B5) Simplicius, *Commentary on Aristotle's* Physics

Since it is in this way that things have separated, one must recognize that all things [i.e. taken in their totality] **are neither less numerous nor more numerous (for it is not possible to be more numerous than all things), but rather the totality of things is always equal** [scil. in quantity].

D17 (< A50) Aristotle, *Physics*

For Anaxagoras [. . .] says that the unlimited maintains itself stable by itself,[1] and that this happens because it is in itself: for nothing else surrounds it [. . .].

[1] The expression "maintains itself stable by itself" might go back to Anaxagoras.

D18 (< A43) Aristotle, *Metaphysics*

Anaxagoras [. . .] says that the principles are unlimited [scil. in number]; for he says, does he not, that all the homeomers (like water and fire) come to be and are destroyed in this way, viz. by aggregation and separation alone, and that they neither come to be nor are destroyed in any other way, but remain, eternal.

D19 (cf. A54) Aëtius

Anaxagoras and his followers [. . .]: mixtures occur by juxtaposition.

D20 (< A52) Arist. *Phys.* 1.4 187a23–29

ἐκ τοῦ μίγματος γὰρ καὶ οὗτοι ἐκκρίνουσι τἆλλα. δια-
φέρουσι δὲ ἀλλήλων τῷ [. . .] ποιεῖν [. . . cf. **EMP. D81**]
τὸν μὲν ἄπειρα τά τε ὁμοιομερῆ καὶ τὰ ἔναντια, τὸν
δὲ τὰ καλούμενα στοιχεῖα μόνον· ἔοικε δὲ Ἀναξαγόρας ἄπειρα οὕτως οἰηθῆναι διὰ τὸ ὑπολαμβάνειν
τὴν κοινὴν δόξαν τῶν φυσικῶν εἶναι ἀληθῆ, ὡς οὐ
γινομένου οὐδενὸς ἐκ τοῦ μὴ ὄντος [. . .].

D21 (< B10) Schol. in Greg. Naz. *Orat.* 9, vol. 36,
p. 911B–C Migne

πῶς γὰρ ἄν, φησίν, ἐκ μὴ τριχὸς γένοιτο[1] θρίξ, καὶ
σὰρξ ἐκ μὴ σαρκός; οὐ μόνον δὲ τῶν σωμάτων ἀλλὰ
καὶ τῶν χρωμάτων ταῦτα κατηγόρει. καὶ γὰρ ἐνεῖναι
τῷ λευκῷ τὸ μέλαν ἔλεγε, καὶ τὸ λευκὸν[2] τῷ μέλανι.
τὸ αὐτὸ δὲ ἐπὶ τῶν ῥοπῶν ἐτίθει, τῷ βαρεῖ τὸ κοῦφον
σύμμικτον εἶναι δοξάζων καὶ τοῦτο αὖθις ἐκείνῳ.

[1] γένοιτο Migne: γένηται mss.   [2] τὸ λευκόν cod. 484:
τῷ λευκῷ cod. 216

All Things Are in All Things (D22–D25)

D22 (B8) Simpl. *In Phys.*, pp. 176.29 (οὐ . . . πελέκει)
et 175.12–14 (οὐδὲ ἀποκέκοπται . . . θερμοῦ)

οὐ κεχώρισται ἀλλήλων τὰ ἐν τῷ ἑνὶ κόσμῳ οὐδὲ
ἀποκέκοπται πελέκει οὔτε τὸ θερμὸν ἀπὸ τοῦ ψυχροῦ οὔτε τὸ ψυχρὸν ἀπὸ τοῦ θερμοῦ.

D20 (< A52) Aristotle, *Physics*

For these men too [i.e. Empedocles and Anaxagoras] say that all other things separate out from the mixture. But they differ from one another in that [. . .] for the one, these are the unlimited [scil. in number] homeomers and the contraries, while for the other [i.e. Empedocles] they are only what are called the elements. Anaxagoras seems to have thought that they are unlimited in this way because he accepted as true the common view of the natural philosophers that nothing can come to be out of what is not [. . .].

D21 (< B10) Scholia on Gregory of Nazianzus

How could it be possible, he says, that out of nonhair hair could ever come to be, and flesh out of nonflesh?[1] He made these assertions not only about bodies but also about colors. For he said that in black there is present white, and white in black. He posited the same thing about weights, supposing that the light is mixed with the heavy and inversely the latter with the former.

1 Scholars disagree on whether or not this is a verbal citation.

All Things Are in All Things (D22–D25)

D22 (B8) Simplicius, *Commentary on Aristotle's* Physics

The things that are in the one world order have not been separated from one another and they have not been chopped apart by an ax, neither the warm from the cold, nor the cold from the warm.

D23 (< B7) Simpl. *In Cael.*, p. 608.26

. . . ὥστε τῶν ἀποκρινομένων μὴ εἰδέναι τὸ πλῆθος
μήτε λόγῳ μήτε ἔργῳ.

D24 (B3) Simpl. *In Phys.*, p. 164.17–20

οὔτε γὰρ τοῦ σμικροῦ ἐστι τό γε ἐλάχιστον, ἀλλ'
ἔλασσον ἀεί· τὸ γὰρ ἐὸν οὐκ ἔστι τὸ μὴ[1] οὐκ εἶναι·[2]
ἀλλὰ καὶ τοῦ μεγάλου ἀεί ἐστι μεῖζον· καὶ ἴσον ἐστὶ
τῷ σμικρῷ πλῆθος· πρὸς ἑαυτὸ δὲ ἕκαστόν ἐστι καὶ
μέγα καὶ σμικρόν.

[1] τὸ μὴ] τομῇ conicit Zeller: τομῇ <μὴ> Jöhrens: τὸ del.
Kranz   [2] εἶναι <οὔτε τὸ μέγιστον> Schorn ex 166.16

D25 (B6) Simpl. *In Phys.*, pp. 164.26–165.1

καὶ ὅτε δὴ[1] ἴσαι μοῖραί εἰσι τοῦ τε μεγάλου καὶ τοῦ
σμικροῦ πλῆθος, καὶ οὕτως ἂν εἴη ἐν παντὶ πάντα·
οὐδὲ χωρὶς ἔστιν εἶναι, ἀλλὰ πάντα παντὸς μοῖραν
μετέχει· ὅτε <δὲ>[2] τοὐλάχιστον μὴ ἔστιν εἶναι, οὐκ
ἂν δύναιτο χωρισθῆναι, οὐδ' ἂν[3] ἐφ' ἑαυτοῦ γενέσθαι, ἀλλ' ὅπωσπερ ἀρχὴν εἶναι καὶ νῦν πάντα
ὁμοῦ. ἐν πᾶσι δὲ πολλὰ ἔνεστι καὶ τῶν ἀποκρινομένων ἴσα πλῆθος ἐν τοῖς μείζοσί τε καὶ ἐλάσσοσι.

[1] δὴ plerique mss.: δὲ EF   [2] <δὲ> ed. Ald.: <τε>
Deichgräber   [3] οὐδ' ἂν E: οὐ λίαν DF: οὐδ' ἂν λίαν
ed. Ald.

D23 (< B7) Simplicius, *Commentary on Aristotle's* On the Heavens

. . . so that of the things that separate out one does not know the quantity either in theory (*logos*) or in deed.

D24 (B3) Simplicius, *Commentary on Aristotle's* Physics

For there is not, of what is small, something that would be the smallest, but rather always something that is smaller: for it is not possible, for what is, not to be. But of what is large too there is always something larger. And it is equal to the small in quantity, but with reference to itself each thing is at the same time both large and small.

D25 (B6) Simplicius, *Commentary on Aristotle's* Physics

And since the portions of both the large and the small are equal in quantity, in this way too all things would be in every thing; and it is not possible to be apart, but all things posses a portion of every thing; and since it is not possible that something be the smallest, it would not be possible that there be separation or existence by itself [i.e. independent], but rather all things, just as at the beginning, so too now are together, and in all things there are also many of the things that are separating out, equal in quantity, both in the larger and in the smaller ones.

Mind (D26–D28)

D26 (B11) Simpl. *In Phys.*, p. 164.23–24

ἐν παντὶ παντὸς μοῖρα ἔνεστι πλὴν νοῦ, ἔστιν οἷσι
δὲ καὶ νοῦς ἔνι.

D27 (B12) Simpl. *In Phys.*, pp. 164.24–25 (τὰ μὲν ἄλλα
. . . μέμικται οὐδενί) et 156.13–157.4 (νοῦς δὲ ἐστιν . . .
ἐστι καὶ ἦν) (et al.)

τὰ μὲν ἄλλα παντὸς μοῖραν μετέχει,[1] νοῦς δέ ἐστιν
ἄπειρον καὶ αὐτοκρατὲς καὶ μέμεικται οὐδενὶ χρήματι, ἀλλὰ μόνος αὐτὸς ἐφ᾿ ἑαυτοῦ ἐστιν. εἰ μὴ γὰρ
ἐφ᾿ ἑαυτοῦ ἦν, ἀλλά τεῳ ἐμέμεικτο ἄλλῳ, μετεῖχεν
ἂν[2] ἁπάντων χρημάτων, εἰ ἐμέμεικτό τεῳ. ἐν παντὶ
γὰρ παντὸς μοῖρα ἔνεστιν, ὥσπερ ἐν τοῖς πρόσθεν
μοι λέλεκται [cf. **D25, D26**]. καὶ ἂν ἐκώλυεν αὐτὸν
τὰ συμμεμειγμένα, ὥστε μηδενὸς χρήματος κρατεῖν
ὁμοίως ὡς καὶ μόνον ἐόντα ἐφ᾿ ἑαυτοῦ. ἔστι γὰρ
λεπτότατόν τε πάντων χρημάτων καὶ καθαρώτατον,
καὶ γνώμην γε περὶ παντὸς πᾶσαν ἴσχει[3] καὶ ἰσχύει
μέγιστον· καὶ ὅσα γε ψυχὴν ἔχει καὶ μείζω καὶ
ἐλάσσω,[4] πάντων νοῦς κρατεῖ· καὶ τῆς περιχωρή-
σιος τῆς συμπάσης νοῦς ἐκράτησεν, ὥστε περιχω-
ρῆσαι τὴν ἀρχήν. καὶ πρῶτον ἀπὸ τοῦ[5] σμικροῦ

---

[1] μέτεχει DE: ἔχει F   [2] μετεῖχεν ἂν ed Ald.: μετεῖχε
μὲν mss.   [3] ἴσχει Simpl. 156.20: ἔχει 177.1

Mind (D26–D28)

D26 (B11), Simplicius, *Commentary on Aristotle's* Physics

In every thing there is a portion of every thing except of mind,[1] but there are things in which mind too is present.

[1] Or: "in every thing except mind there is a portion of every thing."

D27 (B12) Simplicius, *Commentary on Aristotle's* Physics

The other things possess a portion of every thing, but mind is unlimited and master of itself, it has not been mixed with any thing, but is the only one to be itself by itself. For if it were not by itself, but had been mixed with some other thing, it would participate in all things, if it had been mixed with any; for in every thing is present a part of every thing, as I said earlier. And the things that would be mixed with it would prevent it from having control over any thing in the same way as it does being alone by itself. For it is at the same time both the thinnest of all things and the purest, and in particular it retains the full decision [or: understanding] **concerning every thing and possesses the greatest power; and of the things that have life, whether they are larger or smaller, of these mind is master; and mind has been master of the whole rotation, so that there would be rotation at the beginning. And the rotation began at**

4 μείζω καὶ ἐλάσσω 156.21: τὰ μείζω καὶ τὰ ἐλάσσω 177.2
5 τοῦ mss.: του Diels

ἤρξατο περιχωρεῖν, ἔπειτε[6] πλεῖον περιχωρεῖ, καὶ
περιχωρήσει ἐπὶ πλέον. καὶ τὰ συμμισγόμενά τε
καὶ ἀποκρινόμενα καὶ διακρινόμενα πάντα ἔγνω
νοῦς. καὶ ὁποῖα ἔμελλεν ἔσεσθαι καὶ ὁποῖα ἦν ἄσσα
νῦν μή ἐστι, καὶ ὅσα[7] νῦν ἔστι καὶ ὁποῖα ἔσται,[8]
πάντα διεκόσμησε νοῦς, καὶ τὴν περιχώρησιν ταύτην, ἣν νῦν περιχωρέει τά τε ἄστρα καὶ ὁ ἥλιος καὶ
ἡ σελήνη καὶ ὁ ἀὴρ καὶ ὁ αἰθὴρ οἱ ἀποκρινόμενοι.
ἡ δὲ περιχώρησις αὕτη ἐποίησεν ἀποκρίνεσθαι. καὶ
ἀποκρίνεται ἀπό τε τοῦ ἀραιοῦ τὸ πυκνὸν καὶ ἀπὸ
τοῦ ψυχροῦ τὸ θερμὸν καὶ ἀπὸ τοῦ ζοφεροῦ τὸ λαμπρὸν καὶ ἀπὸ τοῦ διεροῦ τὸ ξηρόν. μοῖραι δὲ πολλαὶ
πολλῶν εἰσι. παντάπασι δὲ οὐδὲν ἀποκρίνεται οὐδὲ
διακρίνεται ἕτερον ἀπὸ τοῦ ἑτέρου πλὴν νοῦ. νοῦς
δὲ πᾶς ὅμοιός ἐστι καὶ ὁ μείζων καὶ ὁ ἐλάττων.
ἕτερον δὲ οὐδέν ἐστιν ὅμοιον οὐδενί, ἀλλ᾽ ὅτῳ[9] πλεῖστα ἔνι, ταῦτα ἐνδηλότατα ἓν ἕκαστόν ἐστι καὶ ἦν.

6 ἔπειτε Ritter: ἐπεὶ δὲ mss.   7 ὅσα] ὁποῖα Sider

8 ἄσσα . . . ἔσται Diels: καὶ ὅσα νῦν ἔστι καὶ ὁποῖα ἔσται
156.26, καὶ ὁπόσα νῦν ἔστι καὶ ἔσται 165.33, ὅσα (ὅσσα I³H)
νῦν μὴ ἔστι, καὶ ὁποῖα ἔσται 174.8, ἄσσα (ὅσσα H) νῦν μὴ
ἔστι, καὶ ὁποῖα ἔσται 177.5   9 ἀλλ᾽ ὅτῳ edd.: ἀλλ᾽ ὅτω
DE: ἄλλῳ τῷ F: ἀλλ᾽ ὅτων Diels

D28 (B14) Simpl. In Phys., p. 157.7–9

ὁ δὲ νοῦς †ὅσα ἐστί τε κάρτα†[1] καὶ νῦν ἐστιν ἵνα καὶ
τὰ ἄλλα πάντα, ἐν τῷ πολλὰ περιέχοντι καὶ ἐν τοῖς
προσκριθεῖσι καὶ ἐν τοῖς ἀποκεκριμένοις.[2]

first from the small, then it rotates more broadly, and it will continue to become even broader. And the things that mix as well as those that are detached and separate out—all these mind decided [or: knew]. And as things were going to be and as all things were that now are not, and as all things are now and as they will be, mind separated and ordered them all, as well as this rotation, which is being performed now by the heavenly bodies, the sun, the moon, the air, and the aether, which are separating out. And the rotation itself caused the detachment. And from the rarefied the dense separates out, from the cold the warm, from the dark the bright, and from the moist the dry. Numerous are the parts of numerous things; yet nothing is completely detached or separates out from one another, except mind. But all mind is similar, the larger and the smaller, and nothing else is similar to anything else, but that of which each thing contains the most, this is what each thing is and was most manifestly.

D28 (B14) Simplicius, *Commentary on Aristotle's* Physics

Mind †. . .† **is now too where all the other things are as well, in the surrounding mass, in the things that have separated more (?) and in those that are separating.**

---

[1] ὡς ἀεί ποτε, κάρτα coni. Diels: ὅσα ἐστί τε ἐκράτησε Sider, alii alia [2] προσκριθεῖσι . . . ἀποκεκριμένοις mss.: ἀποκριθεῖσι . . . ἀποκρινομένοις Adam

Cosmogony (D29–D32)

D29

a (A59* Lanza) Arist. *Phys.* 8.1 250b24–26

φησὶν γὰρ ἐκεῖνος, ὁμοῦ πάντων ὄντων καὶ ἠρεμούν-
των τὸν ἄπειρον χρόνον, κίνησιν ἐμποιῆσαι τὸν νοῦν
καὶ διακρῖναι.

b (B13) Simpl. *In Phys.*, pp. 300.31–301.1

καὶ ἐπεὶ ἤρξατο ὁ νοῦς κινεῖν, ἀπὸ τοῦ κινουμένου
παντὸς ἀπεκρίνετο, καὶ ὅσον ἐκίνησεν ὁ νοῦς, πᾶν
τοῦτο διεκρίθη· κινουμένων δὲ καὶ διακρινομένων ἡ
περιχώρησις πολλῷ μᾶλλον ἐποίει διακρίνεσθαι.

D30 (B15) Simpl. *In Phys.*, p. 179.3–6 [μετ᾽ ὀλίγα]

τὸ μὲν πυκνὸν [. . .] καὶ ⟨τὸ⟩¹ διερὸν καὶ τὸ² ψυχρὸν
καὶ τὸ ζοφερὸν ἐνθάδε συνεχώρησεν ἔνθα νῦν γῆ,
τὸ δὲ ἀραιὸν καὶ τὸ θερμὸν³ καὶ τὸ ξηρὸν ἐξεχώρησεν εἰς τὸ πρόσω τοῦ αἰθέρος.

¹ ⟨τὸ⟩ Diels   ² τὸ ΔW: om. cett.
³ ⟨καὶ τὸ λαμπρὸν⟩ post θερμὸν Schorn

Cosmogony (D29–D32)

D29

a (≠ DK) Aristotle, *Physics*

For he says that, when all things were together and at rest for an infinite time, mind introduced motion and separated them.

b (B13) Simplicius, *Commentary on Aristotle's* Physics

And when mind began to cause motion, there was separating out from all that was moving, and whatever mind moved, all this was separated. But the rotation of the things that were moving and separating resulted in the production of a much greater separating.

D30 (B15) Simplicius, *Commentary on Aristotle's* Physics ["shortly after" **D27**]

What is dense and what is moist and what is cold and what is dark came together to where earth [or: the earth] **is now, while what is thin and what is warm and what is dry went outward to the farthest part of the aether.**

D31 (B16) Simpl. *In Phys.*, pp. 179.8–10 (ἀπὸ τουτέων
. . . ψυχροῦ) et 155.21–23 (ἐκ μὲν γὰρ τῶν νεφελῶν . . .
μᾶλλον τοῦ ὕδατος) [ἐν τῷ πρώτῳ τῶν Φυσικῶν 155.
21]

ἀπὸ τουτέων ἀποκρινομένων συμπήγνυται γῆ· ἐκ
μὲν γὰρ τῶν νεφελῶν ὕδωρ ἀποκρίνεται, ἐκ δὲ τοῦ
ὕδατος γῆ, ἐκ δὲ τῆς γῆς λίθοι συμπήγνυνται[1] ὑπὸ
τοῦ ψυχροῦ, οὗτοι δὲ ἐκχωρέουσι μᾶλλον τοῦ ὕδατος.

[1] λίθοι συμπήγνυνται 179.10: λίθος συμπήγνυται 155.22

D32 (< A67) Aët. 2.8.1 (Ps.-Plut.) [τίς ἡ αἰτία τοῦ τὸν
κόσμον ἐγκλιθῆναι]

[. . .] Ἀναξαγόρας μετὰ τὸ συστῆναι τὸν κόσμον καὶ
τὰ ζῷα ἐκ τῆς γῆς ἐξαγαγεῖν ἐγκλιθῆναί πως τὸν
κόσμον ἐκ τοῦ αὐτομάτου εἰς τὸ μεσημβρινὸν αὐτοῦ
μέρος [. . . = **R30**].

Cosmology (D33–D52)
The World Order (D33–D35)

D33 (< A63) Aët. 2.1.2 (Stob.) [περὶ κόσμου]

[. . .] Ἀναξαγόρας [. . .] ἕνα τὸν κόσμον.

D34 (A64) Simpl. *In Phys.*, p. 154.29–31

[. . .] τὸν Ἀναξαγόραν λέγειν ἅπαξ γενόμενον τὸν

D31 (B16) Simplicius, *Commentary on Aristotle's* Physics ["in the first book of the *Physics*"]

Out of these things, as they separate out, earth solidifies: for from the clouds water separates out, and from the water earth; and from earth stones solidify by the effect of the cold, and these go farther outward than water.[1]

---
[1] Probably referring to the distance of the heavenly bodies.

D32 (< A67) Aëtius

[. . .] Anaxagoras: after the world had been formed and animals had come out of the earth, the world inclined somehow on its own toward its southern part [. . .].

Cosmology (D33–D52)
The World Order (D33–D35)

D33 (< A63) Aëtius

[. . .] Anaxagoras [. . .]: there is [scil. only] one world.

D34 (A64) Simplicius, *Commentary on Aristotle's* Physics

[. . .] Anaxagoras says that the world, once it has come

*κόσμον ἐκ τοῦ μίγματος διαμένειν λοιπὸν ὑπὸ τοῦ νοῦ
ἐφεστῶτος διοικούμενόν τε καὶ διακρινόμενον* [. . .].

D35

a (< A65) Aët. 2.4.6 (Stob.) [*εἰ ἄφθαρτος ὁ κόσμος*]

[. . .] Ἀναξαγόρας [. . .] *φθαρτὸν τὸν κόσμον.*

b (≠ DK) Alex. *In Phys.* 250b18, p. 529 Rashed

ἕνα κόσμον γενητὸν καὶ ἄφθαρτον ἐξ ἡσυχίας· [. . .].

Astronomy (D36–D52)
Aether (D36–D37)

D36 (A71) Aët. 2.13.3 (Stob.) [*τίς ἡ οὐσία τῶν ἄστρων,
πλανητῶν καὶ ἀπλανῶν*]

Ἀναξαγόρας *τὸν περικείμενον αἰθέρα πύρινον μὲν εἶναι κατὰ τὴν οὐσίαν, τῇ δὲ εὐτονίᾳ τῆς περιδινήσεως
ἀναρπάσαντα πέτρους ἀπὸ τῆς γῆς καὶ καταφλέ-
ξαντα τούτους ἠστερωκέναι.*

D37

a (A73* Lanza) Arist. *Meteor.* 1.3 339b21–24

[. . .] *ὁ γὰρ λεγόμενος αἰθὴρ παλαιὰν εἴληφε τὴν
προσηγορίαν, ἣν Ἀναξαγόρας μὲν τῷ πυρὶ ταὐτὸν*

about out of the mixture, continues thereafter to be administered and to separate by the controlling mind [. . .].

D35

a (< A65) Aëtius

[. . .] Anaxagoras [. . .]: the world is destructible.

b (≠ DK) Alexander of Aphrodisias, Scholia on Aristotle's *Physics*

one world, ungenerated and indestructible, coming from inactivity [. . .].[1]

[1] Either **D35a** or **D35b** must be erroneous, probably the latter.

Astronomy (D36–D52)
Aether (D36–D37)

D36 (A71) Aëtius

Anaxagoras: the surrounding aether is of fire according to its substance and, having snatched up stones from the earth by the vigor of its rotation and having ignited them, it has turned them into heavenly bodies.

D37

a (≠ DK) Aristotle, *Meteorology*

[. . .] for what is called 'aether' received in ancient times its name, which Anaxagoras, I believe, thought meant the

ἡγήσασθαί μοι δοκεῖ σημαίνειν· τά τε γὰρ ἄνω
πλήρη πυρὸς εἶναι κἀκείνους[1] τὴν ἐκεῖ δύναμιν αἰθέρα
καλεῖν ἐνόμισεν [. . .].

  [1] κἀκεῖνος mss., corr. Thurot

b (A73) Arist. *Cael.* 1.3 270b24

Ἀναξαγόρας δὲ καταχρῆται τῷ ὀνόματι τούτῳ οὐ κα-
λῶς· ὀνομάζει γὰρ αἰθέρα ἀντὶ πυρός.

c (A73) Simpl. *In Cael.*, p. 119.2–4

αἰτιᾶται δὲ τὸν Ἀναξαγόραν οὐ καλῶς ἐτυμολογή-
σαντα τὸ τοῦ αἰθέρος ὄνομα ἀπὸ τοῦ αἴθειν, ὅ ἐστι τὸ
καίειν, καὶ διὰ τοῦτο ἐπὶ τοῦ πυρὸς αὐτῷ χρώμενον.

Sun and Moon (D38–D45)

D38 (< A18) Plut. *Nic.* 23

ὁ γὰρ πρῶτος σαφέστατόν τε[1] πάντων καὶ θαρρα-
λεώτατον περὶ σελήνης καταυγασμῶν καὶ σκιᾶς λόγον εἰς γραφὴν καταθέμενος Ἀναξαγόρας [. . . cf.
P25b].

  [1] γε mss., corr. Reiske

same thing as 'fire.' For he considered that the upper regions are full of fire and that they [i.e. the ancients] had called the property (dunamis) that is found there 'aether' [. . .].

b (A73) Aristotle, *On the Heavens*

Anaxagoras uses this word [i.e. 'aether'] incorrectly; for he says 'aether' instead of 'fire.'[1]

[1] For Aristotle, aether is the element that 'continually runs' (*aei thein*) and not the one that 'burns' (*aithein*).

c (A73) Simplicius, *Commentary on Aristotle's* On the Heavens

He accuses Anaxagoras of mistakenly deriving the word 'aither' from *aithein,* that is, 'to burn,' and using it for this reason for 'fire.'

Sun and Moon (D38–D45)

D38 (< A18) Plutarch, *Nicias*

Anaxagoras, the first person to have put into writing the clearest and boldest explanation of all concerning the illuminations and darkenings of the moon [. . .].

D39 (< A75) Procl. *In Tim.* 4 *ad* 38d (vol. 3, p. 63.26–30 Diehl)

[. . .] καὶ οὐδὲ ταύτης ἦρξεν αὐτὸς τῆς ὑποθέσεως, ἀλλ᾽ Ἀναξαγόρας τοῦτο πρῶτος ὑπέλαβεν, ὡς ἱστόρη-σεν Εὔδημος [Frag. 147 Wehrli].

D40 (B18) Plut. *Fac. orb. lun.* 16 929B

ἥλιος ἐντίθησι τῇ σελήνῃ τὸ λαμπρόν.

D41 (A76) Plat. *Crat.* 409a–b

[. . .] ὃ ἐκεῖνος νεωστὶ ἔλεγεν, ὅτι ἡ σελήνη ἀπὸ τοῦ ἡλίου ἔχει τὸ φῶς [. . .]. νέον δέ που καὶ ἔνον ἀεί ἐστι περὶ τὴν σελήνην τοῦτο τὸ φῶς, εἴπερ ἀληθῆ οἱ Ἀναξαγόρειοι λέγουσι· κύκλῳ γάρ που ἀεὶ αὐτὴν περιιὼν νέον ἀεὶ ἐπιβάλλει, ἔνον δὲ ὑπάρχει τὸ τοῦ προτέρου μηνός.

D42 (< A77) Aët. 2.25.9 (Ps.-Plut., Stob.) [περὶ οὐσίας σελήνης]

Ἀναξαγόρας [. . .] στερέωμα διάπυρον ἔχον ἐν ἑαυτῷ πεδία καὶ ὄρη καὶ φάραγγας.

D43 (A77) Schol. in Apoll. Rhod. 1.498

τὴν δὲ σελήνην ὁ αὐτὸς Ἀναξαγόρας χώραν πλατεῖαν ἀποφαίνει,[1] ἐξ ἧς δοκεῖ ὁ Νεμεαῖος λέων πεπτωκέναι.

D39 (< A75) Proclus, *Commentary on Plato's* Timaeus

[. . .] but he [i.e. Plato] was not the originator of this doctrine [scil. the 'conjunctive introduction' of the sun and moon in the world] either: Anaxagoras was the first person to have thought of this, as Eudemus has reported.

D40 (B18) Plutarch, *On the Face in the Moon*

The sun puts brightness into the moon.

D41 (A76) Plato, *Cratylus*

[. . .] what that man [i.e. Anaxagoras] recently said, viz. that the moon receives its light from the sun [. . .]. And this light in the case of the moon is always in some way both new (*neon*) and old (*henon*), if what the Anaxagoreans say is true; for since it [i.e. the sun] is always going around it in a circle, it always casts a new [scil. light] upon it, while the one [scil. the light] of the previous month is old.[1]

---

[1] It is uncertain whether the latter point goes back to Anaxagoras himself.

D42 (< A77) Aëtius

Anaxagoras [. . .]: [scil. the moon is] a fiery solid possessing in itself plains, mountains, and precipices.

D43 (A77) Scholia on Apollonius Rhodius

The same Anaxagoras declares that the moon is a flat place, from which he [or: one] thinks that the Nemean lion fell.

---

[1] ἀποφαίνει Meineke: ἀποφαίνεται L: ἔφη P

D44 (< A77) Aët. 2.30.2 (Stob.) [περὶ ἐμφάσεως αὐτῆς καὶ διὰ τί γεῶδες φαίνεται]

Ἀναξαγόρας ἀνωμαλότητα συγκρίματος διὰ τὸ ψυχρομιγὲς ἅμα καὶ γεῶδες, τὰ μὲν ἐχούσης ὑψηλὰ τὰ δὲ ταπεινὰ τὰ δὲ κοῖλα [. . .].

D45 (A77) Aët. 2.29.6, 7 (Stob.) [περὶ ἐκλείψεως σελήνης]

a

[6] [. . .] Ἀναξαγόρας [. . .] τὰς μὲν μηνιαίους ἀποκρύψεις συνοδεύουσαν αὐτὴν ἡλίῳ καὶ περιλαμπομένην ποιεῖσθαι, τὰς δ' ἐκλείψεις εἰς τὸ σκίασμα τῆς γῆς ἐμπίπτουσαν, μεταξὺ μὲν ἀμφοτέρων τῶν ἀστέρων γενομένης, μᾶλλον δὲ τῆς σελήνης ἀντιφραττομένης.

b

[7] Ἀναξαγόρας, ὥς φησι Θεόφραστος [Frag. 236 FSH&G], καὶ τῶν ὑποκάτω τῆς σελήνης ἔσθ' ὅτε σωμάτων ἐπιπροσθούντων.

Other Heavenly Bodies (D46–D49)

D46 (< A12) Plut. *Lys.* 12

[. . . = **P7**] εἶναι δὲ καὶ τῶν ἄστρων ἕκαστον οὐκ ἐν ᾗ πέφυκε χώρᾳ· λιθώδη γὰρ ὄντα καὶ βαρέα λάμπειν μὲν ἀντερείσει καὶ περικλάσει τοῦ αἰθέρος, ἕλκεσθαι

D44 (< A77) Aëtius

Anaxagoras: [scil. the reason the moon has the same appearance as the earth is] the irregularity of its aggregate, because it is mixed with cold and at the same time is earthy, itself having some places that are high, others low, and others hollow [. . .].[1]

   [1] The continuation of this notice is almost identical with the entry on Parmenides in this same chapter (= **PARM. D31**); its presence in the entry on Anaxagoras is probably due to an error.

D45 (< A77) Aëtius

a

[. . .] Anaxagoras [. . .]: [scil. the moon] disappears every month because it follows the sun's path and is illuminated [scil. by it], and it undergoes eclipses because it falls into the shadow of the earth when this latter comes between the two heavenly bodies, or rather when the moon is occulted [scil. by the earth].

b

Anaxagoras, as Theophrastus says, [scil. says that eclipses occur] also when it happens that the bodies that are below the moon are sometimes interposed.

Other Heavenly Bodies (D46–D49)

D46 (< A12) Plutarch, *Lysander*

[. . .] Each of the heavenly bodies is not in its natural place. For, being made of stone and heavy, they shine because of the resistance and refraction (*periklasis*) of the aether, but

δὲ ὑπὸ βίας σφιγγόμενα δίνῃ καὶ τόνῳ τῆς περιφορᾶς, ὥς που καὶ τὸ πρῶτον ἐκρατήθη μὴ πεσεῖν δεῦρο
τῶν ψυχρῶν καὶ βαρέων ἀποκρινομένων τοῦ παντός
[. . .].

D47 (< A78) Aët. 2.16.1 (Ps.-Plut.) [περὶ τῆς τῶν ἀστέρων φορᾶς καὶ κινήσεως]

Ἀναξαγόρας [. . .] ἀπ᾽ ἀνατολῶν ἐπὶ δυσμὰς φέρεσθαι
πάντας τοὺς ἀστέρας.

D48 (< A79) Ach. Tat. *Introd. Arat.* 1.13

τοὺς ἀστέρας δὲ ζῷα εἶναι οὔτε Ἀναξαγόρᾳ οὔτε [. . .
cf. **ATOM. D90**] δοκεῖ.

D49 (< A80) Arist. *Meteor.* 1.8 345a25–31

οἱ δὲ περὶ Ἀναξαγόραν καὶ [. . . cf. **ATOM. D97**] φῶς
εἶναι τὸ γάλα λέγουσιν ἄστρων τινῶν· τὸν γὰρ ἥλιον
ὑπὸ τὴν γῆν φερόμενον οὐχ ὁρᾶν ἔνια τῶν ἄστρων.
ὅσα μὲν οὖν περιορᾶται ὑπ᾽ αὐτοῦ, τούτων μὲν οὐ
φαίνεσθαι τὸ φῶς (κωλύεσθαι γὰρ ὑπὸ τῶν τοῦ ἡλίου
ἀκτίνων)· ὅσοις δ᾽ ἀντιφράττει ἡ γῆ ὥστε μὴ ὁρᾶσθαι
ὑπὸ τοῦ ἡλίου, τὸ τούτων οἰκεῖον φῶς εἶναί φασι τὸ
γάλα.

Comets and Meteors (D50–D52)

D50 (< A81) Arist. *Meteor.* 1.6 342b27–29

Ἀναξαγόρας μὲν οὖν καὶ [. . . cf. **ATOM. D99**] φασιν

they are dragged along by force, bound by the vortex and the tension of the revolution, just as at the beginning they were dominated so that they did not fall here when the cold and heavy things were being detached from the whole [. . .].

D47 (< A78) Aëtius

Anaxagoras [. . .]: all the heavenly bodies move from east to west.

D48 (A79) Achilles Tatius, *Introduction to Aratus'* Phaenomena

Neither Anaxagoras nor [. . .] thinks that the heavenly bodies are living beings.

D49 (< A80) Aristotle, *Meteorology*

The followers of Anaxagoras and [. . .] say that the Milky Way is the light of certain heavenly bodies; for the sun, when it moves under the earth, does not see certain heavenly bodies. The light of the ones it sees is not visible (for this is prevented by the sun's rays); but the light belonging to those in front of which the earth is interposed in such a way that the sun does not see them is, they say, the Milky Way.

Comets and Meteors (D50–D52)

D50 (< A81) Aristotle, *Meteorology*

Anaxagoras and [. . .] say that comets are the conjunctive

εἶναι τοὺς κομήτας σύμφασιν τῶν πλανήτων ἀστέρων, ὅταν διὰ τὸ πλησίον ἐλθεῖν δόξωσι θιγγάνειν ἀλλήλων.

D51 (A83) Sen. *Quaest. nat.* 7.5.3

Charmander quoque in eo libro, quem de cometis composuit, ait Anaxagorae visum grande insolitumque caelo lumen magnitudine amplae trabis, et id per multos dies fulsisse.

D52 (A82) Aët. 3.2.9 (Ps.-Plut.) [περὶ κομητῶν καὶ διᾳττόντων καὶ δοκίδων]

Ἀναξαγόρας τοὺς καλουμένους διᾴττοντας ἀπὸ τοῦ αἰθέρος σπινθήρων δίκην καταφέρεσθαι· διὸ καὶ παραυτίκα σβέννυσθαι.[1]

[1] σβέννυσθαι m: κατασβέννυσθαι MΠ

Meteorology (D53–D57)
Thunder, Lightning, and Related
Phenomena (D53)

D53

a (A84) Arist. *Meteor.* 2.9 369b11–19

Ἀναξαγόρας δὲ τοῦ ἄνωθεν αἰθέρος, ὃ δὴ ἐκεῖνος καλεῖ πῦρ, κατενεχθὲν ἄνωθεν κάτω. τὴν μὲν οὖν διάλαμψιν ἀστραπὴν εἶναι τὴν τούτου τοῦ πυρός, τὸν δὲ

shining of the planets when, by coming close together, they seem to touch one another.

D51 (A83) Seneca, *Natural Questions*

Charmander too, in the book he wrote about comets, says that Anaxagoras saw in the sky a large and unusual light, of the size of a large plank, and that it shined brightly for many days.

D52 (A82) Aëtius

Anaxagoras: the so-called shooting stars descend from the aether like sparks, and that is why they are extinguished at once.

Meteorology (D53–D57)
Thunder, Lightning, and Related
Phenomena (D53)

D53

a (A84) Aristotle, *Meteorology*

Anaxagoras [scil. says that the fire that is found in the clouds comes] from the higher aether, which he calls 'fire,' descended from above downward. The flash of this fire,

ψόφον ἐναποσβεννυμένου καὶ τὴν σίξιν βροντήν, ὡς
καθάπερ φαίνεται καὶ γιγνόμενον οὕτως, καὶ πρότερον τὴν ἀστραπὴν οὖσαν τῆς βροντῆς.

b (A84) Aët. 3.3.4 (Ps.-Plut.) [περὶ βροντῶν ἀστραπῶν
κεραυνῶν πρηστήρων τε καὶ τυφώνων]

ὅταν τὸ θερμὸν εἰς τὸ ψυχρὸν ἐμπέσῃ (τοῦτο δ' ἐστὶν
αἰθέριον μέρος εἰς ἀερῶδες), τῷ μὲν ψόφῳ τὴν βροντὴν ἀποτελεῖ, τῷ δὲ παρὰ τὴν μελανίαν τοῦ νεφώδους
χρώματι τὴν ἀστραπήν, τῷ δὲ πλήθει καὶ μεγέθει τοῦ
φωτὸς τὸν κεραυνόν, τῷ δὲ πολυσωματωτέρῳ πυρὶ τὸν
τυφῶνα, τῷ δὲ νεφελομιγεῖ[1] τὸν πρηστῆρα.

[1] νεφελομιγεῖ m: νεφελοειδεῖ ΜΠ

Clouds, Snow, and Hail (D54)

D54

a (A85) Arist. *Meteor.* 1.12 348a14–20

τοῖς μὲν οὖν δοκεῖ τοῦ πάθους αἴτιον εἶναι τούτου καὶ
τῆς γενέσεως, ὅταν ἀπωσθῇ τὸ νέφος εἰς τὸν ἄνω
τόπον μᾶλλον ὄντα ψυχρὸν διὰ τὸ λήγειν ἐκεῖ τὰς
ἀπὸ τῆς γῆς τῶν ἀκτίνων ἀνακλάσεις, ἐλθὸν δ' ἐκεῖ
πήγνυσθαι τὸ ὕδωρ· διὸ καὶ θέρους μᾶλλον καὶ ἐν
ταῖς ἀλεειναῖς χώραις γίγνεσθαι τὰς χαλάζας, ὅτι ἐπὶ
πλέον τὸ θερμὸν ἀνωθεῖ ἀπὸ τῆς γῆς τὰς νεφέλας.

then, is lightning, the noise and the hissing when it is extinguished inside is thunder—on the idea that this happens just as it appears—and that lightning precedes thunder.

b (A84) Aëtius

When what is warm falls onto what is cold (that is, the part of aether onto the part of air), this produces thunder by its noise, lightning by its color in contrast against the blackness of the cloud, the thunderbolt by the quantity and size of the light, the whirlwind by fire containing a much more abundant bodily mass, and the lightning storm (*prêstêr*) by the mixture of the cloudy matter.

See also **D63**

Clouds, Snow, and Hail (D54)

D54

a (A85) Aristotle, *Meteorology*

Some people[1] think that the cause of this phenomenon [i.e. hail] and of its formation is that a cloud is repelled toward the higher region, which is colder because the reflections of the rays coming from the earth stop there, and the water that arrives there solidifies. That is why hailstorms occur more during the summer and in torrid areas, because the heat pushes the clouds up all the higher away from the earth.

---

[1] Alexander of Aphrodisias names Anaxagoras in his commentary on this passage (p. 49.13).

b (A85) Aët. 3.4.2 (Stob.) [περὶ νεφῶν ὁμίχλης ὑετῶν δρόσου χιόνος πάχνης χαλάζης]

Ἀναξαγόρας νέφη μὲν καὶ χιόνα παραπλησίως· χάλαζαν δ' ὅταν ἀπὸ τῶν παγέντων νεφῶν προωσθῇ τινα πρὸς τὴν γῆν, ἃ δὴ[1] ταῖς καταφοραῖς ἀποψυχρούμενα στρογγυλοῦται.

[1] ἃ δὴ Usener: ἤδη mss.

Rainbows and Related Phenomena (D55–D56)

D55 (B19) Schol. BT in *Il.* 17.547

ἶριν δὲ καλέομεν τὸ ἐν τῇσι νεφέλῃσι ἀντιλάμπον τῷ ἡλίῳ. χειμῶνος οὖν ἐστι σύμβολον· τὸ γὰρ περιχεόμενον[1] ὕδωρ τῷ νέφει ἄνεμον ἐποίησεν ἢ ἐξέχεεν ὄμβρον.[2]

[1] περιεχόμενον Solmsen
[2] χειμῶνος . . . ὄμβρον abiudic. Anaxag. Jöhrens

D56 (A86) Aët. 3.5.11 (Ps.-Plut.) [περὶ ἴριδος]

Ἀναξαγόρας ἀνάκλασιν ἀπὸ νέφους πυκνοῦ τῆς ἡλιακῆς περιφεγγείας, καταντικρὺ δὲ τοῦ κατοπτρίζοντος αὐτὴν[1] ἀστέρος διὰ παντὸς ἵστασθαι. παραπλησίως δὲ αἰτιολογεῖται[2] τὰ καλούμενα παρήλια, γινόμενα δὲ κατὰ τὸν Πόντον.

[1] αὐτὴν Mm: αὐτὸν Π: αὐτὸ Reiske
[2] αἰτιολογεῖται Mm: φυσιολογεῖται Π

b (A85) Aëtius

Anaxagoras: clouds and snow [scil. occur] in the same way [scil. as Anaximenes says, cf. **ANAXIMEN. D21**], and hail [scil. occurs] when some [scil. drops of water] are expelled from solidified clouds toward the earth and become spherical when they cool down during their descent.

Rainbows and Related Phenomena (D55–D56)

D55 (B19) Scholia on Homer's *Iliad*

We call 'iris' [i.e. the rainbow] **what shines in return in the clouds facing the sun. Therefore it is a sign of a storm: for the water pouring around the cloud causes wind or pours out rain.**[1]

[1] Some scholars assign only the first sentence to Anaxagoras.

D56 (A86) Aëtius

Anaxagoras: [scil. the rainbow is] the reflection of the radiance of the sun by a dense cloud, and it is always located exactly opposite to the heavenly body that shows it as in a mirror. It is in the same way that he explains the so-called 'parhelia' that occur in the region of the Black Sea.

Winds (D57)

D57 (< A86a) Schol. in Aesch. *Prom.* 88

οἱ ἄνεμοι κατὰ μὲν Ἀναξαγόραν ἐκ τῆς γῆς γίνονται
[. . .].

The Earth (D58–D67)
The Earth Rests Upon Air (D58–D61)

D58 (< 13 A20, A88* Lanza) Arist. *Cael.* 2.13 294b13–23

[. . . cf. **ANAXIMEN. D19**] καὶ Ἀναξαγόρας καὶ [. . . cf.
ATOM. D110] τὸ πλάτος αἴτιον εἶναί φασι τοῦ μένειν
αὐτήν. οὐ γὰρ τέμνειν ἀλλ' ἐπιπωμάζειν τὸν ἀέρα τὸν
κάτωθεν, ὅπερ φαίνεται τὰ πλάτος ἔχοντα τῶν σωμάτων ποιεῖν· ταῦτα γὰρ καὶ πρὸς τοὺς ἀνέμους ἔχει
δυσκινήτως διὰ τὴν ἀντέρεισιν. ταὐτὸ δὴ τοῦτο ποιεῖν
τῷ πλάτει φασὶ τὴν γῆν πρὸς τὸν ὑποκείμενον ἀέρα,
(τὸν δ' οὐκ ἔχοντα[1] μεταστῆναι τόπον ἱκανὸν[2] ἀθρόως[3]
κάτωθεν ἠρεμεῖν), ὥσπερ τὸ ἐν ταῖς κλεψύδραις ὕδωρ.
ὅτι δὲ δύναται πολὺ βάρος φέρειν ἀπολαμβανόμενος
καὶ μένων ὁ ἀήρ, τεκμήρια πολλὰ λέγουσιν.

  [1] ἔχοντα ⟨τοῦ⟩ Diels   [2] an τόπον ἱκανὸν μεταστῆναι?
[3] τῷ post ἀθρόως utrum delendum an ante ἀθρόως ponendum
dub. Moraux

D59 (< A68) Arist. *Cael.* 4.2 309a19–21

ἔνιοι μὲν οὖν τῶν μὴ φασκόντων εἶναι κενὸν οὐδὲν

Winds (D57)

D57 (< A86a) Scholia on Aeschylus' *Prometheus Bound*

The winds, according to Anaxagoras, come about from the earth [. . .].

The Earth (D58–D67)
The Earth Rests Upon Air (D58–D61)

D58 (< 13 A20) Aristotle, *On the Heavens*

[. . .] and Anaxagoras and [. . .] say that its [i.e. the earth's] flatness is the cause for its stationary position. For it does not cut the air beneath it but covers it like a lid, which is what one sees bodies possessing flatness to do; for winds have difficulty moving these bodies too, because of their resistance. And they say that it is in exactly the same way that the earth acts with regard to the air underlying it, because of its flatness, and that since it [i.e. the air] does not have sufficient room to move, it remains motionless below [scil. the earth] in a dense mass, just like the water in clepsydras. And for the fact that air that is enclosed and stationary can bear a great weight, they provide many proofs.

D59 (< A68) Aristotle, *On the Heavens*

Some of those people who deny the existence of the void

διώρισαν περὶ κούφου καὶ βαρέος, οἷον Ἀναξαγόρας
[. . .].

D60 (< A68) Arist. *Phys.* 4.6 213a22–27

οἱ μὲν οὖν δεικνύναι πειρώμενοι ὅτι οὐκ ἔστιν, οὐχ ὃ
βούλονται λέγειν οἱ ἄνθρωποι κενόν, τοῦτ᾽ ἐξελέγχου-
σιν [. . .], ὥσπερ Ἀναξαγόρας καὶ οἱ τοῦτον τὸν τρόπον ἐλέγχοντες. ἐπιδεικνύουσι γὰρ ὅτι ἐστίν τι ὁ ἀήρ,
στρεβλοῦντες τοὺς ἀσκοὺς καὶ δεικνύντες ὡς ἰσχυρὸς
ὁ ἀήρ, καὶ ἐναπολαμβάνοντες ἐν ταῖς κλεψύδραις.

D61 (< A69) Ps.-Arist. *Probl.* 16.8 914b9–15

τῶν περὶ τὴν κλεψύδραν συμβαινόντων τὸ μὲν ὅλον
ἔοικεν εἶναι αἴτιον καθάπερ Ἀναξαγόρας λέγει· ὁ γὰρ
ἀήρ ἐστιν αἴτιος ἐναπολαμβανόμενος ἐν αὐτῇ τοῦ μὴ
εἰσιέναι τὸ ὕδωρ ἐπιληφθέντος τοῦ αὐλοῦ[1] [. . . cf.
R22].

[1] ἄλλου mss., corr. Bussemaker

Earthquakes (D62–D63)

D62 (A89)

a Arist. *Meteor.* 2.7 365a19–25

Ἀναξαγόρας μὲν οὖν φησι τὸν αἰθέρα πεφυκότα φέρεσθαι ἄνω, ἐμπίπτοντα δ᾽ εἰς τὰ κάτω τῆς γῆς καὶ
κοῖλα κινεῖν αὐτήν· τὰ μὲν γὰρ ἄνω συναληλεῖφθαι

did not define anything about what is light and heavy, like Anaxagoras [. . .].

D60 (< A68) Aristotle, *Physics*

Those people who try to prove that it [i.e. the void] does not exist do not refute what men mean by 'void' [. . .]; this is the case of Anaxagoras and of those people who refute in this way. For they demonstrate that air is something by twisting wineskins, showing that air is strong, and by enclosing it in clepsydras.

D61 (< A69) Ps.-Aristotle, *Problems*

For on the whole, the cause for what happens with the clepsydra seems to be what Anaxagoras says. For the air enclosed within it is the cause for the water's not penetrating when the tube is closed [. . .].

Earthquakes (D62–D63)

D62 (A89)

a Aristotle, *Meteorology*

Anaxagoras says that aether moves upward by nature and that, when it collides with the lower parts of the earth and its cavities, it shakes it: for the upper parts have been

διὰ τοὺς ὄμβρους (ἐπεὶ φύσει γε ἄπασαν ὁμοίως εἶναι σομφήν), ὡς ὄντος τοῦ μὲν ἄνω τοῦ δὲ κάτω τῆς ὅλης σφαίρας, καὶ ἄνω μὲν τούτου ὄντος τοῦ μορίου ἐφ᾽ οὗ τυγχάνομεν οἰκοῦντες, κάτω δὲ θατέρου.

b Aët. 3.15.4 (Ps.-Plut.) [περὶ σεισμῶν γῆς]

Ἀναξαγόρας ἀέρος ὑποδύσει τῇ μὲν πυκνότητι τῆς ἐπιφανείας προσπίπτοντος, τῷ δ᾽ ἔκκρισιν λαβεῖν μὴ δύνασθαι τρόμῳ τὸ περιέχον κραδαίνοντος.[1]

> [1] κραιδαίνοντος Π: κραδαίνεσθαι Mm

D63 (A89) Sen. *Quaest. nat.* 6.9.1

[. . .] Anaxagoras [. . .] existimat simili paene ex causa et aëra concuti et terram, cum in[1] inferiore parte spiritus crassum aëra et in nubes coactum eadem vi, qua[2] apud nos quoque nubila frangi solent, rupit,[3] et ignis ex hoc collisu nubium cursuque elisi aëris emicuit, hic ipse in obvia incurrit exitum quaerens, ac divellit repugnantia, donec per angustum[4] aut nactus est viam exeundi ad caelum aut vi et iniuria fecit.

> [1] in *Cam DEST, om. cett.*   [2] eadem vi qua *Fortunatus:* eadem via qua Zθπ: cadere in aqua *AB:* eadem in aqua V
> [3] rumpit *mss., corr. Gertz*   [4] angustum *T:* -tam *AVθπ:* -ta *B:* -tiam Z

clogged by the rains (since by nature at least it is all equally porous)—on the idea that there is a higher part and a lower one of the totality of the sphere and that the higher part is the one on which we happen to live, while the other is the lower one.

b Aëtius

Anaxagoras: [scil. earthquakes occur] because the air that has penetrated [scil. under the earth] collides with its dense surface and, not finding an exit, shakes what surrounds it with a tremor.

D63 (A89) Seneca, *Natural Questions*

[. . .] Anaxagoras [. . .] thinks that the earth is shaken for almost a similar reason as air is, when, in the lower part [i.e. under the earth], wind has broken a thick air condensed into clouds with the same force as, where we are, a cloudy formation too customarily breaks apart, and that the fire has flashed because of this collision of clouds and the expulsion of the air that is driven out, that this latter, seeking an exit, encounters obstacles and tears apart whatever opposes it, until, by a narrow passage, it either finds a way to escape to the sky or else creates one by force and violence.

The Sea (D64–D65)

D64 (A90) Aët. 3.16.2 (Ps.-Plut.) [περὶ θαλάττης πῶς συνέστη καὶ πῶς ἐστι πικρά]

Ἀναξαγόρας τοῦ κατ᾽ ἀρχὴν λιμνάζοντος ὑγροῦ περικαέντος ὑπὸ τῆς ἡλιακῆς περιφορᾶς καὶ τοῦ λεπτοτάτου[1] ἐξατμισθέντος εἰς ἁλυκίδα καὶ πικρίαν τὸ λοιπὸν ὑποστῆναι.

> [1] λιπαροῦ mss., corr. Gomperz, alii alia

D65 (A 90) Alex. *In Meteor.*, p. 67.17–21

τρίτη δὲ δόξα περὶ θαλάσσης ἐστὶν ὡς ἄρα τὸ ὕδωρ τὸ διὰ τῆς γῆς διηθούμενον καὶ διαπλῦνον αὐτὴν ἁλμυρὸν γίνεται τῷ ἔχειν τὴν γῆν τοιούτους χυμοὺς ἐν αὐτῇ· οὗ σημεῖον ἐποιοῦντο τὸ καὶ ἅλας ὀρύττεσθαι ἐν αὐτῇ καὶ νίτρα· εἶναι δὲ καὶ ὀξεῖς χυμοὺς πολλαχοῦ τῆς γῆς. ταύτης πάλιν τῆς δόξης ἐγένετο Ἀναξαγόρας [. . .].

The Flooding of the Nile (D66)

D66

a (A91) Aët. 4.1.3 (Ps.-Plut.) [περὶ Νείλου ἀναβάσεως]

Ἀναξαγόρας[1] ἐκ τῆς χιόνος τῆς ἐν τῇ Αἰθιοπίᾳ τηκομένης μὲν τῷ θέρει, ψυχομένης δὲ τῷ χειμῶνι.

ANAXAGORAS

The Sea (D64–D65)

D64 (A90) Aëtius

Anaxagoras: when the stagnant water at the beginning was strongly heated by the sun's revolution and its thinnest part evaporated, the remaining residue became salty and bitter.

D65 (A90) Alexander of Aphrodisias, *Commentary on Aristotle's* Meteorology

The third doctrine about the sea is that the water that filters through the earth and cleans it becomes brackish because the earth contains within itself these kinds of flavors; they have cited as evidence the extraction of salts and soda from it and the existence of acidic fluids in many places of the earth. Of this opinion in turn was Anaxagoras [. . .].

The Flooding of the Nile (D66)

D66

a (A91) Aëtius

Anaxagoras: [scil. the Nile floods] because of the snow in Ethiopia, which melts in the summer and becomes cold in the winter.

---

1 Ἀναξιμένης m

101

b (A91) Sen. *Quaest. nat.* 4a.2.17

Anaxagoras ait ex Aethiopiae iugis solutas nives ad Nilum usque decurrere.

c (A91* Lanza) Anon. Flor. *Inund. Nili* (cod. Laur. 56.1), p. 538 Landi

Ἀναξαγόρας δὲ ὁ φυσικός φησι τῆς χιόνος τηκο-μένης τὴν ἀναπλήρωσιν τοῦ Νείλου γίνεσθαι· [. . .].

d (≠ DK) Tzetz. *In Il.* 1.427 (p. 188 Lasserre)

Ἀναξαγόρας πάλιν δὲ μετὰ τοῦ Δημοκρίτου
καί τις ἀνὴρ Ἀρχέλαος [. . .]
[. . .] συντρέχουσιν Ὁμήρῳ·
[. . .]
ἐξ ὄμβρων καὶ χιόνος τε τῆς ἐν Αἰθιοπίᾳ
συντηκομένης λέγοντες κατάρδεσθαι τὸν Νεῖλον.

Stones (D67)

D67 (< A98a) Psell. *Lapid.* 26 (p. 119.105–7 Duffy)

τούτων δὲ τῶν παρὰ τοῖς λίθοις δυνάμεων αἰτίας πολ-λοὶ ἐθάρρησαν ἀποδοῦναι, τῶν μὲν ἀρχαιοτέρων σο- ·
φῶν Ἀναξαγόρας [. . .].

b (A91) Seneca, *Natural Questions*

Anaxagoras says that melted snows flow down from the mountains of Ethiopia all the way to the Nile.

c (≠ DK) Anonymous, *On the Flooding of the Nile*

Anaxagoras the natural philosopher says that the flooding of the Nile occurs when the snow melts [. . .].

d (≠ DK) Tzetzes, *Commentary on Homer's* Iliad

Anaxagoras in turn with Democritus
and a certain Archelaus [. . .]
[. . .] they agree with Homer:
[. . .]
When they say that it is from rains and the snow
That melts in Ethiopia that the Nile is watered. [cf.
ATOM. D120; ARCH. D17; Hom. *Od.* 4.581]

Stones (D67)

D67 (< A98a) Psellus, *On the Powers of Stones*

Many people have ventured to explain the causes for these powers of stones: among the more ancient sages Anaxagoras [. . .].

Biology (D68–D95)
Zoogony (D68)

D68 (< A113) Iren. *Adv. haer.* 2.14.2

Anaxagoras autem [. . .] dogmatizavit facta animalia deci-
dentibus e caelo in terram seminibus.

Soul (D69)

D69 (< A93) Aët. 4. 3. 2 (Stob.) [εἰ σῶμα ἡ ψυχὴ καὶ
τίς ἡ οὐσία αὐτῆς]

[. . .] Ἀναξαγόρας [. . .] ἀερώδη.

Sensations (D70–D79)
General Principles (D70–D71)

D70 (< A92) Theophr. *Sens.* 27

Ἀναξαγόρας δὲ γίνεσθαι μὲν τοῖς ἐναντίοις· τὸ γὰρ
ὅμοιον ἀπαθὲς ὑπὸ τοῦ ὁμοίου. καθ᾽ ἑκάστην δ᾽ ἰδίᾳ
πειρᾶται διαριθμεῖν [. . . = **D72**].

D71 (A93* Lanza) Aët. 4.9.6 (Stob., Ps.-Plut.) [εἰ ἀληθεῖς
αἱ αἰσθήσεις καὶ φαντασίαι]

[. . .] Ἀναξαγόρας[1] [. . .] παρὰ τὰς συμμετρίας τῶν
πόρων τὰς κατὰ μέρος αἰσθήσεις γίνεσθαι, τοῦ οἰ-
κείου τῶν αἰσθητῶν ἑκάστου ἑκάστῃ ἐναρμόττοντος.[2]

Biology (D68–D95)
Zoogony (D68)

D68 (< A113) Irenaeus, *Against Heresies*

But Anaxagoras [. . .] maintained that animals were produced by seeds that fell from the sky onto the earth.

Soul (D69)

D69 (< A93) Aëtius

[. . .] Anaxagoras [. . .]: [scil. the soul is made] of air.

Sensations (D70–D79)
General Principles (D70–D71)

D70 (< A92) Theophrastus, *On Sensations*

Anaxagoras [scil. says that sensations] occur by means of contraries: for what is similar is not affected by what is similar. He tries to go through each one [i.e. sense] separately [. . .].

D71 (≠ DK) Aëtius

[. . .] Anaxagoras [. . .]: particular sensations occur as a function of the adaptation of the passages, each of the appropriate perceptibles adjusting to each one of them.

---

[1] Ἀναξαγόρας non hab. Plut.   [2] ἐναρμόττοντος Diels: ἀναρμόττοντος Stob.: ἁρμόζοντος Plut.

Sight (D72)

D72 (< A92) Theophr. *Sens.* 27

[. . . = **D70**] ὁρᾶν μὲν γὰρ τῇ ἐμφάσει τῆς κόρης, οὐκ ἐμφαίνεσθαι δὲ εἰς τὸ ὁμόχρων, ἀλλ' εἰς τὸ διάφορον· καὶ τοῖς μὲν πολλοῖς μεθ' ἡμέραν, ἐνίοις δὲ νύκτωρ εἶναι τὸ ἀλλόχρων, διοξυωπεῖν δέ·[1] ἁπλῶς δὲ τὴν νύκτα μᾶλλον ὁμόχρων εἶναι τοῖς ὀφθαλμοῖς. ἐμφαίνεσθαι δὲ μεθ' ἡμέραν, ὅτι τὸ φῶς συναίτιον τῆς ἐμφάσεως·[2] τὴν δὲ χρόαν τὴν κρατοῦσαν μᾶλλον εἰς τὴν ἑτέραν ἐμφαίνεσθαι [. . . = **D73**].

[1] διοξυωπεῖν δὲ mss.: διὸ ὀξυωπεῖν τότε Schneider
[2] ἐπιφάσεως mss., corr. Schneider

Touch and Taste (D73)

D73 (< A92) Theophr. *Sens.* 28

[. . . = **D72**] τὸν αὐτὸν δὲ τρόπον καὶ τὴν ἀφὴν καὶ τὴν γεῦσιν κρίνειν· τὸ γὰρ ὁμοίως θερμὸν καὶ ψυχρὸν οὔτε θερμαίνειν οὔτε ψύχειν πλησιάζον οὐδὲ δὴ[1] τὸ γλυκὺ καὶ τὸ ὀξὺ δι' αὐτῶν γνωρίζειν, ἀλλὰ τῷ μὲν θερμῷ τὸ ψυχρόν, τῷ δ' ἁλμυρῷ τὸ πότιμον, τῷ δ' ὀξεῖ τὸ γλυκὺ κατὰ τὴν ἔλλειψιν τὴν ἑκάστου· πάντα γὰρ ἐνυπάρχειν ἐστὶν[2] ἐν ἡμῖν. [. . . = **D74**]

[1] δεῖ mss., corr. Stephanus
[2] ἐστὶν secl. Philippson: πάντῃ Usener: φησὶν Diels

Sight (D72)

D72 (< A92) Theophrastus, *On Sensations*

[. . .] For seeing is due to reflection in the pupil, but reflection does not occur in what is of the same color, but in what is different. And in most [scil. animals] it is by day, but in some at night, that the difference in color occurs and that their vision is keen. But in general it is rather the night that is of the same color as the eyes; reflection occurs by day because light is a concomitant cause of the reflection, and it is the dominant color that is reflected more in the other [. . .].

Touch and Taste (D73)

D73 (< A92) Theophrastus, *On Sensations*

[. . .] It is in the same way that touch and taste discern: for things that are hot or cold to the same degree do not heat or cool when they come near one another; and it is not by themselves that we know what is sweet or bitter either, but the cold by the hot, the drinkable by the brackish, the sweet by the bitter, as a function of what each one lacks; for it is possible that everything is present in us. [. . .]

Smell and Hearing (D74–D77)

D74 (< A92) Theophr. *Sens.* 28

[. . . = **D73**] ὡσαύτως δὲ καὶ ὀσφραίνεσθαι καὶ ἀκούειν
τὸ μὲν ἅμα τῇ ἀναπνοῇ, τὸ δὲ τῷ διικνεῖσθαι τὸν
ψόφον ἄχρι τοῦ ἐγκεφάλου· τὸ γὰρ περιέχον ὀστοῦν
εἶναι κοῖλον, εἰς ὃ ἐμπίπτειν τὸν ψόφον. [. . . = **D79b**]

D75 (A106) Aët. 4.19.5 (Ps.-Plut.) [περὶ φωνῆς]

Ἀναξαγόρας τὴν φωνὴν γίνεσθαι πνεύματος ἀντιπε-
σόντος μὲν στερεμνίῳ ἀέρι, τῇ δ' ὑποστροφῇ τῆς
πλήξεως μέχρι τῶν ἀκοῶν προσενεχθέντος· καθὸ καὶ
τὴν λεγομένην ἠχὼ γίνεσθαι.

D76 (A74) Ps.-Arist. *Probl.* 11.33 903a7–10

διὰ τί εὐηκοωτέρα ἡ νὺξ τῆς ἡμέρας ἐστίν; πότερον,
ὥσπερ Ἀναξαγόρας φησί, διὰ τὸ τῆς μὲν ἡμέρας σί-
ζειν καὶ ψοφεῖν τὸν ἀέρα θερμαινόμενον ὑπὸ τοῦ
ἡλίου, τῆς δὲ νυκτὸς ἡσυχίαν ἔχειν ἅτε ἐκλελοιπότος
τοῦ θερμοῦ [. . .];

D77 (A74) Plut. *Quaest. conv.* 8.3.3 722A

[. . .] τὸν Ἀναξαγόραν ὑπὸ τοῦ ἡλίου λέγοντα κινεῖσθαι τὸν ἀέρα κίνησιν τρομώδη καὶ παλμοὺς ἔχου-
σαν, ὡς δῆλόν ἐστι τοῖς διὰ τοῦ φωτὸς ἀεὶ διάττουσι
ψήγμασι μικροῖς καὶ θραύσμασιν, ἃ δή τινες τίλας

Smell and Hearing (D74–D77)

D74 (< A92) Theophrastus, *On Sensations*

[. . .] It is in the same way that smell and hearing occur, the former together with breathing, the latter by sound (*psophos*) penetrating to the brain, for the bone that surrounds it is hollow, and it is into this that sound falls. [. . .]

D75 (A106) Aëtius

Anaxagoras: sound (*phônê*) occurs when breath encounters compact air, and because of its recoil from the blow it is carried as far as the ears; it is in this way too that what is called the echo occurs.

D76 (A74) Ps.-Aristotle, *Problems*

Why is hearing easier at night than during the day? Is it, as Anaxagoras says, because during the day the air hisses and buzzes because it is heated by the sun, whereas at night it is quiet, since the heat has ceased [. . .]?

D77 (A74) Plutarch, *Table Talk*

[. . .] Anaxagoras, who says that the sun makes the air tremble and vibrate, as is clear from the bits of dust and the particles that are always flying through the light, and which some people call 'motes.' That man says that during

καλοῦσιν· ταῦτ᾽ οὖν φησιν ὁ ἀνὴρ πρὸς τὴν θερμό-
τητα σίζοντα καὶ ψοφοῦντα δι᾽ ἡμέρας δυσηκόους τῷ
ψόφῳ τὰς φωνὰς ποιεῖν, νυκτὸς δὲ †φαίνεσθαι†[1] τὸν
σάλον αὐτῶν καὶ τὸν ἦχον.

[1] μαραίνεσθαι Bernardakis: ἀφανίζεσθαι Castiglioni: an
φθίνεσθαι?

Relation between an Animal's Size and the
Acuity of Its Perception (D78)

D78 (< A92) Theophr. *Sens.* 29–30

[. . . = **D79b**] [29] αἰσθητικώτερα δὲ τὰ μείζω ζῷα καὶ
ἁπλῶς εἶναι κατὰ τὸ μέγεθος τὴν αἴσθησιν.[1] ὅσα μὲν
γὰρ μεγάλους καὶ καθαροὺς καὶ λαμπροὺς ὀφθαλ-
μοὺς ἔχει, μεγάλα τε καὶ πόρρωθεν ὁρᾶν, ὅσα δὲ μι-
κρούς, ἐναντίως. [30] ὁμοίως δὲ καὶ ἐπὶ τῆς ἀκοῆς. τὰ
μὲν γὰρ μεγάλα τῶν μεγαλῶν καὶ τῶν πόρρωθεν
ἀκούειν, τὰ δ᾽ ἐλάττω λανθάνειν, τὰ δὲ μικρὰ τῶν
μικρῶν καὶ τῶν ἐγγύς. καὶ ἐπὶ τῆς ὀσφρήσεως ὁμοίως·
ὄζειν μὲν γὰρ μᾶλλον τὸν λεπτὸν ἀέρα, θερμαινόμενον μὲν γὰρ καὶ μανούμενον ὄζειν. ἀναπνέον δὲ τὸ
μὲν μέγα ζῷον ἅμα τῷ μανῷ καὶ τὸ πυκνὸν ἕλκειν, τὸ
δὲ μικρὸν αὐτὸ τὸ μανόν, διὸ καὶ τὰ μεγάλα μᾶλλον
αἰσθάνεσθαι. καὶ γὰρ τὴν ὀσμὴν ἐγγὺς εἶναι μᾶλλον[2]
ἢ πόρρω διὰ τὸ πυκνοτέραν[3] εἶναι, σκεδαννυμένην δὲ
ἀσθενῆ. σχεδὸν δὲ ὡς εἰπεῖν οὐκ αἰσθάνεσθαι τὰ μὲν
μεγάλα τῆς λεπτῆς ἀέρος,[4] τὰ δὲ μικρὰ τῆς πυκνῆς.
[. . .= **R23**]

the day these things, hissing and buzzing because of the heat, make sounds hard to hear because of the noise, whereas at night their agitation and resonance †appear†.[1]

---

[1] One expects a word like 'disappear.'

Relation between an Animal's Size and the Acuity of Its Perception (D78)

D78 (< A92) Theophrastus, *On Sensations*

[29] The larger animals have better perception, and in general perception depends on size. For those that have large, clear, and bright eyes see large and distant objects, while the inverse is the case for those that have small ones. [30] The same applies to hearing. For large ones hear what is large and distant while they do not notice what is smaller, while small ones hear what is small and nearby. The same applies to smell. For thin air has a stronger odor, for it is when it is heated and becomes rarefied that it emits an odor. And when a large animal breathes it inhales the dense together with the rarefied, while a small one inhales just the rarefied; that is why large ones have a more intense perception. For it is because it is denser that a nearby odor is stronger than a distant one, while when it is dispersed it is weak. One could almost say that large animals do not perceive thin air, small ones dense air.

---

[1] αἴσθησιν ‹τῶν αἰσθητηρίων› Schneider   [2] μᾶλλον ‹ἰσχυρὰν› vel ‹κρῖναι› μᾶλλον coni. Diels   [3] πυκνότερα mss., corr. Camotius   [4] ἀέρος ut glossema del. Diels: ὀσμῆς Philippson

Sensation Is Painful (D79)

D79

a   (> A94) Arist. *EN* 7.15 1154b7–9

ἀεὶ γὰρ πονεῖ τὸ ζῷον, ὥσπερ καὶ οἱ φυσιολόγοι[1]
μαρτυροῦσι, τὸ ὁρᾶν,[2] τὸ ἀκούειν φάσκοντες εἶναι λυ-
πηρόν· ἀλλ᾽ ἤδη συνήθεις ἐσμέν, ὥς φασιν.

---

[1] φυσιολόγοι Aspasius *In EN*, p. 156.13: φυσικοὶ K[b]: φυσικοὶ λόγοι cett.   [2] post ὁρᾶν add. καὶ M[b]

b   (< A92) Theophr. *Sens.* 29

[. . . = **D74**] ἅπασαν δ᾽ αἴσθησιν μετὰ λύπης, ὅπερ ἂν
δόξειεν ἀκόλουθον εἶναι τῇ ὑποθέσει· πᾶν γὰρ τὸ
ἀνόμοιον ἁπτόμενον πόνον παρέχει. φανερὸν δὲ τοῦτο
τῷ τε τοῦ ὕπνου[1] πλήθει καὶ τῇ τῶν αἰσθητῶν ὑπερ-
βολῇ. τά τε γὰρ λαμπρὰ χρώματα καὶ τοὺς ὑπερβάλ-
λοντας ψόφους λύπην ἐμποιεῖν καὶ οὐ πολὺν χρόνον
δύνασθαι τοῖς αὐτοῖς ἐπιμένειν. [. . . = **D78**]

---

[1] ὕπνου mss.: χρόνου Schneider

c   (A94) Aët. 4.9.16 (Stob.) [εἰ ἀληθεῖς αἱ αἰσθήσεις]

Ἀναξαγόρας πᾶσαν αἴσθησιν μετὰ πόνου.

Sensation Is Painful (D79)

D79

a (> A94) Aristotle, *Nicomachean Ethics*

A living being is always experiencing suffering, as is testified to by the natural philosophers, who say that seeing, hearing are painful; but we have now become accustomed to this, as they say.[1]

[1] As is shown by **D79b** and **c** (and by Aspasius' commentary on this passage in Aristotle), Aristotle is generalizing here to all the natural philosophers a typically Anaxagorean doctrine.

b (< A92) Theophrastus, *On Sensations*

[. . .] Every sense perception is accompanied by pain, which would seem to correspond to the hypothesis: for everything that is dissimilar causes suffering when it comes into contact. This is clear both from the quantity of sleep and from the excess of perceptible objects: for bright colors and excessive sounds cause a pain and it is impossible to remain exposed for a long time to the same ones [scil. impressions of this sort].

c (A94) Aëtius

Anaxagoras: every sensation is accompanied by pain.

Humans and Animals (D80–D81)

D80 (< A102) Arist. *PA* 4.10 687a7–9

Ἀναξαγόρας μὲν οὖν φησι διὰ τὸ χεῖρας ἔχειν φρο-
νιμώτατον εἶναι τῶν ζῴων ἄνθρωπον [. . .].

D81 (B21b) Plut. *Fort.* 3 98F

ἀλλ᾽ ἐν πᾶσι τούτοις ἀτυχέστεροι τῶν θηρίων ἐσμέν·
ἐμπειρίᾳ δὲ καὶ μνήμῃ καὶ σοφίᾳ καὶ τέχνῃ κατὰ
Ἀναξαγόραν †σφῶν τι†[1] αὐτῶν χρώμεθα καὶ βλίττο-
μεν καὶ ἀμέλγομεν καὶ φέρομεν[2] καὶ ἄγομεν συλλαμ-
βάνοντες [. . .].

---

[1] ἐρίῳ τε Bernardakis: ⟨τῷ⟩ τε σφῶν Fränkel, alii alia
[2] φέρομεν corrupt. videtur

Sleep and Death (D82)

D82 (A103) Aët. 5.25.2 (Ps.-Plut.; cf. Ps.-Gal.) [*ποτέρου
ἐστὶν ὕπνος καὶ θάνατος, ψυχῆς ἢ σώματος*]

Ἀναξαγόρας κατὰ κόπον[1] τῆς σωματικῆς ἐνεργείας
γίνεσθαι τὸν ὕπνον· σωματικὸν γὰρ εἶναι τὸ πάθος,
οὐ ψυχικόν· εἶναι δὲ καὶ ψυχῆς θάνατον τὸν διαχωρι-
σμόν.

---

[1] κατὰ κόπον Gal.: om. Plut.

Humans and Animals (D80–D81)

D80 (< A102) Aristotle, *Parts of Animals*

Anaxagoras says that the human being is the most intelligent of the animals because he has hands [. . .].

D81 (B21b) Plutarch, *On Fortune*

In all these regards [scil. relative to physical strength] we are less fortunate than the wild beasts, but, according to Anaxagoras, thanks to experience, memory, cleverness, and skill we make use of their †. . .†,[1] we collect their honey and take their milk, and, gathering them together, we drive (?) and lead them away [. . .].[2]

[1] Many conjectures have been suggested, e.g. "wool."

[2] Diels considered the whole sentence beginning "thanks to experience" to be a verbal citation from Anaxagoras, but it is likelier to be a paraphrase.

Sleep and Death (D82)

D82 (A103) Aëtius

Anaxagoras: sleep occurs on account of fatigue caused by bodily activity, for it is a process belonging to the body, not to the soul. But complete separation is the death of the soul too.[1]

[1] Starting from "not to the soul," this is probably the doxographer's commentary.

Respiration (D83)

D83 (A115) Arist. *Resp.* 2 470b30–471a2

Ἀναξαγόρας δὲ καὶ Διογένης, πάντα φάσκοντες ἀναπνεῖν, περὶ τῶν ἰχθύων καὶ τῶν ὀστρέων λέγουσι τίνα
τρόπον ἀναπνέουσιν. καί φησιν Ἀναξαγόρας μέν,
ὅταν ἀφῶσι τὸ ὕδωρ διὰ τῶν βραγχίων, τὸν ἐν τῷ
στόματι γινόμενον ἀέρα ἕλκοντας ἀναπνεῖν τοὺς
ἰχθῦς· οὐ γὰρ εἶναι κενὸν οὐδέν. [. . . = **DIOG. D46**]

Reproduction (D84–D92)
Origin of the Semen (D84)

D84 (< A107; < 24 A13) Cens. *Die nat.* 5.3–4

sed hanc opinionem nonnulli refellunt, ut Anaxagoras
[. . .]; hi enim post gregum[1] contentionem[2] non medullis
modo, verum et adipe multaque carne mares exhauriri
respondent [. . . = **D85**].

[1] gregum *H:* graecam (gre- *V*) *C:* crebram *coni. Ald.*
[2] conventionem *Gruber:* coitionem *coni. Ald.*

Respective Contributions of the
Father and the Mother (D85–D87)

D85 (< A107; < 24 A13) Cens. *Die nat.* 5.3–4

[. . . = **D84**] illud quoque ambiguam facit inter auctores
opinionem, utrumne ex patris tantummodo semine partus

Respiration (D83)

D83 (A115) Aristotle, *On Respiration*

Anaxagoras [. . .] and Diogenes, who say that all [scil. animals] breathe, explain in what way fish and oysters breathe. According to Anaxagoras, fish breathe when they expel water through their gills and draw in the air that is formed in their mouths: for there does not exist any void.

Reproduction (D84–D92)
Origin of the Semen (D84)

D84 (< A107; < 24 A13) Censorinus, *The Birthday*

But some people, like Anaxagoras [. . .] refute this opinion [scil. that semen comes from the marrow]: they object that after the exertion [i.e. the copulation] of the flocks, the males are drained not only of their marrow but also of their fat and of much of their flesh [. . .].

Respective Contributions of the
Father and the Mother (D85–D87)

D85 (< A107; < 24 A13) Censorinus, *The Birthday*

[. . .] The following question too causes a difference of opinion among the authorities: whether the offspring is

117

nascatur, [. . .], an etiam ex matris, quod Anaxagorae [. . .]
visum est.

D86 (A107) Arist. *GA* 4.1 763b30–764a1

φασὶ γὰρ οἱ μὲν ἐν τοῖς σπέρμασιν εἶναι ταύτην τὴν
ἐναντίωσιν εὐθύς, οἷον Ἀναξαγόρας καὶ ἕτεροι τῶν
φυσιολόγων· γίνεσθαί τε γὰρ ἐκ τοῦ ἄρρενος τὸ
σπέρμα, τὸ δὲ θῆλυ παρέχειν τὸν τόπον, καὶ εἶναι τὸ
μὲν ἄρρεν ἐκ τῶν δεξιῶν τὸ δὲ θῆλυ ἐκ τῶν ἀριστερῶν, καὶ τῆς ὑστέρας τὰ μὲν ἄρρενα ἐν τοῖς δεξιοῖς
εἶναι τὰ δὲ θήλεα ἐν τοῖς ἀριστεροῖς.

D87 (A111) Cens. *Die nat.* 6.8

Anaxagoras autem eius parentis faciem referre liberos
iudicavit, qui seminis amplius contulisset.

Embryology (D88–D90)

D88 (A109) Cens. *Die nat.* 6.2

sunt qui aetherium calorem inesse arbitrentur, qui mem-
bra disponat, Anaxagoran secuti.

D89 (A108) Cens. *Die nat.* 6.1

Anaxagoras cerebrum, unde omnes sunt sensus.

born only from the father's seed [. . .] or also from the mother's, as was Anaxagoras' view [. . .]?

D86 (A107) Aristotle, *Generation of Animals*

Some people, like Anaxagoras and other natural philosophers, say that this opposition [scil. between male and female] exists from the outset in the semen. For the semen comes from the male, while the female provides the place; and the male comes from the right side, the female from the left, and in the womb the males are on the right side, and the females on the left.

See also **EMP. D175**

D87 (A111) Censorinus, *The Birthday*

Anaxagoras believed that children have the facial features of that parent who contributed more of the seed.

Embryology (D88–D90)

D88 (A109) Censorinus, *The Birthday*

Some people, who follow Anaxagoras, think that there exists inside [scil. the semen] an aethereal heat that orders the limbs.

D89 (A108) Censorinus, *The Birthday*

Anaxagoras [scil. says that the first part formed in the embryo is] the brain, from which all the senses come.

D90 (A110) Cens. *Die nat.* 6.3

Anaxagorae enim ceterisque conpluribus per umbilicum cibus administrari videtur.

Peculiarities of Animal Reproduction (D91–D92)

D91 (< A114) Arist. *GA* 3.6 756b13–17

εἰσὶ γάρ τινες οἳ λέγουσι κατὰ τὸ στόμα μίγνυσθαι τούς τε κόρακας καὶ τὴν ἶβιν καὶ τῶν τετραπόδων τίκτειν κατὰ τὸ στόμα τὴν γαλῆν. ταῦτα γὰρ καὶ Ἀναξαγόρας καὶ τῶν ἄλλων τινὲς φυσικῶν λέγουσι [. . .].

D92 (B22) Aristoph. Byz. *Epit.* 2.57D

Ἀναξαγόρας[1] ἐν τοῖς Φυσικοῖς τὸ καλούμενόν φησιν ὄρνιθος γάλα τὸ ἐν τοῖς ᾠοῖς εἶναι λευκόν.

[1] Ἀλκμαίων coni. Sider

Botany (D93–D95)

D93 (A116) Plut. *Quaest. nat.* 1 911D

ζῷον γὰρ ἔγγαιον τὸ φυτὸν εἶναι [. . .] οἱ περὶ [. . .] Ἀναξαγόραν [. . .] οἴονται.

D90 (A110) Censorinus, *The Birthday*

Anaxagoras and many other people think that nourishment is supplied through the umbilical cord.

Peculiarities of Animal Reproduction (D91–D92)

D91 (< A114) Aristotle, *Generation of Animals*

Some people say that ravens and the ibis have sexual congress through the mouth, and that among four-footed animals the weasel gives birth through the mouth. This is what both Anaxagoras and some of the other natural philosophers say [. . .].

D92 (B22) Aristophanes of Byzantium, *Epitome of Aristotle's* History of Animals

Anaxagoras says in his books *On Nature* that what is called 'bird's milk' is the white of eggs.

Botany (D93–D95)

D93 (A116) Plutarch, *Natural Questions*

[. . .] Anaxagoras' followers [. . .] think that a plant is an animal in the earth.

D94 (A117) Theophr. *HP* 3.1.4

[. . .] Ἀναξαγόρας μὲν τὸν ἀέρα πάντων φάσκων ἔχειν σπέρματα καὶ ταῦτα συγκαταφερόμενα τῷ ὕδατι γεννᾶν τὰ φυτά [. . .].

D95 (cf. A117) Nic. Dam. *Plant.*

a 1.3, p. 127 Drossaart Lulofs (cf. Ps.-Arist. *Plant.* 1.1 815a15–21)

أما أنكساغورس وهمفدوقلس فزعما أن للنبات شهوة وحسا وغما ولذة وزعم أنكساغورس أنه حيوان وأنه يفرح ويحزن وزعم أن دليله على ذلك انتثار ورقه في حينه.

b p. 449.54–56 Drossaart Lulofs

אמר אמנם אנכסגוריש ואבן דקליס חשבו שלצמח תאוה והרגש וצער והנאה. וחשב אנכסגוריש שהוא בעל חיים ושמח ויתאבל. וחשב שראיתו על זה התפשט עליו וענפיו שעלתו אל הלחות וברחו מההפך.

c 1.10, p. 129 (cf. Ps.-Arist. *Plant.* 1.1 815b16–17)

فأما أنكساغورس وهمفدوقلس وديمقراطيس فزعموا أن للنبات عقلا وفهما.

d 1.44, p. 141

أنكساغورس زعم أن بزره من الهواء[. . .].

D94 (A117) Theophrastus, *History of Plants*

[. . .] Anaxagoras, who asserts that the air contains seeds of all things and that these, when they descend together with water, generate plants [. . .].

D95 (cf. A117) Nicolaus of Damascus, *On Plants*

a

Now, Anaxagoras and Empedocles assert that plants have desire and sensation, pain and pleasure, and Anaxagoras asserts that they are animals and that they feel joy and sorrow, and he cites as evidence that they shed their leaves in due season.

b

He [i.e. Aristotle as cited by Nicolaus of Damascus] says that Anaxagoras and Empedocles assert that plants have desire, sensation, pain, and pleasure. Anaxagoras asserts that they are animals, and that they feel joy and sorrow. And he says that his evidence for this is that they stretch out their leaves and branches at the due season toward moisture and withdraw from the opposite.

c

Anaxagoras, Empedocles and Democritus maintained that plants possess reason and understanding.

d

Anaxagoras maintains that their [i.e. plants'] seeds are carried down from the air [. . .].

123

e pp. 449.65–66

וההבדל בין אנכסגוריש ואבן דקליס שאאנכסגוריש לא יניח בצמח זכרים
ונקבות שהעושים פרי כל המין עושה פרי [EMP. **250b** = . . .]

Mathematics (D96–D97)

D96 (< A9) Procl. *In Eucl., Prol.* 2, p. 65.21–66.1

μετὰ δὲ τοῦτον Ἀναξαγόρας [. . .] πολλῶν ἐφήψατο
τῶν κατὰ γεωμετρίαν [. . .].

D97 (< A39) Vitruv. 7 *Praef.* 11

[. . .] Democritus et Anaxagoras de eadem re scripserunt,
quemadmodum oporteat ad aciem oculorum radiorumque
extentionem certo loco centro constituto lineas ratione
naturali respondere, uti de incerta re certae imagines
aedificiorum in scaenarum picturis redderent speciem et
quae in directis planisque frontibus sint figurata, alia
abscedentia alia prominentia esse videantur.

e

The difference between Anaxagoras and Empedocles is that Anaxagoras did not allow that plants have males and females, since the whole species of those [scil. plants] that bear fruit is fructiferous [. . .].[1]

---

[1] Texts **a** (modified), **c**, and **d** translated by H. J. Drossaart Lulofs, **b** and **e** by Elisa Coda.

Mathematics (D96–D97)

D96 (< A9) Proclus, *Commentary on the* First Book *of Euclid's* Elements

After him [i.e. Pythagoras], Anaxagoras [. . .] applied himself to many questions of geometry [. . .].

D97 (< A39) Vitruvius, *On Architecture*

[. . .] Democritus [= **ATOM. D216**] and Anaxagoras wrote about the same subject [scil. as Agatharchus, viz. scene painting]: how, by taking a certain point as the center, to make the lines correspond by a natural ratio to the visual angle and the projection of the rays, in such a way that, in virtue of an object without reality, real images would produce the appearance of buildings on the scene painting, and so that what was represented on vertical and plane surfaces would seem in some cases to recede and in others to project outward.

See also **P26a**

A Moralizing Interpretation of Homer (D98)

D98 (< A1) Diog. Laert. 2.11

δοκεῖ δὲ πρῶτος, καθά φησι Φαβωρῖνος ἐν Παντοδαπῇ ἱστορίᾳ [Frag. 66 Amato], τὴν Ὁμήρου ποίησιν
ἀποφήνασθαι εἶναι περὶ ἀρετῆς καὶ δικαιοσύνης· ἐπὶ
πλεῖον δὲ προστῆναι τοῦ λόγου Μητρόδωρον τὸν
Λαμψακηνόν, γνώριμον ὄντα αὐτοῦ, ὃν καὶ πρῶτον
σπουδάσαι περὶ τὴν τοῦ ποιητοῦ φυσικὴν πραγμα-
τείαν.

A Moralizing Interpretation of Homer (D98)

D98 (< A1) Diogenes Laertius

According to what Favorinus says in his *Miscellaneous History,* he seems to have been the first person to declare that the poetry of Homer is about virtue and justice; and Metrodorus of Lampsacus, who was his student [cf. **P27**], defended this interpretation further and was the first person to study the poet's treatment of nature.[1]

[1] Metrodorus of Lampsacus, mentioned for the first time by Plato, *Ion* 530c, is known for his physical exegeses of Homer [61 DK].

ANAXAGORAS [59 DK]

R

Earliest References and Allusions to
Anaxagoras (R1–R3)
Democritus (R1–R2)

R1 (< A5) Diog. Laert. 9.34–35

Φαβωρῖνος δέ φησιν ἐν Παντοδαπῇ ἱστορίᾳ [Frag. 81 Amato] λέγειν Δημόκριτον περὶ Ἀναξαγόρου ὡς οὐκ εἴησαν αὐτοῦ αἱ δόξαι αἵ τε περὶ ἡλίου καὶ σελήνης, ἀλλὰ ἀρχαῖαι, τὸν δὲ ὑφῃρῆσθαι· [35] διασύρειν τε αὐτοῦ τὰ περὶ τῆς διακοσμήσεως καὶ τοῦ νοῦ, ἐχθρῶς ἔχοντα πρὸς αὐτόν, ὅτι δὴ μὴ προσήκατο αὐτόν. πῶς οὖν κατά τινας ἀκήκοεν αὐτοῦ;

R2 (B21a) Sext. Emp. *Adv. Math.* 7.140

ὄψις γὰρ τῶν ἀδήλων τὰ φαινόμενα, ὥς φησιν Ἀναξαγόρας [**D6**], ὃν ἐπὶ τούτῳ Δημόκριτος ἐπαινεῖ [. . .].

ANAXAGORAS

R

Earliest References and Allusions to
Anaxagoras (R1–R3)
Democritus (R1–R2)

R1 (< A5) Diogenes Laertius

Favorinus reports in his *Miscellaneous History* that Democritus said about Anaxagoras that the opinions he expressed about the sun and moon were not his own but were ancient, and that he had stolen them; and that he [i.e. Democritus] tore to pieces what he [i.e. Anaxagoras] said about the cosmic ordering and mind, displaying hostility toward him because he [i.e. Anaxagoras] had not accepted him to his company. So how could he have been his student, as some people maintain?[1]

[1] The relation between this report and **P10** (cf. **ATOM. R8**) is problematic: was it Anaxagoras who rejected Democritus, or was it the other way around?

R2 (B21a) Sextus Empiricus, *Against the Logicians*

For **"appearances: vision of things that are invisible"** [**D6**], as is said by Anaxagoras, whom Democritus praises for this [. . .] [cf. **ATOM. D14–D23**].

Herodotus (R3)

R3 (A91) Hdt. 2.22

ἡ δὲ τρίτη τῶν ὁδῶν πολλὸν ἐπιεικεστάτη ἐοῦσα μάλιστα ἔψευσται· λέγει γὰρ δὴ οὐδ᾽ αὕτη οὐδέν, φαμένη τὸν
Νεῖλον ῥέειν ἀπὸ τηκομένης χιόνος.

Euripides

See **DRAM. T75–T80**

Aeschines the Socratic

See **PROD. R3**

*Plato's and Xenophon's Evaluations of
Anaxagoras' Teleology (R4–R7)
Plato (R4–R6)*

R4 (A35) Plat. *Apol.* 26d–e

[ΜΕ.] [. . .] ἐπεὶ τὸν μὲν ἥλιον λίθον φησὶν εἶναι, τὴν δὲ
σελήνην γῆν.
[ΣΩ.] Ἀναξαγόρου οἴει κατηγορεῖν [. . .] καὶ οἴει αὐτοὺς
ἀπείρους γραμμάτων εἶναι ὥστε οὐκ εἰδέναι ὅτι τὰ
Ἀναξαγόρου βιβλία τοῦ Κλαζομενίου γέμει τούτων τῶν
λόγων [. . .]. καὶ δὴ καὶ οἱ νέοι ταῦτα παρ᾽ ἐμοῦ μαν-
θάνουσιν, ἃ ἔξεστιν ἐνίοτε εἰ πάνυ πολλοῦ δραχμῆς ἐκ

Herodotus (R3)

R3 (A91) Herodotus, *Histories*

The third way [scil. in which people explain the floods of
the Nile], though it is by far the most plausible, is the most
mistaken: for it too does not say anything worthwhile when
it asserts that the Nile's flow comes from melting snow [cf.
D4[5], D66].

Euripides

See **DRAM. T75–T80**

Aeschines the Socratic

See **PROD. R3**

Plato's and Xenophon's Evaluations of
Anaxagoras' Teleology (R4–R7)
Plato (R4–R6)

R4 (A35) Plato, *Apology*

[Meletus:] [. . .] for he [i.e. Socrates] says that the sun is a
stone and that the moon is earth.
[Socrates:] You think that you are accusing Anaxagoras
[. . .] and you think that they [i.e. the jurors] are so illiter-
ate that they do not know that the books of Anaxagoras of
Clazomenae are filled with such assertions [. . .]. And what
is more, I suppose that it is from me that the young learn
these things—when they can buy them at the marketplace

τῆς ὀρχήστρας πριαμένοις Σωκράτους καταγελᾶν, ἐὰν
προσποιῆται ἑαυτοῦ εἶναι [. . .].

R5 (> A47) Plat. *Phaed.* 97b–98c

[ΣΩ.] ἀλλ᾽ ἀκούσας μέν ποτε ἐκ βιβλίου τινός, ὡς ἔφη,
Ἀναξαγόρου ἀναγιγνώσκοντος, [97c] καὶ λέγοντος ὡς
ἄρα νοῦς ἐστιν ὁ διακοσμῶν τε καὶ πάντων αἴτιος, ταύτῃ
δὴ τῇ αἰτίᾳ ἥσθην καὶ ἔδοξέ μοι τρόπον τινὰ εὖ ἔχειν τὸ
τὸν νοῦν εἶναι πάντων αἴτιον, καὶ ἡγησάμην, εἰ τοῦθ᾽
οὕτως ἔχει, τόν γε νοῦν κοσμοῦντα πάντα κοσμεῖν καὶ
ἕκαστον τιθέναι ταύτῃ ὅπῃ ἂν βέλτιστα ἔχῃ· εἰ οὖν τις
βούλοιτο τὴν αἰτίαν εὑρεῖν περὶ ἑκάστου ὅπῃ γίγνεται
ἢ ἀπόλλυται ἢ ἔστι, τοῦτο δεῖν περὶ αὐτοῦ εὑρεῖν, ὅπῃ
βέλτιστον αὐτῷ ἐστιν ἢ εἶναι ἢ ἄλλο ὁτιοῦν πάσχειν ἢ
ποιεῖν· [97d] ἐκ δὲ δὴ τοῦ λόγου τούτου οὐδὲν ἄλλο
σκοπεῖν προσήκειν ἀνθρώπῳ, καὶ περὶ αὐτοῦ ἐκείνου
καὶ περὶ ἄλλων, ἀλλ᾽ ἢ τὸ ἄριστον καὶ τὸ βέλτιστον.
ἀναγκαῖον δὲ εἶναι τὸν αὐτὸν τοῦτον καὶ τὸ χεῖρον
εἰδέναι. τὴν αὐτὴν γὰρ εἶναι ἐπιστήμην περὶ αὐτῶν.

ταῦτα δὲ λογιζόμενος ἅσμενος ηὑρηκέναι ᾤμην διδάσκαλον τῆς αἰτίας περὶ τῶν ὄντων κατὰ νοῦν ἐμαυτῷ,
τὸν Ἀναξαγόραν, καί μοι φράσειν πρῶτον μὲν πότερον
ἡ γῆ πλατεῖά ἐστιν ἢ στρογγύλη, [97e] ἐπειδὴ δὲ
φράσειεν, ἐπεκδιηγήσεσθαι τὴν αἰτίαν καὶ τὴν ἀνάγκην, λέγοντα τὸ ἄμεινον καὶ ὅτι αὐτὴν ἄμεινον ἦν
τοιαύτην εἶναι· καὶ εἰ ἐν μέσῳ φαίη εἶναι αὐτήν,

for sometimes barely a drachma and make fun of Socrates
if he pretends that these are his own ideas [. . .].[1]

[1] The Platonic Socrates is imagining possible speeches to the
jury by, first, his accuser Meletus, and, then, himself.

R5 (> A47) Plato, *Phaedo*

[Socrates:] But once, having heard someone reading from
a book of Anaxagoras, as he said, [97c] and saying that
mind is what orders and causes all things, I was pleased at
this causality. It seemed to me to be right in a certain way
that mind be the cause of all things; and I supposed that,
if this was right, then ordering mind orders all things and
establishes each one in the best way possible. If then
someone wanted to find the cause for each thing—why it
comes about, or is destroyed, or is—he would have to find
out why it is best for it to be or to undergo or to do anything
whatsoever. [97d] It follows from this argument that it is
appropriate for a human being to investigate nothing else,
both about this very question and about all other ones,
than what is best and finest; and this same man must necessarily know what is worse too. For it is the same science
that deals with both of these things.

While I was reflecting in this way, I was pleased because I thought that I had found in Anaxagoras someone
who would teach me the cause of the things that are in
accord with [or: with my] mind, and who would tell me
first whether the earth is flat or round, [97e] and then,
once he had indicated this, would add the detailed explanation of the cause and the necessity, speaking of what is
better and saying that it was better that it be like this. And
if he said that it is in the center, he would add the detailed

133

ἐπεκδιηγήσεσθαι ὡς ἄμεινον ἦν αὐτὴν ἐν μέσῳ εἶναι·
καὶ εἴ μοι ταῦτα ἀποφαίνοι, παρεσκευάσμην ὡς οὐκέτι
ποθεσόμενος[1] αἰτίας ἄλλο εἶδος. [98a] καὶ δὴ καὶ περὶ
ἡλίου οὕτω παρεσκευάσμην ὡσαύτως πευσόμενος, καὶ
σελήνης καὶ τῶν ἄλλων ἄστρων, τάχους τε πέρι πρὸς
ἄλληλα καὶ τροπῶν καὶ τῶν ἄλλων παθημάτων, πῇ ποτε
ταῦτ᾽ ἄμεινόν ἐστιν ἕκαστον καὶ ποιεῖν καὶ πάσχειν ἃ
πάσχει. οὐ γὰρ ἄν ποτε αὐτὸν ᾤμην, φάσκοντά γε ὑπὸ
νοῦ αὐτὰ κεκοσμῆσθαι, ἄλλην τινὰ αὐτοῖς αἰτίαν
ἐπενεγκεῖν ἢ ὅτι βέλτιστον αὐτὰ οὕτως ἔχειν ἐστὶν
ὥσπερ ἔχει· [98b] ἑκάστῳ οὖν αὐτὸν ἀποδιδόντα τὴν
αἰτίαν καὶ κοινῇ πᾶσι τὸ ἑκάστῳ βέλτιστον ᾤμην καὶ τὸ
κοινὸν πᾶσιν ἐκδιηγήσεσθαι ἀγαθόν· καὶ οὐκ ἂν
ἀπεδόμην πολλοῦ τὰς ἐλπίδας, ἀλλὰ πάνυ σπουδῇ
λαβὼν τὰς βίβλους ὡς τάχιστα οἷός τ᾽ ἦ ἀνεγίγνωσκον,
ἵν᾽ ὡς τάχιστα εἰδείην τὸ βέλτιστον καὶ τὸ χεῖρον. ἀπὸ
δὴ θαυμαστῆς ἐλπίδος, ὦ ἑταῖρε, ᾠχόμην φερόμενος,
ἐπειδὴ προιὼν καὶ ἀναγιγνώσκων ὁρῶ ἄνδρα τῷ μὲν νῷ
οὐδὲν χρώμενον οὐδέ τινας αἰτίας ἐπαιτιώμενον εἰς τὸ
διακοσμεῖν τὰ πράγματα, [98c] ἀέρας δὲ καὶ αἰθέρας
καὶ ὕδατα αἰτιώμενον καὶ ἄλλα πολλὰ καὶ ἄτοπα.

---

[1] ποθεσόμενος T: ὑποθέμενος B

R6 (≠ DK) Plat. *Phil.* 28c–e

[ΣΩ.] πάντες γὰρ συμφωνοῦσιν οἱ σοφοί, ἑαυτοὺς
ὄντως σεμνύνοντες, ὡς νοῦς ἐστι βασιλεὺς ἡμῖν οὐρανοῦ
τε καὶ γῆς. καὶ ἴσως εὖ λέγουσι. [. . .] [28d] πότερον, ὦ

explanation of the reason why it is better for it to be in the center. And if he showed me this, I would be ready to desire no other kind of cause any longer. [98a] And then I was ready to allow myself to be taught in the same way, regarding the sun, the moon, and the other heavenly bodies, about their relative speeds, their returns [i.e. solstices], and other vicissitudes, the reason for which it is better that each one both do and undergo what it undergoes. For I would never have thought that this man, who said that these things are put in order by mind, would attribute any other cause to them than that it is best that they be as they are. [98b] So I thought that he would explain in detail, assigning the cause to each of them and to all in common, what is best for each one and what is the common good for all. And I would not have sold my hopes for any price, and getting hold of the books with great eagerness, I read them as quickly as I could, in order to find out as quickly as possible what is best and what is worse. But from this marvelous hope, my friend, I fell far, when, going further in my reading, I saw that this man made no use at all of mind and that he did not make certain causes responsible for putting things in order, [98c] but instead attributed the responsibility to airs, aethers, waters, and many other strange things.

R6 (≠ DK) Plato, *Philebus*

[Socrates:] For all the sages agree (taking themselves very seriously indeed) that mind reigns for us over heaven and earth. And perhaps they are right. [. . .] [28d] Should we

Πρώταρχε, τὰ σύμπαντα καὶ τόδε τὸ καλούμενον ὅλον
ἐπιτροπεύειν φῶμεν τὴν τοῦ ἀλόγου καὶ εἰκῇ δύναμιν
καὶ τὸ ὅπῃ ἔτυχεν, ἢ τἀναντία, καθάπερ οἱ πρόσθεν
ἡμῶν ἔλεγον, νοῦν καὶ φρόνησίν τινα θαυμαστὴν συν-
τάττουσαν διακυβερνᾶν; [28e]

[ΠΡΩ.] οὐδὲν τῶν αὐτῶν, ὦ θαυμάσιε Σώκρατες· ὃ μὲν
γὰρ σὺ νῦν λέγεις, οὐδὲ ὅσιον εἶναί μοι φαίνεται. τὸ δὲ
νοῦν πάντα διακοσμεῖν αὐτὰ φάναι καὶ τῆς ὄψεως τοῦ
κόσμου καὶ ἡλίου καὶ σελήνης καὶ ἀστέρων καὶ πάσης
τῆς περιφορᾶς ἄξιον, καὶ οὐκ ἄλλως ἔγωγ' ἄν ποτε περὶ
αὐτῶν εἴποιμι οὐδ' ἂν δοξάσαιμι.

Xenophon (R7)

R7 (A73) Xen. *Mem.* 4.7.6–7

ὅλως δὲ τῶν οὐρανίων, ᾗ ἕκαστα ὁ θεὸς μηχανᾶται,
φροντιστὴν γίγνεσθαι ἀπέτρεπεν· [. . .] κινδυνεῦσαι δ'
ἂν ἔφη καὶ παραφρονῆσαι τὸν ταῦτα μεριμνῶντα οὐδὲν
ἧττον ἢ Ἀναξαγόρας παρεφρόνησεν ὁ μέγιστον φρο-
νήσας ἐπὶ τῷ τὰς τῶν θεῶν μηχανὰς ἐξηγεῖσθαι. [7]
ἐκεῖνος γὰρ λέγων μὲν τὸ αὐτὸ εἶναι πῦρ τε καὶ ἥλιον
ἠγνόει ὅτι τὸ μὲν πῦρ οἱ ἄνθρωποι ῥᾳδίως καθορῶσιν,
εἰς δὲ τὸν ἥλιον οὐ δύνανται ἀντιβλέπειν, καὶ ὑπὸ μὲν
τοῦ ἡλίου καταλαμπόμενοι τὰ χρώματα μελάντερα
ἔχουσιν, ὑπὸ δὲ τοῦ πυρὸς οὔ· ἠγνόει δὲ καὶ ὅτι τῶν ἐκ
τῆς γῆς φυομένων ἄνευ μὲν ἡλίου αὐγῆς οὐδὲν δύναται
καλῶς αὔξεσθαι, ὑπὸ δὲ τοῦ πυρὸς θερμαινόμενα πάντα

say, Protarchus, that it is the force of irrationality and of randomness and chance that administer the totality of things and what is called the whole, or on the contrary, as our predecessors used to say, that mind and a marvelous intelligence put them in order and govern them? [28e] [Protarchus:] It is not at all the same thing, my marvelous Socrates, for what you were saying just now does not seem to me pious either. But to say that it is mind that organizes all these things is justified by the spectacle presented by the cosmos, sun, moon, heavenly bodies and the whole rotation, and I for one would never think or speak otherwise about them.

Xenophon (R7)

R7 (A73) Xenophon, *Memorabilia*

Generally speaking, he [i.e. Socrates] refused to reason about the way in which god succeeds in regulating the mechanism of each of the celestial phenomena. [. . .] He said that someone who worries about these matters even runs the risk of going crazy, not less than Anaxagoras, who reasoned most of all about the explanation of the mechanisms the gods employ. [7] For when he said that fire and the sun are identical, he failed to recognize that human beings easily watch a fire but cannot look directly at the sun; and that the color of the skin of those on whom the sun shines is darker, while this is not the case with fire; and he failed to recognize that none of the things that grow from the earth can increase properly without the sun's shining, while everything that is heated by fire is de-

ἀπόλλυται· φάσκων δὲ τὸν ἥλιον λίθον διάπυρον εἶναι
καὶ τοῦτο ἠγνόει, ὅτι λίθος μὲν ἐν πυρὶ ὢν οὔτε λάμπει
οὔτε πολὺν χρόνον ἀντέχει, ὁ δὲ ἥλιος τὸν πάντα χρόνον
πάντων λαμπρότατος ὢν διαμένει.

*Peripatetic Reconstructions and Evaluations of
Anaxagoras' Doctrines (R8–R23)
Comparison with Anaximander (cf. R19)
Comparison with Empedocles (R8)*

R8 (< A43) Arist. *Metaph.* A3 984a11

Ἀναξαγόρας δὲ ὁ Κλαζομένιος τῇ μὲν ἡλικίᾳ πρότε-
ρος ὢν τούτου, τοῖς δ᾽ ἔργοις ὕστερος [. . . = **D18**].

Teleology (R9–R10)

R9 (A58) Arist. *Metaph.* A3 984b15–18

νοῦν δή τις εἰπὼν ἐνεῖναι, καθάπερ ἐν τοῖς ζῴοις, καὶ ἐν
τῇ φύσει τὸν αἴτιον τοῦ κόσμου καὶ τῆς τάξεως πάσης
οἷον νήφων ἐφάνη παρ᾽ εἰκῇ λέγοντας τοὺς πρότερον.
φανερῶς μὲν οὖν Ἀναξαγόραν ἴσμεν ἁψάμενον τούτων
τῶν λόγων, αἰτίαν δ᾽ ἔχει πρότερον Ἑρμότιμος ὁ Κλαζομένιος εἰπεῖν.

stroyed. And when he said that the sun is a fiery stone he
failed to recognize that a stone placed in a fire does not
shine or resist for long, while the sun remains for all time
as the brightest thing of all.

> *Peripatetic Reconstructions and Evaluations of*
> *Anaxagoras' Doctrines (R8–R23)*
> *Comparison with Anaximander (cf. R19)*
> *Comparison with Empedocles (R8)*

R8 (< A43) Aristotle, *Metaphysics*

Anaxagoras of Clazomenae, who was earlier than him [i.e.
Empedocles] in age but more advanced with regard to his
works [. . .].[1]

[1] The meaning of this sentence is controversial. According to
the most plausible interpretation, Aristotle is judging Anaxagoras
to be superior to Empedocles by reason of his doctrine of mind
(*nous*). Others take it to mean that Anaxagoras' writings are posterior to Empedocles'.

See also **R15, R16; EMP. D81**

Teleology (R9–R10)

R9 (A58) Aristotle, *Metaphysics*

That man, whoever he was, who said that mind is present
in nature too, just as in living beings, as the cause of the
world and of all order, appeared like a sober man compared to his predecessors who were speaking at random.
We know that Anaxagoras manifestly broached these arguments, but it is imputed to Hermotimus of Clazomenae to
have said it first.

R10 (A47) Arist. *Metaph.* A4 985a18–21

Ἀναξαγόρας τε γὰρ μηχανῇ χρῆται τῷ νῷ πρὸς τὴν
κοσμοποιίαν, καὶ ὅταν ἀπορήσῃ διὰ τίν' αἰτίαν ἐξ
ἀνάγκης ἐστί, τότε παρέλκει αὐτόν, ἐν δὲ τοῖς ἄλλοις
πάντα μᾶλλον αἰτιᾶται τῶν γιγνομένων ἢ νοῦν.

Mind (R11–R13)

R11 (A56) Arist. *Phys.* 8.5 256b24–27

διὸ καὶ Ἀναξαγόρας ὀρθῶς λέγει, τὸν νοῦν ἀπαθῆ
φάσκων καὶ ἀμιγῆ εἶναι, ἐπειδή γε κινήσεως ἀρχὴν
αὐτὸν εἶναι ποιεῖ· οὕτω γὰρ μόνως ἂν κινοίη ἀκίνητος
ὢν καὶ κρατοίη ἀμιγὴς ὤν.

R12 (A100) Arist. *An.* 1.2 404b1–7

Ἀναξαγόρας δ' ἧττον διασαφεῖ περὶ αὐτῶν· πολλαχοῦ μὲν γὰρ τὸ αἴτιον τοῦ καλῶς καὶ ὀρθῶς τὸν νοῦν
λέγει, ἑτέρωθι δὲ τὸν νοῦν εἶναι ταὐτὸν τῇ ψυχῇ· ἐν
ἅπασι γὰρ ὑπάρχειν αὐτὸν τοῖς ζῴοις, καὶ μεγάλοις
καὶ μικροῖς, καὶ τιμίοις καὶ ἀτιμοτέροις· οὐ φαίνεται
δ' ὅ γε κατὰ φρόνησιν λεγόμενος νοῦς πᾶσιν ὁμοίως
ὑπάρχειν τοῖς ζῴοις, ἀλλ' οὐδὲ τοῖς ἀνθρώποις πᾶσιν.

R10 (A47) Aristotle, *Metaphysics*

The use that Anaxagoras makes of the mind for the organization of the world is that of an artificial device,[1] and he
drags it in whenever he is at a loss to explain for what cause
something is of necessity; but in the other cases he attri-
butes the cause of what belongs to becoming to everything
rather than to mind.

[1] Perhaps Aristotle has in mind the theatrical *deus ex machina*.

Mind (R11–R13)

R11 (A56) Aristotle, *Physics*

That is why Anaxagoras is right when he says that mind is
impassible and unmixed, since he makes it the principle
of motion: for it is only in this way that it could cause motion, by itself being immobile, and that it could dominate,
by being unmixed itself.

R12 (A100) Aristotle, *On the Soul*

Anaxagoras is less clear [scil. than Democritus] about
them [i.e. soul and thought]: for he often says that mind is
the cause of what is fine and correct, but elsewhere he says
that mind is the same thing as the soul; for it is present in
all the animals, big ones and little ones, honored ones and
less honored ones. But it does not appear to be the case
that mind, at least that which is spoken of in relation to
wisdom (*phronêsis*), is equally present in all animals—for
that matter, not even in all human beings.

R13 (A55) Arist. *An.* 1.2 405a13–19

Ἀναξαγόρας δ᾽ ἔοικε μὲν ἕτερον λέγειν ψυχήν τε καὶ
νοῦν [. . .], χρῆται δ᾽ ἀμφοῖν ὡς μιᾷ φύσει, πλὴν ἀρχὴν γε τὸν νοῦν τίθεται μάλιστα πάντων· μόνον γοῦν
φησιν αὐτὸν τῶν ὄντων ἁπλοῦν εἶναι καὶ ἀμιγῆ τε καὶ
καθαρόν. ἀποδίδωσι δ᾽ ἄμφω τῇ αὐτῇ ἀρχῇ, τό τε
γινώσκειν καὶ τὸ κινεῖν, λέγων νοῦν κινῆσαι τὸ πᾶν.

*Anaxagoras' Ultimate Components Identified with
Aristotelian 'Homeomers' (R14–R15)*

R14 (A46) Arist. *GC* 1.1 314a18–20

ὁ μὲν γὰρ τὰ ὁμοιομερῆ στοιχεῖα τίθησιν, οἷον ὀστοῦν
σάρκα μυελὸν[1] καὶ τῶν ἄλλων ὧν ἑκάστῳ συνώνυμον τὸ
μέρος ἐστίν [. . .].

[1] μυελὸν καὶ ξύλον HW

R15 (A43) Arist. *Cael.* 3.3 302a28–b5

Ἀναξαγόρας δ᾽ ἐναντίως Ἐμπεδοκλεῖ λέγει περὶ τῶν
στοιχείων. ὁ μὲν γὰρ πῦρ καὶ γῆν καὶ τὰ σύστοιχα
τούτοις στοιχεῖά φησιν εἶναι τῶν σωμάτων καὶ συγ-
κεῖσθαι πάντ᾽ ἐκ τούτων, Ἀναξαγόρας δὲ τοὐναντίον· τὰ
γὰρ ὁμοιομερῆ στοιχεῖα (λέγω δ᾽ οἷον σάρκα[1] καὶ
ὀστοῦν καὶ τῶν τοιούτων ἕκαστον), ἀέρα δὲ καὶ πῦρ
μίγματα τούτων καὶ τῶν ἄλλων σπερμάτων πάντων·
εἶναι γὰρ ἑκάτερον αὐτῶν ἐξ ἀοράτων τῶν ὁμοιομερῶν

R13 (A55) Aristotle, *On the Soul*

Anaxagoras seems to say that soul is different from mind
[. . .] but he makes use of both of them as though of a
single nature, except that, at least with regard to the principle of all things, it is mind that he posits most of all—at
least he says that this, alone of the things that are, is simple, unmixed, and pure. He assigns to the same principle
both things, knowing and causing motion, saying that it is
mind that moves the whole.

Anaxagoras' Ultimate Components Identified with
Aristotelian 'Homeomers' (R14–R15)

R14 (A46) Aristotle, *On Generation and Corruption*

For he posits as elements the homeomers, for example
bone, flesh, marrow, and the other things of which the part
has the same name as each one [. . .].

R15 (A43) Aristotle, *On the Heavens*

Anaxagoras maintains the opposite to Empedocles with
regard to the elements. For the latter says that fire, earth,
and the terms belonging to the same series are the elements of bodies and that all things are composed out of
them [cf. e.g. **EMP. D73.269**]. But Anaxagoras says the
opposite: for the homeomers are the elements, I mean for
example flesh, bone, and each of the things of this sort;
while air and fire are mixtures of these things and of all
the other seeds, for each of these is an aggregate of all the
invisible homeomers. That is why all things come from

---

[1] σάρκα EHS^p: ξύλα σάρκα J

πάντων ἠθροισμένον. διὸ καὶ γίγνεσθαι πάντ᾽ ἐκ τού-
των· τὸ γὰρ πῦρ καὶ τὸν αἰθέρα προσαγορεύει ταὐτό.

Aristotle's Criticisms of Anaxagoras' Infinitism (R16–R17)

R16 (< A52* Lanza) Arist. *Phys.* 1.4 187b7–188a18

εἰ δὴ τὸ μὲν ἄπειρον ᾗ ἄπειρον ἄγνωστον, τὸ μὲν κατὰ
πλῆθος ἢ κατὰ μέγεθος ἄπειρον ἄγνωστον πόσον τι, τὸ
δὲ κατ᾽ εἶδος ἄπειρον ἄγνωστον ποιόν τι. τῶν δ᾽ ἀρχῶν
ἀπείρων οὐσῶν καὶ κατὰ πλῆθος καὶ κατ᾽ εἶδος, ἀδύνατον εἰδέναι τὰ ἐκ τούτων. οὕτω γὰρ εἰδέναι τὸ σύνθετον
ὑπολαμβάνομεν, ὅταν εἰδῶμεν ἐκ τίνων καὶ πόσων
ἐστίν.

[187b13] ἔτι δ᾽ εἰ ἀνάγκη, οὗ τὸ μόριον ἐνδέχεται
ὁπηλικονοῦν εἶναι κατὰ μέγεθος καὶ μικρότητα, καὶ
αὐτὸ ἐνδέχεσθαι (λέγω δὲ τῶν τοιούτων τι μορίων, εἰς ὃ
ἐνυπάρχον διαιρεῖται τὸ ὅλον), εἰ δὴ ἀδύνατον ζῷον ἢ
φυτὸν ὁπηλικονοῦν εἶναι κατὰ μέγεθος καὶ μικρότητα,
φανερὸν ὅτι οὐδὲ τῶν μορίων ὁτιοῦν· ἔσται γὰρ καὶ τὸ
ὅλον ὁμοίως. σὰρξ δὲ καὶ ὀστοῦν καὶ τὰ τοιαῦτα μόρια
ζῴου, καὶ οἱ καρποὶ τῶν φυτῶν. δῆλον τοίνυν ὅτι ἀδύνατον σάρκα ἢ ὀστοῦν ἢ ἄλλο τι ὁπηλικονοῦν εἶναι τὸ
μέγεθος ἢ ἐπὶ τὸ μεῖζον ἢ ἐπὶ τὸ ἔλαττον.

[187b22] ἔτι εἰ πάντα μὲν ἐνυπάρχει τὰ τοιαῦτα ἐν
ἀλλήλοις, καὶ μὴ γίγνεται ἀλλ᾽ ἐκκρίνεται ἐνόντα,
λέγεται δὲ ἀπὸ τοῦ πλείονος, γίγνεται δὲ ἐξ ὁτουοῦν

these [i.e. from air and fire]; for he calls the same thing fire and aether [cf. **D37**].

*Aristotle's Criticisms of Anaxagoras'
Infinitism (R16–R17)*

R16 (≠ DK) Aristotle, *Physics*

If, then, the unlimited inasmuch as unlimited is unknowable, then what is unlimited in quantity or in size is an unknowable quantity, and what is unlimited in form is an unknowable quality. If the principles are unlimited both in quantity and in form, it is impossible to know what comes from them. For we suppose that we know what is composed when we know out of what [scil. components] and in what quantity it is composed.

[187b13] Furthermore, if it is necessary that that of which the part can be of any extent whatsoever in size or smallness can also itself be [scil. of any extent whatsoever in size or smallness] (I mean one of those parts existing in the whole and into which it is divided), and if it is impossible for an animal or a plant to be of any extent whatsoever in size or smallness, it is clear that this will not be the case either of any one of its parts; for it will be the same for the whole too. Now flesh, bone, and things of this sort are parts of an animal, and fruits are those of plants. So it is clear that it is impossible for flesh or bone or anything else to be of any extent whatsoever in size, whether this is toward the larger or toward the smaller.

[187b22] Furthermore, if all the things of this sort are present in each other, and they do not become but, present in the interior, they separate out, and if they are called

145

ότιοῦν (οἷον ἐκ σαρκὸς ὕδωρ ἐκκρινόμενον καὶ σὰρξ ἐξ
ὕδατος), ἅπαν δὲ σῶμα πεπερασμένον ἀναιρεῖται ὑπὸ
σώματος πεπερασμένου, φανερὸν ὅτι οὐκ ἐνδέχεται ἐν
ἑκάστῳ ἕκαστον ὑπάρχειν. ἀφαιρεθείσης γὰρ ἐκ τοῦ
ὕδατος σαρκός, καὶ πάλιν ἄλλης γενομένης ἐκ τοῦ λοι-
ποῦ ἀποκρίσει, εἰ καὶ ἀεὶ ἐλάττων ἔσται ἡ ἐκκρινομένη,
ἀλλ᾽ ὅμως οὐχ ὑπερβαλεῖ μέγεθός τι τῇ μικρότητι. ὥστ᾽
εἰ μὲν στήσεται ἡ ἔκκρισις, οὐχ ἅπαν ἐν παντὶ ἐνέσται
(ἐν γὰρ τῷ λοιπῷ ὕδατι οὐκ ἐνυπάρξει σάρξ), εἰ δὲ μὴ
στήσεται ἀλλ᾽ ἀεὶ ἕξει ἀφαίρεσιν, ἐν πεπερασμένῳ
μεγέθει ἴσα πεπερασμένα ἐνέσται ἄπειρα τὸ πλῆθος·
τοῦτο δ᾽ ἀδύνατον.

[187b35] πρὸς δὲ τούτοις, εἰ ἅπαν μὲν σῶμα ἀφαι-
ρεθέντος τινὸς ἔλαττον ἀνάγκη γίγνεσθαι, τῆς δὲ σαρκὸς ὥρισται τὸ ποσὸν καὶ μεγέθει καὶ μικρότητι, φανερὸν ὅτι ἐκ τῆς ἐλαχίστης σαρκὸς οὐθὲν ἐκκριθήσεται
σῶμα· ἔσται γὰρ ἐλάττων τῆς ἐλαχίστης.

[188a2] ἔτι δ᾽ ἐν τοῖς ἀπείροις σώμασιν ἐνυρπάρχοι
ἂν ἤδη σὰρξ ἄπειρος καὶ αἷμα καὶ ἐγκέφαλος, κεχω-
ρισμένα μέντοι ἀπ᾽ ἀλλήλων ‹οὔ›,[1] οὐθὲν δ᾽ ἧττον ὄντα,
καὶ ἄπειρον ἕκαστον· τοῦτο δ᾽ ἄλογον.

[188a5] τὸ δὲ μηδέποτε διακριθήσεσθαι οὐκ εἰδότως
μὲν λέγεται, ὀρθῶς δὲ λέγεται· τὰ γὰρ πάθη ἀχώριστα·
εἰ οὖν μέμικται τὰ χρώματα καὶ αἱ ἕξεις, ἐὰν διακριθῶ-
σιν, ἔσται τι λευκὸν καὶ ὑγιεινὸν οὐχ ἕτερόν τι ὂν οὐδὲ
καθ᾽ ὑποκειμένου. ὥστε ἄτοπος τὰ ἀδύνατα ζητῶν ὁ

[1] ‹οὔ› Ross

according to what is most abundant, and anything whatsoever comes to be from anything whatsoever (for example,
water that separates out from flesh, and flesh that separates out from water), and every limited body is abolished
by a limited body, then it is clear that it is not possible that
each thing be found in each thing. For if flesh is removed
from water, and another flesh in turn comes from the rest
by separation, even if that which separates out is always
smaller, nonetheless it will not exceed a certain size in
smallness. So that if the separation comes to a stop, everything will not be in everything (for in the remaining water
there will not be any flesh); and if it does not come to a
stop but there is always a subtraction, there will be in a
limited size an unlimited number of limited equal [scil.
components]—but this is impossible.

[187b35] Besides, if it is necessary that every body
become smaller when something is removed from it, and
that the quantity of flesh is defined in size and in smallness, it is clear that from the smallest flesh no body will be
able to be extracted by separation: for it would be smaller
than the smallest.

[188a2] Furthermore, in unlimited bodies there would
already exist an unlimited flesh, blood, and brain, ⟨not⟩
separated from each other but nonetheless existing, and
each one unlimited—and this is absurd.

[188a5] As for the assertion that there will never be
complete separation, this is said without knowledge, but
it is correct: for the affections are not separable. If then
there is mixture of colors and of manners of being, then,
if there is complete separation, there will be something
white and healthy that will not be something else and will
not be said of a substrate. So that mind that seeks the

147

νοῦς, εἴπερ βούλεται μὲν διακρῖναι, τοῦτο δὲ ποιῆσαι
ἀδύνατον καὶ κατὰ τὸ ποσὸν καὶ κατὰ τὸ ποιόν, κατὰ μὲν
τὸ ποσὸν ὅτι οὐκ ἔστιν ἐλάχιστον μέγεθος, κατὰ δὲ τὸ
ποιὸν ὅτι ἀχώριστα τὰ πάθη.

[188a13] οὐκ ὀρθῶς δὲ οὐδὲ τὴν γένεσιν λαμβάνει
τῶν ὁμοειδῶν. ἔστι μὲν γὰρ ὡς ὁ πηλὸς εἰς πηλοὺς
διαιρεῖται, ἔστι δ' ὡς οὔ. καὶ οὐχ ὁ αὐτὸς τρόπος, ὡς
πλίνθοι ἐξ οἰκίας καὶ οἰκία ἐκ πλίνθων, οὕτω καὶ ὕδωρ
καὶ ἀὴρ ἐξ ἀλλήλων καὶ εἰσὶ καὶ γίγνονται.

[188a17] βέλτιόν τε ἐλάττω καὶ πεπερασμένα λαβεῖν, ὅπερ ποιεῖ Ἐμπεδοκλῆς.

R17 (≠ DK) Simpl. *In Phys.*, p. 173.8–16

"ἀλλὰ μήποτε," φησὶν Ἀλέξανδρος, "οὐχ οὕτως χρὴ τὸν
λόγον εὐθύνειν· τὸ γὰρ πάντα ἐν πᾶσι μεμῖχθαι οὐκ ἐπὶ
τῶν ἀρχῶν ἴσως ἔλεγεν Ἀναξαγόρας, ὡς ἐν ἑκάστῃ τῶν
ἀρχῶν πάντων ὄντων (οὕτως γὰρ οὐδὲ ἀρχαὶ ἂν ἦσαν
ἔτι, εἴπερ συγκρίματα ἦν), ἀλλ' ἐν ἑκάστῳ τῶν αἰσθητῶν σωμάτων τῶν ἐκ τῶν ἀρχῶν συγκεκριμένων πάντα
ἔλεγε μεμῖχθαι· ἐκ τούτων γὰρ καὶ αἱ γενέσεις καὶ αἱ
ἐκκρίσεις· τὰ γὰρ στοιχεῖα τὰ εἰλικρινῆ μήτε αἰσθητὰ
εἶναι τὴν ἀρχήν, ἀλλὰ μηδὲ εἶναι καθ' αὑτά· μηδὲ
γὰρ διακριθῆναι ταῦτα δύνασθαι." ἀλλ' ὁ ταῦτα λέγων
οὐδὲν ἄλλο ἢ μεταφέρει τὸν ἔλεγχον εἰς τὰ συγκρίματα
[. . .].

impossible is an absurdity: since it wishes to separate completely, but it is impossible to do this both according to quantity and according to quality—according to quantity because what is smallest does not exist, according to quality because the affections are not separable.

[188a13] He does not conceive correctly the coming into being of things of the same species either. For in one way it is possible for mud to divide into mud, but in another way it is not. And it is not in the same way that bricks come from a building, and a building from bricks, and that water and air are [scil. constituted] and come to be from each other.

[188a17] And it is better to assume a smaller number [scil. of principles] and limited ones, which is what Empedocles does.

R17 (≠ DK) Alexander of Aphrodisias in Simplicius, *Commentary on Aristotle's* Physics

"But perhaps," says Alexander, "it is not necessary to refute the argument in this way. For perhaps it was not with reference to the principles that Anaxagoras said that all things are mixed with all things, on the idea that all things are in each of the principles (for in this way they would no longer be principles, since they would be composites), but he was saying that all things are mixed in each of the perceptible bodies, which come from the principles by combination. For it is from these that come both comings-to-be and separations. For pure elements are absolutely imperceptible, and they do not exist by themselves either; for these cannot be completely separated either." But to say this is to do nothing other than to transfer the refutation to the composites [. . .].

*Anaxagoras' Principles Can Be
Reduced to Two (R18–R19)*

R18 Arist. *Metaph.*

a (A61) A8 989a30–33

Ἀναξαγόραν δ᾽ εἴ τις ὑπολάβοι δύο λέγειν στοιχεῖα,
μάλιστ᾽ ἂν ὑπολάβοι κατὰ λόγον, ὃν ἐκεῖνος αὐτὸς μὲν
οὐ διήρθρωσεν, ἠκολούθησε μέντ᾽ ἂν ἐξ ἀνάγκης τοῖς
λέγουσιν[1] αὐτόν.

> [1] λέγουσιν E: ἐπάγουσιν A[b]

b (˃ A61) Λ2 1069b18–23

[. . .] ὥστε οὐ μόνον κατὰ συμβεβηκὸς ἐνδέχεται
γίγνεσθαι ἐκ μὴ ὄντος, ἀλλὰ καὶ ἐξ ὄντος γίγνεται
πάντα, δυνάμει μέντοι ὄντος, ἐκ μὴ ὄντος δὲ ἐνεργείᾳ.
καὶ τοῦτ᾽ ἔστι τὸ Ἀναξαγόρου ἕν· βέλτιον γὰρ ἢ ὁμοῦ
πάντα [cf. **D9**] [. . .] "ἦν ὁμοῦ πάντα δυνάμει, ἐνεργείᾳ
δ᾽ οὔ."

R19 (12 A9a) Simpl. *In Phys.*, p. 154.14–23

καὶ Θεόφραστος δὲ [Frag. 228B FSH&G] τὸν Ἀναξαγόραν εἰς τὸν Ἀναξίμανδρον συνωθῶν καὶ οὕτως ἐκλαμ-
βάνει τὰ ὑπὸ Ἀναξαγόρου λεγόμενα, ὡς δύνασθαι μίαν
αὐτὸν φύσιν λέγειν τὸ ὑποκείμενον. γράφει δὲ οὕτως ἐν
τῇ Φυσικῇ ἱστορίᾳ· "οὕτω μὲν οὖν λαμβανόντων δόξειεν
ἂν ποιεῖν τὰς μὲν ὑλικὰς ἀρχὰς ἀπείρους, ὥσπερ εἴρη-

Anaxagoras' Principles Can Be
Reduced to Two (R18–R19)

R18 Aristotle, *Metaphysics*

a (A61)

If someone were to suppose that Anaxagoras was speaking of two elements [scil. mind and matter], his supposition would be completely in accordance with an argument that he himself did not articulate but would necessarily have accepted from those who would have stated it.

b (> A61)

[. . .] so that not only is it possible for something to come about accidentally from what is not, but also everything comes about from what is—from what is potentially, however, and is not actually. And this is the 'one' of Anaxagoras; for better than **"all things together"** [cf. **D9**] [. . .] [scil. would be] "all things were together potentially, but not actually."

R19 (12 A9a) Theophrastus in Simplicius, *Commentary on Aristotle's* Physics

And Theophrastus, pushing Anaxagoras toward Anaximander, understands in this way too what Anaxagoras says, viz. that it is possible that he is saying that the substrate is a single nature. He writes as follows in his *Inquiry on Nature:* "If we take him in this way, he would seem to posit material principles that are unlimited [scil. in number], as

151

ται, τὴν δὲ τῆς κινήσεως καὶ τῆς γενέσεως αἰτίαν μίαν.
εἰ δέ τις τὴν μῖξιν τῶν ἀπάντων ὑπολάβοι μίαν εἶναι
φύσιν ἀόριστον καὶ κατ᾽ εἶδος καὶ κατὰ μέγεθος, ὅπερ
ἂν δόξειε βούλεσθαι λέγειν, συμβαίνει δύο τὰς ἀρχὰς
αὐτῷ λέγειν, τήν τε τοῦ ἀπείρου φύσιν καὶ τὸν νοῦν,
ὥστε πάντως φαίνεται τὰ σωματικὰ στοιχεῖα παραπλησίως ποιῶν Ἀναξιμάνδρῳ."

The Beginning of the Cosmogonic
Process (R20–R21)

R20 (< A50) Arist. *Phys.* 3.5 205b1–2

Ἀναξαγόρας δ᾽ ἀτόπως λέγει περὶ τῆς τοῦ ἀπείρου
μονῆς [. . . = **D17**].

R21 (A59) Simpl. *In Phys.*, p. 1185.9–15

ὁ δὲ Εὔδημος [Frag. 111 Wehrli] μέμφεται τῷ Ἀναξαγόρᾳ
οὐ μόνον ὅτι μὴ πρότερον οὖσαν ἄρξασθαί ποτε λέγει
τὴν κίνησιν, ἀλλ᾽ ὅτι καὶ περὶ τοῦ διαμένειν ἢ λήξειν
ποτὲ παρέλιπεν εἰπεῖν, καίπερ οὐκ ὄντος φανεροῦ. "τί
γὰρ κωλύει," φησί, "δόξαι ποτὲ τῷ νῷ στῆσαι πάντα
χρήματα, καθάπερ ἐκεῖνος εἶπεν κινῆσαι;" καὶ τοῦτο δὲ
αἰτιᾶται τοῦ Ἀναξαγόρου ὁ Εὔδημος· "πῶς ἐνδέχεται
στέρησίν τινα προτέραν εἶναι τῆς ἀντικειμένης ἕξεως;
εἰ οὖν ἡ ἠρεμία στέρησις κινήσεώς ἐστιν, οὐκ ἂν εἴη πρὸ
τῆς κινήσεως."

has been said, but a single cause of motion and of generation. But if one supposed that the mixture of all things is a single nature, undefined both in shape and in size, which is what he would seem to have meant, then the result is that he is saying that there are two principles, the nature of the unlimited and mind, so that he seems indeed to conceive of corporeal elements in the same way as Anaximander" [= **ANAXIMAND. R8**].

The Beginning of the Cosmogonic Process (R20–R21)

R20 (< A50) Aristotle, *Physics*

What Anaxagoras says about the lack of motion of the unlimited is absurd [. . .].

R21 (A59) Eudemus in Simplicius, *Commentary on Aristotle's* Physics

Eudemus blames Anaxagoras not only because he says that the motion that did not exist previously began at a certain moment, but also because he has neglected to say whether it would continue or would stop sometime, even though this is not evident. For he says, "What prevents us from thinking that all things are brought to a stop sometime by mind, just as he said that it set them in motion?" And Eudemus also criticizes this point of Anaxagoras: "How is it possible for a privation to exist before the state to which it is opposed? If then rest is a privation of motion, then it could not exist before motion."

The Clepsydra (R22)

R22 (< A69) Ps.-Arist. *Probl.* 16.8 914b9–15

τῶν περὶ τὴν κλεψύδραν συμβαινόντων τὸ μὲν ὅλον
ἔοικεν αἴτιον εἶναι καθάπερ Ἀναξαγόρας λέγει· [. . . cf.
D61] οὐ μὴν ἁπλῶς γε αἴτιος· κἂν γάρ τις αὐτὴν
πλαγίαν ἐνῇ εἰς τὸ ὕδωρ, ἐπιλαβὼν τὸν αὐλόν, εἴσεισι
τὸ ὕδωρ. διόπερ οὐ λέγεται ὑπ᾽ αὐτοῦ ἱκανῶς ᾗ αἴτιόν
ἐστιν.

Theophrastus' Criticisms of Anaxagoras'
Theory of Sensations (R23)

R23 (≠ DK) Theophr. *Sens.* 31–37

[On the principle of the theory]
[31] τὸ μὲν οὖν τοῖς ἐναντίοις ποιεῖν τὴν αἴσθησιν
ἔχει τινὰ λόγον [. . .]· δοκεῖ γὰρ ἡ ἀλλοίωσις οὐχ ὑπὸ
τῶν ὁμοίων, ἀλλ᾽ ὑπὸ τῶν ἐναντίων εἶναι. καίτοι καὶ
τοῦτο δεῖται πίστεως, εἰ[1] ἀλλοίωσις ἡ αἴσθησις εἴ τε[2]
τὸ ἐναντίον τοῦ ἐναντίου κριτικόν.

<hr />

[1] ἡ mss., corr. Schneider   [2] οὔτε mss., corr. Schneider

[On the assertion that every sensation is
accompanied by pain]
τὸ δὲ μετὰ λύπης ἅπασαν εἶναι[1] οὔτ᾽ ἐκ τῆς χρήσεως
ὁμολογεῖται (τὰ μὲν <γὰρ>[2] μεθ᾽ ἡδονῆς τὰ δὲ πλεῖ-

The Clepsydra (R22)

R22 (< A69) Ps.-Aristotle, *Problems*

For on the whole the cause of what happens with the clepsydra seems to be what Anaxagoras says. [. . .] And yet this is not the cause speaking absolutely: for if one closes the tube and puts it into the water aslant, the water will penetrate in. That is why he does explain sufficiently to what extent this is the cause.

Theophrastus' Criticisms of Anaxagoras' Theory of Sensations (R23)

R23 (≠ DK) Theophrastus, *On Sensations*

[On the principle of the theory]
[31] That he explains sensation by the contraries has a certain degree of reasonableness [. . .]: for it seems that there is alteration by the effect not of the similar but of the contraries. Nonetheless, whether sensation is an alteration and whether the contrary is able to discern the contrary—this too requires confirmation.

[On the assertion that every sensation is accompanied by pain]
As for the assertion that every sensation is accompanied by pain, this cannot be accepted either on the basis of experience (for some of them are accompanied by plea-

---

[1] ψεῦδος post εἶναι hab. mss, secl. Wimmer
[2] ⟨γὰρ⟩ Diels

στα ἄνευ λύπης ἐστίν), οὔτ᾽ ἐκ τῶν εὐλόγων. ἡ μὲν
γὰρ αἴσθησις κατὰ φύσιν, οὐδὲν δὲ τῶν φύσει βίᾳ
καὶ μετὰ λύπης, ἀλλὰ μᾶλλον μεθ᾽ ἡδονῆς, ὅπερ καὶ
φαίνεται συμβαῖνον. τὰ³ γὰρ πλείω καὶ πλεονάκις
ἡδόμεθα καὶ αὐτοὶ⁴ δὲ τὸ αἰσθάνεσθαι χωρὶς τῆς περὶ
ἕκαστον ἐπιθυμίας διώκομεν. [32] ἔτι δ᾽ ἐπεὶ καὶ ἡδονὴ
καὶ λύπη γίνεται διὰ τῆς αἰσθήσεως, ἅπαν δὲ φύσει
πρὸς τὸ βέλτιόν ἐστι, καθάπερ ἡ ἐπιστήμη,⁵ μᾶλλον
ἂν εἴη μεθ᾽ ἡδονῆς ἢ μετὰ λύπης. ἁπλῶς δ᾽ εἴπερ
μηδὲ τὸ διανοεῖσθαι μετὰ λύπης, οὐδὲ τὸ αἰσθάνε-
σθαι· τὸν αὐτὸν γὰρ⁶ ἔχει λόγον ἑκάτερον πρὸς τὴν
αὐτὴν χρείαν. ἀλλὰ μὴν οὐδὲ αἱ τῶν αἰσθητῶν ὑπερ-
βολαὶ καὶ τὸ τοῦ χρόνου πλῆθος οὐδὲν σημεῖον ὡς
μετὰ λύπης ἐστίν, ἀλλὰ μᾶλλον ὡς ἐν συμμετρίᾳ τινὶ
καὶ κράσει⁷ πρὸς τὸ αἰσθητὸν ἡ αἴσθησις. διόπερ
ἴσως τὸ μὲν ἐλλεῖπον ἀναίσθητον, τὸ δ᾽ ὑπερβάλλον
λύπην τε ποιεῖ καὶ φθείρει. [33] συμβαίνει τοίνυν τὸ
κατὰ φύσιν ἐκ τοῦ παρὰ φύσιν σκοπεῖν· ἡ γὰρ ὑπερ-
βολὴ παρὰ φύσιν. ἐπεὶ τό γε ἀπ᾽ ἐνίων καὶ ἐνίοτε
λυπεῖσθαι, καθάπερ καὶ ἥδεσθαι, φανερὸν καὶ ὁμολο-
γούμενον· ὥστ᾽ οὐδὲν μᾶλλον διά γε τοῦτο μετὰ λύπης ἢ μεθ᾽ ἡδονῆς ἐστιν, ἀλλ᾽ ἴσως μετ᾽ οὐδετέρου
κατά γε τὸ ἀληθές· οὐδὲ γὰρ ἂν δύναιτο κρίνειν,

---

³ τῇ mss., corr. Schneider   ⁴ αὐτὸ Schneider

⁵ καθάπερ ἡ ἐπιστήμη del. Schneider: καθάπερ καὶ ἡ ἐπιστήμη prop. Diels   ⁶ γὰρ F: om. P   ⁷ πράξει mss.,
corr. Koraïs

sure, while most of them are free of pain) or on that of plausible arguments. For sensation occurs by nature; now, nothing of what is by nature occurs by violence or together with pain, but rather it occurs together with pleasure, and it is evident too that this is what occurs. For in most cases and for most of the time, we feel pleasure and we ourselves pursue sensation for itself independently of the desire for each of its objects. [32] Furthermore, given that pleasure as well as pain occur by means of sensation, and that every thing tends by nature toward what is better, like knowledge, it [scil. sensation] would be accompanied by pleasure rather than by pain. In general, if thinking is not accompanied by pain either, then neither is perceiving, for each of the two has the same relation with regard to the same usage. Moreover, the excesses of the perceptibles and the quantity of time does not supply the slightest indication that sensation is accompanied by pain, but rather that sensation resides in a certain adaptation and blending with regard to the perceptible. This is surely why the perceptible is not perceived when it is insufficient, whereas it causes pain and destroys when it is excessive. [33] So it comes about that he examines what is by nature according to what is against nature: for excess is against nature. For the fact that, from some things and sometimes, one feels pain, like pleasure too, is evident and is generally recognized; so that, on account of this at least, sensation is not any more accompanied by pain than by pleasure, but doubtless neither by the one nor by the other, at least according to the truth. For it would not be able to discern, and neither would thought either, if it were continually

ὥσπερ οὐδὲ ἡ διάνοια συνεχῶς οὖσα μετὰ λύπης ἢ
ἡδονῆς. ἀλλὰ τοῦτο μὲν ἀπὸ μικρᾶς ἀρχῆς ἐφ᾽ ὅλην
μετήνεγκε τὴν αἴσθησιν.

[The criterion of size]

[34] ὅταν δὲ λέγῃ τὰ μείζω μᾶλλον αἰσθάνεσθαι καὶ
ἁπλῶς κατὰ τὸ μέγεθος τῶν αἰσθητηρίων εἶναι τὴν
αἴσθησιν, τὸ μὲν αὐτῶν ἔχει[1] τινὰ ἀπορίαν, οἷον πότερον τὰ μικρὰ μᾶλλον ἢ τὰ μεγάλα τῶν ζῴων αἰσθη-
τικά· δόξειε[2] γὰρ ἂν ἀκριβεστέρας αἰσθήσεως εἶναι
τὰ μικρὰ μὴ λανθάνειν, καὶ ἅμα τὸ τὰ ἐλάττω δυνά-
μενον καὶ τὰ μείζω κρίνειν οὐκ ἄλογον. ἅμα δὲ καὶ
δοκεῖ περὶ ἐνίας[3] αἰσθήσεις βέλτιον ἔχειν τὰ μικρὰ
τῶν μεγάλων, ὥστε ταύτῃ μὲν χείρων ἡ τῶν μειζόνων
αἴσθησις. [35] εἰ δ᾽ αὖ φαίνεται καὶ πολλὰ λανθάνειν
τὰ μικρὰ τῶν μειζόνων[4] οἷον οἱ ψόφοι, χρώματα,[5] βελ-
τίων ἡ τῶν μειζόνων· ἅμα δὲ καὶ εὔλογον, ὥσπερ καὶ
τὴν ὅλην τοῦ σώματος κρᾶσιν, ὁμοίως ἔχειν καὶ τὰ
περὶ τὰς αἰσθήσεις. τοῦτο μὲν οὖν, ὥσπερ ἐλέχθη,
διαπορήσειεν ἄν τις, εἰ ἄρα καὶ δεῖ λέγειν οὕτως· οὐ
γὰρ ἐν τοῖς ὁμοίοις γένεσιν ἀφώρισται κατὰ τὸ μέγεθος, ἀλλὰ κυριώτατα ἴσως ἡ τοῦ σώματος διάθεσίς
τε καὶ κρᾶσις. τὸ δὲ πρὸς τὰ μεγέθη τὴν συμμετρίαν
ἀποδιδόναι τῶν αἰσθητῶν ἔοικεν ὁμοίως λέγειν Ἐμπε-

---

[1] ἔχειν mss., corr. Vossianus et Camotius   [2] δόξει mss.
corr. Stephanus   [3] περὶ ἐνία mss., corr. Stephanus: πρὸς
ἐνίας coni. Usener   [4] τῶν μειζόνων del. Schneider
[5] οἷον οἱ ψόφοι, χρώματα del. Philippson

accompanied by pain or by pleasure. With regard to this idea, then, he started from a tenuous starting point and transferred it to the totality of sensation.

[The criterion of size]

[34] But when he asserts that larger animals have better sensation and that, in general, sensation depends on the size of the sense organs, the former assertion comports a difficulty, viz. whether it is not the small ones among animals that perceive more than the large ones. For it would seem to be the case that what belongs to a more precise sensation is that small things do not escape it, and it is not unreasonable either to think that one who can discern the smaller things can equally discern the larger ones. At the same time, it does indeed seem to be the case that, in the case of certain sensations, small animals are superior to large ones, so that, in this regard, the sensation of the larger ones is inferior. [35] But if, inversely, it appears that likewise many of the larger objects escape the notice of the small ones, for example sounds, colors, that of the larger ones is superior; now at the same time it is also reasonable to think that the sensations are in the same state as the entire mixture of the body. On this point then, as has been said, one could raise a difficulty, viz. whether one must really express oneself as he does: for in similar species, the distinction is not made according to size, and the most important things are doubtless the arrangement and mixture of the body. As for explaining the adaptation (*summetria*) of the perceptibles with reference to sizes, he seems to say the same things as Empedocles; for the fact

δοκλεῖ· τῷ[6] γὰρ ἐναρμόττειν τοῖς πόροις ποιεῖ τὴν αἴσθησιν. πλὴν ἐπὶ τῆς ὀσφρήσεως ἴδιον συμβαίνει
δυσχερές· ὄζειν μὲν γάρ φησι τὸν λεπτὸν ἀέρα μᾶλλον, ὀσφραίνεσθαι δὲ ἀκριβέστερον ὅσα τὸν πυκνὸν
ἢ τὸν μανὸν[7] ἕλκει.

6 τὸ mss., corr. Philippson
7 μανὸν Wimmer: μικρὸν mss.

[On the theory of reflection]

[36] περὶ δὲ τῆς ἐμφάσεως κοινή τίς ἐστιν ἡ δόξα·
σχεδὸν γὰρ οἱ πολλοὶ τὸ ὁρᾶν οὕτως ὑπολαμβάνουσι
διὰ τὴν γινομένην ἐν τοῖς ὀφθαλμοῖς ἔμφασιν. τοῦτο
δὲ οὐκέτι συνεῖδον ὡς οὔτε τὰ μεγέθη σύμμετρα τὰ
ὁρώμενα τοῖς ἐμφαινομένοις οὔτε ἐμφαίνεσθαι πολλὰ
ἅμα καὶ τἀναντία δυνατόν, ἔτι δὲ κίνησις καὶ διά-
στημα καὶ μέγεθος ὁρατὰ μέν, ἔμφασιν δὲ οὐ ποιοῦσιν. ἐνίοις δὲ τῶν ζῴων οὐδὲν ἐμφαίνεται,[1] καθάπερ
τοῖς σκληροφθάλμοις καὶ τοῖς ἐνύδροις. ἔτι δὲ καὶ
τῶν ἀψύχων διά γε τοῦτο πολλὰ ἂν ὁρῷεν· καὶ γὰρ
ἐν ὕδατι καὶ χαλκῷ καὶ ἑτέροις πολλοῖς ἐστιν ἀνάκλα-
σις. [37] φησὶ δὲ καὶ αὐτὸς ἐμφαίνεσθαι μὲν εἰς ἄλληλα ⟨τὰ⟩[2] χρώματα, μᾶλλον δὲ τὸ ἰσχυρὸν εἰς τὸ
ἀσθενές· ὥστε ἑκάτερον μὲν ἐχρῆν ὁρᾶν, μᾶλλον δὲ
⟨τὸ⟩[3] μέλαν καὶ ὅλως ⟨τὸ⟩[4] ἀσθενέστερον. διὸ καὶ τὴν
ὄψιν ὁμόχρων ποιεῖ τῇ νυκτὶ καὶ τὸ φῶς αἴτιον τῆς
ἐμφάσεως. καίτοι πρῶτον μὲν τὸ φῶς ὁρῶμεν αὐτὸ δι᾽
οὐδεμιᾶς ἐμφάσεως, ἔπειτα οὐδὲν ἧττον τὰ μέλανα

of being adapted (*enarmottein*) to the passages produces sensation. Except that, in the case of smelling, a difficulty arises which is peculiar to him: for he says that thin air has a stronger odor, but he states that those that inhale dense air have a more precise sense of smell than do those that inhale rarefied air.

[On the theory of reflection]

[36] With regard to reflection (*emphasis*) there is a common opinion: for most people suppose that sight occurs in this way, by the reflection that is produced in the eyes. But what they have not seen is that neither do the sizes that one sees correspond to the objects reflected nor is it possible that things that are multiple and opposed be reflected simultaneously; furthermore, motion, distance, and size are quite visible but do not produce a reflection. And in certain animals nothing is reflected, as in those that have hard eyes or live in water. Furthermore, to follow this idea, many inanimate things would possess sight, for there is also refraction in water, on bronze, and in many other kinds of material. [37] And he himself says that colors are reflected in each other, but the strong one more in the weak one; so that each of these two ought to see, but the dark one more, and, in general, the weaker one. That is why he makes the eye to be of the same color as the night, and makes light the cause of reflection. However, to begin with, we see light itself, without this happening by means of a reflection; and then, dark-colored objects are not less

---

¹ φαίνεται mss., corr. Schneider   ² ⟨τὰ⟩ Schneider
3–4 ⟨τὸ⟩ bis Schneider

τῶν λευκῶν οὐκ ἔχει φῶς. ἔτι δὲ κἂν⁵ τοῖς ἄλλοις ἀεὶ
τὴν ἔμφασιν ὁρῶμεν εἰς τὸ λαμπρότερον καὶ καθαρώτερον γινομένην, ὥσπερ καὶ αὐτὸς λέγει τοὺς ὑμέ-
νας τῶν ὀμμάτων λεπτοὺς εἶναι καὶ λαμπρούς. τιθέασι δὲ καὶ τὴν ὄψιν αὐτὴν οἱ πολλοὶ πυρός, <ὡς>⁶
τούτου⁷ τὰς⁸ χρόας μετεχούσας μᾶλλον.

Ἀναξαγόρας μὲν οὖν, ὥσπερ ἐλέχθη, κοινήν τινα
ταύτην καὶ παλαιὰν δόξαν ἀναφέρει. πλὴν ἰδίως⁹ ἐπὶ
πάσαις λέγει ταῖς αἰσθήσεσι καὶ μάλιστα ἐπὶ τῇ
ὄψει, διότι τὸ μέγα¹⁰ αἰσθανόμενόν ἐστιν, οὐ δηλοῖ δὲ
τὰς σωματικωτέρας¹¹ αἰσθήσεις.

⁵ κἂν Diels: γ' ἐν mss.   ⁶ <ὡς> Diels   ⁷ ταύτης
mss., corr. Usener   ⁸ τῆς mss., corr. Schneider   ⁹ ἴδιον
mss., corr. Diels   ¹⁰ μὲν mss., corr. Diels   ¹¹ σωματι-
κωτάτας mss., corr. Diels et Usener

Various Doxographical Reports Influenced by
Later Doctrines (R24–R30)
Platonico-Aristotelian Interpretations (R24–R25)

R24 (A93) Aët.

a 4.7.1 (Theod. 5.23) [περὶ ἀφθαρσίας ψυχῆς]

[. . .] Ἀναξαγόρας [. . .] ἄφθαρτον εἶναι τὴν ψυχὴν
ἀπεφήναντο.

deprived of light than bright-colored ones are. Furthermore, in other cases we always see the reflection occurring in what is more brilliant and purer, as he himself says that the membranes of the eyes are fine and brilliant. And most people posit that sight itself belongs to fire, on the idea that colors participate more in this latter.

So Anaxagoras, as has been said, takes up a common and ancient opinion in this case. Except that he says something peculiar to himself about all the sensations, and especially about sight, viz. that it is the large [scil. animal] that perceives. But he does not explain the sensations that are of a more corporeal nature.

*Various Doxographical Reports Influenced by
Later Doctrines (R24–R30)
Platonico-Aristotelian Interpretations (R24–R25)*

R24 (A93) Aëtius

a

[. . .] Anaxagoras [. . .] asserted that the soul is imperishable.

b 4.5.11 (Stob.) [περὶ τοῦ ἡγεμονικοῦ]

[. . .] Ἀναξαγόρας [. . .] θύραθεν εἰσκρίνεσθαι τὸν νοῦν.

R25 (A86a) Schol. in Aesch. *Prom.* 88

οἱ ἄνεμοι κατὰ μὲν Ἀναξαγόραν ἐκ τῆς γῆς γίνονται [. . .], καθ᾽ Ὅμηρον δὲ "πατρὸς Διὸς ἐκ νεφελάων." ἀλλ᾽ ὁ μὲν Ἀναξαγόρας τὸ ὑλικόν φησιν αἴτιον τῶν ἀνέμων, Ὅμηρος δὲ τὸ ποιητικόν, μᾶλλον δὲ ἀμφότερα τό τε ὑλικὸν καὶ τὸ ποιητικόν.

The Skeptic Arcesilaus Includes Anaxagoras
Among His Predecessors (R26)

R26 (< A95) Cic. *Acad.* 1.12.44

[. . .] earum rerum obscuritate, quae ad confessionem ignorationis adduxerant Socratem et iam ante Socratem [. . .] Anaxagoram [. . .] omnes paene veteres, qui nihil cognosci nihil percipi nihil sciri posse dixerunt, angustos sensus, imbecillos animos, brevia curricula vitae [. . .].

An Eclectic Reading (R27)

R27 (A66) Aët. 1.29.7 (Ps.-Plut.) [περὶ τύχης]

Ἀναξαγόρας [. . .] ἄδηλον αἰτίαν ἀνθρωπίνῳ λογισμῷ· ἃ μὲν γὰρ εἶναι κατ᾽ ἀνάγκην, ἃ δὲ καθ᾽ εἱμαρμένην, ἃ δὲ κατὰ προαίρεσιν, ἃ δὲ κατὰ τύχην, ἃ δὲ κατὰ τὸ αὐτόματον.

b

[. . .] Anaxagoras [. . .]: [scil. mind] enters from outside.

R25 (A86a) Scholia on Aeschylus' *Prometheus Bound*

Winds, according to Anaxagoras, come from the earth [. . .], but, according to Homer, "from the clouds of Father Zeus" (*Il.* 2.146). But Anaxagoras is speaking about the material cause of winds, Homer about the efficient cause, or more exactly about both of them, the material cause and the efficient cause.

The Skeptic Arcesilaus Includes Anaxagoras
Among His Predecessors (R26)

R26 (< A95) Cicero, *Posterior Academics*

[. . .] by the obscurity of these matters, which led Socrates to confess his ignorance and, even before Socrates, [. . .] Anaxagoras, [. . .] and almost all the ancients, who said that nothing can be recognized, or perceived, or known; that the senses are constricted, the spirit weak, the course of life brief [. . .].[1]

[1] Cicero also names Democritus (**ATOM. R100**) and Empedocles (cf. also **EMP. R38**).

An Eclectic Reading (R27)

R27 (A66) Aëtius

Anaxagoras [. . .]: [scil. chance is] a cause that is unclear to human reason; for some things happen by necessity, others according to fate, others by choice, others by chance, and others spontaneously.

The Epicureans (R28–R29)
Epicurus (R28)

R28 (A26) Diog. Laert. 10.12

μάλιστα δὲ ἀπεδέχετο, φησὶ Διοκλῆς, τῶν ἀρχαίων
Ἀναξαγόραν, καίτοι ἔν τισιν ἀντειρηκὼς αὐτῷ [. . . cf.
ARCH. R3].

Lucretius (R29)

R29 (> A44) Lucr. 1.859–96

praeterea quoniam cibus auget corpus alitque,
860   scire licet nobis venas et sanguen et ossa
⟨. . .⟩
sive cibos omnis commixto corpore dicent
esse et habere in se nervorum corpora parva
ossaque et omnino venas partisque cruoris,
fiet uti cibus omnis, et aridus et liquor ipse,
865   ex alienigenis rebus constare putetur,
ossibus et nervis sanieque et sanguine mixto.
praeterea quaecumque e terra corpora crescunt
si sunt in terris, terram constare necessest

post 860 lac. pos. Lambinus
866 mixto Lachmann: mixta OQG: misto Lambinus

The Epicureans (R28–R29)
Epicurus (R28)

R28 (A26) Diogenes Laertius

More than anyone else, says Diocles, he [i.e. Epicurus] preferred Anaxagoras among the ancients, even if he contradicted him on certain points [. . .].

Lucretius (R29)

R29 (> A44) Lucretius, *On the Nature of Things*

Furthermore, since food makes the body grow and
    nourishes it,
We can know that veins, blood, bones,   860
⟨and sinews are made up of heterogeneous parts⟩;[1]
Or if they say that all foodstuffs are made up of a
    mixed body
And contain corpuscles of sinews,
Bones, and moreover veins and parts of blood,
Then the result will be that one must think that every
    foodstuff,
Both dry and liquid, is made up of heterogeneous   865
    things,
Bones, sinews, humors, and blood mixed together.
Furthermore, if all the bodies that grow from the
    earth
Already exist in the earth, then the earth must be
    made

---

[1] At least one verse seems to have been lost; the words in brackets indicate the probable meaning.

ex alienigenis, quae terris exoriuntur.

870 transfer item, totidem verbis utare licebit:
in lignis si flamma latet fumusque cinisque,
ex alienigenis consistant ligna necessest

[874] ex alienigenis, quae lignis exoriuntur.

[873] praeterea tellus quae corpora cumque alit auget
⟨ . . . ⟩

875 linquitur hic quaedam latitandi copia tenuis,
id quod Anaxagoras sibi sumit, ut omnibus omnis
res putet immixtas rebus latitare, sed illud
apparere unum cuius sint plurima mixta
et magis in promptu primaque in fronte locata.

880 quod tamen a vera longe ratione repulsumst.
conveniebat enim fruges quoque saepe, minaci
robore cum saxi franguntur, mittere signum
sanguinis aut aliquid, nostro quae corpore aluntur,
cum lapidi in lapidem terimus, manare cruorem.

885 consimili ratione herbas quoque saepe decebat
et latices dulcis guttas similique sapore

873–74 transp. Diels et lac. post 874 pos.: post 873 lac. pos.
Munro: 873 secl. Lambinus, 873–74 Marullus
882 post cum hab. OQ in, del. Marullus
885 herbis OQ, corr. Marullus

---

[2] This passage is corrupt; one or more verses seem to have
been lost. The words in brackets indicate the probable meaning.

Of the heterogeneous things that arise from the
    earth.
Apply this to another case and you can use the very   870
    same words:
If flame, smoke, and ash lie concealed in logs,
Then it is necessary that logs are made of
    heterogeneous things,
Of heterogeneous things that arise from the wood.   [874]
Furthermore, whatever bodies the earth nourishes,   [873]
    makes grow,
‹must consist of heterogeneous things containing
    other heterogeneous things.›[2]
There remains here a slight possibility of hiding,   875
To which Anaxagoras has recourse: to think that all
    things
Are mixed, hiding, in every thing, but that the one
That appears is the one of which there is the most in
    the mixture
And that is located most visibly and in the very front.
But this is very far distant from right reasoning.   880
For in that case wheat too, when it is crushed
By the threatening force of a stone, should often emit
    a trace
Of blood or one of the things that are nourished in
    our body,
And when we rub it on one stone against another,
    blood should flow forth.
According to the same reasoning, grass too and pools   885
    of water
Should often send forth sweet drops with a taste
    similar

mittere, lanigerae quali sunt ubere lactis,
scilicet et glebis terrarum saepe friatis
herbarum genera et fruges frondisque videri
890   dispertita inter terram latitare minute,
postremo in lignis cinerem fumumque videri,
cum praefracta forent, ignisque latere minutos.
quorum nil fieri quoniam manifesta docet res,
scire licet non esse in rebus res ita mixtas,
895   verum semina multimodis inmixta latere
multarum rerum in rebus communia debent.

A Stoicizing Interpretation (R30)

R30 (< A67) Aët. 2.8.1 (Ps.-Plut.) [τίς ἡ αἰτία τοῦ τὸν κόσμον ἐγκλιθῆναι]

[. . .] ἐγκλιθῆναί πως τὸν κόσμον [. . . cf. **D32**], ἴσως ὑπὸ προνοίας, ἵνα ἃ μὲν¹ ἀοίκητα γένηται, ἃ δὲ² οἰκητὰ μέρη τοῦ κόσμου κατὰ ψύξιν καὶ ἐκπύρωσιν καὶ εὐκρασίαν.

¹ post ἃ μέν hab. mss. τινα, ut glossema del. Diels: τὰ μὲν Eus. 15.39.1   ² ἃ δὲ mss.: τὰ δὲ Eus.

Anaxagoras in Simplicius (R31–R34)
Simplicius Nuances Plato's Criticism of Anaxagoras (R31)

R31 (≠ DK) Simpl. *In Phys.*, p. 177.9–17

καὶ ὅπερ δὲ ὁ ἐν Φαίδωνι Σωκράτης ἐγκαλεῖ τῷ Ἀναξ-

170

To the richness of the milk from the udder of fleece-
    bearing animals;
And indeed, when clods of earth are crumbled
Kinds of grass, wheat, and leaves should often
    become visible,
Their minute parts hiding, scattered throughout the   890
    earth;
And finally ash and smoke should become visible in
    logs
When they are broken, and minute flames hiding.
But since reality manifestly indicates that none of this
    happens,
We can know that things are not mixed in this way in
    other things,
But rather that seeds common to many things   895
Must lie hidden intermingled in things in many ways.

A Stoicizing Interpretation (R30)

R30 (< A67) Aëtius

[. . .] the world inclined [. . .], perhaps from providence,
so that some parts of the world would become uninhabited
and others inhabited, as a function of extreme cold or heat,
or of a temperate climate.

Anaxagoras in Simplicius (R31–R34)
Simplicius Nuances Plato's Criticism of
Anaxagoras (R31)

R31 (≠ DK) Simplicius, *Commentary on Aristotle's*
Physics

And what Socrates reproaches Anaxagoras with in the

171

ἀγόρᾳ, τὸ ἐν ταῖς τῶν κατὰ μέρος αἰτιολογίαις μὴ τῷ νῷ
κεχρῆσθαι ἀλλὰ ταῖς ὑλικαῖς ἀποδόσεσιν, οἰκεῖον ἦν
φυσιολογίᾳ. τοιγαροῦν καὶ αὐτὸς ὁ Πλάτων ἐν Τιμαίῳ
τὴν ποιητικὴν πάντων αἰτίαν ὁλικῶς παραδοὺς ἐν τοῖς
κατὰ μέρος διαφορὰς ὄγκων καὶ σχημάτων αἰτιᾶται τῆς
τε θερμότητος καὶ ψυχρότητος καὶ ἐπὶ τῶν ἄλλων ὡσαύτως. ὁ μέντοι Σωκράτης τὴν ἀπὸ τοῦ τελικοῦ ἀπόδοσιν
ὑποδεῖξαι βουλόμενος ἐμνημόνευσεν Ἀναξαγόρου ὡς
τῇ ὑλικῇ μᾶλλον ἀλλ' οὐ τελικῇ αἰτίᾳ χρωμένου.

Simplicius Defends Anaxagoras Against
Aristotle's Criticisms (R32–R33)

R32 (> A53) Simpl. *In Phys.*, p. 461.10–16, 20–27

ὅτι δὲ ὁ μὲν Ἀριστοτέλης τὸ προφαινόμενον ἱστορεῖ τῆς
Ἀναξαγόρου δόξης, ὁ δὲ Ἀναξαγόρας σοφὸς ὢν διττὴν
ᾐνίττετο τὴν διακόσμησιν, τὴν μὲν ἡνωμένην καὶ
νοητὴν προυπάρχουσαν οὐ χρόνῳ[1] (οὐ γὰρ ἔγχρονος
ἐκείνη), ἀλλ' ὑπεροχῇ οὐσίας καὶ δυνάμεως, τὴν δὲ δια-
κεκριμένην ἀπὸ ταύτης καὶ κατὰ ταύτην ὑφίστασθαι
ὑπὸ τοῦ δημιουργικοῦ νοῦ, εἴρηται καὶ ἐν ταῖς εἰς τὸ
πρῶτον σχολαῖς, ἐν αἷς τὰς πίστεις ἀπ' αὐτῶν ἐπειράθην
παραγράψαι τῶν Ἀναξαγόρου ῥημάτων. [...] διό φησιν
Ἀναξαγόρας μηδ' ἐνδέχεσθαι πάντα διακριθῆναι· οὐ
γὰρ παντελὴς διασπασμός ἐστιν ἡ διάκρισις. διὸ οὐχ
οἷόν τε βάδισιν ἢ χρόαν ἢ ὅλως τὰ πάθη καὶ τὰς ἕξεις

[1] οὐ χρόνῳ Diels: οὐ χρόμο sic E: om. F

Phaedo [cf. **R5**], viz. that he made use not of mind but of material reasons in the causal explanation of particular phenomena—this was appropriate for natural science. Indeed, Plato himself in the *Timaeus,* having begun by indicating universally the efficient cause of all things, then when he comes to particular things makes differences of volume and shape the cause of heat and cold, and so too in the other cases [cf. *Timaeus* 53c]. But Socrates, who wanted to indicate explanation on the basis of finality, has mentioned Anaxagoras as someone who had recourse rather to the material cause and not to the final cause.

Simplicius Defends Anaxagoras Against
Aristotle's Criticisms (R32)

R32 (> A53) Simplicius, *Commentary on Aristotle's* Physics

As I already said as well in my lectures on Book 1, in which I made an effort to cite evidence drawn from Anaxagoras' own words [cf. **R34**], Aristotle reports the visible surface of Anaxagoras' doctrine; but Anaxagoras, in his wisdom, alludes enigmatically to a double organization of the world, the one unified and intelligible, preceding not in time (for it is not within time) but by superiority of being and power, the other divided, which derives from this one and is in conformity with it, and whose existence is due to a demiurgic mind. [. . .] That is why Anaxagoras says that it is not possible either for all things to be completely separated: for dissociation is not a complete disintegration. That is why it is impossible that walking, color, or in general affections and conditions be separated from the

173

χωρισθῆναι τῶν ὑποκειμένων. τὸ δὲ χρονικὴν δοκεῖν
λέγεσθαι τὴν τῆς διακρίσεως ἀρχὴν σύνηθες ἦν τοῖς
πάλαι φυσιολόγοις τε καὶ θεολόγοις συγκαταβαίνουσι
τῇ ἀσθενείᾳ τῆς ἡμετέρας νοήσεως· οὐ γὰρ δυνάμεθα τῇ
ἀιδίῳ παρατάσει συμπαρατείνειν τὴν νόησιν, ἀλλ᾽
ἀπαιτοῦμεν ἀρχῆς τινος ὑποτιθεμένης ἐφεξῆς θεωρεῖν
τὰ ἀκόλουθα.[2]

[2] τὰ ἀκόλουθα F: τὰ καθόλου E

R33 (ad B16, B15) Simpl. *In Phys.*, pp. 178.28–179.12

ἀλλ᾽ ὅτι μὲν οὐχ οὕτως ἄπειρα ὡς ἀπερίηγητα τῷ πλήθει
καὶ Ἀναξαγόρας τὰ στοιχεῖά φησι, πρότερον ἐπειράθην
πιστώσασθαι [cf. p. 174.14]. κἂν πεπερασμένα δὲ
κατὰ τὰ εἴδη φησίν, ἀλλ᾽ ἀρχοειδέστερον Ἐμπεδοκλῆς
ἁπλούστερα τῶν γινομένων στοιχεῖα γῆν καὶ ὕδωρ καὶ
ἀέρα καὶ πῦρ ὑπέθετο τοῦ καὶ ταῦτα ὁμοίως ἔχειν τοῖς
ἐξ αὐτῶν συντεθεῖσιν νομίσαντος. εἰ μὴ ἄρα καὶ Ἀναξαγόρας τὰς ἁπλᾶς καὶ ἀρχοειδεῖς ποιότητας ὑπέθετο
στοιχεῖα, ἄλλα[1] τὰ σύνθετα ἐν οἷς φησιν "ἡ δὲ περιχώρησις [. . .] καὶ ἀπὸ τοῦ διεροῦ τὸ ξηρόν" [cf. **D27**].
καὶ μετ᾽ ὀλίγα δὲ "τὸ μὲν πυκνόν [. . .] τοῦ αἰθέρος"
[**D30**]. καὶ τὰ μὲν ἀρχοειδῆ ταῦτα καὶ ἁπλούστατα ἀποκρίνεσθαι λέγει, ἄλλα δὲ τούτων συνθετώτερα ποτὲ μὲν
συμπήγνυσθαι λέγει ὡς σύνθετα, ποτὲ δὲ ἀποκρίνεσθαι
ὡς τὴν γῆν. οὕτως γάρ φησιν "ἀπὸ τουτέων ἀποκρινο-

[1] ἄλλα coni. Diels: ἀλλ᾽ οὐ ed. Ald.: ἀλλὰ mss.

substrates. As for seeming to say that the beginning of the dissociation is temporal, this was a habit among the ancient natural philosophers and theologians, for they were accommodating themselves to the weakness of our thought: for we are not able to extend our own thought to the extension of eternity, but we need to posit a certain beginning in order to consider what follows from it step by step.

R33 (ad B16, B15) Simplicius, *Commentary on Aristotle's* Physics

I tried to demonstrate earlier that Anaxagoras too says that the elements are unlimited in the sense of a quantity that cannot be traversed. But even if he says that they are limited according to their forms, nonetheless Empedocles has posited in a way more appropriate for principles elements that are simpler for the things that come about (earth, water, air, and fire) than he [i.e. Anaxagoras] has done, who thinks that these latter are constituted in the same way as what is composed out of them—if Anaxagoras too was not positing as elements the simple elements, the ones that are principles, and the composites as different, when he says, **"And the rotation** [. . .] **and from the moist the dry"** [cf. **D27**], and a little later, **"What is dense** [. . .] **of the aether"** [**D30**]; and he says that these things, which are principles and are the simplest, separate, while for others, which are more complex, he says that sometimes they coalesce like composites, while at other times they separate, like earth. For he says, **"Out of these**

μένων [. . .] ὑπὸ τοῦ ψυχροῦ" [cf. **D31**]. οὕτως μὲν οὖν
ἐπὶ τὰ ἁπλᾶ εἴδη ἀναδραμὼν Ἀναξαγόρας ἀρχοειδέστερον δόξει τοῦ Ἐμπεδοκλέους τὰ περὶ τῶν στοιχείων
φιλοσοφεῖν.

The Transmission of the Fragments of
Anaxagoras: An Example (R34)

R34 (cf. ad B1, B2) Simpl. *In Phys.*, pp. 155.23–157.24

ὅτι δὲ Ἀναξαγόρας ἐξ ἑνὸς[1] μίγματος ἄπειρα τῷ πλήθει
ὁμοιομερῆ ἀποκρίνεσθαί φησιν πάντων μὲν ἐν παντὶ
ἐνόντων, ἑκάστου δὲ κατὰ τὸ ἐπικρατοῦν χαρακτηριζομένου, δηλοῖ διὰ τοῦ πρώτου τῶν Φυσικῶν λέγων ἀπ᾽
ἀρχῆς "ὁμοῦ χρήματα πάντα ἦν [. . .] καὶ πλήθει καὶ
μεγέθει" [**D9**]. καὶ μετ᾽ ὀλίγον "καὶ γὰρ ἀὴρ [. . .]
ἄπειρόν ἐστι τὸ πλῆθος" [**D10**]. καὶ μετ᾽ ὀλίγα "τούτων
δὲ οὕτως ἐχόντων [. . .] χροιὰς καὶ ἡδονάς" [cf. **D13**].
"πρὶν δὲ ἀποκριθῆναι," φησί, "πάντων ὁμοῦ ἐόντων
[. . .] τὸ ἕτερον τῷ ἑτέρῳ" [cf. **D12**].

ὅτι δὲ οὐδὲ γίνεται οὐδὲ φθείρεταί τι τῶν ὁμοιομερῶν,
ἀλλ᾽ ἀεὶ τὰ αὐτά ἐστι, δηλοῖ λέγων "τούτων δὲ οὕτω
διακεκριμένων [. . .] πάντα ἴσα ἀεί" [**D16**].

ταῦτα μὲν οὖν περὶ τοῦ μίγματος καὶ τῶν ὁμοιομε-
ρειῶν. περὶ δὲ τοῦ νοῦ τάδε γέγραφε· "νοῦς δέ ἐστιν
ἄπειρον καὶ αὐτοκρατὲς [. . .] ταῦτα ἐνδηλότατα ἓν
ἕκαστόν ἐστι καὶ ἦν" [cf. **D27**].

---

[1] ἐξ ἑνὸς DE: ἔκ τινος F

things [. . .] **of the cold**" [cf. **D31**]. And in this way Anaxagoras, going back to the simple forms, will seem to provide a philosophical account with regard to the elements in a way that is more appropriate for principles than Empedocles does.

The Transmission of the Fragments of Anaxagoras: An Example (R34)

R34 (cf. ad B1, B2) Simplicius, *Commentary on Aristotle's* Physics

The fact that Anaxagoras says that homeomers unlimited in quantity separate out from a single mixture and that, all things being in every thing, each one is characterized according to what predominates—he makes this clear throughout book 1 of his *Physics,* saying at the beginning, **"All things were together** [. . .] **both in quantity and in magnitude"** [**D9**]; and shortly after, **"For both the air** [. . .] **unlimited in quantity"** [**D10**]; and shortly after, **"These things being so** [. . .] **colors and flavors"** [cf. **D13**]; **"Before these things separated out,"** he says, **"all things being together** [. . .] **to each other"** [cf. **D12**].

   The fact that none of the homeomers ever comes to be or is destroyed, but that they are always the same, he makes clear by saying, **"Since it is in this way that these things have separated** [. . .] **the totality of things is always equal"** [**D16**].

   This then is what he says about the mixture and the homeomers. As for mind, he has written the following: **"but mind is unlimited and master of itself** [. . .] **this is and was most manifestly each thing"** [cf. **D27**].

ὅτι δὲ διττήν τινα διακόσμησιν ὑποτίθεται τὴν μὲν
νοεράν, τὴν δὲ αἰσθητὴν ἀπ᾽ ἐκείνης, δῆλον μὲν καὶ ἐκ
τῶν εἰρημένων, δῆλον δὲ καὶ ἐκ τῶνδε· "ὁ δὲ νοῦς [. . .]
ἐν τοῖς ἀποκεκριμένοις" [**D28**]. καὶ μέντοι εἰπὼν
"ἐνεῖναι πολλά τε καὶ παντοῖα [. . .] καὶ τὰ ἄλλα ζῷα
ὅσα ψυχὴν ἔχει" [cf. **D13**], ἐπάγει "καὶ τοῖς γε
ἀνθρώποισιν [. . .] χρῶνται" [cf. **D13**]. καὶ ὅτι μὲν
ἑτέραν τινὰ διακόσμησιν παρὰ τὴν παρ᾽ ἡμῖν αἰνίττε-
ται, δηλοῖ τὸ "**ὥσπερ παρ᾽ ἡμῖν**" οὐχ ἅπαξ μόνον
εἰρημένον. ὅτι δὲ οὐδὲ αἰσθητὴν μὲν ἐκείνην οἴεται, τῷ
χρόνῳ δὲ ταύτης προηγησαμένην, δηλοῖ τὸ "**ὧν ἐκεῖνοι
τὰ ὀνήιστα συνενεικάμενοι εἰς τὴν οἴκησιν χρῶνται.**"
οὐ γὰρ "ἐχρῶντο" εἶπεν, ἀλλὰ "**χρῶνται.**" ἀλλ᾽ οὐδὲ ὡς
νῦν κατ᾽ ἄλλας τινὰς οἰκήσεις ὁμοίας οὔσης καταστά-
σεως τῇ παρ᾽ ἡμῖν· οὐ γὰρ εἶπε "τὸν ἥλιον καὶ τὴν
σελήνην εἶναι καὶ παρ᾽ ἐκείνοις ὥσπερ καὶ[2] παρ᾽ ἡμῖν,"
ἀλλ᾽ "**ἥλιον καὶ σελήνην, ὥσπερ παρ᾽ ἡμῖν**" ὡς δὴ περὶ
ἄλλων λέγων.

ἀλλὰ ταῦτα μὲν εἴτε οὕτως εἴτε ἄλλως ἔχει, ζητεῖν
ἄξιον.

[2] καὶ om. DE

The fact that he accepts a double organization of the world, the one intelligible and the other perceptible deriving from the former, is clear both from what I have already said and also from the following: **"Mind** [. . .] **in those that are separating"** [**D28**]. Furthermore, having said, **"that many things and of all kinds, are present** [. . .] **and all the other living things that possess soul"** [cf. **D13**], he adds, **"and that these human beings** [. . .] **make use of them"** [cf. **D13**]. And the fact that he is alluding enigmatically to a different organization of the world from the one among us is made clear by the phrase **"just as among us,"** which is said more than once. And the fact that he thinks that that one is not perceptible, but that it precedes this one in time, is made clear by the phrase, **"of which they gather the most useful ones into their household and make use of them."** For he did not say "made use," but rather **"make use."** But he did not speak either as though the state of things in the other households was similar to the one among us now; for he did not say, "they have the sun and the moon, just as among us," but rather, **"a sun and a moon, just as among us,"** which suggests that he is speaking about other ones [i.e. sun and moon].

But whether these matters are like this or different would be worth investigating.

A Judgment on Anaxagoras' Style (R35)

R35 (< A1) Diog. Laert. 2.6

[. . .] ἀρξάμενος οὕτω τοῦ συγγράμματος, ὅ ἐστιν
ἡδέως καὶ μεγαλοφρόνως ἡρμηνευμένον [. . . cf. **P42**].

*An Aphorism Attributed to Anaxagoras
in Syriac (R36)*

R36 (B23) *Studia Sinaitica* 1, p. 33

O = Oxford, New College, Syr. 331, fol. 97v
S = Monastery of Saint Catherine on Mount Sinai, Syr. 16, fol.
147v

¹ O om. S

A Judgment on Anaxagoras' Style (R35)

R35 (< A1) Diogenes Laertius

[. . .] beginning in the following way his treatise, which is written in an agreeable and elevated style [. . .].

An Aphorism Attributed to Anaxagoras in Syriac (R36)

R36 (B23) From a Syriac collection of Greek sayings

Anaxagoras said, "Death, which seems at first sight to humans to be bitter, is, when things are examined more closely, very beautiful: it grants peace to old age, which lacks strength, to youth, which pains assail, and to childhood, which it prevents from tormenting and exhausting itself, from constructing, planting, and installing for other people; it frees debtors from their creditors, who demand capital and interest. We should not grieve because of something that is fixed and determined, for grief cannot eliminate it, whereas a good mood can conceal it, even if only for a certain time, for there is no suffering in the port when one spends time there. And even if the sight of death is hateful to the eyes of those who see it, then close your eyes for a moment. And so: you have seen how beautiful death is—death, which those who are afflicted and tormented call for. This provides testimony for how calm and marvelous the habitation of the Underworld is."[1]

[1] Translated from the French translation by Henri Hugonnard-Roche.

Anaxagoras in The Assembly of
Philosophers *(R37)*

R37 (≠ DK) *Turba Phil.* Sermo III, p. 49.1–7 Plessner

ait Anaxagoras: "dico quod principium omnium, quae Deus creavit, est pietas et ratio, eo quod pietas regit omnia, et in ratione apparuit pietas et spissum terrae; pietas autem non videtur nisi in corpore. et scitote, omnis Turba, quod spissitudo quatuor elementorum in terra quiescit, eo quod ignis spissum in aëra cadit, aëris vero spissum et quod ex ignis spisso congregatur, in aquam incidit, aquae quoque spissum et quod ex ignis et aëris spisso coadunatur, in terra quiescit."

Anaxagoras in The Assembly of Philosophers (R37)

R37 (≠ DK) *The Assembly of Philosophers*

Anaxagoras said: "I say to you that the beginning of all things that God creates is piety and reason, since piety rules all things and it is in reason that piety and the density of earth [?] appeared; but piety manifests itself only in a body. And know, you the whole Assembly, that the density of the four elements comes to rest in earth, because the density of fire falls onto air, while the density of air and of what is aggregated from the density of fire falls onto water, and the density of water and what is united out of the density of fire and of air comes to rest in earth."

26. ARCHELAUS [ARCH.]

Archelaus' dates are not indicated by any ancient source, so he can be situated only relatively, as Anaxagoras' disciple and as Socrates' teacher (**P1**). Thus he may be supposed to have been active at the beginning of the second half of the fifth century BC. What we can tell about his doctrine allows us to characterize it as a revision regarding the two neuralgic points of Anaxagoras' system: the elementary constituents that Aristotle calls 'homeomers' and the role of Mind (*nous*). From this point of view, he belongs to the same post-Anaxagorean movement as does Diogenes of Apollonia, who is surely younger than him and who shares with him the importance assigned to air in the cosmogonic process. The fact that ancient sources present him as the last natural philosopher is surely only the counterpart of the statement that he already concerned himself with ethical questions (**R2**), making him a kind of bridge between Anaxagoras and Socrates. But even if this information should happen to be correct, it is no longer possible to provide anything more than a very sketchy outline of his thought.

BIBLIOGRAPHY

Editions

At the time of this writing (2016), there is no edition of the fragments of Archelaus besides that in Diels-Kranz.

Studies

G. Betegh. "Socrate et Archélaos dans les *Nuées.* Philosophie naturelle et éthique," in A. Laks and R. Saetta Cottone, eds., *Comédie et philosophie. Socrate et les 'Présocratiques' dans les* Nuées *d'Aristophane* (Paris, 2013), pp. 87–106.

OUTLINE OF THE CHAPTER

ARCHELAUS [60DK]

P

Origin and Intellectual Lines of Descent (P1–P4)

P1 (<A1) Diog. Laert. 2.16

Ἀρχέλαος Ἀθηναῖος ἢ Μιλήσιος, πατρὸς Ἀπολλοδώρου, ὡς δέ τινες, Μίδωνος, μαθητὴς Ἀναξαγόρου, δι-
δάσκαλος Σωκράτους. οὗτος πρῶτος ἐκ τῆς Ἰωνίας
τὴν φυσικὴν φιλοσοφίαν μετήγαγεν Ἀθήναζε[1] καὶ
ἐκλήθη φυσικός [. . . = **R2**].

   [1] οὗτος . . . Ἀθήναζε ut glossema ad Anaxagoram referens
secl. Menagius

P2 (≠ DK) Eus. *PE* 10.14.13

Ἀναξαγόρου δὲ ἐγένοντο γνώριμοι τρεῖς, Περικλῆς,
Ἀρχέλαος, Εὐριπίδης. [. . .] ὁ δὲ Ἀρχέλαος ἐν Λαμψάκῳ διεδέξατο τὴν σχολὴν τοῦ Ἀναξαγόρου, μετα-
βὰς δ' εἰς Ἀθήνας ἐκεῖ ἐσχόλασε καὶ πολλοὺς ἔσχεν
Ἀθηναίων γνωρίμους, ἐν οἷς καὶ Σωκράτην.

ARCHELAUS

P

Origin and Intellectual Lines of Descent (P1–P4)

P1 (<A1) Diogenes Laertius

Archelaus of Athens or of Miletus; his father was Apollodorus or, as some say, Midon; disciple of Anaxagoras, teacher of Socrates. This man was the first to transfer natural philosophy from Ionia to Athens[1] and he was called a 'natural philosopher' (*phusikos*) [. . .].

    [1] Some scholars believe that this last phrase refers to Anaxagoras (cf. **ANAXAG. P13**).

P2 (≠ DK) Eusebius, *Evangelical Preparation*

Anaxagoras had three disciples: Pericles, Archelaus, and Euripides. [. . .] Archelaus was the successor at the school of Anaxagoras in Lampsacus, and after he moved to Athens he taught there and had many Athenian pupils, including Socrates.

P3 (< A2) *Suda* A.4084

Ἀρχέλαος, Ἀπολλοδώρου ἢ Μίδωνος, Μιλήσιος, φιλόσοφος, φυσικὸς τὴν αἵρεσιν κληθεὶς ὅτι ἀπὸ Ἰωνίας πρῶτος τὴν φυσιολογίαν ἤγαγεν, Ἀναξαγόρου
μαθητὴς τοῦ Κλαζομενίου, τοῦ δὲ μαθητὴς Σωκράτης·
οἱ δὲ καὶ Εὐριπίδην[1] φασίν.

[1] Εὐριπίδην Kuster: Εὐριπίδης A: Εὐριπίδου ITM

P4 (A3) Diog. Laert. 2.23

Ἴων δὲ ὁ Χῖος [Frag. 11 Blumenthal] καὶ νέον ὄντα εἰς
Σάμον σὺν Ἀρχελάῳ ἀποδημῆσαι.

Socrates' Lover (P5–P6)

P5 (> A3) *Suda* Σ.829

Ἀριστόξενος δὲ Ἀρχελάου πρῶτον αὐτὸν διακοῦσαι
λέγει [Frag. 52b Wehrli]· γεγονέναι δὲ αὐτοῦ καὶ παι-
δικά, σφοδρότατόν τε περὶ τὰ ἀφροδίσια [. . . = **P6b**].

P6 Porph. *Hist. phil.*

a (A3) Theod. *Cur.* 12.66 [= Porph. Frag. 215 Smith]

ἐλέγετο δὲ περὶ αὐτοῦ ὡς ἄρα παῖς ὢν οὐκ εὖ βιώ-
σειεν οὐδὲ εὐτάκτως [. . .]. ἤδη δὲ περὶ τὰ ἑπτακαίδεκα
ἔτη προσελθεῖν αὐτῷ Ἀρχέλαον, τὸν Ἀναξαγόρου μα-
θητήν, φάσκοντα ἐραστὴν εἶναι· τὸν δὲ Σωκράτην οὐκ

P3 (< A2) *Suda*

Archelaus, son of Apollodorus or of Midon, from Miletus, a philosopher, called 'natural' with regard to his school, because he was the first to bring the philosophy of nature (*phusiologia*) from Ionia; disciple of Anaxagoras of Clazomenae; Socrates was his disciple, some say that Euripides was too.

P4 (A3) Ion of Chios in Diogenes Laertius

Ion of Chios also [scil. says that] when he [i.e. Socrates] was young he traveled to Samos with Archelaus.

Socrates' Lover (P5–P6)

P5 (> A3) *Suda*

Aristoxenus says that he [scil. Socrates] at first studied with Archelaus, and that he also became his beloved, with a very passionate sexual love [. . .].

P6 Porphyry, *History of Philosophy*

a (A3) Theodoret, *Greek Maladies*

It was said of him [i.e. Socrates] that when he was very young he did not live in a proper or well-ordered way [. . .]. When he was already about seventeen years old [= 452 BC], Archelaus, Anaxagoras' disciple, came to him, saying that he was in love with him. Socrates did not refuse these

ἀπώσασθαι τὴν ἔντευξίν τε καὶ ὁμιλίαν τὴν πρὸς τὸν
Ἀρχέλαον, ἀλλὰ γενέσθαι παρ' αὐτῷ ἔτη συχνά. καὶ
οὕτως[1] ὑπὸ τοῦ Ἀρχελάου προτραπῆναι ἐπὶ τὰ φιλό-
σοφα.

[1] οὕτως Μγρ.: ὅπως L: πως ΚΜ

b (≠ DK) *Suda* Σ.829 [= Porph. Frag. 215a Smith]

[. . . = **P5**] ἀλλὰ ἀδικήματος χωρίς, ὡς Πορφύριος ἐν
τῇ Φιλοσόφῳ ἱστορίᾳ φησίν.

advances or Archelaus' company, but spent a number of years with him. And it was in this way that he was directed toward philosophical questions by Archelaus.

b (≠ DK) Suda

[. . . a very passionate sexual love, cf. **P5**], but one that was free of wrongdoing, as Porphyry says in his *History of Philosophy.*

ARCHELAUS [60 DK]

D

Writings (D1)

D1 (< A2) *Suda* A.4084

συνέταξε δὲ φυσιολογίαν [. . .]. συνέταξε καὶ ἄλλα
τινά.

Two General Summaries Going Back
Ultimately to Theophrastus (D2–D3)

D2 (< A4) (Ps.-?) Hippol. *Ref.* 1.9

[1] [. . .] οὗτος ἔφη τὴν μῖξιν τῆς ὕλης ὁμοίως Ἀναξαγόρᾳ τάς τε ἀρχὰς ὡσαύτως· οὗτος δὲ τῷ νῷ ἐνυπάρχειν τι εὐθέως μῖγμα. [2] εἶναι <δ᾽>[1] ἀρχὰς[2] τῆς κινήσεως <τῷ>[3] ἀποκρίνεσθαι ἀπ᾽ ἀλλήλων τὸ θερμὸν καὶ
τὸ ψυχρόν, καὶ τὸ μὲν θερμὸν κινεῖσθαι, τὸ δὲ ψυχρὸν
ἠρεμεῖν· τηκόμενον δὲ τὸ ὕδωρ εἰς μέσον ῥεῖν, ἐν ᾧ
καὶ κατακαιόμενον ἀέρα γίνεσθαι καὶ γῆν, ὧν τὸ μὲν

ARCHELAUS

D

Writings (D1)

D1 (< A2) *Suda*

He composed a treatise on nature (*phusiologia*) [. . .]. He also composed some other works.

Two General Summaries Going Back Ultimately to Theophrastus (D2–D3)

D2 (< A4) (Ps.-?) Hippolytus, *Refutation of All Heresies*

[1] [. . .] This man spoke of the mixture of matter in a way similar to Anaxagoras, and so too of the principles. But as for himself he said that a certain mixture was present in mind (*nous*) from the beginning. [2] The principles of motion are the hot and the cold, by separating from each other; and the hot moves, while the cold remains at rest. Water melts and flows toward the center, where, when it is also burned, air and earth come to be, of which the

───────────────

¹ ‹δ'› Schneidewin-Duncker   ² ἀρχὰς mss.: ἀρχὰς τῆς κινήσεως ‹δύο ἃς› ἀποκρίνεσθαι Diels: ἀρχὴν Roeper
³ ‹τῷ› nos: ‹τὸ› Ritter

ἄνω φέρεσθαι, τὸ δὲ ὑφίστασθαι κάτω. [3] τὴν μὲν
οὖν γῆν ἠρεμεῖν καὶ γενέσθαι διὰ ταῦτα, κεῖσθαι δ᾽
ἐν μέσῳ οὐδὲν μέρος οὖσαν, ὡς εἰπεῖν, τοῦ παντός·
‹τὸν δ᾽ ἀέρα›[4] ἐκδεδομένον ἐκ τῆς πυρώσεως, ἀφ᾽ οὗ
πρῶτον ἀποκαιομένου τὴν τῶν ἀστέρων εἶναι φύσιν,
ὧν μέγιστον μὲν ἥλιον, δεύτερον δὲ σελήνην, τῶν δὲ
ἄλλων τὰ μὲν ἐλάττω, τὰ δὲ μείζω. [4] ἐπικλιθῆναι δὲ
τὸν οὐρανόν φησι, καὶ οὕτως τὸν ἥλιον ἐπὶ τῆς γῆς
ποιῆσαι φῶς καὶ τόν τε ἀέρα ποιῆσαι διαφανῆ καὶ
τὴν γῆν ξηράν. λίμνην γὰρ εἶναι τὸ πρῶτον, ἅτε
κύκλῳ μὲν οὖσαν ὑψηλήν, μέσον δὲ κοίλην. σημεῖον
δὲ φέρει τῆς κοιλότητος, ὅτι ὁ ἥλιος οὐχ ἅμα ἀνατέλ-
λει τε καὶ δύεται πᾶσιν, ὅπερ ἔδει συμβαίνειν, εἴπερ
ἦν ὁμαλή. [5] περὶ δὲ ζῴων φησί, ὅτι θερμαινομένης
τῆς γῆς τὸ πρῶτον ἐν τῷ κάτω μέρει,[5] ὅπου τὸ θερμὸν
καὶ τὸ ψυχρὸν ἐμίσγετο, ἀνεφαίνετο τά τε ἄλλα ζῷα
πολλὰ καὶ οἱ ἄνθρωποι, ἅπαντα[6] τὴν αὐτὴν δίαιταν
ἔχοντα ἐκ τῆς ἰλύος τρεφόμενα—ἦν δὲ ὀλιγοχρόνια—
ὕστερον δὲ αὐτοῖς ἥ[7] ἐξ ἀλλήλων γένεσις συνέστη·[8]
[6] καὶ διεκρίθησαν ἄνθρωποι ἀπὸ τῶν ἄλλων καὶ
ἡγεμόνας καὶ νόμους καὶ τέχνας καὶ πόλεις καὶ τὰ
ἄλλα συνέστησαν. νοῦν δὲ λέγει πᾶσιν ἐμφύεσθαι
ζῴοις ὁμοίως. χρῆσθαι[9] γὰρ ἕκαστον τῶν σωμάτων
ὅσῳ ‹δυνατόν›,[10] τὸ μὲν βραδυτέρως, τὸ δὲ ταχυ-
τέρως.

[4] ‹τὸν δ᾽ ἀέρα› [scil. γενέσθαι] nos post Roeper, qui ‹τὸν δ᾽
ἀέρα κρατεῖν τοῦ παντὸς› suppl.
[5] κάτω μέρει Cedrenus 1.278 (ex Hipp.): κατὰ μέρος mss.

former rises upward while the latter sinks downward. [3]
Thus the earth remains at rest and comes to be for these
reasons, and it lies in the center since it is not at all, as it
were, a part of the whole. ⟨The air⟩ [scil. comes to be]
once it has been restored from the conflagration; from its
burning comes first the nature of the heavenly bodies, of
which the largest is the sun, then the moon; and as for the
other heavenly bodies, some are smaller and others larger.
[4] He says that the heavens inclined and that in this way
the sun produced light on the earth and made the air
transparent and the earth dry. For at first it was a marsh,
being elevated in its circumference and sunken in the center. He cites as evidence for its being sunken the fact that
the sun does not rise and set at the same time for every-
one, something that would have to be the case if it were
uniform. [5] With regard to animals, he says that, the earth
having been warmed at first in its lower part, where the
warm and the cold mixed, there appeared, together with
many other animals, also human beings, and that they all
lived in the same way, nourishing themselves from the
mud (they lived only a short time), but that afterward their
reproduction was from each other. [6] And the humans
separated from the other ones [scil. animals] and established leaders, laws, arts, cities, and the rest. He says that
mind (*nous*) is equally present by nature in all animals. For
each of their bodies uses as much of it ⟨as is possible⟩, the
ones more slowly, the others more quickly.

---

⁶ οἱ ἄνθρωποι, ἅπαντα Cedrenus: ἀνόμοια πάντα mss.

⁷ ἡ Cedrenus: καὶ mss.   ⁸ συνέστη OT: ἀνέστη LB:
ἐπηκολούθησεν Cedrenus   ⁹ χρῆσθαι Zeller: χρήσασθαι
LO: χρήσεσθαι B   ¹⁰ τῶν σωμάτων ὅσω ⟨δυνατόν⟩ e.g.
nos: τῶν σωμάτων ὅσω (ὅσα BO) mss.: τῶν ζῴων τῷ νῷ Diels

D3 (< A1) Diog. Laert. 2.17

τηκόμενόν φησι τὸ ὕδωρ[1] ὑπὸ τοῦ θερμοῦ, καθὸ μὲν
εἰς τὸ ‹μέσον διὰ τὸ›[2] πυρῶδες συνίσταται, ποιεῖν
γῆν· καθὸ δὲ περιρρεῖ, ἀέρα γεννᾶν. ὅθεν ἡ μὲν ὑπὸ
τοῦ ἀέρος, ὁ δὲ ὑπὸ τῆς τοῦ πυρὸς περιφορᾶς κρατεῖται. γεννᾶσθαι δέ φησι τὰ ζῷα ἐκ θερμῆς τῆς γῆς
καὶ ἰλὺν παραπλησίαν γάλακτι οἷον τροφὴν ἀνιείσης·
οὕτω δὴ καὶ τοὺς ἀνθρώπους ποιῆσαι. πρῶτος δὲ εἶπε
φωνῆς γένεσιν τὴν τοῦ ἀέρος πλῆξιν. τὴν δὲ θάλατ-
ταν ἐν τοῖς κοίλοις διὰ τῆς γῆς ἠθουμένην συνεστά-
ναι. μέγιστον τῶν ἄστρων τὸν ἥλιον, καὶ τὸ πᾶν ἄπειρον.

  [1] ὕδωρ P: ὑγρὸν B   [2] ‹μέσον διὰ τὸ› Kranz, alii alia

The Principles (D4–D8)
The First Principles (D4–D5)

D4 (< A5) Simpl. *In Phys.*, p. 27.26–28

[. . . = **R1**] οὗτοι μὲν οὖν ἀπείρους τῷ πλήθει καὶ ἀνομογενεῖς τὰς ἀρχὰς λέγουσι, τὰς ὁμοιομερείας τιθέν-
τες ἀρχάς.

D5 (A10) August. *Civ. Dei* 8.2

Anaxagorae successit auditor eius Archelaus. etiam ipse
de particulis inter se similibus, quibus singula quaeque
fierent, ita putavit constare omnia, ut inesse etiam mentem

D3 (< A1) Diogenes Laertius

He says that the water, melting by the effect of heat, produced the earth ‹because of the› fiery element to the extent that it reached the ‹center›, and that it generated the air to the extent that it flowed around the periphery. That is why the one is dominated by the air, the other by the revolution of the fire. He says that the animals were generated out of the warm earth, which sent up a mud similar to milk as a form of nourishment. It is in this way too that it [i.e. the earth] made humans. He was the first person to say that it is the striking of air that produces sound. The sea was filtered through the earth and was deposited in its cavities. The largest of the heavenly bodies is the sun, and the whole is unlimited.

The Principles (D4–D8)
The First Principles (D4–D5)

D4 (< A5) Simplicius, *Commentary on Aristotle's* Physics

These people [i.e. Anaxagoras and Archelaus] say that the principles are unlimited in number and are not homogeneous; they posit that the homoeomeries are principles.

D5 (A10) Augustine, *City of God*

Anaxagoras was followed by his disciple Archelaus: he too thought that all the things that come to be are composed of particles similar to each other, but in such a way, he said, that mind (*mens*) is also present in them; these eternal

199

diceret, quae corpora aeterna, id est illas particulas, con-
iungendo et dissipando ageret omnia.

Further Principles (D6–D8)

D6 (< A7) Aët. 1.3.6 (Ps.-Plut.) [περὶ ἀρχῶν τί εἰσιν]

Ἀρχέλαος [. . .] ἀέρα ἄπειρον καὶ τὴν περὶ αὐτὸν
πυκνότητα καὶ μάνωσιν· τούτων δὲ τὸ μὲν εἶναι πῦρ
τὸ δ᾽ ὕδωρ.

D7 (< A1) Diog. Laert. 2.16

ἔλεγε δὲ δύο αἰτίας εἶναι γενέσεως, θερμὸν καὶ ψυχρόν [. . . = **D19**].

D8 (< A9) Epiph. *Pan.* 3.2.9.5

Ἀρχέλαος [. . .] ἐκ γῆς τὰ πάντα λέγει γεγενῆσθαι.
αὕτη γὰρ ἀρχὴ τῶν ὅλων ἐστίν, ὥς φησι.

The Formation of the World and the
Role of Mind (D9–D11)

D9 (A12) Aët. 1.7.14 (Stob.) [τίς ὁ θεός;]

Ἀρχέλαος ἀέρα καὶ νοῦν τὸν θεόν, οὐ μέντοι κοσμο-
ποιὸν τὸν νοῦν.

bodies, that is, those particles, direct all things by combining and separating.

Further Principles (D6–D8)

D6 (< A7) Aëtius

Archelaus [. . .]: [scil. the principle is] unlimited air and the condensation and rarefaction it undergoes; of these, the one is fire, the other water.

D7 (< A1) Diogenes Laertius

He said that the causes of generation are two, hot and cold [. . .].

D8 (< A9) Epiphanius, *Against Heresies*

Archelaus [. . .] says that everything is generated out of the earth. For it is this that is the origin of all things, as he says.

*The Formation of the World and the
Role of Mind (D9–D11)*

D9 (A12) Aëtius

Archelaus: god is air and mind, but mind is not what made the world.

D10 (A14) Aët. 2.4.5 (Stob.) [εἰ ἄφθαρτος ὁ κόσμος]

Ἀρχέλαος ὑπὸ θεοῦ[1] καὶ ἐμψυχίας[2] συστῆναι τὸν κόσμον.

  [1] θερμοῦ Heeren   [2] ἐμψυχρίας Meineke

D11 (A11) Clem. Alex. *Protr.* 5.66.1

τούτω μέν γε ἄμφω τὸν νοῦν ἐπεστησάτην τῇ ἀπειρίᾳ.

Infinity of Worlds (D12)

D12 (< A13) Aët. 2.1.3 (Stob.; cf. Ps-Plut.) [περὶ κόσμου]

[. . .] Ἀρχέλαος [. . .] ἀπείρους κόσμους ἐν τῷ ἀπείρῳ κατὰ πᾶσαν περίστασιν.[1]

  [1] περίστασιν Plut.: περιαγωγήν Stob.

The Formation of the Earth (D13)

D13 (< B1a) Plut. *Prim. frig.* 21.6 954F

[. . .] ἧς ἡ ψυχρότης **δεσμός** ἐστιν, ὡς Ἀρχέλαος ὁ φυσικὸς εἶπεν [. . .].

D10 (A14) Aëtius

Archelaus: the world was formed by god and animation.[1]

  [1] Or, emending the text: "by heat and cooling." But the god that creates the world can be air, rather than mind, cf. **D9,** and air is a principle of animation (cf. **D20**).

D11 (A11) Clement of Alexandria, *Protreptic*

These two [i.e. Anaxagoras and Archelaus] both set mind in control over the infinite.

Infinity of Worlds (D12)

D12 (< A13) Aëtius

[. . .] Archelaus [. . .]: the worlds are unlimited [scil. in number] in the unlimited throughout the entire surrounding area.

The Formation of the Earth (D13)

D13 (B1a) Plutarch, *On the Principle of Cold*

[. . .] the cold is the **bond** [scil. of the earth], as Archelaus the natural philosopher says [. . .].

Is the World Destructible? Two Incompatible
Doxographical Reports (D14)

D14

a (< A14) Aët. 2.4.6 (Stob.) [εἰ ἄφθαρτος ὁ κόσμος]

[. . .] Ἀρχέλαος [. . .] φθαρτὸν τὸν κόσμον.

b (≠ DK) Alex. *In Phys.* 539 ad 250b18, p. 487 Rashed

ἕνα κόσμον γενητὸν καὶ ἄφθαρτον ἐξ ἡσυχίας· [. . .]
Ἀρχέλαος [. . .].

The Heavenly Bodies (D15)

D15 (A15) Aët. 2.13.6 (Stob.) [περὶ οὐσίας ἄστρων]

Ἀρχέλαος μύδρους ἔφησεν εἶναι τοὺς ἀστέρας, δια-
πύρους δέ.

Thunder and Lightning (D16)

D16 (A16) Aët. 3.3.5 (Stob.) [περὶ βροντῶν ἀστραπῶν
κεραυνῶν πρηστήρων τε καὶ τυφώνων]

Ἀρχέλαος ταὐτὸ[1] λέγει παρατιθεὶς τὸ τῶν διαπύρων
λίθων καθιεμένων εἰς ψυχρὸν ὕδωρ πάθος.

---

[1] τοῦτο mss., corr. Meineke

Is the World Destructible? Two Incompatible
Doxographical Reports (D14)

D14

a (< A14) Aëtius

[. . .] Archelaus [. . .]: the world is destructible.

b (≠ DK) Alexander of Aphrodisias, *Scholia on Aristotle's Physics*

One world, created and indestructible, coming from a state of rest: [. . .] Archelaus [. . .].

The Heavenly Bodies (D15)

D15 (A15) Aëtius

Archelaus said that the heavenly bodies are lumps of stone, and that they are on fire.

Thunder and Lightning (D16)

D16 (A16) Aëtius

Archelaus says the same thing [scil. as Anaxagoras about thunder, lightning, etc.], comparing them to what happens to red-hot stones when they are plunged into cold water.

The Flooding of the Nile (D17)

D17 (≠DK) Tzetz. *In Il.* 1.427 (p. 188 Lasserre)

[. . . = **ANAXAG. D66d**]

καὶ τις ἀνὴρ Ἀρχέλαος [. . .]

[. . .] συντρέχουσιν Ὁμήρῳ·

[. . .]

ἐξ ὄμβρων καὶ χιόνος τε τῆς ἐν Αἰθιοπίᾳ
συντηκομένης λέγοντες κατάρδεσθαι τὸν Νεῖλον.

Earthquakes (D18)

D18 (A16a) Sen. *Quaest. nat.* 6.12.1–2

Archelaus †antiquitatis†[1] diligens ait ita: "venti in concava
terrarum deferuntur; deinde, ubi iam omnia spatia plena
sunt et in quantum aër potuit densatus est, is qui supervenit
spiritus priorem premit et elidit ac frequentibus plagis
primo cogit, deinde proturbat; [2] tunc ille quaerens locum omnes angustias dimovet et claustra sua conatur
effringere: sic evenit, ut terrae spiritu luctante et fugam
quaerente moveantur. itaque cum terrae motus futurus
est, praecedit aëris tranquillitas et quies, videlicet quia vis
spiritus, quae concitare ventos solet, in inferna[2] sede
retinetur."

[1] inter antiquos satis *Gertz*: auctor ueritatis *Schultess*
[2] in (in *om.* λ) inferni *mss.*, *corr. Fortunatus*

The Flooding of the Nile (D17)

D17 (≠ DK) Tzetzes, *Commentary on Homer's* Iliad

[. . .]
And a certain Archelaus [. . .]
[. . .] they agree with Homer:
[. . .]
When they say that it is from rains and the snow
That melts in Ethiopia that the Nile is watered. [cf.
   ANAXAG. D66d]

Earthquakes (D18)

D18 (A16a) Seneca, *Natural Questions*

Archelaus, esteeming †. . .†, says the following: "winds penetrate into the cavities of the earth; then, when all the spaces are full and the air has been condensed as far as is possible, the air that arrives subsequently presses the air that was already there and strikes it, and by means of frequent blows first it forces it, then it repels it. Then the earlier one, trying to find some room, splits open all the narrow passageways and tries to break open the barriers that enclose it: and so it comes about that the earth moves, as the air struggles and tries to escape. And this is why, when an earthquake is about to happen, the air is calm and tranquil beforehand, since the force of the air, which usually stirs up the winds, is being kept back in the subterranean region."

The Birth of Animals (D19)

D19 (< A1) Diog. Laert. 2.16

[. . . = **D7**] καὶ τὰ ζῷα ἀπὸ τῆς ἰλύος γεννηθῆναι.

The Soul (D20)

D20 (< A17) Aët. 4.3.2 (Stob.) [εἰ σῶμα ἡ ψυχὴ καὶ τίς ἡ οὐσία αὐτῆς]

[. . .] Ἀρχέλαος [. . .] ἀερώδη.

Politics and Ethics (D21–D22)

D21 (A6) Sext. *Adv. Math.* 7.14

[. . .] Ἀρχέλαος δὲ ὁ Ἀθηναῖος τὸ φυσικὸν καὶ ἠθικόν.

D22 (< A1) Diog. Laert. 2.16

[. . . cf. **R2**] καὶ γὰρ περὶ νόμων πεφιλοσόφηκε καὶ καλῶν καὶ δικαίων· [. . . = **R2**] καὶ τὸ δίκαιον εἶναι καὶ τὸ αἰσχρὸν οὐ φύσει ἀλλὰ νόμῳ.

The Birth of Animals (D19)

D19 (< A1) Diogenes Laertius

[. . .] and the animals were born from mud.

The Soul (D20)

D20 (< A17) Aëtius

[. . .] Archelaus [. . .]: it [scil. the soul is] of air.

Politics and Ethics (D21–D22)

D21 (A6) Sextus Empiricus, *Against the Logicians*

[. . .] Archelaus of Athens [scil. broached] questions of physics and ethics.

D22 (< A1) Diogenes Laertius

[. . .] for he also philosophized about laws and what is fine and just; [. . .] what is just and what is shameful exist not by nature but by convention.

ARCHELAUS [60 DK]

R

Earliest Attestation: Ion of Chios

See **P4**

Theophrastus' Judgment (R1)

R1 (< A5) Simpl. *In Phys.*, p. 27.23–26 [cf. Theophr. Frag. 228A FSH&G]

καὶ Ἀρχέλαος ὁ Ἀθηναῖος [. . .] ἐν μὲν τῇ γενέσει τοῦ κόσμου καὶ τοῖς ἄλλοις πειρᾶταί τι φέρειν ἴδιον, τὰς ἀρχὰς δὲ τὰς αὐτὰς ἀποδίδωσιν ἅσπερ Ἀναξαγόρας [. . . = **D4**].

The Construction of a Philosophical Succession (R2)

R2 (<A1) Diog. Laert. 2.16

[. . . = **P1**] παρὸ καὶ ἔληξεν ἐν αὐτῷ ἡ φυσικὴ φιλοσοφία, Σωκράτους τὴν ἠθικὴν εἰσαγαγόντος. ἔοικε δὲ

ARCHELAUS

R

Earliest Attestation: Ion of Chios

See **P4**

Theophrastus' Judgment (R1)

R1 (< A5) Simplicius, *Commentary on Aristotle's* Physics

Archelaus of Athens too [. . .] tries to say something of his own on the generation of the world and on other matters, but he assigns the same principles as Anaxagoras does.

The Construction of a Philosophical Succession (R2)

R2 (<A1) Diogenes Laertius

[. . .] that is also why natural philosophy came to an end with him, with Socrates introducing ethics. But it seems

καὶ οὗτος ἅψασθαι τῆς ἠθικῆς [. . . = **D22**]· παρ' οὗ
λαβὼν Σωκράτης τῷ αὐξῆσαι εἷς ὁ εὑρὼν[1] ὑπελήφθη.

[1] εἷς ὁ εὑρὼν nos: εἰς τὸ εὑρεῖν mss.: εἰς τὸ ⟨ἄκρον⟩ εὑρεῖν
Diels

Epicurus, a Reader of Archelaus (R3)

R3 (< 59 A26) Diog. Laert. 10.12

μάλιστα δὲ ἀπεδέχετο [Epic. Frag. 240 Usener], φησὶ
Διοκλῆς, τῶν ἀρχαίων Ἀναξαγόραν [. . . cf. **ANAXAG.
R28**] καὶ Ἀρχέλαον τὸν Σωκράτους διδάσκαλον.

An Objection by Seneca to Archelaus' Explanation of Earthquakes (R4)

R4 (≠ DK) Sen. *Quaest. nat.* 6.12.3

[. . . = **D18**] "quid ergo? numquam flante vento terra
concussa est?" "admodum raro: ⟨nam raro⟩[1] duo simul
flavere venti: fieri tamen et potest et solet. quod si re-
cipimus, et constat duos ventos rem simul gerere, quidni[2]
accidere possit, ut alter superiorem aëra agitet, alter in-
fernum?"

[1] ⟨nam⟩ *Hine*, ⟨raro⟩ *Shackleton Bailey*
[2] quidni *Erasmus*: quidnam Zθπ: quid (quod B) inde δ

that he too touched upon ethics. [. . .] Socrates took it over from him, but was considered to have been it sole discoverer it because he had developed it.

Epicurus, a Reader of Archelaus (R3)

R3 (< 59 A26) Diogenes Laertius

More than anyone else, says Diocles, he [i.e. Epicurus] preferred Anaxagoras among the ancients [. . .], and Archelaus, Socrates' teacher.

An Objection by Seneca to Archelaus' Explanation of Earthquakes (R4)

R4 (≠ DK) Seneca, *Natural Questions*

[. . .] "Well then? Has there never been an earthquake while the wind was blowing?" "It is very rare: for it is rare that two winds blow at the same time. But this can happen and it does happen customarily. If we accept that, and it is a fact that two winds are acting at the same time, why then could it not happen that one agitates the higher air, the other the lower air?"

Elegiac Poems? (R5)

R5 (< B1) Plut. *Cim.* 4.8

[. . .] εἴ τι δεῖ τεκμαίρεσθαι [. . .] ταῖς γεγραμμέναις
ἐπὶ παρηγορίᾳ τοῦ πένθους ἐλεγείαις πρὸς αὐτόν, ὧν
Παναίτιος ὁ φιλόσοφος οἴεται [Frag. 125 van Straaten]
ποιητὴν γεγονέναι τὸν φυσικὸν Ἀρχέλαον, οὐκ ἀπὸ
τρόπου τοῖς χρόνοις εἰκάζων.

Alchemical Forgeries (R6)

R6 (< B2) *Coll. Alchim.* I, p. 25.6–13

γίνωσκε, ὦ φίλε, καὶ τὰ ὀνόματα τῶν ποιητῶν· [. . .]
Ἀρχέλαος [. . .].

Archelaus in The Assembly of Philosophers *(R7)*

R7 (≠ DK) *Turba Phil.*

a p. 109.1–9 Ruska

liber, in quo discipulorum suorum prudentiores Arisleus
congregavit, Pitagoram sc. philosophum et sapientum
verba, qui in tertia synodo Pitagorica qui artifex dicitur

Elegiac Poems? *(R3)*

R5 (< B1) Plutarch, *Cimon*

[. . .] if one must judge [. . .] from the elegiac poems written to console him [scil. Cimon] for his grief [scil. for the death of his lover Isodice], of which the philosopher Panaetius, conjecturing not implausibly on the basis of the chronology, thinks that the natural philosopher Archelaus was the author.

Alchemical Forgeries (R6)

R6 (< B2) *Collection of Ancient Greek Alchemists*

Learn as well, dear friend, the names of those who make [scil. gold]: [. . .] Archelaus [. . .].[1]

[1] Archelaus' name appears twenty-second in a list of twenty-seven names (including those of Plato, Aristotle, Democritus, etc.). A collection of 336 early Byzantine iambs is preserved in Archelaus the Philosopher, *On the Same Sacred Art* [scil. of making gold], cf. DK I, p. 48.

Archelaus in The Assembly of Philosophers *(R7)*

R7 (≠ DK) *The Crowd of Philosophers*

a The beginning

The book, in which Arisleus (i.e. Archelaus) has gathered together the wiser among his students, viz. [scil. the students of] the philosopher Pythagoras, who is called 'the master of the art [i.e. alchemy],' and the discourses of the wise men who met in the third Pythagorean synod.

sunt coadunati. quem librum vix legit intellectum habens vel aliquantulum prius in hac arte investigans, qui in nobile propositum non pervenit.[1]

huius autem codicis principium est:

Arisleus genitus Pitagorae, discipulus ex discipulis Hermetis gratia triplicis, expositionem scientiae docens omnibus posteris residuis salutem et misericordiam.

[1] liber . . . pervenit *textus valde incertus*

b Sermo V, p. 57.1–58.9 Plessner

ait Arisleus: scitote, quod terra est collis et non est plana, unde non ascendit sol super climata terrae una hora. nam si plana esset, uno ascenderet momento super totam terram.

inquit Parmenides: breviter locutus es, Arislee.

respondit: numquid Magister dimisit nobis aliud dicendum? dico tamen, quod Deus unus est, numquam genuit nec genitus est; et quod omnium caput post se est terra et ignis, eo quod ignis tenuis et levis regit omnia, terra autem cum sit ponderosa et spissa, fert omnia, quae regit ignis.

Scarcely anyone who has understanding or who has some prior experience in this art reads this book without arriving at his noble goal.[1]

Of this codex the beginning is as follows:

Arisleus, the son of Pythagoras, a student from among the students of the thrice blessed Hermes [i.e. Hermes Trismegistus], teaching the exposition of his science: health and compassion for all posterity. [cf. **PYTHS. R73**]

[1] Our translation of this very difficult and probably corrupt text follows the tentative suggestions of Ruska, cf. p. 173, n. 1.

b

Arisleus said: Know that the earth is a hill and not flat, which is why the sun does not rise above the regions of the earth at one time. For if it were flat, it would rise in one moment above the whole earth.

Parmenides said: You have spoken briefly, Arisleus.

He answered: Yes indeed, for has our Teacher left us anything else to say? Nevertheless I say that God is one, He never begot nor was he ever begotten; and that the beginning of all things after Him is earth and fire, since fire, being rarefied and light, rules over all things, while the earth, which is heavy and dense, bears all the things over which fire rules.

28. DIOGENES OF APOLLONIA
[DIOG.]

For Diogenes' chronology we do not possess any precise dates, but an indication that goes back to Theophrastus presents him as one of the last, indeed as "virtually the youngest," of the natural philosophers (**P2**), and the very content of his doctrine allows us to consider him a younger contemporary of Anaxagoras. He is also one of the probable targets of Aristophanes' *Clouds*, which was staged in 423 BC. For a long time disparaged as an eclectic and naïve thinker, his importance is now recognized, for the teleological program he sketches out, for his explicit argumentation in favor of a monism of which the foundation is called 'air,' and for the detailed description he gives, in relation with his general theory, of the system of distribution of blood and air in the human body. His monism of air and the concrete turn of his thought suggest that Diogenes occupies a place analogous, with regard to Anaxagoras, to that which Anaximenes had occupied with regard to Anaximander. His central term, *noêsis* ('intelligence'), which clearly echoes Anaxagoras' *nous*, is difficult to translate univocally: in various contexts it can apply either to intelligence or to mind or to other forms of apprehension, like perception.

BIBLIOGRAPHY

Edition

A. Laks. *Diogène d'Apollonie. Édition, traduction et commentaire des fragments et témoignages* (Sankt-Augustin, 2008²).

Studies

D. W. Graham. *Explaining the Cosmos: The Ionian Tradition of Scientific Philosophy* (Princeton, 2006), ch. 10.

OUTLINE OF THE CHAPTER

DIOGENES OF
APOLLONIA [64 DK]

P

Chronology and Philosophical Affiliations (P1–P2)

P1 (< A1) Diog. Laert. 9.57

Διογένης Ἀπολλοθέμιδος[1] Ἀπολλωνιάτης, ἀνὴρ φυσικὸς καὶ ἄγαν ἐλλόγιμος. ἤκουσε δέ, φησὶν Ἀντισθέ-
νης [FGrHist 508 F15], Ἀναξιμένους. ἦν δὲ ἐν τοῖς
χρόνοις κατ᾽ Ἀναξαγόραν [. . . = **P4**].

 [1] ἀπολλοθέμιδος F: -μιτος BP

P2 (< A5) Simpl. *In Phys.*, p. 25.1–3 (cf. Theophr. Frag.
226A FHS&G)

καὶ Διογένης δὲ ὁ Ἀπολλωνιάτης, σχεδὸν νεώτατος
γεγονὼς τῶν περὶ ταῦτα σχολασάντων, τὰ μὲν πλεῖστα συμπεφορημένως γέγραφε,[1] τὰ μὲν κατὰ Ἀναξαγόραν, τὰ δὲ κατὰ Λεύκιππον λέγων [. . . = **D8**].

 [1] γέγραφε E^aF: ἔγραφε DE

DIOGENES OF
APOLLONIA

P

Chronology and Philosophical Affiliations (P1–P2)

P1 (< A1) Diogenes Laertius

Diogenes of Apollonia, son of Apollothemis, a natural philosopher and a man of great reputation. Antisthenes says that he studied with Anaximenes; but in chronological terms he lived at the time of Anaxagoras [. . .].

P2 (< A5) Simplicius, *Commentary on Aristotle's* Physics

Diogenes of Apollonia, virtually the youngest of those who taught on this subject [i.e. the principle from which the world came], wrote about most subjects in a composite manner, sometimes following Anaxagoras, other times Leucippus.

City of Origin (P3)

P3 (A3) Steph. Byz. *Ethn.* s.v. Ἀπολλωνία

Ἀπολλωνία. [. . .] κγ´ Κρήτης, ἡ πάλαι Ἐλεύθερνα,
Λίνου πατρίς. ἐκ ταύτης ὁ φυσικὸς Διογένης.

Diogenes in Danger at Athens? (P4)

P4 (< A1) Diog. Laert. 9.57

[. . . = **P1**] τοῦτόν φησιν ὁ Φαληρεὺς Δημήτριος ἐν τῇ
Σωκράτους ἀπολογίᾳ [Frag. 91 Wehrli] διὰ μέγαν φθό-
νον μικροῦ κινδυνεῦσαι Ἀθήνησιν.

City of Origin (P3)

P3 (A3) Stephanus of Byzantium, *Ethnica*

Apollonia: [. . .] (23) of Crete, the former Eleutherna, the homeland of Linus; Diogenes the natural philosopher came from this city.[1]

----

[1] This is not certain; there were many other cities named Apollonia, notably one in Thrace, on the Black Sea, to which Diogenes is connected most often.

Diogenes in Danger at Athens? (P4)

P4 (< A1) Diogenes Laertius

[. . .] Demetrius of Phaleron says in his *Apology of Socrates* that he almost died at Athens because he was the object of great ill will.[1]

----

[1] The "he"'s could also refer to Anaxagoras, mentioned in the preceding sentence (**P1**). Cf. **ANAXAG. P23.**

DIOGENES OF
APOLLONIA [64 DK]

D

More Than One Treatise? (D1)

D1 (< A4) Simpl. *In Phys.*, p. 151.24–29

[. . .] ἰστέον ὡς γέγραπται μὲν πλείονα τῷ Διογένει
τούτῳ συγγράμματα (ὡς αὐτὸς ἐν τῷ Περὶ φύσεως
ἐμνήσθη καὶ πρὸς φυσιολόγους ἀντειρηκέναι λέγων,
οὓς καλεῖ καὶ αὐτὸς σοφιστάς, καὶ Μετεωρολογίαν
γεγραφέναι, ἐν ᾗ καὶ λέγει περὶ τῆς ἀρχῆς εἰρηκέναι,
καὶ μέντοι καὶ Περὶ ἀνθρώπου φύσεως), ἐν δέ γε τῷ
Περὶ φύσεως, ὃ τῶν αὐτοῦ μόνον εἰς ἐμὲ ἦλθε, προτίθεται μὲν διὰ πολλῶν δεῖξαι ὅτι [. . . = **D5a, R7**].

The Beginning of the Treatise:
A Metholodogical Remark (D1)

D2 (B1) Diog. Laert. 9.57

λόγου παντὸς ἀρχόμενον δοκεῖ μοι χρεὼν εἶναι τὴν

226

DIOGENES OF
APOLLONIA

D

More Than One Treatise? (D1)

D1 (< A4) Simplicius, *Commentary on Aristotle's* Physics

[. . .] one must know that this Diogenes wrote a number of treatises, as he himself says in his *On Nature,* when he says that he wrote a reply against the natural philosophers, whom he himself calls 'sophists' [or: 'wise men,' *sophistai*], and also wrote a *Meteorology,* in which he says that he has spoken about the principle, and also *On the Nature of Man;* but at least in his *On Nature,* which is the only book of his that has reached me, he proposes to demonstrate by means of numerous arguments that [. . .].[1]

[1] The existence of more than one treatise by Diogenes is not attested elsewhere. This might be merely a hypothesis of Simplicius' intended to resolve an interpretative problem (see **R7**).

The Beginning of the Treatise:
A Methodological Remark (D2)

D2 (B1) Diogenes Laertius

It is my view that it is necessary, when one begins (*arkhesthai*) any discourse, to provide a beginning

ἀρχὴν ἀναμφισβήτητον παρέχεσθαι, τὴν δ' ἑρμη-
νείαν ἁπλῆν καὶ σεμνήν.

The Principle (D3–D13)
The Justification of Monism (D3)

D3 (B2) Simpl. *In Phys.*, pp. 151.31–152.7 [immediately
after the proem; cf. **R7**]

ἐμοὶ δὲ δοκεῖ τὸ μὲν ξύμπαν εἰπεῖν πάντα τὰ ὄντα
ἀπὸ τοῦ αὐτοῦ ἑτεροιοῦσθαι καὶ τὸ αὐτὸ εἶναι. καὶ
τοῦτο εὔδηλον· εἰ γὰρ τὰ ἐν τῷδε τῷ κόσμῳ ἐόντα
νῦν, γῆ καὶ ὕδωρ καὶ ἀὴρ καὶ πῦρ καὶ τὰ ἄλλα ὅσα
φαίνεται ἐν τῷδε τῷ κόσμῳ ἐόντα, εἰ τούτων τι ἦν
ἕτερον τοῦ ἑτέρου, ἕτερον ὂν τῇ ἰδίᾳ φύσει, καὶ μὴ
τὸ αὐτὸ ἐὸν μετέπιπτε πολλαχῶς καὶ ἡτεροιοῦτο,
οὐδαμῇ οὔτε μίσγεσθαι ἀλλήλοις ἠδύνατο, οὔτε
ὠφέλησις τῷ ἑτέρῳ ⟨γενέσθαι ἀπὸ τοῦ ἑτέρου⟩[1] οὔτε
βλάβη, οὐδ' ἂν οὔτε φυτὸν ἐκ τῆς γῆς φῦναι οὔτε
ζῷον οὔτε ἄλλο γενέσθαι οὐδέν, εἰ μὴ οὕτω συν-
ίστατο ὥστε ταὐτὸ εἶναι. ἀλλὰ πάντα ταῦτα ἐκ τοῦ
αὐτοῦ ἑτεροιούμενα ἄλλοτε ἀλλοῖα γίνεται καὶ εἰς
τὸ αὐτὸ ἀναχωρεῖ.

[1] ⟨γενέσθαι ἀπὸ τοῦ ἑτέρου⟩ Diels

(*arkhê*) **that is free of ambiguity, and a style that is simple and dignified.**

The Principle (D3–D13)
The Justification of Monism (D3)

D3 (B2) Simplicius, *Commentary on Aristotle's* Physics [Immediately after the proem; cf. **R7**]

It is my view, to say it as a whole, that all the things that are are differentiated out of the same thing and are the same thing. And this is manifest: for if the things that exist now in this world—earth, water, air, fire, and all the other things of which it is visible that they exist in this world—if any one of these were different from the other, being different by its own nature, and it were not the case that it was transformed and was differentiated in many ways, being the same thing, then it would not be possible in any way either that things would mix with one another or that benefit or harm ‹would come about from the one› **to the other, or that any plant could grow from the earth either, or any animal or anything else come to be, if they were not constituted in such a way that they were the same thing. But all these things come about, sometimes of one sort, sometimes of another, by being differentiated out of the same, and they return to the same.**

Eternity of the Principle (D4)

D4 (B7) Simpl. *In Phys.*, p. 153.19–20

καὶ αὐτὸ μὲν τοῦτο καὶ ἀίδιον καὶ ἀθάνατον σῶμα,
τῷ¹ δὲ τὰ μὲν γίνεται, τὰ δὲ ἀπολείπει.

¹ τῷ DE: τὸ F

Intelligence of the Principle (D5–D6)

D5 Simpl. *In Phys.*

a (cf. 3 Laks) p. 151.28–30

ἐν δέ γε τῷ Περὶ φύσεως [. . . cf. **D1**], προτίθεται μὲν
διὰ πολλῶν δεῖξαι ὅτι ἐν τῇ ὑπ᾽ αὐτοῦ τεθείσῃ ἀρχῇ
ἐστι "νόησις πολλή."

b (B3) p. 152.11–16

ἐφεξῆς δὲ δείξας ὅτι ἐστὶ ἐν τῇ ἀρχῇ ταύτῃ νόησις
πολλή—οὐ γὰρ ἄν, φησίν, οἷόν τε ἦν οὕτω δεδάσθαι
ἄνευ νοήσιος ὥστε πάντων μέτρα ἔχειν, χειμῶνός
τε καὶ θέρους καὶ νυκτὸς καὶ ἡμέρας καὶ ὑετῶν καὶ
ἀνέμων καὶ εὐδιῶν· καὶ τὰ ἄλλα εἴ τις βούλεται
ἐννοεῖσθαι, εὑρίσκοι ἂν οὕτω διακείμενα ὡς ἀνυστὸν κάλλιστα, ἐπάγει [. . . paraphrase and citation of
D9].

Eternity of the Principle (D4)

D4 (B7) Simplicius, *Commentary on Aristotle's* Physics

And this is itself a body both eternal and deathless, but it is by means of it that some things come to be and others cease to exist.

Intelligence of the Principle (D5–D6)

D5 Simplicius, *Commentary on Aristotle's* Physics

a (≠ DK)

[. . .] in his *On Nature* [. . .] he proposes to show by means of numerous arguments that in the principle which he posits there exists **"much intelligence** [or: cognitive activity, *noêsis*]**."**

b (B3)

Then, after having shown that there exists in this principle **much intelligence** (*noêsis*)—**"for,"** he says, **"without intelligence it would not be possible for it to be distributed in such a way as to possess the measures of all things, of winter and summer, of night and day, of rains and winds and fine weather; and the other things, if one wishes to think intelligently about them** (*ennoeisthai*)**, one would find that they are arranged in the finest way that could be achieved"**—, he adds that: [. . . paraphrase and citation of **D9**].

D6 (B8) Simpl. *In Phys.*, p. 153.20–22

ἀλλὰ τοῦτό μοι δῆλον δοκεῖ εἶναι, ὅτι καὶ μέγα καὶ ἰσχυρὸν καὶ ἀίδιόν τε καὶ ἀθάνατον καὶ πολλὰ εἰδός ἐστι.

The Principle Is Air (D7–D8)

D7 (13 A4) Arist. *Metaph.* A3 984a 5–7

Ἀναξιμένης δὲ ἀέρα καὶ Διογένης πρότερον ὕδατος καὶ μάλιστ᾽ ἀρχὴν τιθέασι τῶν ἁπλῶν σωμάτων.

D8 (< A5) Simpl. *In Phys.*, p. 25.4–8 (cf. Theophr. Frag. 226A FHS&G)

[. . . = **P2**] τὴν δὲ τοῦ παντὸς φύσιν ἀέρα καὶ οὗτός φησιν ἄπειρον εἶναι καὶ ἀίδιον, ἐξ οὗ πυκνουμένου καὶ μανουμένου καὶ μεταβάλλοντος τοῖς πάθεσι τὴν τῶν ἄλλων γίνεσθαι μορφήν. καὶ ταῦτα μὲν Θεόφραστος ἱστορεῖ περὶ τοῦ Διογένους, καὶ τὸ εἰς ἐμὲ ἐλθὸν αὐτοῦ σύγγραμμα Περὶ φύσεως ἐπιγεγραμμένον ἀέρα σαφῶς λέγει τὸ ἐξ οὗ πάντα γίνεται τὰ ἄλλα [. . . = **R6**].

Air Is the Principle of Life (D9–D12)

D9 (B4) Simpl. *In Phys.*, p. 152.18–21

ἔτι δὲ πρὸς τούτοις καὶ τάδε μεγάλα σημεῖα· ἄνθρω-

D6 (B8) Simplicius, *Commentary on Aristotle's* Physics

But this seems to me to be evident: that it is vast and powerful, eternal and deathless, and that it knows many things.

The Principle Is Air (D7–D8)

D7 (13 A4) Aristotle, *Metaphysics*

Anaximenes [**ANAXIMEN. D4**] as well as Diogenes posits air before water and as that one among the simple bodies that is most of all a principle.

D8 (< A5) Theophrastus in Simplicius, *Commentary on Aristotle's* Physics

[. . .] As for the nature of the whole, he too [scil. like Anaximenes] says that it is unlimited and eternal air, from which, through condensation, rarefaction, and transformation of its conditions, comes the form of the other things. And this is what Theophrastus reports about Diogenes, and the latter's treatise that has reached me, entitled *On Nature,* states clearly that what all other things come from is air [. . .].

Air Is the Principle of Life (D9–D12)

D9 (B4) Simplicius, *Commentary on Aristotle's* Physics

Moreover, besides those [scil. proofs]**, there are also these important proofs: human beings and the other**

ποι γὰρ καὶ τὰ ἄλλα ζῷα ἀναπνέοντα ζώει τῷ ἀέρι
καὶ τοῦτο αὐτοῖς καὶ ψυχή ἐστι καὶ νόησις, ὡς δε-
δηλώσεται ἐν τῇδε τῇ συγγραφῇ ἐμφανῶς, καὶ ἐὰν
τοῦτο ἀπαλλαχθῇ, ἀποθνῄσκει καὶ ἡ νόησις ἐπιλείπει.

D10 (B5) Simpl. *In Phys.*, pp. 152.22–153.16

καί μοι δοκεῖ τὸ τὴν νόησιν ἔχον εἶναι ὁ ἀὴρ κα-
λούμενος ὑπὸ τῶν ἀνθρώπων, καὶ ὑπὸ τούτου πάντας[1] καὶ κυβερνᾶσθαι καὶ πάντων κρατεῖν· αὐτὸ[2]
γάρ μοι τοῦτο θεὸς[3] δοκεῖ εἶναι καὶ ἐπὶ πᾶν ἀφῖχθαι
καὶ πάντα διατιθέναι καὶ ἐν παντὶ ἐνεῖναι. καὶ ἔστιν
οὐδὲ ἓν ὅ τι μὴ μετέχει τούτου· μετέχει δὲ οὐδὲ ἓν
ὁμοίως τὸ ἕτερον τῷ ἑτέρῳ, ἀλλὰ πολλοὶ τρόποι καὶ
αὐτοῦ τοῦ ἀέρος καὶ τῆς νοήσιός[4] εἰσιν· ἔστι γὰρ
πολύτροπος, καὶ θερμότερος καὶ ψυχρότερος καὶ ξηρότερος καὶ ὑγρότερος καὶ στασιμώτερος καὶ ὀξυ-
τέρην κίνησιν ἔχων, καὶ ἄλλαι πολλαὶ ἑτεροιώσιες
ἔνεισι καὶ ἡδονῆς καὶ χροιῆς ἄπειροι. καὶ πάντων
τῶν ζῴων δὲ ἡ ψυχὴ τὸ αὐτό ἐστιν, ἀὴρ θερμότερος
μὲν τοῦ ἔξω ἐν ᾧ ἐσμεν, τοῦ μέντοι παρὰ τῷ ἡλίῳ
πολλὸν ψυχρότερος· ὅμοιον δὲ τοῦτο τὸ θερμὸν
οὐδενὸς τῶν ζῴων ἐστίν (ἐπεὶ οὐδὲ τῶν ἀνθρώπων
ἀλλήλοις), ἀλλὰ διαφέρει μέγα μὲν οὔ, ἀλλ' ὥστε

---

[1] πάντα Panzebieter   [2] ἀπὸ mss., corr. Usener   [3] ἔθος
mss., corr. Usener   [4] καὶ τῆς νοήσιός F: καὶ τῆς κινήσιός
D: κατὰ τῆς νοήσιός E

animals that breathe live by means of air, and this is for them both life and mental activity (*noêsis*), as will be made manifestly clear in this treatise; and if this departs, they die and the mental activity (*noêsis*) ceases to exist.

D10 (B5) Simplicius, *Commentary on Aristotle's* Physics

And it is my view that that what possesses cognitive activity (*noêsis*) is what humans call 'air,' and that it is by this that all are steered and at the same time dominate over all.[1] For it is my view that it is this itself that is god, and that it arrives everywhere, arranges all things, and exists in every thing. And there is not even one thing that does not have a share in this. But neither is there any one that has a share in the same way as another has, but there are many forms both of the air itself and of mental activity (*noêsis*), for it is multiform, hot and cold, dry and moist, immobile and possessing quick motion, and many other differentiations are in it, unlimited both in flavor (*hêdonê*) and in color. And for all the animals, the soul is the same thing: air that is warmer than the external one in which we exist, but much colder than the one that is near the sun. But this warmth is not similar in any of the animals (since it is not either among human beings compared with one another); but it differs not very much, but enough

---

[1] Or, emending: "it is by this that all is steered and that it [i.e. air] dominates over all."

παραπλήσια εἶναι· οὐ μέντοι γε⁵ ἀτρεκέως γε ὅμοιον
οὐδὲν οἷόν τε γενέσθαι τῶν ἑτεροιουμένων ἕτερον τῷ
ἑτέρῳ, πρὶν τὸ αὐτὸ γένηται. ἅτε οὖν πολυτρόπου
ἐούσης τῆς ἑτεροιώσιος πολύτροπα καὶ τὰ ζῷα καὶ
πολλὰ καὶ οὔτε ἰδέαν ἀλλήλοις ἐοικότα οὔτε δίαιταν
οὔτε νόησιν ὑπὸ τοῦ πλήθεος τῶν ἑτεροιώσεων·
ὅμως δὲ πάντα τῷ αὐτῷ καὶ ζῇ καὶ ὁρᾷ καὶ ἀκούει,
καὶ τὴν ἄλλην νόησιν ἔχει ἀπὸ τοῦ αὐτοῦ πάντα.

⁵ γε DE: om. F

D11 (< A20) Arist. *An.* 1.2 405a 21–25

Διογένης [. . .] τοῦτον οἰηθεὶς πάντων λεπτότατον¹ εἶναι καὶ ἀρχήν· καὶ διὰ τοῦτο γινώσκειν τε καὶ κινεῖν
τὴν ψυχήν, ᾗ μὲν πρῶτόν ἐστι καὶ ἐκ τούτου τὰ λοιπά,
γινώσκειν, ᾗ δὲ λεπτότατον,² κινητικὸν εἶναι.

¹ λεπτομερέστερον X
² λεπτότατον ESUX: λεπτομερέστατον CVWy

D12 (5b Laks) Aët. 4.3.8 (Stob.) [εἰ σῶμα ἡ ψυχὴ καὶ
τίς ἡ οὐσία αὐτῆς]

Διογένης ὁ Ἀπολλωνιάτης ἐξ ἀέρος τὴν ψυχήν.

Divinity of the Principle (D13)

D13 (< A19) Theophr. *Sens.* 42

ὅτι δὲ ὁ ἐντὸς ἀὴρ αἰσθάνεται μικρὸν ὢν μόριον τοῦ
θεοῦ, σημεῖον εἶναι· [. . . = **D34b**].

that they are very similar—except that it is not possible for any of the things that are differentiated to become perfectly similar to another one, unless it becomes the same thing. Since therefore differentiation is multiform, multiform are the animals too and numerous, and they resemble one another neither in their shape nor in their way of life nor in their mental activity (*noêsis*), because of the multitude of differentiations. And yet they all live, see, and hear by means of the same thing, and they all possess from the same thing the rest of their mental activity (*noêsis*).

D11 (< A20), Aristotle, *On the Soul*

Diogenes [. . .] [scil. says that the soul is air,] thinking that this is of all things the one that is most rarefied and that it is a principle. And it is for this reason that the soul both knows and moves: because it is first and everything else comes from it, it knows, and because it is the most rarefied, it is able to impart motion.

D12 (≠ DK) Aëtius

Diogenes of Apollonia: the soul is [scil. made] of air.

Divinity of the Principle (D13)

D13 (< A19) Theophrastus, *On Sensations*

There is evidence that the inner air, **a small portion of god,** is what perceives [. . .].

237

Cosmogony (D14–D17)
The Formation of Worlds: Two General
Summaries (D14–D15)

D14 (< A1) Diog. Laert. 9.57

ἐδόκει αὐτῷ τάδε· στοιχεῖον εἶναι τὸν ἀέρα, κόσμους
ἀπείρους καὶ κενὸν ἄπειρον· τόν τε ἀέρα πυκνούμενον
καὶ ἀραιούμενον γεννητικὸν εἶναι τῶν κόσμων· οὐδὲν
ἐκ τοῦ μὴ ὄντος γίνεσθαι οὐδὲ εἰς τὸ μὴ ὂν φθείρεσθαι. τὴν γῆν στρογγύλην, ἠρεισμένην ἐν τῷ μέσῳ,
τὴν σύστασιν εἰληφυῖαν κατὰ τὴν ἐκ τοῦ θερμοῦ
περιφορὰν καὶ πῆξιν ὑπὸ τοῦ ψυχροῦ.

D15 (A6) Ps.-Plut. *Strom.* (in Eus. *PE* 1.8.12)

[12] Διογένης ὁ Ἀπολλωνιάτης ἀέρα ὑφίσταται στοι-
χεῖον· κινεῖσθαι δὲ[1] τὰ πάντα, ἀπείρους τε εἶναι τοὺς
κόσμους. κοσμοποιεῖ δὲ οὕτως· ὅτι τοῦ παντὸς κινουμένου καὶ ᾗ μὲν ἀραιοῦ, ᾗ δὲ πυκνοῦ γενομένου, ὅπου
συνεκύρησεν τὸ πυκνὸν συστροφὴν ποιῆσαι, καὶ οὕτως τὰ λοιπὰ κατὰ τὸν αὐτὸν λόγον· τὰ κουφότατα,
τὴν ἄνω τάξιν λαβόντα, τὸν ἥλιον ἀποτελέσαι. [11]
[. . .] πυκνούμενον δὲ τὸν αἰθέρα ποιεῖν νεφέλας, εἶτα
ὕδωρ, ὃ καὶ κατιὸν ἐπὶ τὸν ἥλιον σβεννύναι αὐτόν·
καὶ πάλιν ἀραιούμενον ἐξάπτεσθαι. χρόνῳ δὲ πήγνυσθαι τῷ ξηρῷ τὸν ἥλιον καὶ ποιεῖν ἐκ τοῦ λαμπροῦ
ὕδατος ἀστέρας, νύκτα τε καὶ ἡμέραν ἐκ τῆς σβέσεως
καὶ ἐξάψεως καὶ καθόλου τὰς ἐκλείψεις ἀποτελεῖν.[2]

---

[1] δὲ AB: τε ONV   [2] πυκνούμενον . . . ἀποτελεῖν, quod
in mss. ad Metrodorum pertinet (1.8.11), Diogeni attrib. Palmer

Cosmogony (D14–D17)
The Formation of Worlds: Two General
Summaries (D14–D15)

D14 (< A1) Diogenes Laertius

He had the following views: the element is air, there exist
an unlimited number of worlds and an unlimited void; the
air is what generates the worlds by condensing and rarefy-
ing; nothing comes to be out of nonbeing or is destroyed
into nonbeing; the earth is spherical, fixed firmly in the
center; its shape is due to circular motion caused by heat
and to solidification caused by cold.

D15 (A6) Ps.-Plutarch, *Stromata*

[12] Diogenes of Apollonia posits air as element; the totality of things is in motion; and the worlds are unlimited in
number. This is how he conceives the formation of the
world: the whole being in motion and becoming rarefied
here and dense there, where the dense happened to come
together it created a concentration, and so too everything
else in the same way. The lightest elements, occupying the
highest position, formed the sun. *[11] [. . .] By becoming
dense, the aether produces clouds, then water, which, de-
scending toward the sun, extinguishes it; and when it becomes rarefied, it is kindled again. With time, the sun was
solidified by dryness and formed stars out of the bright
water; it produced night and day out of extinction and il-
lumination, and in general eclipses.*[1]

---

[1] The passage printed in italics appears in the notice dedicated to Metrodorus of Lampsacus, but it is difficult to assign this
doctrine to him. The transposition, proposed by Palmer, *Classical
Quarterly* 51 (2001): 7–17, is plausible but not certain.

*An Infinite Number of Worlds or
Only One? (D16)*

D16

a (< A10) Aët. 2.1.3 (Stob.; cf. Ps.-Plut.) [περὶ κόσμου]

[. . .] Διογένης [. . .] ἀπείρους κόσμους ἐν τῷ ἀπείρῳ
κατὰ πᾶσαν περίστασιν.[1]

> [1] περίστασιν Plut.: περιαγωγήν Stob.

b (< 13 A11) Simpl. *In Phys.*, p. 1121.12–15

γενητὸν δὲ καὶ φθαρτὸν τὸν ἕνα κόσμον ποιοῦσιν
ὅσοι ἀεὶ μέν φασιν εἶναι κόσμον, οὐ μὴν τὸν αὐτὸν
ἀεί, ἀλλὰ ἄλλοτε ἄλλον γινόμενον κατά τινας χρόνων
περιόδους, ὡς [. . .] Διογένης [. . .].

The Inclination of the Poles (D17)

D17 (< A11, cf. 59 A67) Aët. 2.8.1 (Ps.-Plut.) [τίς ἡ αἰτία
τοῦ τὸν κόσμον ἐγκλιθῆναι]

Διογένης καὶ Ἀναξαγόρας [**ANAXAG. D32**] μετὰ τὸ
συστῆναι τὸν κόσμον καὶ τὰ ζῷα ἐκ τῆς γῆς ἐξαγαγεῖν ἐγκλιθῆναί πως τὸν κόσμον ἐκ τοῦ αὐτομάτου εἰς
τὸ μεσημβρινὸν αὐτοῦ μέρος [. . . = **R15**].

DIOGENES OF APOLLONIA

An Infinite Number of Worlds or Only One? (D16)

D16

a (< A10) Aëtius

[. . .] Diogenes [. . .]: worlds unlimited [scil. in number] in the unlimited, throughout the entire surrounding area.

b (< 13 A11) Simplicius, *Commentary on Aristotle's Physics*

Those who say that the world always exists but without always being the same, but becoming different at different times according to certain periods of time—these people make the one world subject to generation and destruction, like [. . .] Diogenes [. . .].

The Inclination of the Poles (D17)

D17 (< A11, cf. 59 A67) Aëtius

Diogenes and Anaxagoras: after the world had been formed and the animals had emerged from the earth, the world inclined somehow on its own toward its southern part [. . .].

Cosmology (D18–D22)
The Heavenly Bodies (D18)

D18 (< A12) Aët. 2.13.5 et 9 (Stob.) [περὶ οὐσίας ἄστρων]

Διογένης κισηροειδῆ τὰ ἄστρα, διαπνοίας δὲ αὐτὰ νομίζει τοῦ κόσμου, εἶναι δὲ διάπυρα· συμπεριφέρεσθαι δὲ τοῖς φανεροῖς ἄστροις ἀφανεῖς λίθους καὶ παρ' αὐτὸ τοῦτ' ἀνωνύμους· πίπτοντα δὲ πολλάκις ἐπὶ τῆς γῆς σβέννυσθαι, καθάπερ τὸν ἐν Αἰγὸς ποταμοῖς πυρωδῶς κατενεχθέντα ἀστέρα πέτρινον.

The Sun (D19–D20)

D19 (A13) Aët. 2.20.10 (Stob.) [περὶ οὐσίας ἡλίου]

Διογένης κισηροειδῆ τὸν ἥλιον, εἰς ὃν ἀπὸ τοῦ αἰθέρος ἀκτῖνες ἐναποστηρίζονται.

D20 (A13) Aët. 2.23.4 (Ps.-Plut.) [περὶ τροπῶν ἡλίου]

Διογένης ὑπὸ τοῦ ἀντιπίπτοντος τῇ θερμότητι ψύχους σβέννυσθαι τὸν ἥλιον.

The Moon (D21)

D21 (A14) Aët. 2.25.10 (Stob.) [περὶ σελήνης οὐσίας]

Διογένης κισηροειδὲς ἄναμμα τὴν σελήνην.

Cosmology (D18–D22)
The Heavenly Bodies (D18)

D18 (< A12) Aëtius

Diogenes: the stars are like pumice stone, and he thinks that they are the world's vents, and that they are aflame; and that stones that are invisible (and for this reason are nameless) accompany the visible heavenly bodies in their revolutions; and that they often fall and are extinguished on the earth, like the heavenly body made of stone that fell burning at Aegospotami.

The Sun (D19–D20)

D19 (A13) Aëtius

Diogenes: the sun is like pumice stone; the rays coming from the aether become fastened to it.

D20 (A13) Aëtius

Diogenes: the sun is extinguished by the cold that collides with the heat.

The Moon (D21)

D21 (A14) Aëtius

Diogenes: the moon is an ignited mass like pumice stone.

Comets (D22)

D22 (A15) Aët. 3.2.8 (Ps.-Plut.) [περὶ κομητῶν καὶ διᾳττόντων καὶ τῶν τοιούτων]

Διογένης ἀστέρας εἶναι τοὺς κομήτας.

Meteorology: Thunder and Lightning (D23)

D23

a (A16) Aët. 3.3.8 (Stob.) [περὶ βροντῶν ἀστραπῶν κεραυνῶν πρηστήρων τε καὶ τυφώνων]

Διογένης ἔμπτωσιν[1] πυρὸς εἰς νέφος ὑγρόν, βροντὴν μὲν τῇ σβέσει ποιοῦν, τῇ δὲ λαμπηδόνι τὴν ἀστρα-πήν. συναιτιᾶται δὲ καὶ τὸ πνεῦμα.

[1] ἐμπύρωσιν mss., corr. Canter

b (A16) Sen. *Quaest. nat.* 2.20.1

Diogenes Apolloniates ait quaedam tonitrua igne, quaedam spiritu fieri; illa ignis facit quae ipse antecedit et nuntiat; illa spiritus quae sine splendore crepuerunt.

The Earth (D24–D26)
The Sea (D24)

D24 (< A17) Alex. *In Meteor.*, p. 67.11–14

[. . . = **ANAXIMAND. D35b**] ταύτης τῆς δόξης ἐγέ-νετο, ὡς ἱστορεῖ Θεόφραστος [Frag. 221 FHS&G],

Comets (D22)

D22 (A15) Aëtius

Diogenes: the comets are heavenly bodies.

Meteorology: Thunder and Lightning (D23)

D23

a (A16) Aëtius

Diogenes: the collision of fire with a moist cloud, producing thunder by extinguishing and lightning by flashing. But he also adduces wind as an auxiliary cause.

b (A16) Seneca, *Natural Questions*

Diogenes of Apollonia says that certain thunders occur because of fire, others because of wind; fire produces the ones that it precedes and announces, wind the ones that rumble without a flash of light.

The Earth (D24–D26)
The Sea (D24)

D24 (A17) Alexander of Aphrodisias, *Commentary on Aristotle's* Meteorology

This opinion [scil. that the sea will dry out one day by the effect of the evaporation caused by the sun], as Theophrastus reports, was maintained by Anaximander [cf.

Ἀναξίμανδρός τε καὶ Διογένης. Διογένης δὲ καὶ τῆς
ἁλμυρότητος ταύτην αἰτίαν λέγει, ὅτι ἀνάγοντος τοῦ
ἡλίου τὸ γλυκὺ τὸ καταλειπόμενον καὶ ὑπομένον ἁλμυρὸν εἶναι συμβαίνει.

The Floods of the Nile (D25)

D25

a (< T35c Laks) Arist. (?), *Inund. Nili* (= Frag. 248 Rose,
p. 192.22–24)

Diogenes autem †Nakithemius† Apolloniates fontibus ait
addi aquam attrahente terra propter arefieri a sole in
estate: natum esse enim indigens trahere ex propinquo
[. . . = **R4**].

b (A18) Sen. *Quaest. nat.* 4a.28–29

Diogenes Apolloniates ait: "sol umorem ad se rapit; hunc
adsiccata tellus ex mari ducit, tum ex ceteris aquis. fieri
autem non potest, ut alia sicca sit tellus, alia abundet; sunt
enim perforata omnia et invicem pervia, et sicca ab umidis
sumunt. alioquin, nisi aliquid terra acciperet, exaruisset.
ergo undique sol trahit, sed ex his quae premit maxime;
haec meridiana sunt. terra cum exaruit, plus ad se umoris
adducit; ut in lucernis oleum illo fluit ubi exuritur, sic aqua
illo incumbit quo vis caloris et terrae aestuantis arcessit.
unde ergo trahit? ex illis scilicet partibus semper hibernis:

ANAXIMAND. D35b] and Diogenes. Diogenes also says that this is the cause of salinity: the sun removing the sweet part, the residue and deposit turn out to be saline.

The Floods of the Nile (D25)

D25

a (≠ DK) Aristotle (?), *On the Flooding of the Nile*

But Diogenes of Apollonia †Nakithemius† says that additional water arrives at its sources, the earth attracting it because it has been made dry by the sun in the summer; for by nature it draws from what is nearest when it is in need [. . .].

b (A18) Seneca, *Natural Questions*

Diogenes of Apollonia says, "The sun attracts to itself the moisture that the dried-out land draws from the sea and also from other waters. But it cannot happen that the land is dry in one place and overflows in another: for the whole is perforated and one part communicates with another, and the dry parts take from the moist ones. Otherwise, if the earth received nothing, it would have completely dried up. Thus the sun attracts [scil. water] from everywhere, but [scil. especially] from those regions that it most oppresses: these are the southerly ones. When the earth has become completely dried up, it attracts more moisture to itself: just as in lanterns the oil flows to the place where it is burning, so too water flows to where the force of heat and of the burning earth summons it. From where then does the latter attract it? Evidently from those regions

septemtrionales semper exundant (ob hoc Pontus in in-
fernum mare assidue fluit rapidus, non, ut cetera maria,
alternatis ultro citro aestibus, in unam partem semper
pronus et torrens); quod nisi factis[1] itineribus quod cuique
deest redderetur, quod cuique superest emitteretur, iam
aut sicca essent omnia aut inundata."

[1] factis *Diels*: faceret his *T*: facit his *PE*

c (T35b Laks) Io. Lyd. *Mens.* 4.107

Διογένης ὁ Ἀπολλωνιάτης φησὶ τοῦ ἡλίου ἁρπάζον-
τος τὴν ὑγρότητα ἕλκεσθαι ὑπὸ[1] τῆς ξηρᾶς τὸν Νεῖλον ἐκ τῆς θαλάττης· σηραγγώδης γὰρ κατὰ φύσιν
ὑπάρχουσα καὶ διατετρημένη ἕλκει πρὸς ἑαυτὴν τὸ
ὑγρόν· καὶ ὅσῳ μᾶλλον ξηροτέρα ἡ γῆ τῆς Αἰγύπτου,
τοσούτῳ πλέον ἕλκει πρὸς ἑαυτὴν τὴν νοτίδα, καθάπερ τὸ ἔλαιον ἐπὶ τῶν λύχνων ἐκεῖσε πλέον ὁρμᾷ, ὅπη
καὶ δαπανᾶται ὑπὸ τοῦ πυρός.

[1] ὑπὸ AB: ἀπὸ T

d (A18) Schol. in Apoll. Rhod. 4.269

Διογένης δὲ ὁ Ἀπολλωνιάτης ὑπὸ τοῦ ἡλίου ἁρπάζε-
σθαι τὸ ὕδωρ τῆς θαλάσσης ὃ τότε εἰς τὸν Νεῖλον
καταφέρεσθαι· οἴεται γὰρ πληροῦσθαι τὸν Νεῖλον ἐν
τῷ θέρει διὰ τὸ τὸν ἥλιον εἰς τοῦτον τὰς ἀπὸ γῆς
ἰκμάδας τρέπειν.

where it is always winter: the northerly ones constantly overflow (that is why the Black Sea runs continuously in a rapid stream into the lower sea [i.e. the Mediterranean] and does not ebb and flow with alternating tides like other seas, but always flows swiftly in the same direction). For if what each one lacks were not restored to it and the excess were not discharged thanks to these passages, then everything would already be either dry or overflowing."

c (≠ DK) John Lydus, *On the Months*

Diogenes of Apollonia says that, the sun taking away the moisture, the Nile draws it from the sea by means of the dry land: for being by nature cavernous and perforated, it [i.e. the land] draws moisture to itself; and as the land of Egypt is drier than the others, it attracts liquid all the more strongly, just as oil in the case of lanterns moves more abundantly to where it is being consumed by the fire.

d (A18) Scholia on Apollonius Rhodius

Diogenes of Apollonia: the water of the sea is drawn away by the sun and then precipitates onto the Nile; for he thinks that the Nile floods in the summer because the sun directs toward it the moistures from the earth.

The Magnet (D26)

D26 (A33) Alex. (?) *Quaest.* 2.23, p. 73

Διογένης τε ὁ Ἀπολλωνιάτης πάντα τὰ ἐλατά φησιν
καὶ ἀφιέναι τινὰ ἰκμάδα ἀφ᾽ αὑτῶν πεφυκέναι καὶ ἕλκειν ἔξωθεν, τὰ μὲν πλείω, τὰ δὲ ἐλάττω, πλείστην δὲ
ἀφιέναι χαλκόν τε καὶ σίδηρον, οὗ σημεῖον τό τε ἀπο-
καίεσθαί τι καὶ ἀπαναλίσκεσθαι ἀπ᾽ αὐτῶν ἐν τῷ
πυρί, καὶ τὸ χριόμενα αὐτὰ ὄξει καὶ ἐλαίῳ ἰοῦσθαι·
τοῦτο γὰρ πάσχειν διὰ τὸ ἕλκειν ἐξ αὐτῶν τὴν ἰκμάδα
τὸ ὄξος· τὸ γὰρ[1] πῦρ καίειν ἄν· καίειν ⟨δὲ⟩ αὐτὸ τῷ[2]
εἰσδυόμενον εἰς ἕκαστον ἕλκειν τε καὶ ἀναλίσκειν τὸ
ἐν αὐτοῖς ὑγρόν· τοῦ σιδήρου ἕλκοντός τε καὶ πλεῖον
ἀφιέντος ὑγρόν, τὴν λίθον οὖσαν ἀραιοτέραν τοῦ σιδήρου καὶ γεωδεστέραν πλεῖον ἕλκειν τὸ ὑγρὸν τὸ
ἀπὸ τοῦ παρακειμένου ἀέρος ἢ ἀφιέναι. τὸ μὲν οὖν
συγγενὲς ἕλκουσαν ἐν αὑτῇ δέχεσθαι τό τε μὴ συγγενὲς ἀπωθεῖν· εἶναι δ᾽ αὐτῇ συγγενῆ τὸν σίδηρον διὰ
τὸ ἀπὸ τούτου ἕλκειν τε καὶ δέχεσθαι ἐν αὑτῇ· καὶ διὰ
τῆς τούτου ἕλξεως καὶ τὸν σίδηρον ἐπισπᾶσθαι διὰ
τὴν ἀθρόαν ἕλξιν τοῦ ἐν αὐτῷ ὑγροῦ, μηκέτι δὲ τὸν
σίδηρον ἕλκειν τὴν λίθον μήθ᾽ οὕτως εἶναι τὸν σίδηρον ἀραιὸν ὡς δέχεσθαι δύνασθαι ἀθρόαν τὴν ἀπ᾽
αὐτῆς ὑγρότητα.

---

[1] τὸ post γὰρ hab. mss., secl. Panzerbieter

The Magnet (D26)

D26 (A33) Alexander of Aphrodisias (?), *Natural Questions*

Diogenes of Apollonia says that by nature all metals both emit a certain moisture from themselves and draw it in from outside, the ones more, the others less, and that copper and iron emit the most. A sign of this is that a part of them burns up and is consumed in fire, and that when they are smeared with vinegar and oil they become rusty: for this happens to them because the vinegar draws the moisture out of them. For the fire burns, but it burns because, penetrating into each of these, it draws in and consumes the moisture that is found in them. Therefore, since iron draws moisture in but emits even more, the magnet, being more rarefied and more earthy than iron, draws in the moisture from the surrounding air more than it emits it. Well, it [i.e. the magnet], drawing material in, welcomes within itself what is related to it and repels what is not related to it. But iron is related to it, because it [i.e. the magnet] draws in and welcomes within itself what comes from it [i.e. the iron]. And it is because of this attraction that the iron itself is displaced toward it because of the massive attraction undergone by the moisture in it; whereas the iron does not draw in the magnet, nor is the iron sufficiently rarefied as to be able to welcome massively the moisture that comes from it.

---

2 καίειν ⟨δέ⟩ αὐτὸ τῷ nos: καίειν ἄν καίειν αὐτῷ τῷ δὲ VFGBᵃᶜ Sᵃᶜ: καίειν τὴν ἐν αὐτῷ ἰκμάδα ἄν καίειν Bᵖᶜ Sᵖᶜ: καὶ γὰρ τὸ πῦρ καίειν ἃ καίει αὐτῶν τῷ Diels

Physiology (D27–D44)
The System of the Vessels in Humans (D27)

D27 (B6) Arist. *HA* 3.2 511b 31–513b 11

αἱ δὲ φλέβες ἐν τῷ ἀνθρώπῳ ὧδ᾽ ἔχουσιν· εἰσὶ δύο
μέγισται· αὗται τείνουσι διὰ τῆς κοιλίας παρὰ τὴν
νωτιαίαν ἄκανθαν, ἡ μὲν ἐπὶ δεξιά, ἡ δ᾽ ἐπ᾽ ἀριστερά,
εἰς τὰ σκέλη, ἑκατέρα παρ᾽ ἑαυτῇ, καὶ ἄνω εἰς τὴν
κεφαλὴν [511b35] παρὰ τὰς κλεῖδας διὰ τῶν σφαγῶν.
ἀπὸ δὲ τούτων καθ᾽ ἅπαν τὸ σῶμα φλέβες διατείνουσιν, ἀπὸ μὲν τῆς δεξιᾶς εἰς τὰ δεξιά, ἀπὸ δὲ τῆς
ἀριστερᾶς εἰς τὰ ἀριστερά, μέγισται μὲν δύο εἰς τὴν
καρδίαν περὶ αὐτὴν τὴν νωτιαίαν ἄκανθαν, ἕτεραι δ᾽
ὀλίγον ἀνωτέρω διὰ τῶν στηθῶν ὑπὸ τὴν μασχάλην
[512a5] εἰς ἑκατέραν τὴν χεῖρα τὴν παρ᾽ ἑαυτῇ· καὶ
καλεῖται ἡ μὲν σπληνῖτις, ἡ δὲ ἡπατῖτις. σχίζεται δ᾽
αὐτῶν ἄκρα ἑκατέρα, ἡ μὲν ἐπὶ τὸν μέγαν δάκτυλον,
ἡ δ᾽ ἐπὶ τὸν ταρσόν, ἀπὸ δὲ τούτων λεπταὶ καὶ πολύο-
ζοι ἐπὶ τὴν ἄλλην χεῖρα καὶ δακτύλους. ἕτεραι δὲ λεπτότεραι ἀπὸ τῶν πρώτων [a10] φλεβῶν τείνουσιν,
ἀπὸ μὲν τῆς δεξιᾶς εἰς τὸ ἧπαρ, ἀπὸ δὲ τῆς ἀριστερᾶς εἰς τὸν σπλῆνα καὶ τοὺς νεφρούς. αἱ δὲ εἰς τὰ
σκέλη τείνουσαι σχίζονται κατὰ τὴν πρόσφυσιν, καὶ
διὰ παντὸς τοῦ μηροῦ τείνουσιν. ἡ δὲ μεγίστη αὐτῶν
ὄπισθεν τείνει τοῦ μηροῦ καὶ ἐκφαίνεται[1] παχεῖα·
ἑτέρα δὲ εἴσω τοῦ μηροῦ [a15] μικρὸν ἧττον παχεῖα
ἐκείνης. ἔπειτα παρὰ τὸ γόνυ τείνουσιν εἰς τὴν κνήμην

DIOGENES OF APOLLONIA

Physiology (D27–D44)
The System of the Vessels in Humans (D27)

D27 (B6) Aristotle, *History of Animals*

The blood vessels in the human are arranged as follows. There are two that are the largest ones. These extend through the belly, along the spinal column, the one on the right, the other on the left, down into the legs, each one on its own side, and up into the head [511b35], along the clavicles, through the throat. Starting from these, vessels extend throughout the whole body, from the one on the right toward the right, from the one on the left toward the left, the two largest ones into the heart near the spinal column itself, and the others a little higher, through the chest, under the armpit [512a5] into that hand located on its own side. And the one is called the 'splenic' vessel, the other the 'hepatic' one. Each of their extremities is divided, the one toward the thumb, the other toward the palm, and from these other thin vessels, with many branches, going toward the rest of the hand and the fingers. Other, thinner vessels extend from the first [a10] vessels, going from the one on the right into the liver, from the one on the left into the spleen and kidneys. Those vessels that extend into the legs are divided at the juncture and extend through the whole thigh. The largest of these extends to the back of the thigh and is seen to be thick; the other one, on the inside of the thigh, [a15] is a little less thick than that one. They then extend along the knee into

---

1 ἐκφαίνεται Cᵃ PDᵃ: ἐμφ- Aᵃ

253

τε καὶ τὸν πόδα καθάπερ καὶ εἰς τὰς χεῖρας. καὶ ἐπὶ
τὸν ταρσὸν τοῦ ποδὸς καθήκουσι καὶ ἐντεῦθεν ἐπὶ
τοὺς δακτύλους διατείνουσιν. σχίζονται δὲ καὶ ἐπὶ
τὴν κοιλίαν καὶ τὸ πλευρὸν πολλαὶ ἀπ' αὐτῶν καὶ
λεπταὶ φλέβες. [a20] αἱ δ' εἰς τὴν κεφαλὴν τείνουσαι
διὰ τῶν σφαγῶν φαίνονται ἐν τῷ αὐχένι μεγάλαι· ἀφ'
ἑκατέρας δ' αὐτῶν, ᾗ τελευτᾷ, σχίζονται εἰς τὴν κεφαλὴν πολλαί, αἱ μὲν ἐκ τῶν δεξιῶν εἰς τὰ ἀριστερά,
αἱ δ' ἐκ τῶν ἀριστερῶν εἰς τὰ δεξιά· τελευτῶσι δὲ
παρὰ τὸ οὖς ἑκάτεραι. ἔστι δ' ἑτέρα [a25] φλὲψ ἐν τῷ
τραχήλῳ παρὰ τὴν μεγάλην ἑκατέρωθεν, ἐλάττων
ἐκείνης ὀλίγον, εἰς ἣν αἱ πλεῖσται ἐκ τῆς κεφαλῆς
συνέχουσιν[2] αὐτῆς·[3] καὶ αὗται τείνουσι διὰ τῶν σφαγῶν εἴσω· καὶ ἀπ' αὐτῶν ἑκατέρας ὑπὸ τὴν ὠμοπλά-
την τείνουσι καὶ εἰς τὰς χεῖρας, καὶ φαίνονται παρά
τε τὴν σπληνῖτιν καὶ τὴν ἡπατῖτιν [a30] ἕτεραι ὀλίγον[4]
ἐλάττους, ἃς ἀποσχῶσιν[5] ὅταν τὸ ὑπὸ τὸ δέρμα λυπῇ·[6]
ἂν δ' ἔτι καὶ περὶ τὴν κοιλίαν, τὴν ἡπατῖτιν καὶ τὴν
σπληνῖτιν. τείνουσι δὲ καὶ ὑπὸ[7] τοὺς μαστοὺς ἀπὸ
[512b1] τούτων ἕτεραι.[8] ἕτεραι δ' εἰσὶν αἱ ἀπὸ ἑκατέρας τείνουσαι διὰ τοῦ νωτιαίου μυελοῦ εἰς τοὺς ὄρχεις λεπταί· ἕτεραι δ' ὑπὸ τὸ δέρμα καὶ διὰ τῆς σαρκὸς τείνουσιν εἰς τοὺς νεφροὺς καὶ τελευτῶσιν εἰς
τοὺς ὄρχεις τοῖς ἀνδράσι, ταῖς δὲ γυναιξὶν εἰς [b5] τὰς

[2] συνέχουσιν A[a] C[a]: συντείνουσιν PD[a]

[3] αὐτῆς PD[a]: αὐταῖς A[a] C[a]

[4] ὀλίγον A[a] P: ὀλίγαι D[a]: ὀλίγον πολλάκις C[a]

the shank and foot, in the same way as into the hands. And
they descend toward the flat of the foot, and from there
they extend to the toes. And many thin vessels coming
from these divide out toward the belly and the flank. [a20]
The ones that extend into the head through the throat are
seen to be large in the neck. From each of these two,
where they terminate, many vessels divide out into the
head, the ones coming from the right side into the left
side, the others from the left side into the right side; and
they both terminate beside the ear. There is another [a25]
vessel in the neck beside the large one on both sides, a
little smaller than that one, to which most of the ones
coming from the head itself are attached; and these extend
through the throat toward the interior, and coming from
each of these two, others extend under the shoulder blade
and into the hands. And others, a little smaller, are visible
beside the splenic blood vessel and the hepatic one; [a30]
these are the ones they bleed when something under the
skin causes pain; but if it is something near the belly [scil.
that causes pain], it is the hepatic and the splenic vessels
[scil. that they bleed]. Other vessels also extend from these
[512b1] under the breasts. There are others too, thin ones,
that extend from each of these two through the spinal
marrow into the testicles; and still others extend under the
skin and through the flesh into the kidneys, and terminate
at the testicles in men and at the uterus in women. [b5]

---

5 ἀποσχῶσιν Dᵃ: ἀποσπῶσιν P: ὑποσχίζουσιν αἱ ὑπερέχουσαι Aᵃ: ἀποσχίζονται καὶ αἱ ὑπερέχουσαι Cᵃ

6 τὸ ὑπὸ τὸ δέρμα λυπῇ PDᵃ: ὑποδράμη λύπη Aᵃ Cᵃ

7 ὑπὸ Aᵃ Cᵃ: εἰς PDᵃ

8 ἔτεραι PDᵃ: ἑκάτεραι Aᵃ Cᵃ

ὑστέρας. αἱ δὲ φλέβες αἱ μὲν πρῶται ἐκ τῆς κοιλίας
εὐρύτεραί εἰσιν, ἔπειτα λεπτότεραι γίγνονται, ἕως ἂν
μεταβάλωσιν ἐκ τῶν δεξιῶν εἰς τὰ ἀριστερὰ καὶ ἐκ
τούτων εἰς τὰ δεξιά. αὗται δὲ σπερματίτιδες καλοῦν-
ται. τὸ δ᾽ αἷμα τὸ μὲν παχύτατον [b10] ὑπὸ τῶν σαρ-
κῶν⁹ ἐκπίνεται, ὑπερβάλλον δὲ εἰς τοὺς τόπους τούτους λεπτὸν καὶ θερμὸν καὶ ἀφρῶδες γίνεται.

⁹ σαρκῶν Aᵃ Cᵃ: σαρκωδῶν PDᵃ

Semen (D28)

D28

a (A24) Clem. Alex. *Paed.* 1.6.48.3

τινὲς δὲ καὶ τὸ σπέρμα τοῦ ζῴου ἀφρὸν εἶναι τοῦ
αἵματος κατ᾽ οὐσίαν ὑποτίθενται, ὃ δὴ τῇ ἐμφύτῳ τοῦ
ἄρρενος θέρμῃ παρὰ τὰς συμπλοκὰς ἐκταραχθὲν
ἐκριπιζόμενον¹ ἐξαφροῦται κἂν ταῖς σπερματίτισιν²
παρατίθεται φλεψίν· ἐντεῦθεν γὰρ ὁ Ἀπολλωνιάτης
Διογένης τὰ ἀφροδίσια κεκλῆσθαι βούλεται.

¹ ἐκριπιζόμενον F: ἐκραπιζόμενον M
² σπερματίσιν mss., corr. Dindorf

b (ad B6) Cod. Brux. 1348–59, fol. 48 (pp. 208–10 Well-
mann)

[1] Alexander [. . .], discipulus Asclepiadis, libro primo de
semine spumam sanguinis eius essentiam dixit, Diogenis

The first of these blood vessels, which come from the belly, are wider, but then they become thinner, until they cross over from the right side to the left and from this latter to the right. They are called 'spermatic.' The thickest blood [b10] is absorbed by the fleshy parts, but when it overflows it flows into these regions in a form that is thin, warm, and foamy.[1]

---

[1] This description is often considered to be a verbal citation, but various indications suggest that Aristotle is summarizing and adapting. Therefore this text is presented here as a testimonium rather than as an original fragment.

Semen (D28)

D28

a (A24) Clement of Alexandria, *Pedagogue*

Some people think that the animal's semen is in its substance foam (*aphron*) of blood, which is greatly agitated during sexual union because of the male's inborn heat, and, fanned [scil. by its breath], becomes foam (*exaphroutai*) and is deposited in the spermatic vessels; Diogenes of Apollonia thinks that the sexual act (*ta aphrodisia*) has received its name from this.

b (ad B6) Brussels fragment on semen

Alexander [. . .] a disciple of Asclepiades, said in his first book on semen that it is in its essence foam of blood, agreeing with the views of Diogenes. [. . .] But as for Di-

placitis consentiens. [. . .] [3] Diogenes autem Apolloniates[1] essentiam similiter spumam sanguinis dixit libro physico. etenim spiratione adductus spiritus sanguinem suspendit, cuius alia pars carne bibitur,[2] alia superans in seminales cadit[3] vias et semen facit, quod ‹non›[4] est aliud quam spuma sanguinis spiritu collisi.

[1] Apollonii *mss., corr. Wellman*   [2] bibitur *Rose*: vivit *ms.*
[3] cadet *ms., corr. Neuenar*   [4] ‹non› *Neuenar*

Embryology (D29–D32)

D29 (A27) Cens. *Die nat.* 5.4

illud quoque ambiguam facit inter auctores opinionem, utrumne ex patris tantummodo semine partus nascatur, ut Diogenes [. . .] scripserunt, an etiam ex matris [. . .].

D30 (A27) Cens. *Die nat.* 6.1

Diogenes Apolloniates ex umore primum carnem fieri existimavit, tum ex carne ossa nervosque et ceteras partis enasci.

D31

a (B9) Gal. *In Hipp. Epid.* 6.2.47, p. 122.3–9

καὶ μέντοι καὶ ὡμολόγηται σχεδὸν ἅπασι τοῖς ἰα-
τροῖς οὐ μόνον διαπλάττεσθαι θᾶττον, ἀλλὰ καὶ κινεῖσθαι τὸ ἄρρεν τοῦ θήλεος. [. . .] Ῥοῦφος δέ φησι
Διογένη τὸν Ἀπολλωνιάτην μόνον ἐναντίως ἀποφήνα-

ogenes of Apollonia, he said the same thing in his book on nature, viz. that its essence is foam of blood: for the air inhaled during respiration lifts up the blood, of which one part is absorbed by the flesh while the other part, over-flowing, falls into the spermatic channels and produces semen, which is ‹nothing› other than foam of blood that has been struck by the air.

Embryology (D29–D32)

D29 (A27) Censorinus, *The Birthday*

The following question too causes a difference of opinion among the authorities: whether the offspring is born only from the father's seed, as Diogenes [. . .] wrote, or also from the mother's [. . .].

D30 (A27) Censorinus, *The Birthday*

Diogenes of Apollonia thought that flesh is produced first from the liquid, and that then from the flesh the bones, the tendons, and the other parts are born.

D31

a (B9) Galen, *Commentary on Hippocrates'* Epidemics

In fact, there is agreement among almost all doctors that the male not only is formed, but also begins to move, more quickly than the female. [. . .] Rufus says that Diogenes of Apollonia is the only one who has expressed the opposite

σθαι κατὰ τὸ Περὶ φύσεως δεύτερον· ἐγὼ δὲ οὐκ ἐν-
έτυχον τῷ βιβλίῳ.

b (> A26) Cens. *Die nat.* 9.2

alii enim plerique, cum omnes partus non uno tempore
fiant maturi, una tamen eademque tempora omnibus
conformandis dederunt; ut Diogenes Apolloniates, qui
masculis corpus ait quattuor mensibus formari et feminis
quinque [. . . = **HIPPO D16**].

D32

a (A25) Cens. *Die nat.* 6.3

at Diogenes et Hippon [**HIPPO D14**] existimarunt esse
in alvo prominens quiddam, quod infans ore adprehendat,
et[1] ex eo alimentum ita trahat ut cum editus est ex matris
uberibus.

    [1] et V[2]: *om. cett.*

b (A25) Aristoph. Byz. *Epit.* 1.78 (p. 23.14–15 Lambros)

[. . .] Διογένην τὸν Ἀπολλωνιάτην εἰρηκότα ταῖς κοτυληδόσι ταῖς ἐν τῇ μήτρᾳ τρέφεσθαι τὰ ἔμβρυα [. . .
= **R12**].

view, in the second book of his *On Nature;* but I myself have not come across this book.

b (> A26) Censorinus, *The Birthday*

Although not all children are ready to be born at the same time, most of the other authorities have determined for the formation of all of them one and the same period of time, like Diogenes of Apollonia, who said that males' bodies are formed in four months and females' in five [. . .].[1]

[1] Rufus' statement in **D31a** contradicts Censorinus'.

D32

a (A25) Censorinus, *The Birthday*

But Diogenes and Hippo thought that there exists in the belly [scil. of the mother] a protrusion that the infant takes in its mouth and from which it draws nourishment in the same way as, after it is born, it does from its mother's breasts.

b (A25) Aristophanes of Byzantium, *Epitome of Aristotle's* History of Animals

[. . .] Diogenes of Apollonia [. . .] says that embryos are nourished by cup-shaped cavities located in the uterus.

Respiration, Life, and Death (D33)

D33 (A29) Aët. 5.24.3 (Ps.-Plut.) [πῶς ὕπνος γίνεται καὶ θάνατος]

Διογένης, εἰ ἐπὶ πᾶν τὸ αἷμα διαχεόμενον πληρώσει μὲν τὰς φλέβας τὸν δ᾽ ἐν αὐταῖς¹ περιεχόμενον² ἀέρα ὤσει εἰς τὰ στέρνα καὶ τὴν ὑποκειμένην γαστέρα, ὕπνον γεγενῆσθαι καὶ θερμότερον ὑπάρχειν τὸν θώρακα· ἐὰν δ᾽ ἅπαν τὸ ἀερῶδες ἐκ τῶν φλεβῶν ἐκλίπῃ, θάνατον συντυγχάνειν.

¹ αὐτοῖς mss., corr. Beck
² περιεχόμενον ΜΠ: περιχεόμενον m

Physiology of Sensations (D34–D42)
The General Principle (D34)

D34 (< A19) Theophr. *Sens.*

a 39

Διογένης δ᾽ ὥσπερ τὸ ζῆν καὶ τὸ φρονεῖν τῷ ἀέρι καὶ τὰς αἰσθήσεις ἀνάπτει [. . . cf. **R10**].

b 43

[. . . = **D42**] ὅτι δὲ ὁ ἐντὸς ἀὴρ αἰσθάνεται μικρὸν ὢν μόριον τοῦ θεοῦ, σημεῖον εἶναι· διὸ πολλάκις πρὸς ἄλλα τὸν νοῦν ἔχοντες οὔθ᾽ ὁρῶμεν οὔτ᾽ ἀκούομεν [. . . cf. **D43**].

Respiration, Life, and Death (D33)

D33 (A29) Aëtius

Diogenes: if the blood, diffusing itself completely, fills the vessels and expels the air that is contained in them toward the chest and the stomach below it, sleep is produced and the thorax is warmer; but if all the air leaves the vessels, death occurs.

See also **D46–D47**

Physiology of Sensations (D34–42)
The General Principle (D34)

D34 (< A19) Theophrastus, *On Sensations*

a

Diogenes, just as he does in the case of life and thought, connects the sensations too with air [. . .].

b

[. . .] There is evidence that the inner air, **a small portion of god** is what perceives: that is the reason why often, when we are paying attention to something else, we neither see nor hear. [. . .]

The Particular Sensations (D35–D41)
Smelling (D35)

D35 (< A19) Theophr. *Sens.* 39

[. . . = **R10**] τὴν μὲν ὄσφρησιν τῷ περὶ τὸν ἐγκέφαλον
ἀέρι· τοῦτον γὰρ ἄθρουν εἶναι καὶ σύμμετρον τῇ ἀκοῇ
(τὸν γὰρ ἐγκέφαλον αὐτὸν μόνον καὶ φλέβια, λεπτότατον δ᾿ ἐν οἷς ἡ θέσις ἀσύμμετρος) καὶ οὐ μίγνυσθαι ταῖς ὀσμαῖς· ὡς εἴ τις εἴη τῇ κράσει σύμμετρος,
δῆλον ὡς αἰσθανόμενον ἄν. [. . . = **D36**]

Hearing (D36–D37)

D36 (< A19) Theophr. *Sens.* 40

[. . . = **D35**] τὴν δ᾿ ἀκοήν, ὅταν ὁ ἐν τοῖς ὠσὶν ἀὴρ
κινηθεὶς ὑπὸ τοῦ ἔξω διαδῷ πρὸς τὸν ἐγκέφαλον [. . .
= **D38**].

D37 (A21) Aët. 4.16.3 (Ps.-Plut.) [περὶ ἀκοῆς]

Διογένης τοῦ ἐν τῇ κεφαλῇ ἀέρος ὑπὸ τῆς φωνῆς τυ-
πτομένου καὶ κινουμένου.

Sight (D38)

D38 (< A19) Theophr. *Sens.* 40

[. . . = **D36**] τὴν δὲ ὄψιν ὁρᾶν ἐμφαινομένην εἰς τὴν
κόρην, ταύτην δὲ μιγνυμένην τῷ ἐντὸς ἀέρι ποιεῖν

The Particular Sensations (D35–D41)
Smelling (D35)

D35 (< A19) Theophrastus, *On Sensations*

[. . .] Smelling [scil. occurs] by means of the air located near the brain: for this is compact and adapted to hearing (?) (for the brain is nothing but this [i.e. air] and vessels, and it is extremely rarefied in those places where its position is not adapted) and it does not mix with smells;[1] so that if one [scil. an air] were adapted in its constitutive mixture, this would clearly be something that perceives. [. . .]

[1] The text of this sentence is very uncertain.

Hearing (D36–D37)

D36 (< A19) Theophrastus, *On Sensations*

[. . .] hearing [scil. occurs] when the air contained in the ears is set in motion by the external air and transmits this to the brain [. . .].

D37 (A21) Aëtius

Diogenes: [scil. hearing occurs] when the air contained in the head is struck by a sound and is set in motion.

Sight (D38)

D38 (< A19) Theophrastus, *On Sensations*

[. . .] one sees the object of vision when a reflection is formed in the pupil: when this is mixed with the internal

αἴσθησιν· σημεῖον δέ· ἐὰν γὰρ φλεγμασία γένηται
τῶν φλεβῶν οὐ μιγνῦσι τῷ ἐντός, οὐχ ὁρᾶν, ὁμοίως
τῆς ἐμφάσεως οὔσης [. . . = **D39**].

Taste (D39–D40)

D39 (< A19) Theophr. *Sens.* 40

[. . . = **D38**] τὴν δὲ γεῦσιν τῇ γλώττῃ διὰ τὸ μανὸν
καὶ ἁπαλόν [. . . = **D41**].

D40 (A22) Aët. 4.18.2 (Ps.-Plut.) [περὶ γεύσεως]

Διογένης τῇ ἀραιότητι τῆς γλώττης καὶ τῇ μαλα-
κότητι καὶ διὰ τὸ συνάπτειν τὰς ἀπὸ τοῦ σώματος εἰς
αὐτὴν φλέβας διαχεῖσθαι τοὺς χυμοὺς ἑλκομένους
ἐπὶ τὴν αἴσθησιν καὶ τὸ ἡγεμονικὸν καθάπερ ἀπὸ
σπογγιᾶς.

Touch (D41)

D41 (< A19) Theophr. *Sens.* 40

[. . . = **D39**] περὶ δὲ ἁφῆς οὐδὲν ἀφώρισεν, οὔτε πῶς
οὔτε τίνων ἐστίν [= **D42**].

air, it produces the sensation. And there is evidence for this: for if there is an inflammation of the vessels in people who for this reason do not achieve the mixture with the internal air, they cannot see, even though the reflection occurs in the same way [. . .].

Taste (D39–D40)

D39 (< A19) Theophrastus, *On Sensations*

[. . .] tasting [scil. occurs] by the tongue, for its consistency is loose and soft [. . .].

D40 (A22) Aëtius

Diogenes: it is by reason of the porosity of the tongue and its softness, and because the vessels that extend from the body to it enter into contact, that the flavors are diffused, drawn toward sensation and the directing principle, as though by a sponge.

Touch (D41)

D41 (< A19) Theophrastus, *On Sensations*

[. . .] regarding touch he defined nothing, neither how it occurs nor to what objects it applies [. . .].

*Intensity and Precision of the
Different Sensations (D42)*

D42 (< A19) Theophr. *Sens.* 40–43

[. . . = **D41**] ἀλλὰ μετὰ ταῦτα πειρᾶται λέγειν, διὰ τί
συμβαίνει τὰς αἰσθήσεις ἀκριβεστέρας εἶναι καὶ τῶν
ποίων.

[41] ὄσφρησιν μὲν οὖν ὀξυτάτην, οἷς[1] ἐλάχιστος ἀὴρ
ἐν τῇ κεφαλῇ· ἥκιστα γὰρ μίγνυσθαι· καὶ πρὸς τούτοις, ἐὰν ἕλκῃ διὰ μακροτέρου καὶ στενωτέρου· θᾶττον γὰρ οὕτω κρίνεσθαι· διόπερ ἔνια τῶν ζῴων
ὀσφραντικώτερα τῶν ἀνθρώπων εἶναι· οὐ μὴν ἀλλὰ
συμμέτρου γε οὔσης τῆς ὀσμῆς τῷ ἀέρι πρὸς τὴν
κρᾶσιν μάλιστα ἂν αἰσθάνεσθαι τὸν ἄνθρωπον.

ἀκούειν δ' ὀξύτατα, ὧν αἵ τε φλέβες λεπταί, καθάπερ τῇ αἰσθήσει, καὶ τῇ ἀκοῇ τέτρηται βραχὺ καὶ
λεπτὸν καὶ ἰθὺ καὶ πρὸς τούτοις τὸ οὖς ὀρθὸν ἔχει καὶ
μέγα. κινούμενον γὰρ τὸν ἐν τοῖς ὠσὶν ἀέρα κινεῖν
τὸν ἐντός. ἐὰν δὲ εὐρύτερα ᾖ, κινουμένου τοῦ ἀέρος
ἦχον εἶναι καὶ τὸν ψόφον ἄναρθρον διὰ τὸ μὴ προσ-
πίπτειν πρὸς ἠρεμοῦν.

[42] ὁρᾶν δ' ὀξύτατον, ὅσα τε τὸν ἀέρα καὶ τὰς φλέβας ἔχει λεπτάς, ὥσπερ ἐπὶ τῶν ἄλλων, καὶ ὅσα τὸν
ὀφθαλμὸν λαμπρότατον. μάλιστα δ' ἐμφαίνεσθαι τὸ
ἐναντίον χρῶμα· διὸ τοὺς μελανοφθάλμους μεθ' ἡμέραν καὶ τὰ λαμπρὰ μᾶλλον ὁρᾶν, τοὺς δ' ἐναντίους
νύκτωρ [. . . = **D34b, D43**].

---

[1] ἧς mss., corr. Schneider

Intensity and Precision of the
Different Sensations (D42)

D42 (< A19) Theophrastus, *On Sensations*

[. . .] after this, he tries to explain for what reason it happens that sensations are more precise, and in what kinds of conformations.

[41] The most acute sense of smell belongs to those whose head contains the least amount of air, for it is mixed the least; and also when respiration occurs through a passageway that is longer and narrower, for in this way one discerns more quickly. This is why certain animals have a better sense of smell than humans do; except that, the smell being adapted to the air with regard to the mixture, it is the human being that would have this sensation most intensely.

The most acute sense of hearing is found in those whose vessels are thin, just as for sensation, and whose passageway, with regard to the organ of hearing, is perforated short, thin, and straight, and whose ear is straight and big: for it is when the air in the ears is set in motion that it moves the internal air. But if they are too wide, an echo occurs when the air is in motion and the sound is inarticulate, because it does not fall upon a body at rest.

[42] The most acute sense of sight is found in those who have both the air and the vessels thin, just as for the other [scil. sensations], and whose eye is very brilliant. It is the opposite color that reflects the most; and that is why those people who have dark eyes see better during the day and [scil. see] bright objects [scil. better], while those with the opposite [scil. color of eyes see better] at night.

[43] κριτικώτατον δὲ ἡδονῆς τὴν γλῶτταν· ἁπαλώτα-
τον γὰρ εἶναι καὶ μανὸν καὶ τὰς φλέβας ἁπάσας
ἀνήκειν εἰς αὐτήν· διὸ σημεῖά τε πλεῖστα τοῖς κάμ-
νουσιν ἐπ᾽ αὐτῆς εἶναι, καὶ τῶν ἄλλων ζῴων τὰ χρώματα μηνύειν· ὁπόσα γὰρ ἂν ᾖ καὶ ὁποῖα, τοσαῦτα
ἐμφαίνεσθαι. [. . . = **D44**]

Pleasure, Pain, and Other Affections (D43)

D43 (< A19) Theophr. *Sens.* 43

[. . . = **D34b**] ἡδονὴν δὲ καὶ λύπην γίνεσθαι τόνδε τὸν
τρόπον. ὅταν μὲν πολὺς ὁ ἀὴρ μίσγηται τῷ αἵματι
καὶ κουφίζῃ κατὰ φύσιν ὢν καὶ κατὰ πᾶν τὸ σῶμα
διεξιών, ἡδονήν· ὅταν δὲ παρὰ φύσιν καὶ μὴ μίσγηται συνισάζοντος[1] τοῦ αἵματος καὶ ἀσθενεστέρου καὶ
πυκνοτέρου γινομένου, λύπην. ὁμοίως καὶ θάρσος καὶ
ὑγίειαν καὶ τἀναντία. [. . . = **D42[43]**]

[1] συνιζάνοντος Schneider

Thought (D44)

D44 (< A19) Theophr. *Sens.* 44–45

[. . . = **D42**] [44] φρονεῖν δ᾽ ὥσπερ ἐλέχθη, τῷ ἀέρι
καθαρῷ καὶ ξηρῷ· κωλύειν γὰρ τὴν ἰκμάδα τὸν νοῦν·
διὸ καὶ ἐν τοῖς ὕπνοις καὶ ἐν ταῖς μέθαις καὶ ἐν ταῖς
πλησμοναῖς ἧττον φρονεῖν. ἔτι δὲ ἡ ὑγρότης ἀφαι-
ρεῖται τὸν νοῦν· σημεῖον δ᾽ ὅτι τὰ ἄλλα ζῷα χείρω

[43] The organ that discerns flavor (*hêdonê*) the best is the tongue, for it is the softest and most relaxed, and all the vessels arrive at it. That is why it shows the largest number of signs in people who are sick and why it reveals the colors of the other animals: for whatever their number and their nature, they are all reflected in it. [. . .]

Pleasure, Pain, and Other Affections (D43)

D43 (< A19) Theophrastus, *On Sensations*

[. . .] pleasure and pain occur in the following way: when a large quantity of air is mixed with the blood and lightens it, acting according to its nature and extending throughout the whole body, this is pleasure; but when it acts against its nature and does not mix, the blood being present in an equal quantity and becoming weaker and thicker, this is pain. And the same applies for vigor, health, and their opposites. [. . .]

Thought (D44)

D44 (< A19) Theophrastus, *On Sensations*

[. . .] [44] Thinking (*phronein*), as has been said, occurs thanks to pure and dry air, for liquid impedes the mind (*nous*): that is why one thinks less during sleep, intoxication, and conditions of fullness. Furthermore, moisture abolishes the mind; evidence for this is that the other animals are inferior with regard to thought (*dianoia*), for

τὴν διάνοιαν· διαπνεῖν τε γὰρ τὸν ἀπὸ τῆς γῆς ἀέρα
καὶ τροφὴν ὑγροτέραν προσφέρεσθαι. τοὺς δὲ ὄρνιθες
ἀναπνεῖν μὲν καθαρόν, φύσιν δὲ ὁμοίαν ἔχειν τοῖς
ἰχθύσι· καὶ γὰρ τὴν σάρκα στιφρὰν[1] καὶ τὸ πνεῦμα
οὐ διέναι διὰ παντός, ἀλλὰ ἱστάναι περὶ τὴν κοιλίαν·
διὸ τὴν μὲν τροφὴν ταχὺ πέττειν, αὐτὸ δ' ἄφρον εἶναι.
συμβάλλεσθαι δ' ἔτι πρὸς τῇ τροφῇ καὶ τὸ στόμα καὶ
τὴν γλῶτταν· οὐ γὰρ δύνασθαι συνεῖναι ἀλλήλων. τὰ
δὲ φυτά, διὰ τὸ μὴ εἶναι κοῖλα μηδὲ ἀναδέχεσθαι τὸν
ἀέρα, παντελῶς ἀφῃρῆσθαι[2] τὸ φρονεῖν. [45] ταὐτὸν δ'
αἴτιον εἶναι καὶ ὅτι τὰ παιδία ἄφρονα. πολὺ γὰρ ἔχειν
τὸ ὑγρόν, ὥστε μὴ δύνασθαι διὰ παντὸς διιέναι τοῦ
σώματος, ἀλλὰ ἐκκρίνεσθαι περὶ τὰ στήθη, διὸ νωθῆ
τε εἶναι καὶ ἄφρονα. ὀργίλα δὲ καὶ ὅλως ὀξύρροπα
καὶ εὐμετάπτωτα διὰ τὸ ἐκ μικρῶν κινεῖσθαι τὸν ἀέρα
πολύν· ὅπερ καὶ τῆς λήθης αἴτιον εἶναι· διὰ γὰρ τὸ
μὴ ἰέναι διὰ παντὸς τοῦ σώματος οὐ δύνασθαι συν-
εῖναι·[3] σημεῖον δέ· καὶ γὰρ τοῖς ἀναμιμνησκομένοις
τὴν ἀπορίαν εἶναι περὶ τὸ στῆθος, ὅταν δὲ εὕρωσιν,
"διασκίδνασθαι" καὶ ἀνακουφίζεσθαι τῆς λύπης [. . .
= **R11**].

---

[1] στιφρὰν Koraïs: στρυφνὰν mss.
[2] ἀφῃρῆσθαι Schneider: ἀναιρεῖσθαι mss.
[3] συνεῖναι P: καὶ συνεῖναι F

the air coming from the earth blows through them and they consume food that is too moist. As for birds, they breathe pure air, to be sure, but their nature is similar to that of fish: for their flesh is firm and does not let the breath pass through the whole body but keeps it in the area of the belly. That is why it digests its food quickly but is itself without intelligence (*aphron*). Besides their food, their mouth and tongue contributes too, for they cannot understand each other. As for plants, because they have no cavities and do not welcome the air, they are entirely devoid of thinking. [45] It is for the same reason too that small children are without intelligence; for they possess moisture in abundance, so that it cannot penetrate throughout the whole body but is repelled in the area of the chest, the reason for which they are obtuse and without intelligence. And they are irascible and, in general, impetuous and unstable, because a large quantity of air is expelled from small passages. This is also the cause of forgetfulness; for it is because the air does not permeate throughout the whole body that it cannot understand. And there is evidence for this: those people who try to remember feel trouble in the area of the chest, and when they find it, there occurs a **"dispersion"** and an alleviation of the pain [. . .].

Animals (D45–D47)

D45 (A30) Aët. 5.20.5 (Ps.-Plut.) [πόσα γένη ζῴων καὶ εἰ πάντα αἰσθητὰ καὶ λογικά]

Διογένης μετέχειν μὲν αὐτὰ τοῦ νοητοῦ καὶ ἀέρος, διὰ δὲ τὸ τὰ μὲν πυκνότητι, τὰ δὲ πλεονασμῷ τῆς ὑγρασίας, μήτε διανοεῖσθαι μήτε αἰσθάνεσθαι, προσφερῶς δὲ αὐτὰ διακεῖσθαι τοῖς μεμηνόσι παρεπταικότος τοῦ ἡγεμονικοῦ.

D46 (A31) Arist. *Resp.* 2 470b28–471a5

Ἀναξαγόρας δὲ καὶ Διογένης, πάντα φάσκοντες ἀναπνεῖν, περὶ τῶν ἰχθύων καὶ τῶν ὀστρέων λέγουσι τίνα τρόπον ἀναπνέουσιν [. . . = **ANAXAG. D83**]. Διογένης δ' ὅταν ἀφῶσι τὸ ὕδωρ διὰ τῶν βραγχίων, ἐκ τοῦ περὶ τὸ στόμα περιεστῶτος ὕδατος ἕλκειν τῷ κενῷ τῷ ἐν τῷ στόματι τὸν ἀέρα, ὡς ἐνόντος ἐν τῷ ὕδατι ἀέρος.

D47 (< A31) Arist. *Resp.* 3 471b15–19

[. . .] φησὶ γὰρ ὅτι τὸν ἀέρα πολὺν ἕλκουσι λίαν ἐν τῷ ἀέρι, ἐν δὲ τῷ ὕδατι μέτριον, καὶ διὰ τοῦτ' ἀποθνῄσκειν· [. . .] [cf. **R3**].

Animals (D45–D47)

D45 (A30) Aëtius

Diogenes: they [i.e. animals] have a share in the intelligible (*noêtos*)[1] and in the air, but because of the fact that some do so with density, and others with an excess of moisture, they neither think nor perceive; their condition is comparable to that of madmen whose directing principle has stumbled.

[1] A post-Platonic expression for the fact that animals, for Diogenes, possess a certain kind of intelligence (*noêsis*).

D46 (A31) Aristotle, *On Respiration*

Anaxagoras and Diogenes, who say that all [scil. animals] breathe, explain in what way fish and oysters breathe [. . .]. For Diogenes, when they [i.e. fish] expel water through their gills, they breathe in the air from the water that is located near their mouth by means of the void that is located in their mouth—for he supposes that there is air in the water.

D47 (< A31) Aristotle, *On Respiration*

[. . .] for he says that when they [scil. fish] are in the air, they breathe in too much of the air, which is present in great quantity, and that that is why they die; but when they are in water, the quantity is moderate.

Plants: Spontaneous Generation (D48)

D48 (A32) Theophr. *HP* 3.1.4

[. . .] καὶ ἔτι τὰς αὐτομάτους, ἃς καὶ οἱ φυσιολόγοι
λέγουσιν, Ἀναξαγόρας μὲν φάσκων [. . . = **ANAXAG.
D94**], Διογένης δὲ σηπομένου τοῦ ὕδατος καὶ μίξιν
τινὰ λαμβάνοντος πρὸς τὴν γῆν.

An Ionic Form Without Context (D49)

D49 (B10) Hdn. *Mon. Lex.* vol. 3, p. 912 Lentz

τὸ δὲ πλῆ εἰρημένον παρὰ Διογένει τῷ Ἀπολλωνιάτῃ
ἀντὶ τοῦ πλέη θηλυκοῦ ἐπιθετικῶς ἄγνωστον τοῖς ἄλλοις.

Plants: Spontaneous Generation (D48)

D48 (A32) Theophrastus, *History of Plants*

[. . .] and also the spontaneous [scil. births], which the natural philosophers speak about: Anaxagoras, who asserts [. . .], and Diogenes, [scil. who asserts that plants are born] when the water putrefies and takes on a certain mixture with regard to the earth.

An Ionic Form Without Context (D49)

D49 (B10) Herodian, *On Particular Usages*

As for the form **plê** (= 'full') that is found in Diogenes of Apollonia for the feminine adjective *pleê,* it is not attested in other authors.

DIOGENES OF APOLLONIA [64 DK]

R

Possible Pre-Aristotelian Echoes

See **MED. T10; DERV. Col. XVII–XIX; DRAM. T10, T81**

Peripatetic Reactions (R1–R12)
Aristotle (R1–R7)
Praise for the Unicity of Diogenes' Principle (R1)

R1 (> A7) Arist. *GC* 1.6 322b9–19

ἀλλὰ μὴν οὐδ' ἀλλοιοῦσθαι δυνατόν, οὐδὲ διακρίνεσθαι καὶ συγκρίνεσθαι, μηδενὸς ποιοῦντος μηδὲ
πάσχοντος· [. . .] καὶ τοῦτο ὀρθῶς λέγει Διογένης, ὅτι
εἰ μὴ ἐξ ἑνὸς ἦν ἅπαντα, οὐκ ἂν ἦν τὸ ποιεῖν καὶ τὸ
πάσχειν ὑπ' ἀλλήλων, οἷον τὸ θερμὸν ψύχεσθαι καὶ
τοῦτο θερμαίνεσθαι πάλιν· οὐ γὰρ ἡ θερμότης μετα-
βάλλει καὶ ἡ ψυχρότης εἰς ἄλληλα, ἀλλὰ δηλόνοτι τὸ
ὑποκείμενον. ὥστε ἐν οἷς τὸ ποιεῖν ἐστι καὶ πάσχειν,
ἀνάγκη τούτων μίαν εἶναι τὴν ὑποκειμένην φύσιν.

DIOGENES OF APOLLONIA

R

Possible Pre-Aristotelian Echoes

See **MED. T10; DERV. Col. XVII–XIX; DRAM. T10, T81**

Peripatetic Reactions (R1–R12)
Aristotle (R1–R7)
Praise for the Unicity of Diogenes' Principle (R1)

R1 (> A7) Aristotle, *On Generation and Corruption*

It is not possible that there be alteration either, any more than separation and reunion, if there is nothing that acts or that undergoes. [. . .] And Diogenes is right to say that if everything did not come from only one thing there would not be either reciprocal acting or undergoing, for example what is warm becoming cold and this becoming warm again: for it is not the warmth and the coldness that are transformed into each other, but, evidently, the substrate. So that in those things in which there is acting and undergoing, the nature that forms the substrate must necessarily be one.

Various Criticisms (R2–R4)

R2 (A25) Arist. *GA* 2.7 746a 19–22

οἱ δὲ λέγοντες τρέφεσθαι τὰ παιδία ἐν ταῖς ὑστέραις
διὰ τοῦ σαρκίδιόν τι βδάλλειν¹ οὐκ ὀρθῶς λέγουσιν·
ἐπί τε γὰρ τῶν ἄλλων ζῴων ταὐτὸν συνέβαινεν ἄν,²
νῦν δ᾽ οὐ φαίνεται (θεωρῆσαι γὰρ τοῦτο ῥᾴδιον διὰ
τῶν ἀνατομῶν) [. . .].

¹ βδάλλειν Oᶜ i.m. (Gaza): βάλλειν ZPSEOᶜ: θάλλειν Y
² ἄν P: om. ZSYEOᶜ

R3 (< A31) Arist. *Resp.* 3 471b11, 15, 17–18

[. . .] διὰ τίν᾽ αἰτίαν ἐν τῷ ἀέρι ἀποθνῄσκουσι [. . .];
ἣν γὰρ λέγει Διογένης αἰτίαν, εὐήθης· [. . . = **D47**].
καὶ γὰρ ἐπὶ τῶν πεζῶν ἔδει δυνατὸν εἶναι τοῦτο συμβαίνειν.

R4 (< T35c Laks) Arist. (?), *Inund. Nili* (= Frag. 248
Rose, p. 192.24–29)

[. . . = **D25a**] accidit autem et huic, unum quidem quod
frigidissimum¹ estate quod secundum terram est, trahit
autem omne calidum existens et quando utique maxime
fuerit calidum. adhuc autem quia alios oportebat fluvios
eos qui in Libia idem facere. non enim singulariter solum
illius dessicat fontes.

¹ frigidissimum *ed. Veneta*: frigidissimi *mss.*

Various Criticisms (R2–R4)

R2 (A25) Aristotle, *Generation of Animals*

Those who say [including Diogenes, cf. **D32**] that children are nourished in the uterus by sucking an appendix of flesh are mistaken; for the same thing would happen in the other animals, but in fact this is seen not to be the case (it is easy to observe this by means of dissections) [. . .].

R3 (< A31) Aristotle, *On Respiration*

[. . .] for what reason do they [i.e. fish] die when they are in the air [. . .]? For the reason that Diogenes gives is silly [. . .]. For this [i.e. death by excess of air breathed in] would have to be possible in the case of terrestrial animals too.

R4 (≠ DK) Aristotle (?), *On the Flooding of the Nile*

[. . .] But it also happens to it,[1] first of all, that what is found in the earth is extremely cold in the summer, for it [scil. the sun] attracts all the existing warmth, and especially when it is hottest. And what is more, the other rivers located in Libya would have to do the same thing, for it does not dry out the sources of only that one river.

[1] The medieval Latin expression, derived awkwardly from the Greek, means, "His doctrine, like that of other philosophers, encounters difficulties, viz. . . ."

*An Exegetical Problem in Aristotle and
Its Consequences for the Transmission
of the Fragments (R5–R7)*

R5 (cf. 63.15–28) Simpl. *In Phys.*, p. 149.3–19

καὶ τῶν ἓν λεγόντων δύο τρόπους εἶναί φησι τῆς ἐκ
τούτου[1] τῶν ὄντων γενέσεως. πάντες μὲν γὰρ σωματι-
κόν τι τὸ ἓν ὑποτίθενται τοῦτο, ἀλλ᾽ οἱ μὲν ἕν τι τῶν
τριῶν στοιχείων, ὥσπερ Ἀναξιμένης δὲ καὶ Διογένης
τὸν ἀέρα, Ἡράκλειτος δὲ καὶ Ἵππασος τὸ πῦρ [. . .]·
τινὲς δὲ ἄλλο τι τῶν τριῶν ὑπέθεντο, ὅ ἐστι πυρὸς μὲν
πυκνότερον, ἀέρος δὲ λεπτότερον, ἢ ὡς ἐν ἄλλοις φησίν, ἀέρος μὲν πυκνότερον, ὕδατος δὲ λεπτότερον. καὶ
ὁ μὲν Ἀλέξανδρος Ἀναξίμανδρον οἴεται τὸν[2] ἄλλην
τινὰ φύσιν σώματος παρὰ τὰ στοιχεῖα τὴν ἀρχὴν
ὑποθέμενον, ὁ μέντοι Πορφύριος [Frag. 137 Smith] ὡς
τοῦ Ἀριστοτέλους ἀντιδιαιροῦντος τοὺς σῶμα τὸ ὑποκείμενον ἀδιορίστως ποιήσαντας πρὸς τοὺς ἢ τῶν
τριῶν τι στοιχείων ἓν ἢ ἄλλο τι τὸ μεταξὺ πυρὸς καὶ
ἀέρος, σῶμα μὲν τὸ ὑποκείμενον ἀδιορίστως Ἀναξίμανδρον λέγειν φησὶν ἄπειρον οὐ διορίσαντα τὸ εἶδος εἴτε πῦρ εἴτε ὕδωρ εἴτε ἀήρ, τὸ δὲ μεταξὺ καὶ
αὐτὸς, ὥσπερ Νικόλαος ὁ Δαμασκηνός, εἰς Διογένην
τὸν Ἀπολλωνιάτην ἀνέπεμψεν.

[1] ἐκ τούτου Diels: ἐκ τούτων DE: ἐκ τοῦ F
[2] τὸν F: τοῦτον DE

*An Exegetical Problem in Aristotle and
Its Consequences for the Transmission
of the Fragments (R5–R7)*

R5 (cf. 63.15–28) Simplicius, *Commentary on Aristotle's*
Physics

He [i.e. Aristotle] says that among those who say that there
is only one element there are two ways in which beings are
generated out of this. For they all posit that this one is
corporeal, but some of them say that it is one of the three
elements, like [. . .] air for Anaximenes and Diogenes, fire
for Heraclitus and Hippasus [. . .]; while for others, it is
different from the three elements, denser than fire but
more rarefied than air, or, as he says elsewhere, denser
than air, but more rarefied than water. Alexander thinks
that Anaximander is the one who posited that the principle is some other corporeal nature besides the elements
[cf. **ANAXIMAND. R4**] ; but Porphyrius thinks that Aristotle's distinction is opposing those who make the substrate a body without defining it further to those who make
it either one of the three elements or some other thing
intermediate between fire and air; and according to him,
Anaximander is the one who says that the substrate is an
unlimited body without defining it further or specifying
whether its form is fire, water, or air; as for what is intermediate, he too, like Nicolaus of Damascus, refers it to
Diogenes of Apollonia.

R6 (< A5) Simpl. *In Phys.*, p. 25.8–9

[. . . = **D8**] Νικόλαος μέντοι τοῦτον ἱστορεῖ μεταξὺ
πυρὸς καὶ ἀέρος τὸ στοιχεῖον τίθεσθαι.

R7 (cf. A4) Simpl. *In Phys.*, pp. 151.20–153.22

ἐπειδὴ δὲ ἡ τῶν πλειόνων ἱστορία Διογένην τὸν
Ἀπολλωνιάτην ὁμοίως Ἀναξιμένει τὸν ἀέρα τίθεσθαι
τὸ πρῶτον στοιχεῖόν φησι, Νικόλαος δὲ ἐν τῇ Περὶ
θεῶν πραγματείᾳ τοῦτον ἱστορεῖ τὸ μεταξὺ πυρὸς καὶ
ἀέρος τὴν ἀρχὴν ἀποφήνασθαι, καὶ τῷ Νικολάῳ συν-
ηκολούθησεν ὁ πολυμαθέστατος τῶν φιλοσόφων
Πορφύριος, ἱστέον ὡς [. . . cf. **D1**] ἐν δέ γε τῷ Περὶ
φύσεως, ὃ τῶν αὐτοῦ μόνον εἰς ἐμὲ ἦλθε [. . .] προτίθεται μὲν διὰ πολλῶν δεῖξαι ὅτι ἐν τῇ ὑπ' αὐτοῦ τεθείσῃ
ἀρχῇ ἐστι "νόησις πολλή" [**D5a**]. γράφει δὲ εὐθὺς
μετὰ τὸ προοίμιον τάδε· [. . . = **D3**] τούτοις καὶ ἐγὼ
πρώτοις ἐντυχὼν ᾠήθην ἄλλο τι λέγειν αὐτὸν παρὰ
τὰ τέτταρα στοιχεῖα τὸ κοινὸν ὑποκείμενον, εἴπερ φησὶν μὴ ἀναμίγνυσθαι ταῦτα μηδὲ μεταπίπτειν εἰς ἄλληλα, εἴπερ ἔν τι αὐτῶν ἦν ἡ ἀρχὴ ἰδίαν φύσιν ἔχον,
καὶ μὴ τὸ αὐτὸ πᾶσιν ὑπέκειτο, ἀφ' οὗ πάντα ἑτεροι-
οῦται. ἐφεξῆς δὲ δείξας ὅτι ἐστὶν ἐν τῇ ἀρχῇ ταύτῃ
νόησις πολλή [. . . = **D5b**] ἐπάγει ὅτι καὶ ἄνθρωποι
καὶ τὰ ἄλλα ζῷα ἐκ τῆς ἀρχῆς ταύτης, ἥτις ἐστὶν ὁ
ἀήρ, καὶ ζῇ καὶ ψυχὴν ἔχει καὶ νόησιν, λέγων οὕτως·
[. . . = **D9**] εἶτα μετ' ὀλίγα σαφῶς ἐπήγαγε [. . . = **D10**]·
καὶ ἐφεξῆς δείκνυσιν ὅτι καὶ τὸ σπέρμα τῶν ζῴων

R6 (< A5) Simplicius, *Commentary on Aristotle's* Physics

[. . .] But Nicolaus reports that the element that he posits is intermediate between fire and air.

R7 (cf. A4) Simplicius, *Commentary on Aristotle's* Physics

But since, according to most authors, Diogenes of Apollonia, like Anaximenes, posited that the first element is air, but Nicolaus, in his treatise *On the Gods,* reports that he maintained that the principle is what is intermediate between fire and air, and Porphyry, the most erudite of the philosophers, has followed Nicolaus, one must know that [. . .] in his *On Nature* at least, which is the only book of his that has reached me (cf. **D1**) [. . .] he proposes to show by means of numerous arguments that in the principle which he posits there exists **"much intelligence** [or: cognitive activity, *noêsis*]" [**D5a**]. Immediately after the proem he writes this: [. . . = **D3**]. When I read these first assertions, I too thought that he was saying that the common substrate is something different from the four elements, since he says that these would not mix together or be transformed into each other if one of them were the principle and possessed its own nature, and if there were not the same substrate for all bodies, from which they were all differentiated. But right after he has shown that there exists in this principle **much intelligence** ("[. . . = **D5b**]"), he adds that both humans and the other animals also live and have their soul and intelligence from this principle, which is air, speaking as follows: "[. . . = **D9**]." Then a little later he adds clearly, "[. . . = **D10**]." And right after this he shows both that the semen of animals is of the

πνευματῶδές ἐστι καὶ νοήσεις γίνονται τοῦ ἀέρος σὺν
τῷ αἵματι τὸ ὅλον σῶμα καταλαμβάνοντος διὰ τῶν
φλεβῶν, ἐν οἷς καὶ ἀνατομὴν ἀκριβῆ τῶν φλεβῶν
παραδίδωσιν [cf. **D27**]. ἐν δὴ τούτοις σαφῶς φαίνεται
λέγων ὅτι ὃν ἄνθρωποι λέγουσιν ἀέρα, τοῦτό ἐστιν ἡ
ἀρχή. θαυμαστὸν δὲ ὅτι κατὰ ἑτεροίωσιν τὴν ἀπ᾽ αὐτοῦ λέγων τὰ ἄλλα γίνεσθαι, ἀίδιον ὅμως αὐτό φησι
λέγων [. . . = **D4**], καὶ ἐν ἄλλοις [. . . = **D6**]. ταῦτα μὲν
οὖν περὶ Διογένους προσιστορήσθω.

Theophrastus (R8–R11)
His Book on Diogenes (R8)

R8 (II, p. 52.28) Diog. Laert. 5.43 [Catalog of the writings
of Theophrastus]

τῶν Διογένους συναγωγὴ α´

Diogenes' Lack of Coherence (R9)

R9 (< A5) Simpl. In Phys., p. 25.1–3 (< Theophr. Frag.
226A FSH&G)

καὶ Διογένης δὲ ὁ Ἀπολλωνιάτης [. . .] τὰ μὲν πλεῖστα
συμπεφορημένως γέγραφε τὰ μὲν κατὰ Ἀναξαγόραν,
τὰ δὲ κατὰ Λεύκιππον λέγων [cf. **P2**].

nature of air and that cognitive acts (*noêseis*) occur when air together with blood occupies the whole body through the vessels; in this section he also provides a detailed description of the vessels. In these passages he is seen to be saying clearly that what humans call 'air' is the principle. But it is surprising that, although he says that the other things come to be from it by differentiation, he nonetheless asserts that it is immortal, saying, "[. . . = **D4**]," and elsewhere, "[. . . = **D6**]." Let this then be what is additionally reported about Diogenes.

Theophrastus (R8–R11)
His Book on Diogenes (R8)

R8 (II, p. 52.28) Diogenes Laertius [Catalog of the writings of Theophrastus]

Collection of Diogenes' Opinions, one book

Diogenes' Lack of Coherence (R9)

R9 (< A5) Simplicius, *Commentary on Aristotle's* Physics

Diogenes of Apollonia [. . .], wrote for the most part in a composite manner, sometimes following Anaxagoras, other times Leucippus.

*Should Diogenes Be Connected with Theories of
the Similar? (R10)*

R10 (< A19) Theophr. *Sens.* 39

Διογένης δ' ὥσπερ τὸ ζῆν καὶ τὸ φρονεῖν τῷ ἀέρι, καὶ
τὰς αἰσθήσεις ἀνάπτει· διὸ καὶ δόξειεν ἂν τῷ ὁμοίῳ
ποιεῖν· οὐδὲ γὰρ τὸ ποιεῖν εἶναι καὶ πάσχειν, εἰ μὴ
πάντ' ἦν ἐξ ἑνός [. . . = **D35**].

*Criticisms of Diogenes'
Doctrine of Cognition (R11)*

R11 (p. 160 Laks) Theophr. *Sens.* 46–48

[. . . = **D44**] [46] Διογένης μὲν οὖν πάντα βουλόμενος
ἀνάπτειν τῷ ἀέρι πολλῶν ἀπολείπεται πρὸς πίστιν.
οὔτε γὰρ τὴν αἴσθησιν οὔτε τὴν φρόνησιν ἴδιον ποιεῖ
τῶν ἐμψύχων.[1] ἴσως γὰρ καὶ ἀέρα τοιοῦτον καὶ κρᾶσιν καὶ συμμετρίαν ἐνδέχεται πανταχοῦ καὶ πᾶσιν
ὑπάρχειν, εἰ δὲ μή, τοῦτο αὐτὸ λεκτέον. ἔτι δὲ καὶ ἐν
αὐταῖς ταῖς διαφόροις αἰσθήσεσιν, ὥστε ἐνδέχεσθαι
τὰ τῆς ὄψεως τὴν ἀκοὴν κρίνειν καὶ ὥσπερ ἡμεῖς τῇ
ὀσφρήσει, ταῦτα ἄλλο τι ζῷον ἑτέρᾳ διὰ τὸ τὴν αὐτὴν
ἔχειν κρᾶσιν· ὥστε καὶ τῇ[2] περὶ τὸν θώρακα ἀναπνοῇ
κρίνειν τότε τὰς ὀσμάς· ἐνδέχεται γὰρ ἐνίοτε σύμμετρον εἶναι ταύταις. [47] εὐήθη δὲ καὶ τὰ περὶ τὴν ὄψιν,
ὡς τῷ ἀέρι τῷ ἐντὸς ὁρῶμεν· ἀλλὰ ἐλέγχει μέν[3] πως

---

[1] ἐμψύχων Wimmer: ὄψεων mss.   [2] τῇ P: τὸ F
[3] ἐλέγχομεν mss., corr. Stephanus

Should Diogenes Be Connected with Theories of the Similar? (R10)

R10 (< A19) Theophrastus, *On Sensations*

Diogenes, just as he does in the case of life and thought, connects the sensations too with air. That is why one might think that he explains them by the action of what is similar, for there would not even be acting or undergoing if all things did not derive from only one principle [. . .].

Criticisms of Diogenes' Doctrine of Cognition (R11)

R11 (≠ DK) Theophrastus, *On Sensations*

[. . .] [46] Diogenes, in wanting to connect everything with air, in many cases fails to persuade. For he makes neither sensation nor thought something that belongs to animated beings as their own. For perhaps air of a certain sort, constitutive mixture, and proportion exists everywhere and in all things; and if not, it is precisely this that needs to be explained. Moreover, it [i.e. this air] might also be found in the different sensations themselves, so that it would be possible for hearing to discern the objects of sight, and as we do by means of the sense of smell, some other living being would discern these things by means of a different sense, because it would possess the same constitutive mixture; so that it would then also be able to discern odors by means of the respiration in its chest; for it is possible that sometimes this would be proportionate to those. [47] Silly, too, is what he says about sight, viz. that we see by means of the internal air. But he does refute in

τοὺς τὴν ἔμφασιν ποιοῦντας, οὐ μὴν αὐτὸς λέγει τὴν αἰτίαν.

ἔπειτα τὸ μὲν αἰσθάνεσθαι καὶ ἥδεσθαι καὶ φρονεῖν τῇ τε[4] ἀναπνοῇ καὶ τῇ μίξει τοῦ αἵματος ἀποδίδωσι. πολλὰ δὲ τῶν ζῴων τὰ μὲν ἄναιμα, τὰ δὲ ὅλως οὐκ ἀναπνεῖ· καὶ εἰ δεῖ διὰ παντὸς τοῦ σώματος διιέναι τὴν ἀναπνοήν, ἀλλὰ μορίων τινῶν (μικροῦ γὰρ ἕνεκα) τοῦτ᾽ ἔστιν, οὐθὲν ἂν κωλύοι[5] διά γε τοῦτο καὶ τὰ πάντα καὶ μεμνῆσθαι καὶ φρονεῖν. ἔτι δὲ εἰ καὶ τοῦτο συνέβαινεν, οὐκ ἂν ἦν ἐμποδών. οὐ γὰρ ἐν ἅπασι τοῖς μέρεσιν ὁ νοῦς, οἷον ἐν τοῖς σκέλεσι καὶ τοῖς ποσίν, ἀλλὰ ἐν ὡρισμένοις,[6] δι᾽ ὧν καὶ οἱ ἐν ἡλικίᾳ καὶ μέμνηνται καὶ φρονοῦσιν. [48] εὔηθες δὲ καὶ τὸ[7] τοὺς ἀνθρώπους διαφέρειν τῷ καθαρώτερον ἀναπνεῖν, ἀλλ᾽ οὐ τὴν φύσιν, καθάπερ καὶ τὰ ἔμψυχα τῶν ἀψύχων. ἐχρῆν γὰρ εὐθὺς μεταλλάξαντα τόπον διαφέρειν τὸ φρονεῖν καὶ τῶν ἀνθρώπων δὲ τοὺς ἐν τοῖς ὑψηλοῖς ἐμφρονεστέρους[8] εἶναι, τῶν πάντων δὲ μάλιστα τοὺς ὄρνιθας· οὐ γὰρ τοσοῦτον ἡ τῆς σαρκὸς διαφέρει φύσις ὅσον ἡ τοῦ ἀέρος καθαριότης. ἔτι δὲ τὰ φυτὰ μὴ φρονεῖν διὰ τὸ μὴ ἔχειν κενόν, οἷς δ᾽ ἐνυπάρχει, ταῦτα πάντα φρονεῖν.

Διογένης μὲν οὖν, ὥσπερ εἴπομεν, ἅπαντα προθυμούμενος ἀνάγειν εἰς τὴν ἀρχὴν πολλὰ διαμαρτάνει τῶν εὐλόγων.

[4] ἔτι δὲ mss., corr. Wimmer
[5] κωλύοι Stephanus: κωλύει F: κωλύῃ P
[6] ὡρισμέναις mss., corr. Camotius

some way those people who have recourse to reflection, even if he himself does not indicate the cause.

Then he goes on to explain sensation, pleasure, and thought by respiration and the mixture of blood. But many animals are either bloodless or do not breathe at all. And if respiration has to permeate throughout the whole body, and this is due to certain parts (because of smallness), then nothing would prevent, on this hypothesis, all the parts from being endowed with both memory and thought. Moreover, even if this happened, it would not be an obstacle. For the mind is not located in all the parts, as for example in the legs and feet, but in certain determinate ones, by means of which those who have reached a suitable age remember and think. [48] It is also silly to say that human beings are distinguished by the fact that they breathe a purer one [scil. air], but not by their nature, as animate beings [scil. are distinguished] from inanimate ones. For it would be necessary that by simply changing places one would be distinguished with regard to thought, and that among humans those in lofty places would be more intelligent, and of all creatures most of all birds; for the nature of their flesh does not differ as much as the purity of the air does. Moreover, [scil. it is silly to say] that plants do not think because they do not contain any void, while all of those beings in which there is some [scil. void] do think.

And so Diogenes, as we said, in his eagerness to reduce everything to the principle, often ends up going far astray from plausible explanations.

---

7 τὸ καὶ mss., corr. Wimmer   8 ἐμφρονεστέρους Schneider: ἐμφανεστέρους P: ἐμφαινεστέρους F

Another Peripatetic Criticism (R12)

R12 (> A25) Aristoph. Byz. *Epit.* 1.78 (p. 23.14–15 Lambros)

διαπίπτειν[1] δὲ Διογένην τὸν Ἀπολλωνιάτην εἰρηκότα ταῖς κοτυληδόσι ταῖς ἐν τῇ μήτρᾳ τρέφεσθαι τὰ ἔμβρυα· οὐδὲν γὰρ τῶν ἀμφωδόντων κοτυληδόνας ἔχει ἐν τῇ μήτρᾳ, ἔστι δὲ ὁ ἄνθρωπος ἀμφόδους.

[1] διαπίπτει mss., corr. Rose

Diogenes Among the Epicureans (R13–R14)
An Obvious Reference to Diogenes in
a Report on Epicurus (R13)

R13 (≠ DK) Aët. 2.20.14 (Stob.) [περὶ οὐσίας ἡλίου]

Ἐπίκουρος γήινον πύκνωμα τὸν ἥλιόν φησιν εἶναι κισηροειδῶς καὶ σπογγοειδῶς ταῖς κατατρήσεσιν ὑπὸ πυρὸς ἀνημμένον.

A Criticism (R14)

R14 (A8) Cic. *Nat. deor.* 1.12.29

quid? aër, quo Diogenes Apolloniates utitur deo, quem sensum habere potest aut quam formam dei?

Another Peripatetic Criticism (R12)

R12 (> A25) Aristophanes of Byzantium, *Epitome of Aristotle's* History of Animals

Diogenes of Apollonia is mistaken when he says that embryos are nourished by cup-shaped cavities located in the uterus [cf. **D32b**]. For among the animals that possess incisors on both jaws, no species possesses cup-shaped cavities in the uterus, and man is one of these.

Diogenes Among the Epicureans (R13–14)
An Obvious Reference to Diogenes in
a Report on Epicurus (R13)

R13 (≠ DK) Aëtius

Epicurus: it [i.e. the sun] is a concentration that, like a pumice stone and a sponge, is inflamed in its openings by the effect of fire.[1]

[1] The term 'pumice stone' is characteristic of Diogenes (cf. **D18, D19, D21**); cf. also 'sponge' at **D40**.

A Criticism (R14)

R14 (A8) Cicero, *On the Nature of the Gods*

[Velleius:] And air, which Diogenes of Apollonia makes a god, what sensation can it have, or what form of a god?

Stoicizing Versions of Diogenes? (R15–R17)

R15 (< A11, cf. 59 A67) Aët. 2.8.1 (Ps.-Plut.) [τίς ἡ αἰτία τοῦ τὸν κόσμον ἐγκλιθῆναι]

[. . . = **D17**] ἐγκλιθῆναί πως τὸν κόσμον [. . .] ἴσως ὑπὸ προνοίας ἵν᾽ ἃ μέν τινα ἀοίκητα γένηται, ἃ δὲ οἰκητὰ μέρη τοῦ κόσμου κατὰ ψῦξιν καὶ ἐκπύρωσιν καὶ εὐκρασίαν.

R16 (< A10) Aët. 2.1.6 (Stob.) [περὶ κόσμου]

Διογένης καὶ [. . .] τὸ μὲν πᾶν ἄπειρον, τὸν δὲ κόσμον πεπεράνθαι.

R17 (< A8) Aët. 1.7.17 (Stob.) [περὶ θεοῦ]

Διογένης καὶ Κλεάνθης [. . .] τὴν τοῦ κόσμου ψυχήν.

Three Divergent Presentations of Diogenes
in Christian Authors (R18–R20)

R18 (T7b Laks) Clem. Alex. *Protr.* 5.64.1–3

στοιχεῖα μὲν οὖν ἀρχὰς ἀπέλιπον[1] ἐξυμνήσαντες [. . .] καὶ Ἀναξιμένης [. . .] τὸν ἀέρα, ᾧ Διογένης ὕστερον ὁ Ἀπολλωνιάτης κατηκολούθησεν. [. . .] ἄθεοι μὲν δὴ καὶ οὗτοι, σοφίᾳ τινὶ ἀσόφῳ τὴν ὕλην προσκυνήσαντες [. . .].

---

[1] ἀπέλειπον ms., corr. Cobet

Stoicizing Versions of Diogenes? (R15–R17)

R15 (< A11, cf. 59 A67) Aëtius

[. . .] the world inclined somehow on its own [. . .]—
perhaps by the working of providence, so that some parts
of the world would be uninhabited and others inhabited,
because of coldness, extreme heat, and a temperate climate.

R16 (< A10) Aëtius

Diogenes and [. . .]: the whole is unlimited, but the world
is limited.

R17 (< A8) Aëtius

Diogenes, Cleanthes [. . .]: [scil. god is] the soul of the
world.[1]

[1] This might perhaps refer to Diogenes the Stoic (but, as Diels
notes, Aëtius never cites him).

Three Divergent Presentations of Diogenes
in Christian Authors (R18–R20)

R18 (≠ DK) Clement of Alexandria, *Protreptic*

They [i.e. the philosophers] have accepted that the
principles are elements, glorifying [. . .] and Anaximenes
[. . .], whom Diogenes of Apollonia later followed, air. [. . .]
These men too are atheists, since, by a kind of unwise
wisdom, they adore matter [. . .].

R19 (A8) August. *Civ. Dei* 8.2

Diogenes quoque Anaximenis alter auditor aërem quidem
dixit rerum esse materiam, de qua omnia fierent; sed eum
esse compotem divinae rationis, sine qua nihil ex eo fieri
posset.

R20 (T7d Laks) Min. Fel. *Octav.* 19.5

Anaximenes deinceps et post Apolloniates Diogenes aëra
deum statuunt infinitum et immensum.

An Alchemical Utilization (R21)

R21 (≠ DK) Ps.-Olymp. *Ars sacra* 22

ὁ δὲ Διογένης τὸν ἀέρα, ἐπειδὴ οὗτος πλούσιός ἐστιν
καὶ γόνιμος· τίκτει γὰρ ὄρνεα· καὶ εὐδιάπλαστος καὶ
αὐτός· ὡς γὰρ θέλεις διαπλάττεις καὶ τοῦτον· ἀλλὰ
καὶ εἷς ἐστιν οὗτος καὶ κινούμενος, καὶ οὐκ ἀίδιος.

R19 (A8) Augustine, *City of God*

Diogenes, Anaximenes' other disciple [scil. besides Anax-
agoras], also says that air is the matter of the things from
which everything comes; but he says that this is endowed
with divine reason, without which nothing could come
from it.

R20 (≠ DK) Minucius Felix, *Octavius*

Then Anaximenes, and later Diogenes of Apollonia, assert
that air is an unlimited and immense god.

An Alchemical Utilization (R21)

R21 (≠ DK) Ps.-Olympiodorus, *On the Sacred Art*

Diogenes [scil. says that the principle] is air, because it is
rich and fertile. For it generates birds. It too [scil. like
water, Thales' principle] is easy to shape. For to this too
you give the shape you wish. But it too is one and in motion, and it is not eternal.

29. EARLY GREEK
MEDICINE (MED.)

Philosophy and medicine, two disciplines that later came to be distinguished clearly from one another, present numerous points of contact throughout antiquity. There is no firm line of demarcation between them during the period presented in this volume: certain authors, such as Alcmaeon, Hippo, and Diogenes of Apollonia, belong just as much to the history of medicine as they do to the history of philosophy; and more generally there are important interferences between the two bodies of texts with regard both to general principles and to particular problems.

In the present chapter we gather together a number of passages of the medical tradition that are useful for situating and explaining, by way of comparison, the doctrines of the early Greek philosophers—and vice versa. Some of these texts illustrate the process of the gradual differentiation between the two disciplines during this period and the relations, sometimes strained, between the two groups of practitioners; others show how certain Hippocratic writers made explicit appeals to cosmological doctrines in order to provide a foundation for their own properly medical theories; still others provide examples of how some medical authors developed their own original epistemo-

logical and methodological principles, ones on which Plato and Aristotle reflected as much as they did for example on Empedocles or Democritus; a final group of texts discuss certain aspects of human physiology that were regularly studied by a number of philosophers.

Given the impossibility of attributing the texts involved to a particular author or of dating them, except relatively, without a large margin of error, these passages—which nonetheless are all located within a span of time between the last third of the fifth and the beginning of the fourth centuries BC—must be used with caution. Furthermore, this is only a selection, to which other passages could certainly be added. But there can be no doubt concerning the general relevance and importance of these extracts in the present context.

In this chapter, more than in the others, we have adopted the texts presented by the editions of reference without indicating the variations and corruptions of the manuscript tradition (which are often quite numerous and of limited interest from the point of view of the present collection) nor even all the corrections made by the various editors.

BIBLIOGRAPHY

Editions

See the list of editions of reference of the various treatises cited in this chapter.

Studies

H. Bartoš. *Philosophy and Dietetics in the Hippocratic* On Regimen (Leiden, 2015).

E. M. Craik. *The 'Hippocratic' Corpus: Content and Context* (Abingdon-New York, 2015).

J. Jouanna. *Hippocrate* (Paris, 1992).

OUTLINE OF THE CHAPTER

T

EARLY GREEK
MEDICINE [≠ DK]

T

Medicine and Natural Philosophy:
Demarcation and Competition (T1–T4)
No Systematic Distinction between Philosophy
and Medicine Before the 5th Century (T1)

T1 (› 68 B300.10) Cels. *Medic.* Prooem. 5–8

ergo etiam post eos, de quibus rettuli, nulli[1] clari viri
medicinam exercuerunt, donec maiore studio litterarum
disciplina agitari coepit [. . .]. primoque medendi scientia
sapientiae pars habebatur, ut et morborum curatio et
rerum naturae contemplatio sub isdem auctoribus nata sit.
[. . .] ideoque multos ex sapientiae professoribus peritos
eius fuisse accipimus, clarissimos vero ex his Pythagoran
et Enpedoclen et Democritum. huius autem, ut quidam
crediderunt, discipulus Hippocrates Cous, primus ex
omnibus memoria dignus, a studio sapientiae disciplinam
hanc separavit, vir et arte et facundia insignis.

 [1] nulli: *VFJ¹T*: nonnulli *F¹J²*

EARLY GREEK
MEDICINE

T

Medicine and Natural Philosophy:
Demarcation and Competition (T1–T4)
No Systematic Distinction between Philosophy
and Medicine Before the 5th Century (T1)

T1 (> 68 B300.10) Celsus, *On Medicine*

Thus after the men about whom I have spoken [i.e. doctors named by Homer], no famous men practiced medicine until the study of letters began to be pursued with greater zeal [. . .]. At first the science of medicine was considered to be a part of wisdom, so that it was among the same authors that the cure of diseases and the observation of natural phenomena first appeared. [. . .] And so we hear about many teachers of wisdom who were experts in this subject [i.e. medicine], but the most celebrated among them were Pythagoras, Empedocles, and Democritus. It was Hippocrates of Cos, the disciple of the last-named, as some have believed [cf. **ATOM. P28**], the first of them all to be worthy of being remembered, a man notable both for his science and for his eloquence, who separated this discipline from the study of wisdom.

*Existence, Discovery, and Progress
of the Medical Discipline (T2–T4)*

T2 (87 B1) Hipp. *Art.* 2

δοκεῖ δή μοι τὸ μὲν σύμπαν τέχνη εἶναι οὐδεμία οὐκ
ἐοῦσα· καὶ γὰρ ἄλογον τῶν ἐόντων τι ἡγεῖσθαι μὴ
ἐνεόν· ἐπεὶ τῶν γε μὴ ἐόντων τίνα ἂν τίς οὐσίην θεη-
σάμενος ἀπαγγείλειεν ὡς ἔστιν; εἰ γὰρ δὴ ἔστι γε
ἰδεῖν τὰ μὴ ἐόντα ὥσπερ τὰ ἐόντα, οὐκ οἶδ᾽ ὅπως ἄν
τις αὐτὰ νομίσειε μὴ ἐόντα ἅ γε εἴη καὶ ὀφθαλμοῖσιν
ἰδεῖν καὶ γνώμῃ νοῆσαι ὡς ἔστιν. ἀλλ᾽ ὅπως μὴ οὐκ
ᾖ τοῦτο τοιοῦτον· ἀλλὰ τὰ μὲν ἐόντα αἰεὶ ὁρᾶταί τε
καὶ γινώσκεται, τὰ δὲ μὴ ἐόντα οὔτε ὁρᾶται οὔτε γινώσκεται. γινώσκεται τοίνυν δεδιδαγμένων[1] ἤδη[2] τῶν
τεχνέων καὶ οὐδεμία ἐστὶν ἥ γε ἔκ τινος εἴδεος οὐχ
ὁρᾶται. οἶμαι δ᾽ ἔγωγε καὶ τὰ ὀνόματα αὐτὰς διὰ τὰ
εἴδεα λαβεῖν· ἄλογον γὰρ ἀπὸ τῶν ὀνομάτων ἡγεῖσθαι τὰ εἴδεα βλαστάνειν καὶ ἀδύνατον· τὰ μὲν γὰρ
ὀνόματα φύσιος[3] νομοθετήματά ἐστιν, τὰ δὲ εἴδεα οὐ
νομοθετήματα, ἀλλὰ βλαστήματα.

---

[1] δεδιδαγμένων A: δεδειγμένων M   [2] ἤδη AM: εἴδεα
Ermerins: ἤδη ‹εἴδεα› Gomperz: ἤδη ‹τῶν εἰδέων ἑκάστη›
Diels   [3] φύσιος M: φύσεως A, secl. Diels, transp. post
βλαστήματα Gomperz

Existence, Discovery, and Progress
of the Medical Discipline (T2–T4)

T2 (87 B1) Hippocrates, *On the Art*

It seems to me that, on the whole, there is no art that does not exist. For it is absurd to think that any of the things that exist is not there; since, of those things that do not exist, what kind of being could one consider in order to proclaim its existence? For if it is possible to see things that do not exist just as well as things that do exist, I do not know how one could think that those things do not exist, the ones that one could both see with one's eyes and know with one's thought as existing. No, it surely cannot be like this, but the things that exist are always seen and known, while things that do not exist are neither seen nor known. Hence it [i.e. the art of medicine] is something known, given that the arts have already been taught, and that there is not one [scil. art] that is not seen on the basis of some form (*eidos*). And I myself think that they have received their names because of their form. For it is absurd to suppose that the forms blossom [scil. like plants, *blastanein*] from the names, and in fact also impossible. For the names are institutions (*nomothetêmata*) of nature, while the forms are not institutions, but blossomings.[1]

---

[1] The transmitted text presupposes that nature manifests itself in two distinct ways, by producing either an institution or a flowering. The editors often emend the text so as to obtain a simple opposition between institution and nature.

T3 (≠ DK) Hipp. *Loc. Hom.* 46

ἰητρικὴ δή μοι δοκεῖ ἤδη ἀνευρῆσθαι ὅλη, ἥτις οὕτως
ἔχει, ἥτις διδάσκει ἕκαστα καὶ τὰ ἤθεα[1] καὶ τοὺς και-
ρούς· ὃς γὰρ οὕτως ἰητρικὴν ἐπίσταται, ἐλάχιστα τὴν
τύχην ἐπιμένει, ἀλλὰ καὶ ἄνευ τύχης καὶ σὺν τύχῃ εὖ
ποιηθείη ἄν. βέβηκε γὰρ ἰητρικὴ πᾶσα, καὶ φαίνεται
τῶν σοφισμάτων τὰ κάλλιστα ἐν αὐτῇ συγκείμενα
ἐλάχιστα τύχης δεῖσθαι.

[1] ἤθεα Heidel: ἔθεα ms.: εἴδεα Ermerins

T4 (≠ DK) Hipp. *Vet. med.* 3

τὴν γὰρ ἀρχὴν οὔτ᾽ ἂν εὑρέθη ἡ τέχνη ἡ ἰητρική, οὔτ᾽
ἂν ἐζητήθη—οὐδὲν γὰρ αὐτῆς ἔδει—εἰ τοῖσι κάμνουσι
τῶν ἀνθρώπων τὰ αὐτὰ διαιτωμένοισί τε καὶ προσφερομένοισιν ἅπερ οἱ ὑγιαίνοντες ἐσθίουσί τε καὶ πί-
νουσι καὶ τἆλλα διαιτέονται συνέφερεν καὶ μὴ ἦν
ἕτερα τούτων βελτίω. νῦν δὲ αὐτὴ ἡ ἀνάγκη ἰητρικὴν
ἐποίησεν ζητηθῆναί τε καὶ εὑρεθῆναι ἀνθρώποισιν,
ὅτι τοῖσι κάμνουσι ταὐτὰ προσφερομένοισιν ἅπερ οἱ
ὑγιαίνοντες οὐ συνέφερεν, ὡς οὐδὲ νῦν συμφέρει. ἔτι
δὲ ἄνωθεν ἔγωγε ἀξιῶ οὐδ᾽ ἂν τῶν ὑγιαινόντων δίαι-
τάν τε καὶ τροφήν, ᾗ νῦν χρέωνται, εὑρεθῆναι, εἰ ἐξ-
ήρκει τῷ ἀνθρώπῳ ταὐτὰ ἐσθίοντι καὶ πίνοντι βοΐ τε
καὶ ἵππῳ καὶ πᾶσιν ἐκτὸς ἀνθρώπου, οἷον τὰ ἐκ τῆς
γῆς φυόμενα, καρπούς τε καὶ ὕλην καὶ χόρτον· ἀπὸ
τούτων γὰρ καὶ τρέφονται καὶ αὔξονται καὶ ἄπονοι

T3 (≠ DK) Hippocrates, *On Places in Man*

Medicine seems to me to have been discovered already as a whole, as it is now, teaching in each instance both the dispositions (*êthea*) and the appropriate times (*kairoi*). For whoever knows medicine in this way waits for luck hardly at all, but both independently of luck and with the help of luck he would be able to do good. For the whole of medicine is well established, and it is manifest that the finest technical resources (*sophismata*) contained within it need luck hardly at all.

T4 (≠ DK) Hippocrates, *Ancient Medicine*

For in the beginning the art of medicine would not have been discovered or sought after—for there would have been no need of it—if it had been useful for sick people to follow the same way of life and diet as what healthy people do with regard to eating, drinking, and the rest of their way of life, and if nothing better than this existed. But in reality necessity itself made medicine sought after and discovered by human beings, for it was not beneficial for sick people to follow the same diet as healthy ones, just as little as it is beneficial nowadays. And, to go back even further, I myself think that the way of life and nourishment used by healthy people nowadays would not have been discovered either, if it had been sufficient for man to eat and drink the same things as an ox, a horse, and all the animals besides man, like for example what grows from the earth: fruits, wood, and grass. For it is thanks to these things that they [i.e. the animals] are nourished and grow

307

διάγουσιν οὐδὲν προσδεόμενοι ἄλλης διαίτης. καί τοι
τήν γε ἀρχὴν ἔγωγε δοκέω καὶ τὸν ἄνθρωπον τοιαύτη
τροφῇ κεχρῆσθαι· τὰ δὲ νῦν διαιτήματα εὑρημένα καὶ
τετεχνημένα ἐν πολλῷ χρόνῳ γεγενῆσθαί μοι δοκεῖ.
ὡς γὰρ ἔπασχον πολλά τε καὶ δεινὰ ὑπὸ ἰσχυρῆς τε
καὶ θηριώδεος διαίτης ὠμά τε καὶ ἄκρητα καὶ με-
γάλας δυνάμιας ἔχοντα ἐσφερόμενοι—οἷά περ ἂν καὶ
νῦν ὑπ᾽ αὐτῶν πάσχοιεν—πόνοισί τε ἰσχυροῖσι καὶ
νούσοισι περιπίπτοντες καὶ διὰ ταχέος θανάτοισιν·
ἧσσον μὲν οὖν ταῦτα τότε εἰκὸς ἦν πάσχειν διὰ τὴν
συνήθειαν, ἰσχυρῶς δὲ καὶ τότε [. . .] διὰ δὴ ταύτην
τὴν χρείην καὶ οὗτοί μοι δοκέουσι ζητῆσαι τροφὴν
ἁρμόζουσαν τῇ φύσει καὶ εὑρεῖν ταύτην ᾗ νῦν χρεώ-
μεθα.

Medicine Contrasted with Charlatanry (T5)

T5 (≠ DK) Hipp. *Morb. sacr.*

a

[1.4] ἐμοὶ δὲ δοκέουσιν οἱ πρῶτοι τοῦτο τὸ νόσημα
ἀφιερώσαντες τοιοῦτοι εἶναι ἄνθρωποι οἷοι καὶ νῦν
εἰσι μάγοι τε καὶ καθάρται καὶ ἀγύρται καὶ ἀλαζόνες,
ὁκόσοι προσποιέονται σφόδρα θεοσεβεῖς εἶναι καὶ
πλέον τι εἰδέναι. οὗτοι τοίνυν παραμπεχόμενοι καὶ
προβαλλόμενοι τὸ θεῖον τῆς ἀμηχανίης τοῦ μὴ ἴσχειν
ὅ τι προσενέγκαντες ὠφελήσουσιν, ὡς μὴ κατάδηλοι

and live free of pain, without having need of any other way of life. And I myself think that, at least at the beginning, man too made use of this kind of nourishment. Certainly, I myself think that at the beginning humans too were nourished in this way, and it seems to me that the present ways of life were discovered and elaborated by art over the course of a long period of time. For they used to suffer many terrible things because of their rough and bestial way of life, eating food that was uncooked, unmixed, and extremely potent (just as would happen to them nowadays too), and falling victim to severe pains, illnesses, and rapid death. To be sure, it is likely that they suffered less then because they had become inured to such conditions, but nonetheless then too they must have suffered severely. [. . .] It was by this need, I think, that they were impelled to seek a nourishment fitting for their nature and to discover what we use nowadays.

Medicine Contrasted with Charlatanry (T5)

T5 (≠ DK) Hippocrates, *On the Sacred Disease*

a

[1.4] To me it seems that the first people who made this disease [i.e. epilepsy] a sacred one were of the same sort as the men who nowadays too are magi, purifiers, vagabonds, and charlatans, all of them people who pretend to be especially pious and to possess greater knowledge. These people, alleging the divine as a pretext and putting it forward so as to conceal their helplessness in not possessing anything they could apply to be useful, consid-

ἔωσιν οὐδὲν ἐπιστάμενοι, ἱρὸν ἐνόμισαν τοῦτο τὸ πάθος εἶναι, καὶ λόγους ἐπιλέξαντες ἐπιτηδείους τὴν
ἴησιν κατεστήσαντο ἐς τὸ ἀσφαλὲς σφίσιν αὐτοῖσι
[. . .]. [1.5] ταῦτα δὲ πάντα τοῦ θείου εἵνεκεν προστι-
θέασιν ὡς πλέον τι εἰδότες καὶ ἄλλας προφάσιας
προλέγοντες ὅπως, εἰ μὲν ὑγιὴς γένοιτο, αὐτῶν ἡ
δόξα εἴη καὶ ἡ δεξιότης, εἰ δ᾽ ἀποθάνοι, ἐν ἀσφαλεῖ
καθίσταιτο αὐτῶν ἡ ἀπολογίη καὶ ἔχοιεν πρόφασιν
ὡς οὐδὲν αἴτιοί εἰσιν αὐτοί, ἀλλ᾽ οἱ θεοί [. . .].

b

[1.8] [. . .] καίτοι ἔμοιγε οὐ περὶ εὐσεβείης δοκέουσι
τοὺς λόγους ποιεῖσθαι, ὡς οἴονται, ἀλλὰ περὶ δυσσε-
βείης μᾶλλον καὶ ὡς οἱ θεοὶ οὐκ εἰσί· τό τε εὐσεβὲς
αὐτῶν καὶ τὸ θεῖον ἀσεβές ἐστι καὶ ἀνόσιον [. . .].
[1.9] εἰ γὰρ σελήνην τε καθαιρεῖν καὶ ἥλιον ἀφανίζειν
καὶ χειμῶνά τε καὶ εὐδίην ποιεῖν καὶ ὄμβρους καὶ
αὐχμοὺς καὶ θάλασσαν ἄφορον καὶ γῆν καὶ τἆλλα τὰ
τοιουτότροπα πάντα ὑποδέχονται ἐπίστασθαι—εἴτε
καὶ ἐκ τελετέων εἴτε καὶ ἐξ ἄλλης τινὸς γνώμης ἢ
μελέτης φασὶ ταῦτα οἷόν τ᾽ εἶναι γενέσθαι—, οἱ ταῦτ᾽
ἐπιτηδεύοντες δυσσεβεῖν ἔμοιγε δοκέουσι καὶ θεοὺς
οὔτ᾽ εἶναι νομίζειν οὔτε ἰσχύειν οὐδὲν οὔτ᾽ εἴργεσθαι
ἂν οὐδενὸς τῶν ἐσχάτων, ὧν ποιέοντες, ὡς οὐ δεινοὶ[1]
αὐτοῖσίν εἰσιν.[2] εἰ γὰρ ἄνθρωπος μαγεύων τε καὶ
θύων σελήνην τε καθαιρήσει καὶ ἥλιον ἀφανιεῖ καὶ

---

[1] ὡς οὐ δεινοὶ θ: ἔνεκά γε· πῶς ἄρ᾽ M   [2] εἰσιν M: ἔωσιν θ

ered this disease to be sacred in order to avoid it being discovered that they knew nothing, and, adding suitable explanations, they established a course of treatment that
served the goal of their own safety [. . .]. [1.5] And all this
they assign to the divine as though they possessed greater
knowledge, and they speak of additional causes so that, if
the patient recovers, the reputation and the skill will be
theirs, whereas, if he dies, their defense will be assured
and they will have the excuse that it is not at all they who
are responsible, but the gods [. . .].

b

[1.8] [. . .] As for me, what they say seems to belong not to
piety, as they suppose, but rather to impiety, and to suggest
that the gods do not exist; and their piety and notion of the
divine is impiety and sacrilege [. . .]. [1.9] For if they swear
that they know how to make the moon fall, to make the
sun disappear, to produce storm and sunshine, rain and
drought, and to make the sea unnavigable and the land
infertile, and everything else of this sort (whether they say
that this can come about from initiatic rites or from some
other knowledge or practice), to me at least those who
behave in this way seem to be impious and to suppose that
the gods do not exist and that they possess no strength,
and it seems that they would not refrain from the worst
extremities: they [i.e. such men] act in this way because
they [i.e. the gods] are not an object of fear for them. For
if a human being, by using magical sacrifices, makes the
moon fall, makes the sun disappear, and produces storm
and sunshine, I myself for my part would not think that

χειμῶνα καὶ εὐδίην ποιήσει, οὐκ ἂν ἔγωγ' ἔτι θεῖον
νομίσαιμι τούτων εἶναι οὐδέν, ἀλλ' ἀνθρώπινον, εἰ δὴ
τοῦ θείου ἡ δύναμις ὑπ' ἀνθρώπου γνώμης κρατεῖται
καὶ δεδούλωται. [1.10] ἴσως δὲ οὐχ οὕτως ἔχει ταῦτα,
ἀλλ' ἄνθρωποι βίου δεόμενοι πολλὰ καὶ παντοῖα
τεχνῶνται καὶ ποικίλλουσιν ἔς τε τἆλλα πάντα καὶ ἐς
τὴν νοῦσον ταύτην, ἑκάστῳ εἴδει τοῦ πάθεος θεῷ τὴν
αἰτίην προστιθέντες. [. . .] [1.13] οὐ μέντοι ἔγωγε ἀξιῶ
ὑπὸ θεοῦ ἀνθρώπου σῶμα μιαίνεσθαι, τὸ ἐπικηρότα-
τον ὑπὸ τοῦ ἁγνοτάτου· ἀλλὰ κἢν τυγχάνῃ ὑφ' ἑτέρου
μεμιασμένον ἤ τι πεπονθός, ὑπὸ τοῦ θεοῦ καθαίρε-
σθαι ἂν αὐτὸ καὶ ἁγνίζεσθαι μᾶλλον ἢ μιαίνεσθαι.

Medicine Contrasted with Philosophy (T6–T7)

T6 (> 30 A6) Hipp. *Nat. hom.* 1

ὅστις μὲν οὖν εἴωθεν ἀκούειν λεγόντων ἀμφὶ τῆς φύσιος τῆς ἀνθρωπίνης προσωτέρω ἢ ὅσον αὐτῆς ἐς
ἰητρικὴν ἀφήκει, τούτῳ μὲν οὐκ ἐπιτήδειος ὅδε ὁ λόγος ἀκούειν· οὔτε γὰρ τὸ πάμπαν ἠέρα λέγω τὸν ἄνθρωπον εἶναι, οὔτε πῦρ, οὔτε ὕδωρ, οὔτε γῆν, οὔτε
ἄλλο οὐδὲν ὅ τι μὴ φανερόν ἐστιν ἐνεὸν ἐν τῷ ἀν-
θρώπῳ· ἀλλὰ τοῖσι βουλομένοισι ταῦτα λέγειν παρ-
ίημι. δοκέουσι μέντοι μοι οὐκ ὀρθῶς γινώσκειν οἱ
ταῦτα λέγοντες· γνώμῃ μὲν γὰρ τῇ αὐτῇ πάντες
χρέωνται, λέγουσι δὲ οὐ ταυτά· ἀλλὰ τῆς μὲν γνώμης
τὸν ἐπίλογον τὸν αὐτὸν ποιέονται—φασί τε γὰρ ἕν τε

any of these actions was divine, but human, since the power of the divine was being dominated and enslaved by a human's thought. [1.10] But perhaps this is not how things are, but certain people, lacking a livelihood, invent and elaborate many contrivances of all kinds, with regard to everything else and also to this disease, assigning the cause for each kind of suffering to a god. [. . .] [1.13] But I myself do not think that a human body, the most corrupt thing of all, can be defiled by a god, the most pure thing of all—on the contrary, if it happened to have been defiled by something else or to have suffered damage from it, then it would be restored to integrity and purity by the god much more than it would be defiled by him.

Medicine Contrasted with Philosophy (T6–T7)

T6 (> 30 A6) Hippocrates, *On the Nature of Man*

For anyone who is accustomed to hear people whose discourses regarding the nature of man go beyond as much of it as pertains to the domain of medicine, to listen to the present discourse is of no utility. For I do not state at all that man is air, fire, water, earth, or anything else that is not visibly present in man—I leave those who wish to make these discourses to do so. But it seems to me that those people who make these discourses do not possess correct knowledge. For while they all share the same conception, they do not say the same things: for regarding the conception, their reflection is the same (for they say that

εἶναι, ὅ τι ἐστί, καὶ τοῦτο εἶναι τὸ ἕν τε καὶ τὸ πᾶν—,
κατὰ δὲ τὰ ὀνόματα οὐχ ὁμολογέουσιν· λέγει δ᾽ αὐτῶν
ὁ μέν τις φάσκων ἠέρα τοῦτο εἶναι τὸ ἕν τε καὶ τὸ
πᾶν, ὁ δὲ ὕδωρ, ὁ δὲ πῦρ, ὁ δὲ γῆν, καὶ ἐπιλέγει ἕκαστος τῷ ἑωυτοῦ λόγῳ μαρτύριά τε καὶ τεκμήρια ἅ
ἐστιν οὐδέν. ὁπότε δὲ γνώμῃ τῇ αὐτῇ πάντες προσ-
χρέωνται, λέγουσι δὲ οὐ ταὐτά, δῆλον ὅτι οὐδὲν[1]
γινώσκουσιν.[2] γνοίη δ᾽ ἂν τόδε τις μάλιστα παρα-
γενόμενος αὐτοῖσιν ἀντιλέγουσιν· πρὸς γὰρ ἀλλήλους
ἀντιλέγοντες οἱ αὐτοὶ ἄνδρες τῶν αὐτῶν ἐναντίον
ἀκροατέων οὐδέποτε τρὶς ἐφεξῆς ὁ αὐτὸς περιγίνεται
ἐν τῷ λόγῳ, ἀλλὰ τοτὲ μὲν οὗτος ἐπικρατεῖ, τοτὲ δὲ
οὗτος, τοτὲ δὲ ᾧ ἂν τύχῃ μάλιστα ἡ γλῶσσα ἐπιρρυ-
εῖσα πρὸς τὸν ὄχλον. καίτοι δίκαιόν ἐστι τὸν φάντα
ὀρθῶς γινώσκειν ἀμφὶ τῶν πρηγμάτων παρέχειν αἰεὶ
ἐπικρατέοντα τὸν λόγον τὸν ἑωυτοῦ, εἴπερ ἐόντα γινώσκει καὶ ὀρθῶς ἀποφαίνεται. ἀλλ᾽ ἔμοιγε δοκέουσιν
οἱ τοιοῦτοι ἄνθρωποι αὐτοὶ ἑωυτοὺς καταβάλλειν ἐν
τοῖσιν ὀνόμασι τῶν λόγων ⟨τῶν⟩[3] ἑωυτῶν ὑπὸ ἀσυνη-
σίης, τὸν δὲ Μελίσσου λόγον ὀρθοῦν.

[1] οὐδὲ mss., corr. Wilamowitz   [2] γινώσκουσι A: γινώσκουσιν αὐτά MV   [3] ⟨τῶν⟩ Jouanna

T7 (> 31 A71) Hipp. *Vet. med.* 1–2

a

[1.1] ὁκόσοι μὲν ἐπεχείρησαν περὶ ἰητρικῆς λέγειν ἢ
γράφειν ὑπόθεσιν αὐτοὶ ἑωυτοῖσιν ὑποθέμενοι τῷ

314

what is, whatever the thing is that is, is one, and that this is the one and the whole), they do not agree with regard to the words. For one of them speaks asserting that this one and whole is air [**ANAXIMEN. D1; DIOG. D7–D8**], another fire [**HER. D86;** cf. **R45**], another water [**THAL. D3–D4**], another earth [**XEN. D25–D27**], and each one alleges in support of his own thesis evidence and proofs that are worth nothing. But if they share the same conception but do not say the same thing, it is clear that they do not know anything. The best way to know this consists in being present when they argue against each other: for when the same men argue against one another before the same listeners, the same man never wins in the discussion three times in a row, but one time this man wins, another time that one, another time someone whose tongue happens to flow most fluently toward the crowd. And yet it would be right for someone who says he has correct knowledge about the matters in question to always ensure the victory of his own discourse, if he really knows what is and delivers correct statements. But to me it seems that these men themselves, in their stupidity, overthrow themselves in the terms of their own arguments, and that they confirm the argument of Melissus [**MEL. R1**].

T7 (> 31 A71) Hippocrates, *Ancient Medicine*

a

[1.1] All those people who have tried to speak or write about medicine by giving themselves as the postulate

λόγῳ θερμὸν ἢ ψυχρὸν ἢ ὑγρὸν ἢ ξηρὸν ἢ ἄλλο τι ὃ
ἂν θέλωσιν, ἐς βραχὺ ἄγοντες τὴν ἀρχὴν τῆς αἰτίης
τοῖσιν ἀνθρώποισι τῶν νούσων τε καὶ τοῦ θανάτου
καὶ πᾶσι τὴν αὐτὴν ἐν ἢ δύο ὑποθέμενοι, ἐν πολλοῖσι
μὲν καὶ οἶσι λέγουσι καταφανεῖς εἰσιν ἁμαρτάνοντες,
μάλιστα δὲ ἄξιον μέμψασθαι, ὅτι ἀμφὶ τέχνης ἐούσης ᾗ χρέωνταί τε πάντες ἐπὶ τοῖσι μεγίστοισι καὶ
τιμῶσι μάλιστα τοὺς ἀγαθοὺς χειροτέχνας καὶ δημι-
ουργούς. [. . .] [1.3] διὸ οὐκ ἠξίουν αὐτὴν ἔγωγε καινῆς
ὑποθέσιος δεῖσθαι, ὥσπερ τὰ ἀφανέα τε καὶ ἀπορεό-
μενα· περὶ ὧν ἀνάγκη ἤν τις ἐπιχειρῇ τι λέγειν ὑπο-
θέσει χρῆσθαι, οἷον περὶ τῶν μετεώρων ἢ τῶν ὑπὸ
γῆν· ἃ εἴ τις λέγοι καὶ γινώσκοι ὡς ἔχει, οὔτ᾽ ἂν αὐτῷ
τῷ λέγοντι οὔτε τοῖσιν ἀκούουσι δῆλα ἂν εἴη, εἴτε
ἀληθέα ἐστὶν εἴτε μή· οὐ γάρ ἐστι πρὸς ὅ τι χρὴ
ἐπανενέγκαντα εἰδέναι τὸ σαφές. [2.1] ἰητρικὴ δὲ πάλαι
πάντα ὑπάρχει, καὶ ἀρχὴ καὶ ὁδὸς εὑρημένη, καθ᾽ ἣν
καὶ τὰ εὑρημένα πολλά τε καὶ καλῶς ἔχοντα εὕρηται
ἐν πολλῷ χρόνῳ, καὶ τὰ λοιπὰ εὑρεθήσεται, ἤν τις
ἱκανός τ᾽ ἐὼν καὶ τὰ εὑρημένα εἰδὼς ἐκ τούτων ὁρμώ-
μενος ζητῇ.

b

[20] [. . .] λέγουσι δέ τινες καὶ ἰητροὶ καὶ σοφισταὶ ὡς
οὐκ εἴη δυνατὸν ἰητρικὴν εἰδέναι ὅστις μὴ οἶδεν ὅ τι

(*hupothesis*) for their discourse the hot or the cold, or the moist or the dry, or whatever else they wish—summarily reducing the principle of what is the cause of diseases and death in human beings and postulating the same one or two [scil. causes] for all—they are manifestly mistaken in what they say on many points; but what makes them most blameworthy is that they do this with regard to an art that exists, to which all people have recourse in the most important situations and in which they honor most of all the good craftsmen and practitioners. [. . .] [1.3] And that is why I myself have thought that it [i.e. this art] does not need a new postulate, as in the case of things that are invisible and cause perplexity, for which it is necessary, if one tries to say something, to have recourse to a postulate, as for example in the case of heavenly or subterranean phenomena. For if one spoke about these matters and knew how they are, neither the speaker nor his listeners would know clearly whether [scil. what he was saying was] true or not [cf. **XEN. D49**]. For there is nothing to refer to in order to know with certainty. [2.1] But medicine has possessed all [scil. it needs] for a long time, a principle has been discovered and also a method, thanks to which many fine discoveries have been made over the course of a long time, and the remaining ones will be discovered if someone who is proficient and knows what has already been discovered uses these as a starting point for his own research.

b

[20] [. . .] Certain doctors and sophists [or: experts] (*sophistai*) say that it is impossible for anyone to know

ἐστὶν ἄνθρωπος [. . .]. τείνει τε αὐτοῖσιν ὁ λόγος ἐς
φιλοσοφίην καθάπερ Ἐμπεδοκλέης ἢ ἄλλοι οἳ περὶ
φύσιος γεγράφασιν ἐξ ἀρχῆς ὅ τι ἐστὶν ἄνθρωπος,
καὶ ὅπως ἐγένετο πρῶτον καὶ ὁπόθεν συνεπάγη. ἐγὼ
δὲ τοῦτο μὲν ὅσα τινὶ εἴρηται ἢ σοφιστῇ ἢ ἰητρῷ ἢ
γέγραπται περὶ φύσιος ἧσσον νομίζω τῇ ἰητρικῇ τέχνῃ προσήκειν ἢ τῇ γραφικῇ, νομίζω δὲ περὶ φύσιος
γνῶναί τι σαφὲς οὐδαμόθεν ἄλλοθεν εἶναι ἢ ἐξ ἰητρικῆς [= **EMP. R6**].

Cosmophysiological Models (T8–T12)
A Pluralist Vision (T8)

T8 (≠ DK) Hipp. *Nat. hom.* 3

[. . . = **T25**] ἀνάγκη τοίνυν, τῆς φύσιος τοιαύτης ὑπαρ-
χούσης καὶ τῶν ἄλλων πάντων καὶ τοῦ ἀνθρώπου, μὴ
ἓν εἶναι τὸν ἄνθρωπον, ἀλλ᾿ ἕκαστον τῶν συμβαλλο-
μένων ἐς τὴν γένεσιν ἔχειν τὴν δύναμιν ἐν τῷ σώματι,
οἵην περ συνεβάλετο. καὶ πάλιν γε ἀνάγκη ἀναχω-
ρεῖν ἐς τὴν ἑωυτοῦ φύσιν ἕκαστον, τελευτῶντος τοῦ
σώματος τοῦ ἀνθρώπου, τό τε ὑγρὸν πρὸς τὸ ὑγρὸν
καὶ τὸ ξηρὸν πρὸς τὸ ξηρὸν καὶ τὸ θερμὸν πρὸς τὸ
θερμὸν καὶ τὸ ψυχρὸν πρὸς τὸ ψυχρόν. τοιαύτη δὲ καὶ
τῶν ζῴων ἐστὶν ἡ φύσις, καὶ τῶν ἄλλων πάντων· γί-
νεταί τε ὁμοίως πάντα καὶ τελευτᾷ ὁμοίως πάντα·
συνίσταταί τε γὰρ αὐτῶν ἡ φύσις ἀπὸ τούτων τῶν
εἰρημένων πάντων, καὶ τελευτᾷ κατὰ τὰ εἰρημένα· ἐς
τωὐτὸ ὅθεν περ συνέστη ἕκαστον, ἐνταῦθα οὖν καὶ
ἀπεχώρησε.

medicine who does not know what a human being is [. . .].
But what they are talking about belongs to philosophy, like
Empedocles or others who have written about nature:
what a human being is from the beginning, how he first
appeared and out of what things he is constituted. But as
for me, I think that whatever has been said or written by
some sophist [or: expert] (*sophistês*) or doctor about nature belongs less to the art of medicine than to that of
painting [or: writing], and I think that there is no other
source than medicine for having some clear knowledge
about nature [= **EMP. R6**].

Cosmophysiological Models (T8–T12)
A Pluralist Vision (T8)

T8 (≠ DK) Hippocrates, *On the Nature of Man*

[. . .] Of necessity then, since the nature of all the other
things and also of the human being is like this [scil. not a
single thing but a composite of warm, cold, moist, and
dry], the human being is not one, but each of the constituents that contributes to generation possesses in the body
the powers that constitute its contribution. And again, of
necessity each one returns to its own nature when the human body dies, the moist to the moist and the dry to the
dry, the warm to the warm and the cold to the cold. The
nature of the animals is like this too, as is that of all other
things. All things come to be in the same way and all things
end in the same way. For their nature is composed out of
all the things I mentioned earlier, and each thing ends in
accordance with what I have said: what each thing has
been composed of, it is into that that it also returns.

An Eclectic Synthesis (T9)

T9 (cf. 22 C1) Hipp. *Vict.*

[2] φημὶ δὲ δεῖν τὸν μέλλοντα ὀρθῶς συγγράφειν περὶ
διαίτης ἀνθρωπηίης πρῶτον μὲν παντὸς φύσιν ἀνθρώπου γνῶναι καὶ διαγνῶναι· γνῶναι μὲν ἀπὸ τίνων
συνέστηκεν ἐξ ἀρχῆς, διαγνῶναι δὲ ὑπὸ τίνων μερέων
κεκράτηται· εἴτε γὰρ τὴν ἐξ ἀρχῆς σύστασιν μὴ γνώ-
σεται, ἀδύνατος ἔσται τὰ ὑπ' ἐκείνων γινόμενα γνῶ-
ναι· εἴτε μὴ διαγνώσεται τὸ ἐπικρατέον ἐν τῷ σώματι,
οὐχ ἱκανὸς ἔσται τὰ συμφέροντα προσενεγκεῖν τῷ
ἀνθρώπῳ. ταῦτα μὲν οὖν δεῖ γινώσκειν τὸν συγγρά-
φοντα, μετὰ δὲ ταῦτα σίτων καὶ ποτῶν ἀπάντων, οἷσι
διαιτώμεθα, δύναμιν ἥντινα ἕκαστα ἔχει καὶ τὴν κατὰ
φύσιν καὶ τὴν δι' ἀνάγκην καὶ τέχνην ἀνθρωπηίην.
[3] συνίσταται μὲν οὖν τὰ ζῷα τά τε ἄλλα πάντα καὶ
ὁ ἄνθρωπος ἀπὸ δυοῖν, διαφόροιν μὲν τὴν δύναμιν,
συμφόροιν δὲ τὴν χρῆσιν, πυρὸς καὶ ὕδατος. [. . .] τὴν
μὲν οὖν δύναμιν αὐτῶν ἔχει ἑκάτερον τοιήνδε· τὸ μὲν
γὰρ πῦρ δύναται πάντα διὰ παντὸς κινῆσαι, τὸ δὲ
ὕδωρ πάντα διὰ παντὸς θρέψαι· ἐν μέρει δὲ ἑκάτερον
κρατεῖ καὶ κρατεῖται ἐς τὸ μήκιστον καὶ τὸ ἐλάχιστον
ὡς ἀνυστόν. οὐδέτερον γὰρ κρατῆσαι παντελῶς δύναται διὰ τόδε· τὸ μὲν πῦρ ἐπεξιὸν ἐπὶ τὸ ἔσχατον τοῦ
ὕδατος ἐπιλείπει ἡ τροφή· ἀποτρέπεται οὖν ὅθεν μέλ-
λει τρέφεσθαι· τὸ δὲ ὕδωρ ἐπεξιὸν ἐπὶ τὸ ἔσχατον τοῦ
πυρός, ἐπιλείπει ἡ κίνησις· ἵσταται οὖν ἐν τούτῳ·

An Eclectic Synthesis (T9)

T9 (cf. 22 C1) Hippocrates, *On Regimen*

[Epistemological considerations]
[2] I say that whoever intends to write a treatise correctly about human regimen must first of all know and discern the nature of the human being as a whole: he must know what it is constituted from at the beginning, and discern by what parts it is controlled. For if he does not know its constitution from the beginning, he will not be capable of knowing the effects that they [i.e. the primary constituents] produce. And if he does not recognize what exercises control in the body, he will not be competent to prescribe what is beneficial for a person. So it is necessary that the author of a treatise know these things, and then the power, both the one that derives from their nature and the one from necessity together with human art, of all the foods and drinks that make up our regimen.

[The primary constituents: fire and water]
[3] Now all animals, including the human being, are composed of two things, different by their power but collaborating in their function: fire and water. [. . .] Each of them then possesses the following powers: fire can always move every thing, while water can always nourish every thing. But each one dominates and is dominated in turn to the greatest or least extent possible. For neither one is capable of dominating completely for the following reason: when fire arrives at the limit of water, it lacks nourishment, and so it turns back to where it will be able to be nourished; while when water arrives at the limit of fire, it lacks movement, and so it stops at this point. But when it stops, it no

321

ὀκόταν δὲ στῇ, οὐκέτι ἐγκρατές ἐστιν, ἀλλ᾽ ἤδη τῷ
ἐμπίπτοντι πυρὶ ἐς τὴν τροφὴν καταναλίσκεται [. . .].
[4] τούτων δὲ πρόσκειται ἑκατέρῳ τάδε· τῷ μὲν πυρὶ
τὸ θερμὸν καὶ τὸ ξηρόν, τῷ δὲ ὕδατι τὸ ψυχρὸν καὶ
τὸ ὑγρόν· ἔχει δὲ ἀπ᾽ ἀλλήλων τὸ μὲν πῦρ ἀπὸ τοῦ
ὕδατος τὸ ὑγρόν· ἔνι γὰρ ἐν πυρὶ ὑγρότης· τὸ δὲ ὕδωρ
ἀπὸ τοῦ πυρὸς τὸ ξηρόν· ἔνι γὰρ ἐν ὕδατι ξηρόν.

οὕτω δὲ τούτων ἐχόντων, ⟨ἐς⟩[1] πολλὰς καὶ παντοδα-
πὰς ἰδέας ἀποκρίνονται ἀπ᾽ ἀλλήλων καὶ σπερμάτων
καὶ ζῴων οὐδὲν ὁμοίων ἀλλήλοισιν οὔτε τὴν ὄψιν οὔτε
τὴν δύναμιν· ἅτε γὰρ οὔποτε κατὰ τωὐτὸ ἱστάμενα,
ἀλλ᾽ αἰεὶ ἀλλοιούμενα ἐπὶ τὰ καὶ ἐπὶ τά, ἀνόμοια ἐξ
ἀνάγκης γίνεται καὶ τὰ ἀπὸ τούτων ἀποκρινόμενα.
ἀπόλλυται μὲν οὖν οὐδὲν ἁπάντων χρημάτων, οὐδὲ
γίνεται ὅ τι μὴ καὶ πρόσθεν ἦν· συμμισγόμενα δὲ καὶ
διακρινόμενα ἀλλοιοῦται· νομίζεται δὲ ὑπὸ τῶν ἀνθρώπων τὸ μὲν ἐξ Ἅιδου ἐς φάος αὐξηθὲν γενέσθαι,
τὸ δὲ ἐκ τοῦ φάεος ἐς Ἅιδην μειωθὲν ἀπολέσθαι·
ὀφθαλμοῖσι γὰρ πιστεύουσι μᾶλλον ἢ γνώμῃ, οὐχ
ἱκανοῖς ἐοῦσιν οὐδὲ περὶ τῶν ὁρεομένων κρῖναι· ἐγὼ
δὲ τάδε γνώμῃ ἐξηγέομαι. ζῷα γὰρ κἀκεῖνα καὶ τάδε·
καὶ οὔτε, εἰ ζῷον, ἀποθανεῖν οἷόν τε, εἰ μὴ μετὰ πά-
ντων· ποῖ[2] γὰρ ἀποθανεῖται; οὔτε τὸ μὴ ἐὸν γενέσθαι·
πόθεν γὰρ ἔσται; ἀλλ᾽ αὔξεται πάντα καὶ μειοῦται ἐς

---

[1] ⟨ἐς⟩ Zwingerus
[2] ποῖ Peck: ποῦ θ: καὶ M

longer dominates anything, but is already completely used up by the fire that attacks it in order to nourish itself [. . .]. [4] The qualities that belong to each of these two are the following: to fire, the hot and the dry; to water, the cold and the moist. And each one receives from the other: in the case of fire, the moist coming from water (for there is moisture in fire); and in the case of water, the dry coming from fire (for there is dryness in water) [cf. **ANAXAG. D27**].

[The process of separation]

Since these things are like this, they separate from one another in many forms of all kinds, both of seeds and of animals, which are not at all similar to one another either in their appearance or in their power [cf. **ANAXAG. D12**]. For since they never remain the same but are always changing to this or to that, the things that separate from them are of necessity dissimilar too. Of the totality of things, then, nothing is destroyed, and nothing comes into being out of what did not exist previously [cf. **ANAXAG. D15**]. Things change by mixing and separating. People think that one thing grows and comes to be out of Hades into the light, and that another decreases and is destroyed, leaving the light for Hades: for they trust their eyes more than their thought, even though these are not competent to make a judgment even about what is seen. But as for me, I explain these matters by means of thought. For living things are so both down there and here [cf. **HER. D70**]. And it is not possible, if something is alive, that it die, unless together with everything else: for to what would it die? Nor can what is not come into being: for from what would come its being? But all things, at least all of

τὸ μήκιστον καὶ ἐς τὸ ἐλάχιστον, τῶν γε δυνατῶν. ὅ
τι δ᾽ ἂν διαλέγωμαι γενέσθαι ἢ ἀπολέσθαι, τῶν πολλῶν εἵνεκεν ἑρμηνεύω· ταῦτα δὲ συμμίσγεσθαι καὶ
διακρίνεσθαι δηλῶ.

ἔχει δὲ ὧδε· γενέσθαι καὶ ἀπολέσθαι τωὐτό, συμμιγῆναι καὶ διακριθῆναι τωὐτό, αὐξηθῆναι καὶ μειωθῆναι
τωὐτό, γενέσθαι συμμιγῆναι τωὐτό, ἀπολέσθαι διακριθῆναι τωὐτό, ἕκαστον πρὸς πάντα καὶ πάντα πρὸς
ἕκαστον τωὐτό, καὶ οὐδὲν πάντων τωὐτό· ὁ νόμος γὰρ
τῇ φύσει περὶ τούτων ἐναντίος.

[5] χωρεῖ δὲ πάντα καὶ θεῖα καὶ ἀνθρώπινα ἄνω καὶ
κάτω ἀμειβόμενα. ἡμέρη καὶ εὐφρόνη ἐπὶ τὸ μήκιστον καὶ ἐλάχιστον· ὡς σελήνη ἐπὶ[1] τὸ μήκιστον καὶ
τὸ ἐλάχιστον, πυρὸς ἔφοδος καὶ ὕδατος, ⟨οὕτως⟩[2]
ἥλιος ἐπὶ τὸ μακρότατον καὶ βραχύτατον, πάντα
ταὐτὰ καὶ οὐ ταὐτά· φάος Ζηνί, σκότος Ἀίδη, φάος
Ἀίδη, σκότος Ζηνί, φοιτᾷ κεῖνα ὧδε, καὶ τάδε κεῖσε,
πᾶσαν ὥρην, πᾶσαν χώρην διαπρησσόμενα κεῖνά τε
τὰ τῶνδε, τάδε τ᾽ αὖ τὰ κείνων. καὶ ἃ μὲν πρήσσουσι
οὐκ οἴδασιν, ἃ δὲ οὐ πρήσσουσι δοκέουσιν εἰδέναι·
καὶ ἃ μὲν ὁρέουσιν οὐ γινώσκουσιν, ἀλλ᾽ ὅμως αὐτοῖσι πάντα γίνεται δι᾽ ἀνάγκην θείην καὶ ἃ βούλονται καὶ ἃ μὴ βούλονται. [. . .]

---

[1] εἴη mss., corr. Diels
[2] ⟨οὕτως⟩ Diels

those capable of doing so, increase and decrease to the greatest and least degree [cf. **ANAXAG. D9**]. Whenever I say that something comes to be or is destroyed, I use this expression for the sake of the majority of people, but what I shall show is that they mix or separate [cf. **EMP. D53**].

[A Heraclitizing perspective]

This is how it is: to come to be and to be destroyed are the same thing; to be mixed and to separate are the same thing; to increase and to decrease are the same thing; to come to be, to mix, the same thing; to be destroyed, to separate, the same thing—each thing in relation to all and all in relation to each one, the same thing; and none of all of them, the same thing [cf. e.g. **HER. D47–D51**]. For in the case of these things, convention (*nomos*) is the opposite of nature (*phusis*).

[5] All things, both divine and human, go upward and downward, exchanging their places: day and night, toward the largest and the smallest; just as the moon goes toward the largest and the smallest, the arrival of fire and of water, so too the sun goes for the longest and the shortest time, all things are the same and not the same: light for Zeus, darkness for Hades, light for Hades, darkness for Zeus, those things come here, and these things go there, every season, in every place those things doing the work of these ones, and these ones in turn doing the work of those. And what they do they do not know, but what they do not do they think that they know; and what they see they do not understand, but nonetheless everything happens for them through divine necessity, both what they want and what they do not want. [. . .] [cf. e.g. **HER. D47–D62, D1–2, D63**]

325

[6] τὰ δὲ ἄλλα πάντα, καὶ ψυχὴ ἀνθρώπου, καὶ σῶμα
ὁκοῖον ἡ ψυχή, διακοσμεῖται. ἐσέρπει δὲ ἐς ἄνθρωπον
μέρεα μερέων, ὅλα ὅλων, ἔχοντα σύγκρησιν πυρὸς
καὶ ὕδατος, τὰ μὲν ληψόμενα, τὰ δὲ δώσοντα· καὶ τὰ
μὲν λαμβάνοντα μεῖον ποιεῖ, τὰ δὲ διδόντα πλέον.
πρίουσιν ἄνθρωποι ξύλον· ὁ μὲν ἕλκει, ὁ δὲ ὠθεῖ, τὸ
δ᾽ αὐτὸ τοῦτο ποιέουσι, μεῖον δὲ ποιέοντες πλεῖον[1]
ποιέουσι. τοιοῦτον φύσις ἀνθρώπου, τὸ μὲν ὠθεῖ, τὸ
δὲ ἕλκει· τὸ μὲν δίδωσι, τὸ δὲ λαμβάνει· καὶ τῷ μὲν
δίδωσι, τοῦ δὲ λαμβάνει· καὶ τῷ μὲν δίδωσι τοσούτῳ
πλέον, τοῦ δὲ[2] λαμβάνει τοσούτῳ μεῖον. [. . .]

[7] περὶ μὲν οὖν τῶν ἄλλων ζῴων ἐάσω, περὶ δὲ ἀνθρώπου δηλώσω. ἐσέρπει γὰρ ἐς ἄνθρωπον ψυχὴ πυρὸς καὶ ὕδατος σύγκρησιν ἔχουσα, μοῖραν σώματος
ἀνθρώπου. ταῦτα δὲ καὶ θήλεα καὶ ἄρσενα πολλὰ καὶ
παντοῖα τρέφεταί τε καὶ αὔξεται διαίτῃ τῇ περὶ τὸν
ἄνθρωπον· ἀνάγκη δὲ τὰ μέρεα ἔχειν πάντα τὰ ἐσι-
όντα· οὗτινος γὰρ μὴ ἐνείη μοῖρα ἐξ ἀρχῆς οὐκ ἂν
αὐξηθείη οὔτε πολλῆς ἐπιούσης τροφῆς οὔτε ὀλίγης,
οὐ γὰρ ἔχει τὸ προσαυξόμενον· ἔχον δὲ πάντα, αὔξεται ἐν χώρῃ τῇ ἑωυτοῦ ἕκαστον, τροφῆς ἐπιούσης
ἀπὸ ὕδατος ξηροῦ καὶ πυρὸς ὑγροῦ, τὰ μὲν εἴσω βια-
ζόμενα, τὰ δὲ ἔξω. ὥσπερ οἱ τέκτονες τὸ ξύλον πρίζουσι,[3] καὶ ὁ μὲν ἕλκει, ὁ δὲ ὠθεῖ, τωὐτὸ ποιέοντες·
κάτω δὲ πιεζόντων ἄνω ἕρπει, οὐ γὰρ ἂν παρὰ <και-

---

[1] μεῖον . . . πλεῖον Diels: πλέον . . . μεῖον mss.
[2] τοῦ δὲ Littré: οὐδὲν mss.

[The human being]

[6] All things are arranged in an orderly fashion, man's soul too, and his body like the soul. Into man penetrate parts of parts, wholes of wholes, possessing a mixture of fire and of water, some going to receive, others to give. And the ones that receive make smaller; those that give, bigger. Men saw a log: one pulls, the other pushes; but they do the same thing, and doing less they do more. The nature of the human being is like this: this pushes, that pulls; this gives, and that takes; and it gives to this and it takes from that, and it gives to one this much more and it takes from that this much less. [. . .]

[7] I shall not speak about the other animals, but I shall demonstrate how it is in the human being. For into the human penetrates a soul containing a mixture of fire and of water, a portion of a human body. These [i.e. the constituents of this mixture], both female and male, many and of all kinds, are nourished and increased by the human's way of life. It is necessary that the parts that enter contain everything: for something of which there was not present from the beginning a portion within would not increase, whether the nourishment that supervened were much or little, for it contains nothing that could be increased [cf. **ANAXAG. D21**]. But if each thing possesses all, it is increased at its own place when nourishment supervenes coming from a dry water and a moist fire, some things being forced to penetrate inside, others to depart outside. Just as carpenters saw a log, and the one pulls while the other pushes, although they are doing the same thing: while they are pressing down, the one moves upward, for

---

³ πρίζουσι θ¹: τρυπῶσιν θM: πρίουσιν Diels

ρὸν⟩[1] δέχοιτο κάτω ἰέναι· ἢν δὲ βιάζηται, παντὸς
ἁμαρτήσεται. τοιοῦτον τροφὴ ἀνθρώπου· τὸ μὲν ἕλκει,
τὸ δὲ ὠθεῖ· εἴσω δὲ βιαζόμενον ἔξω ἕρπει· ἢν δὲ βιῆ-
ται παρὰ καιρόν, παντὸς ἀποτεύξεται.

[8] [. . .] χώρην δὲ ἀμείψαντα καὶ τυχόντα ἁρμονίης
ὀρθῆς ἐχούσης συμφωνίας τρεῖς, συλλαβήν, δι᾽
ὀξέων,[2] διὰ πασέων, ζώει καὶ αὔξεται τοῖσιν αὐτοῖσιν
οἷσι καὶ πρόσθεν· ἢν δὲ μὴ τύχῃ τῆς ἁρμονίης, μηδὲ
σύμφωνα τὰ βαρέα τοῖσιν ὀξέσι γένηται ἐν τῇ πρώτῃ
συμφωνίῃ ἢ τῇ δευτέρῃ ἢ τῇ διὰ παντός,[3] ἑνὸς ἀπο-
γενομένου πᾶς ὁ τόνος μάταιος· οὐ γὰρ ἂν προσαεί-
σαι· ἀλλ᾽ ἀμείβει ἐκ τοῦ μέζονος ἐς τὸ μεῖον πρὸ
μοίρης· διότι οὐ γινώσκουσιν ὅ τι ποιέουσιν.

[10] ἑνὶ δὲ λόγῳ πάντα διεκοσμήσατο κατὰ τρόπον
αὐτὸ ἑωυτῷ τὰ ἐν τῷ σώματι τὸ πῦρ, ἀπομίμησιν τοῦ
ὅλου, μικρὰ πρὸς μεγάλα καὶ μεγάλα πρὸς μικρά·
κοιλίην μὲν τὴν μεγίστην, ὕδατι ξηρῷ καὶ ὑγρῷ τα-
μιεῖον, δοῦναι πᾶσι καὶ λαβεῖν παρὰ πάντων, θαλάσσης δύναμιν, ζώων συμφόρων[4] τροφόν, ἀσυμφόρων
δὲ φθορόν· περὶ δὲ ταύτην ὕδατος ψυχροῦ καὶ ὑγροῦ
σύστασιν, διέξοδον πνεύματος ψυχροῦ καὶ θερμοῦ,
ἀπομίμησιν γῆς, τὰ ἐπεσπίπτοντα πάντα ἀλλοιού-
σης. καὶ τὰ μὲν ἀνάλισκον, τὰ δὲ αὖξον,[5] σκέδασιν
ὕδατος λεπτοῦ καὶ πυρὸς ἐποιήσατο ἠερίου, ἀφανέος

---

¹ ⟨καιρὸν⟩ Diels   ² συλλήβδην διεξιὼν vel διεξιῶν mss.,
corr. Bernays   ³ ἐν τῇ πρώτῃ . . . διὰ παντὸς Diels: locum
corruptum in mss.   ⁴ συμφόρων Wilamowitz: συντρόφων
θ: ἐν-M   ⁵ καταναλίσκοντα δὲ αὖξον mss., corr. Diels

otherwise it [scil. the saw] would refuse to go downward at the wrong ⟨moment⟩; and if it is forced to do so, then it will fail completely. A human being's nourishment is something similar: one thing pulls, the other pushes; what is forced in slips out; but if it is imposed by force at the wrong moment, it will founder completely.

[8] [. . .] And when they [i.e. the constituents] change their place, if they happen to find a correct harmony, one containing three concords, the fourth, the fifth, and the octave [cf. **PHILOL. D14**], then they live and increase by the same things as previously. But if they do not happen to find the harmony, so that the low-pitched ones are not concordant with the high-pitched ones in the first concord, the second one, or the octave, then the whole tuning is futile because of the absence of a single element, for it could not serve as accompaniment, but they change from the greater to the lesser before their allotted portion. And that is why they do not know what they are doing.

> [Fire has fashioned the body on
> the model of the universe]

[10] To state it in a word, fire ordered all the things in the body in the same way by itself: an imitation of the whole, small things in relation to large ones and large ones in relation to small ones: the largest is the [scil. abdominal] cavity, a reservoir of dry and moist water, to give to all and to receive from all—the power of the sea, the nourishment of animals that are useful and the destruction of those that are not; and around this, an assembly of cold and moist water, a passage of cold and hot breath, an imitation of the earth, which changes everything that falls onto it. Using up this, increasing that, it made the rarefied water and aerial fire scatter, the invisible and the visible, separation

καὶ φανεροῦ, ἀπὸ τοῦ συνεστηκότος ἀπόκρισιν, ἐν ᾧ
φερόμενα ἐς τὸ φανερὸν ἀφικνεῖται ἕκαστον μοίρῃ
πεπρωμένῃ. ἐν δὲ τούτῳ ἐποιήσατο τὸ πῦρ[1] περιόδους
τρισσάς, περαινούσας πρὸς ἀλλήλας καὶ εἴσω καὶ
ἔξω· αἱ μὲν πρὸς τὰ κοῖλα τῶν ὑγρῶν, σελήνης δύναμιν, αἱ δὲ πρὸς τὴν ἔξω περιφορήν,[2] πρὸς τὸν περι-
έχοντα πάγον, ἄστρων δύναμιν, αἱ δὲ μέσαι καὶ εἴσω
καὶ ἔξω περαίνουσαι ⟨ἡλίου δύναμιν⟩.[3] τὸ θερμότατον
καὶ ἰσχυρότατον πῦρ, ὅπερ πάντων κρατεῖ, διέπον
ἅπαντα κατὰ φύσιν, ἄθικτον[4] καὶ ὄψει καὶ ψαύσει, ἐν
τούτῳ ψυχή, νόος, φρόνησις, αὔξησις, μείωσις, κίνησις, διάλλαξις,[5] ὕπνος, ἔγερσις· τοῦτο πάντα διὰ παντὸς κυβερνᾷ, καὶ τάδε καὶ ἐκεῖνα, οὐδέκοτε ἀτρεμίζον.
[11] [. . .] πάντα γὰρ ὅμοια, ἀνόμοια ἐόντα· καὶ σύμ-
φορα πάντα, διάφορα ἐόντα· διαλεγόμενα, οὐ διαλε-
γόμενα· γνώμην ἔχοντα, ἀγνώμονα· ὑπεναντίος ὁ τρόπος ἑκάστων, ὁμολογεόμενος. νόμος γὰρ καὶ φύσις,
οἷσι πάντα διαπρησσόμεθα, οὐχ ὁμολογεῖται ὁμολο-
γεόμενα· νόμον μὲν ἄνθρωποι ἔθεσαν αὐτοὶ ἑωυτοῖσιν, οὐ γινώσκοντες περὶ ὧν ἔθεσαν, φύσιν δὲ πάντων θεοὶ διεκόσμησαν. τὰ μὲν οὖν ἄνθρωποι διέθεσαν
οὐδέποτε κατὰ τωὐτὸ ἔχει οὔτε ὀρθῶς οὔτε μὴ ὀρθῶς·
ὅσα δὲ θεοὶ[6] διέθεσαν αἰεὶ ὀρθῶς ἔχει· καὶ τὰ ὀρθὰ
καὶ τὰ μὴ ὀρθὰ τοσοῦτον διαφέρει.

---

[1] τὸ πῦρ Bernays: πυρὸς mss.   [2] πρὸς τὴν ἔξω περιφορήν del. Joly suad. Jones   [3] ⟨ἡλίου δύναμιν⟩ Joly
[4] ἄθικτον Bernays: ἄοικτον θ: ἄψοφον Μ
[5] μείωσις, κίνησις, διάλλαξις Joly: κ., μ., δ. Μ, om. θ

of the assembly in which each thing arrives to become visible in conformity with its allotted portion. Within this the fire produced three circular trajectories, limiting with regard to one another both inside and outside: some toward the cavities filled with moisture—the power of the moon—, others toward the outer circuit, toward the solid envelope—the power of the heavenly bodies; and those in the middle, limiting both inside and outside ‹—the power of the sun›. The hottest and strongest fire, which dominates all things, which directs all things in conformity with nature, unattainable by sight or by touch, in this reside the soul, the mind, thought, growth, decrease, motion, change of place, sleep, waking. It is this that governs everything always, the things here and the things there, and it is never at rest.

[11] [. . .] For all things are similar, even though they are dissimilar; and all things converge, even though they diverge; they converse, they do not converse; they possess thought, they do not think; the manner of each is opposed, yet agreeing [cf. e.g. **HER. D49**]. For custom (*nomos*) and nature (*phusis*), by which we do everything, are not in accord with one another, even though they are in accord: for human beings instituted custom for themselves without knowing the matters regarding which they were instituting it, whereas it is the gods who put in order the nature of all things. So what humans have established never stays the same, whether it was established correctly or not correctly; but everything that the gods have established is always correct—so great is the difference between what is correct and what is not correct.

---

6 ὅσα δὲ θεοὶ Diels: ὁκόσα θεοὶ M: ὅσα δὲ ὅσοι θ

The Power of Breath (T10)

T10 (> 64 C2) Hipp. *Flat.* 3–4

[3.1] τὰ σώματα καὶ τὰ τῶν ἄλλων ζῴων καὶ τὰ τῶν
ἀνθρώπων ὑπὸ τρισσῶν τροφέων τρέφεται· τῇσι δὲ
τροφῇσι τάδε ὀνόματά ἐστι· σῖτα, ποτά, πνεῦμα.
πνεῦμα δὲ τὸ μὲν ἐν τοῖσι σώμασιν φῦσα καλεῖται,
τὸ δὲ ἔξω τῶν σωμάτων ἀήρ. [2] οὗτος δὲ μέγιστος ἐν
τοῖσι πᾶσι τῶν πάντων δυνάστης ἐστίν. ἄξιον δ᾽ αὐτοῦ θεήσασθαι τὴν δύναμιν. ἄνεμος γάρ ἐστιν ἠέρος
ῥεῦμα καὶ χεῦμα· ὅταν οὖν πολλὸς ἀὴρ ἰσχυρὸν τὸ
ῥεῦμα ποιήσῃ, τά τε δένδρεα ἀνασπαστὰ πρόρριζα
γίνεται διὰ τὴν βίην τοῦ πνεύματος, τό τε πέλαγος
κυμαίνεται, ὁλκάδες τε ἀπείρατοι μεγέθει διαρριπτεῦν-
ται· τοιαύτην μὲν οὖν ἐν τούτοισιν ἔχει δύναμιν. [3]
ἀλλὰ μήν ἐστί γε τῇ μὲν ὄψει ἀφανής, τῷ δὲ λογισμῷ
φανερός. τί γὰρ ἄνευ τούτου γένοιτ᾽ ἄν; ἢ τίνος οὗτος
ἄπεστιν; ἢ τίνι οὐ συμπάρεστιν; ἅπαν γὰρ τὸ μεταξὺ
γῆς τε καὶ οὐρανοῦ πνεύματος σύμπλεόν ἐστιν. τοῦτο
καὶ χειμῶνος καὶ θέρεος αἴτιον, ἐν μὲν τῷ χειμῶνι
πυκνὸν καὶ ψυχρὸν γινόμενον, ἐν δὲ τῷ θέρει πρηὺ
καὶ γαληνόν. ἀλλὰ μὴν ἡλίου γε[1] καὶ σελήνης καὶ
ἄστρων ὁδὸς διὰ τοῦ πνεύματός ἐστιν· τῷ γὰρ πυρὶ
τὸ πνεῦμα τροφή· πῦρ δὲ ἠέρος στερηθὲν οὐκ ἂν δύναιτο ζώειν· ὥστε καὶ τὸν τοῦ ἡλίου βίον[2] ἀέναον ὁ
ἀὴρ ἀέναος καὶ λεπτὸς ἐὼν παρέχεται. ἀλλὰ μὴν ὅτι
γε καὶ τὸ πέλαγος μετέχει πνεύματος, φανερόν· οὐ

The Power of Breath (T10)

T10 (> 64 C2) Hippocrates, *On Breaths*

[3.1] Bodies, both those of the other animals and those of humans, are nourished by three kinds of nourishment. The names of those nourishments are the following: food, drink, and breath (*pneuma*). The breath inside bodies is called 'air flow' (*phusa*), the one outside bodies 'air' (*aêr*). [2] This latter has the strongest power of all things in all things; and it is worth considering its power. A wind (*anemos*) is a flow and flux of air. So when a large quantity of air produces a strong flow, trees are torn up by their roots by the violence of the breath, the sea swells with waves, cargo ships of vast magnitude are hurled about. So this is the kind of power it has in these cases. [3] And yet it is invisible to the eye—but visible to reason. For what could possibly exist without this? From what is it absent? What thing does it is not accompany? For the whole space between the earth and the sky is full of breath (*pneuma*). This is the cause of winter and of summer, becoming dense and cold in the winter, gentle and serene in the summer. Furthermore, the course of the sun, the moon, and the heavenly bodies is due to breath (*pneuma*). For breath is the nourishment of fire, and fire, deprived of air, would not be able to live. Hence it is air, being eternal and subtle, that makes the life of the sun eternal. Moreover, it is evident that the sea too has a share in moving breath:

---

[1] γε Jouanna: τε A, om. M
[2] βίον A: δρόμον M: βίον καὶ δρόμον coni. Jouanna

γὰρ ἄν ποτε τὰ πλωτὰ ζῷα ζώειν ἐδύνατο μὴ μετ-
έχοντα πνεύματος· μετέχοι δ' ἂν πῶς ἂν ἄλλως ἀλλ'
ἢ διὰ τοῦ ὕδατος κἀκ τοῦ ὕδατος ἕλκοντα τὸν ἠέρα;
καὶ μὴν ἥ τε γῆ τούτῳ βάθρον, οὗτός τε γῆς ὄχημα,
κενεόν τε οὐδέν ἐστι τούτου. [4] διότι μὲν οὖν ἐν τοῖσιν ὅλοισιν[3] ὁ ἀὴρ ἔρρωται, εἴρηται· τοῖσι δ' αὖ θνη-
τοῖσιν οὗτος αἴτιος τοῦ βίου καὶ τῶν νούσων τοῖσι
νοσέουσι.

3 ὅλοισιν Schneider: ὁδοῖς A: ἄλλοισιν M

*A Cosmophysiology Founded
on the Principle of Heat (T11)*

T11 (> 64 C3) Hipp. *Carn.* 1–3

[1] ἐγὼ τὰ μέχρι τοῦ λόγου τούτου κοινῇσι γνώμῃσι
χρέωμαι ἑτέρων τε τῶν ἔμπροσθεν, ἀτὰρ καὶ ἐμεωυ-
τοῦ· ἀναγκαίως γὰρ ἔχει κοινὴν ἀρχὴν ὑποθέσθαι
τῇσι γνώμῃσι βουλόμενον συνθεῖναι τὸν λόγον τόνδε
περὶ τῆς τέχνης τῆς ἰητρικῆς. περὶ δὲ τῶν μετεώρων
οὐδέν[1] δέομαι λέγειν, ἢν μὴ τοσοῦτον ἐς ἄνθρωπον
ἀποδείξω καὶ τὰ ἄλλα ζῷα, ὅπως[2] ἔφυ καὶ ἐγένετο, καὶ
ὅ τι ψυχή[3] ἐστιν, καὶ ὅ τι τὸ ὑγιαίνειν, καὶ ὅ τι τὸ
κάμνειν, καὶ ὅ τι τὸ[4] ἐν ἀνθρώπῳ κακὸν καὶ ἀγαθόν,
καὶ ὅθεν ἀποθνῄσκει. νῦν δὲ ἀποφαίνομαι αὐτὸς
⟨τὰς⟩[5] ἐμεωυτοῦ γνώμας.

varias corruptelas in ms. sanarunt edd.: [1] οὐδὲν Heidel
[2] ὅπως Ermerins   [3] ⟨ἡ⟩ ψυχὴ Heidel

334

for the animals that swim would not be able to live at all if they did not have a share in breath. But how could they have a share in any other way than by drawing in the air through the water and out of the water? Moreover, the earth is a foundation for this, and this is the vehicle of the earth, and nothing is empty of this. [4] So it has now been stated that air is strong in the universe; but it is also the cause of life for mortals, and of sicknesses for those who are sick [cf. **DIOG. D9**].

A Cosmophysiology Founded
on the Principle of Heat (T11)

T11 (> 64 C3) Hippocrates, *Fleshes*

[1] For my part, it is to conceptions commonly held, both by my predecessors and by myself, that I have recourse before undertaking the present discourse. For it is necessary, since I wish to compose this discourse about the art of medicine, that I set as a basis for my own conceptions a principle that is shared in common. I need say nothing about celestial phenomena except insofar as I shall indicate their relevance to humans and the other animals— how they are born by nature and came to exist, what the soul is, what it is to be healthy, what it is to be sick, what is bad and good in the human, and whence it comes that he dies. And now I myself shall declare my own conceptions.

---

⁴ τὸ edd.
⁵ ⟨τὰς⟩ Ermerins

[2] δοκεῖ δέ μοι ὃ καλέομεν θερμὸν ἀθάνατόν τε εἶναι
καὶ νοεῖν πάντα καὶ ὁρῆν καὶ ἀκούειν καὶ εἰδέναι
πάντα καὶ τὰ ἐόντα τε καὶ μέλλοντα ἔσεσθαι· τοῦτο
οὖν τὸ πλεῖστον, ὅτε ἐταράχθη πάντα, ἐξεχώρησεν ἐς
τὴν ἀνωτάτω περιφορήν· καὶ ὀνομῆναί μοι αὐτὸ δοκέουσιν οἱ παλαιοὶ αἰθέρα. ἡ ⟨δὲ⟩[1] δευτέρη μοῖρα
κάτωθεν αὐτῆς[2] καλεῖται μὲν γῆ, ψυχρὸν[3] καὶ ξηρὸν
καὶ πολὺ κινεόμενον·[4] καὶ ἐν τούτῳ ἔνι δὴ[5] πολὺ τοῦ
θερμοῦ. ἡ δὲ τρίτη μοῖρα ἡ τοῦ ἠέρος τοῦ ἐγγυτάτω
πρὸς τῇ γῇ, ὑγρότατόν τε καὶ παχύτατον.

[3] κυκλεομένων δὲ τούτων, ὅτε συνεταράχθη, ἀπελεί-
φθη τοῦ θερμοῦ πολὺ ἐν τῇ γῇ ἄλλοθι ⟨καὶ ἄλλοθι⟩,[6]
τὰ μὲν μεγάλα, τὰ δὲ ἐλάσσω, τὰ δὲ καὶ πάνυ σμικρὰ
πλῆθος πολλά. καὶ τῷ χρόνῳ ὑπὸ τοῦ θερμοῦ ξηραι-
νομένης τῆς γῆς, ταῦτα ⟨τὰ⟩[7] καταλειφθέντα[8] περὶ
αὐτὰ σηπεδόνας ποιεῖ οἷόν περ[9] χιτῶνας. καὶ πολλῷ
χρόνῳ θερμαινόμενον, ὅσον μὲν ἐτύγχανεν ἐκ τῆς γῆς
σηπεδόνος λιπαρόν τε ἐὸν καὶ ὀλίγιστον τοῦ ὑγροῦ
ἔχον, τάχιστα ἐξεκαύθη καὶ ἐγένετο ὀστέα. ὁπόσα δὲ
ἐτύγχανε κολλωδέστερα ἐόντα καὶ τοῦ ψυχροῦ μετ-
έχοντα, ταῦτα δὲ θερμαινόμενα οὐκ ἐδύνατο ἐκκαυθῆναι, οὐδὲ ξηρὰ γενέσθαι· οὐ γὰρ ἦν τοῦ λιπαροῦ ὡς
ἐκκαυθῆναι, οὐδὲ μὴν τοῦ ὑγροῦ ὡς ἐκκαυθὲν ξηρὸν
γενέσθαι. διὰ τοῦτο ἰδέην[10] ἀλλοιοτέρην ἔλαβε τῶν
ἄλλων καὶ ἐγένετο νεῦρα καὶ φλέβες. αἱ μὲν φλέβες

---

[1] ⟨δὲ⟩ Ermerins   [2] αὐτῆς Deichgräber
[3] ψυχρὸν ⟨δὲ⟩ Deichgräber

[2] It seems to me that what we call heat is immortal and that it thinks everything, sees, hears, and knows everything, both what is and what will be. Of this, when all things were in agitation, the greatest part escaped to the most distant rotation; and it is this that the ancients seem to me to have named 'aether.' Its second, lower part is called 'earth'—something cold, dry, and subject to numerous motions; and there is much heat present in this too. The third part is the air that is located closest to the earth, and this is the most moist and dense thing.

[3] While these things were rotating, at the time when they were in agitation, much of the heat remained here ‹and there› in the earth, in some places a lot, in others less, in others very little but in number very many. And then, in the course of time, as the earth dried out because of the heat, these remainders produced around themselves putrefactions, like cloaks. And if the matter that came from the putrefaction of the earth happened to be fat and to possess the least amount of moisture, when it was heated for a long time it was quickly burned up and became bones. But whatever happened to be more glutinous and had a share of cold could not be completely burned up or become dry when it was heated: for it had no fat that could be burned up nor any moisture that, being burned up, could become dry. That is why it took on a form different from the rest, and became sinews and vessels. The

---

4 πολὺ κινεόμενον Deichgräber

5 ἔνι δὴ Littré   6 ‹καὶ ἄλλοθι› Littré

7 ‹τὰ› Ermerins   8 καταλειφθέντα Deichgräber

9 περ Cornarius   10 ἰδέην Ermerins

κοῖλαι, τὰ δὲ νεῦρα στερεά· οὐδὲ γὰρ ἐνῆν πολὺ τοῦ
ψυχροῦ αὐτοῖσιν.[1] αἱ δὲ φλέβες τοῦ ψυχροῦ εἶχον
πολύ· καὶ τούτου τοῦ ψυχροῦ τὸ μὲν πέριξ ὅσον κολ-
λωδέστατον ἦν, ὑπὸ τοῦ θερμοῦ ἐξοπτηθὲν μῆνιγξ
ἐγένετο, τὸ δὲ ψυχρὸν ἐνεὸν[2] κρατηθὲν ὑπὸ τοῦ θερμοῦ
διελύθη καὶ ἐγένετο ὑγρὸν διὰ τοῦτο [. . .]. περὶ μὲν
τούτων οὕτως· τὸ μὲν ψυχρὸν πήγνυσι· τὸ δὲ θερμὸν
διαχεῖ, ἐν δὲ τῷ πολλῷ καὶ ξηραίνει χρόνῳ· ὅπου δὲ
⟨ἂν⟩[3] τοῦ λιπαροῦ συνίῃ τι τούτοισι, θᾶσσον ἐκκαίει
καὶ ξηραίνει· ὅπου δὲ ἂν τὸ κολλῶδες συνίῃ τῷ ψυχρῷ ἄνευ τοῦ λιπαροῦ, οὐκ ἐθέλει ἐκκαίεσθαι, ἀλλὰ
τῷ χρόνῳ θερμαινόμενον πήγνυται.

[1] αὐτοῖσιν Ermerins   [2] ἐνεὸν Zwingerus
[3] ⟨ἂν⟩ Littré

A Resolutely Heraclitizing Doctor (T12)

T12 (< 22 C2) Hipp. *Nutrim.*

a

[1] τροφὴ καὶ τροφῆς εἶδος μία καὶ πολλαί· μία μὲν
ᾗ γένος ἕν, εἶδος δὲ ὑγρότητι καὶ ξηρότητι· καὶ ἐν
τούτοις ἰδέαι καὶ πόσον ἐστὶ καὶ ἐς τίνα καὶ ἐς τοσαῦτα.

vessels are hollow, the sinews are solid; for there was not much cold in the latter; but the vessels had much cold, and of this cold the external part, which was most glutinous, was completely baked by the heat and became membrane while the internal cold, overcome by the heat, was dissolved and became liquid for this reason. [. . .][1] This is how things are in these matters: cold condenses; heat diffuses and, at the end of a long period of time, dries out; where some fat is associated with these, it [scil. heat] burns and dries it out quickly; but where something glutinous is associated with cold but without fat, it tends not to be burned up, but if it is heated, with time it becomes condensed.

[1] The author goes on to use the same principles to explain the formation of the trachea, the viscera, and the bladder.

Cf. **T9[10–11]**

A Resolutely Heraclitizing Doctor (T12)[1]

[1] The language of these passages is staunchly Heraclitean, but we have only indicated the more evident parallels with the preserved fragments of Heraclitus.

T12 (< 22 C2) Hippocrates, *On Nutriment*

a

[1] Nutriment and form of nutriment, one and many: one inasmuch as it is one kind, but its form [scil. varies] as a function of moisture and dryness. And in these too there exist forms, how much, for what, and for how many.

b

[2] αὔξει δὲ καὶ ῥώννυσι καὶ σαρκοῖ καὶ ὁμοιοῖ καὶ ἀνομοιοῖ τὰ ἐν ἑκάστοισι κατὰ φύσιν τὴν ἑκάστου καὶ τὴν ἐξ ἀρχῆς δύναμιν.

c

[9] ἀρχὴ δὲ πάντων μία καὶ τελευτὴ πάντων μία καὶ ἡ αὐτὴ τελευτὴ καὶ ἀρχή.

d

[13] δυνάμιος δὲ ποικίλαι φύσιες.

e

[14] χυμοὶ φθείροντες καὶ ὅλον καὶ μέρος καὶ ἔξωθεν καὶ ἔνδοθεν, αὐτόματοι καὶ οὐκ αὐτόματοι, ἡμῖν μὲν αὐτόματοι, αἰτίῃ δὲ οὐκ αὐτόματοι. αἰτίης δὲ τὰ μὲν δῆλα, τὰ δὲ ἄδηλα, καὶ τὰ μὲν δυνατά, τὰ δὲ ἀδύνατα.

f

[15] φύσις ἐξαρκεῖ πάντα πᾶσιν.

g

[17] [. . .] μία φύσις ἐστὶ πάντα ταῦτα καὶ οὐ μία· πολλαὶ φύσιές εἰσι πάντα ταῦτα καὶ μία.

b

[2] It increases, strengthens, develops the flesh, makes similar and dissimilar what is found in each one according to the nature of each one and its original power.

c

[9] The beginning of all things is one, the end of all things is one, and the end and the beginning are the same [cf. **HER. D54**].

d

[13] Of power, the natures are various.

e

[14] Humors: destructive totally and in part, from outside and from inside, spontaneous and not spontaneous, spontaneous for us but not spontaneous as far as their cause. Of the cause, certain aspects are clear and certain ones are unclear; and certain things are possible and certain ones are impossible.

f

[15] Nature suffices in all things for all.

g

[17] [. . .] All these things are one nature and not one; all these things are many natures and one.

h

[23] σύρροια μία, σύμπνοια μία, συμπαθέα πάντα. κατὰ μὲν οὐλομελίην πάντα, κατὰ μέρος δὲ τὰ ἐν ἑκάστῳ μέρει μέρεα πρὸς τὸ ἔργον.

i

[24] ἀρχὴ μεγάλη εἰς ἔσχατον μέρος ἀφικνεῖται· ἐξ ἐσχάτου μέρεος ἐς ἀρχὴν μεγάλην ἀφικνεῖται· μία φύσις εἶναι καὶ μὴ εἶναι.

j

[32] δύναμις μία καὶ οὐ μία, ᾗ πάντα ταῦτα καὶ τὰ ἑτεροῖα διοικεῖται, ἡ μὲν ἐς ζωὴν ὅλου καὶ μέρεος, ἡ δὲ ἐς αἴσθησιν ὅλου καὶ μέρεος.

k

[40] [. . .] τὸ σύμφωνον διάφωνον, τὸ διάφωνον σύμφωνον [. . .].

l

[45] ὁδὸς ἄνω κάτω, μία.

h

[23] Conjoined flowing, one; conjoined breathing, one; conjoined affections, all things. With regard to the totality, all things; but with regard to the part, the parts in each of the parts with regard to their function.

i

[24] A great starting point arrives at the farthest part; from the farthest part it arrives at the great starting point. A single nature, to be and not to be.

j

[32] The power is one and not one, by which all these things and those that are different are governed, the one for the life of the whole and the part, the other for the perception of the whole and the part.

k

[40] [. . .] what is harmonious is dissonant, what is dissonant is harmonious [cf. **HER. D47**] [. . .].

l

[45] The way upward and downward: one [cf. **HER. D51**].

Questions of Method (T13–T22)
Invisible/Visible (T13–T14)

T13 (> 68 B11) Hipp. *Art.* 11.1

οὐ γὰρ δὴ ὀφθαλμοῖσί γ᾽ ἰδόντι τούτων τῶν εἰρημένων οὐδενὶ οὐδὲν ἔστιν εἰδέναι. διὸ καὶ ἄδηλα ἐμοί
τε ὠνόμασται καὶ τῇ τέχνῃ κέκριται εἶναι· οὐ μὴν ὅτι
ἄδηλα κεκράτηκεν, ἀλλ᾽ ᾗ δυνατὸν κεκράτηται· δυνατὸν δὲ ὡς αἵ τε τῶν νοσεόντων φύσιες ἐς τὸ σκεφθῆ-
ναι παρέχουσιν, αἵ τε τῶν ἐρευνησόντων ἐς τὴν ἔρευ-
ναν πεφύκασιν. μετὰ πλείονος μὲν γὰρ πόνου καὶ οὐ
μετ᾽ ἐλάσσονος χρόνου ἢ εἰ τοῖσιν ὀφθαλμοῖσιν ἑώ-
ρατο, γινώσκεται· ὅσα γὰρ τὴν τῶν ὀμμάτων ὄψιν
ἐκφεύγει, ταῦτα τῇ τῆς γνώμης ὄψει κεκράτηται. καὶ
ὅσα δ᾽ ἐν τῷ μὴ ταχὺ ὀφθῆναι οἱ νοσέοντες πάσχου-
σιν, οὐχ οἱ θεραπεύοντες αὐτοὺς αἴτιοι, ἀλλ᾽ ἡ φύσις
ἥ τε τοῦ νοσέοντος ἥ τε τοῦ νοσήματος.

T14 (< 22 C1) Hipp. *Vict.* 1.11–12

[11] οἱ δὲ ἄνθρωποι ἐκ τῶν φανερῶν τὰ ἀφανέα
σκέπτεσθαι οὐκ ἐπίστανται· τέχνῃσι γὰρ χρεώμενοι
ὁμοίῃσιν ἀνθρωπίνῃ φύσει οὐ γινώσκουσιν· θεῶν
γὰρ νόος ἐδίδαξε μιμεῖσθαι τὰ ἑωυτῶν, γινώσκοντας
ἃ ποιέουσι, καὶ οὐ γινώσκοντας ἃ μιμέονται. [. . .] [12]
ἐγὼ δὲ δηλώσω τέχνας φανερὰς ἀνθρώπου παθήμα-
σιν ὁμοίας ἐούσας καὶ φανεροῖσι καὶ ἀφανέσι. μαν-
τικὴ τοιόνδε· τοῖσι μὲν φανεροῖσι τὰ ἀφανέα γι-

Questions of Method (T13–T22)
Invisible/Visible (T13–T14)

T13 (> 68 B11) Hippocrates, *On the Art*

None of those [scil. internal cavities] that I have spoken of can be known by anyone with his eyes; that is the reason why I call them 'invisible' (*adêla*) and why they are judged to exist by the art. But it is not that they are masters because they are invisible, but instead they have been mastered as far as possible; and this is possible insofar as the patients' nature lends itself to examination and as the investigators' possesses a natural disposition for investigation. For it requires greater effort and not less time to recognize them than if they were seen with the eyes: for whatever escapes the sight of the eyes is mastered by the sight of thought. And what patients suffer from the observation's not being rapid is the fault not of those who are treating them, but of the patient's nature and the disease's.

T14 (< 22 C1) Hippocrates, *On Regimen*

[11] People do not understand how to examine invisible things (*aphanea*) on the basis of visible ones. For although they are using arts that are similar to human nature, they do not know this. For the mind of the gods taught them to imitate their own activities by knowing what they do, but not by knowing what they imitate. [. . .] [12] But I shall show that the manifest arts are similar to human affections, both manifest ones and not manifest ones. Divination is like this: for it knows things that are not mani-

νώσκει, καὶ τοῖσιν ἀφανέσι τὰ φανερά, καὶ τοῖσιν
ἐοῦσι τὰ μέλλοντα, καὶ τοῖσιν ἀποθανοῦσι τὰ ζῶντα,
καὶ τοῖσιν ἀσυνέτοισι συνιᾶσιν, ὁ μὲν εἰδὼς αἰεὶ ὀρθῶς, ὁ δὲ μὴ εἰδὼς ἄλλοτε ἄλλως. φύσιν ἀνθρώπου
καὶ βίον ταῦτα μιμεῖται· ἀνὴρ γυναικὶ συγγενόμενος
παιδίον ἐποίησε· τῷ φανερῷ τὸ ἄδηλον γινώσκει ὅτι
οὕτως ἔσται. γνώμη ἀνθρώπου ἀφανὴς γινώσκουσα
τὰ φανερά, ἐκ παιδὸς ἐς ἄνδρα μεθίσταται· τῷ ἐόντι
τὸ μέλλον γινώσκει [. . .].

Diagnosis: The Search for the Cause (T15–T17)

T15 (≠ DK) Hipp. *Flat.* 1.4

ἐν δὲ δή τι τῶν τοιούτων ἐστὶν τόδε· τί ποτε τὸ αἴτιόν
ἐστι τῶν νούσων καὶ τίς ἀρχὴ καὶ πηγὴ γίνεται τῶν
ἐν τῷ σώματι κακῶν; εἰ γάρ τις εἰδείη τὴν αἰτίην τοῦ
νοσήματος, οἷός τ᾽ ἂν εἴη τὰ συμφέροντα προσφέρειν
τῷ σώματι ἐκ τῶν ἐναντίων ἐπιστάμενος τῷ νοσήματι.
αὕτη γὰρ ἡ ἰητρικὴ μάλιστα κατὰ φύσιν ἐστίν.

T16 (≠ DK) Hipp. *Art.* 6.3–4

[. . .] οὐκ ἔστιν ἔτι οὐδενὶ τῶν ἄνευ ἰητροῦ ὑγιαζο-
μένων τὸ αὐτόματον αἰτιήσασθαι ὀρθῷ λόγῳ. τὸ μὲν
γὰρ αὐτόματον οὐδὲν φαίνεται ἐὸν ἐλεγχόμενον· πᾶν
γὰρ τὸ γινόμενον διά τι εὑρίσκοιτ᾽ ἂν γινόμενον, καὶ

fest by means of ones that are manifest, and things that are manifest by means of ones that are not manifest, and things of the future by means of ones of the present, and things that are living by means of ones that are dead; and they [i.e. the diviners] understand by means of what is not understood—he who knows, always correctly; he who does not know, sometimes correctly, sometimes not. All this imitates a human being's nature and life. A man has intercourse with a woman and makes a child; by means of what is manifest, he knows what is invisible: that it will be like this. A human being's thought, not manifest, knowing manifest things, passes from the child to the man; by means of the present, it knows the future [. . .].

Diagnosis: The Search for the Cause (T15–T17)

T15 (≠ DK) Hippocrates, *On Breaths*

One of the questions of this sort [scil. particularly difficult ones] is this: what is the cause of diseases, and what is the origin and source of the ills in the body? For if someone knew the cause of a disease, he would be able to administer to the body what is beneficial to it by opposing the disease on the basis of the contraries. For this is the medicine that is most in accord with nature.

T16 (≠ DK) Hippocrates, *On the Art*

[. . .] it is not possible either, for anyone who recovers his health without a doctor, to assign the cause by a correct reasoning to spontaneity. For the spontaneous, if it is examined closely, reveals itself to be nothing: for everything

ἐν τῷ διά τι τὸ αὐτόματον οὐ φαίνεται οὐσίην ἔχον
οὐδεμίαν ἀλλ᾽ ἢ ὄνομα· ἡ δὲ ἰητρικὴ καὶ ἐν τοῖσι διά
τι καὶ ἐν τοῖσι προνοευμένοισι φαίνεταί τε καὶ φα-
νεῖται αἰεὶ οὐσίην ἔχουσα.

T17 (≠ DK) Hipp. *Vet. med.* 19.3–4

δεῖ δὲ δήπου ταῦτα αἴτια ἑκάστου ἡγεῖσθαι εἶναι, ὧν
παρεόντων μὲν τοιουτότροπον ἀνάγκη γίνεσθαι, μετα-
βαλλόντων δ᾽ ἐς ἄλλην κρῆσιν παύεσθαι. ὁκόσα τε
οὖν ἀπ᾽ αὐτῆς τῆς θέρμης εἰλικρινέος ἢ ψύξιος γίνεται καὶ μὴ μετέχει ἄλλης δυνάμιος μηδεμιῆς, οὕτω
παύοιτ᾽ ἂν ὅταν μεταβάλλῃ ἐκ τοῦ θερμοῦ ἐς τὸ ψυχρὸν καὶ ἐκ τοῦ ψυχροῦ ἐς τὸ θερμόν.

The Natural Origin of Diseases (T18)

T18 (≠ DK) Hipp. *Morb. sacr.*

a 1.1

περὶ τῆς ἱερῆς νούσου καλεομένης ὧδε ἔχει· οὐδέν τί
μοι δοκεῖ τῶν ἄλλων θειοτέρη εἶναι νούσων οὐδὲ ἱε-
ρωτέρη, ἀλλὰ φύσιν μὲν ἔχει καὶ τὰ λοιπὰ νοσήματα
ὅθεν γίνεται, φύσιν δὲ αὕτη καὶ πρόφασιν. οἱ δ᾽ ἄνθρωποι ἐνόμισαν θεῖόν τι πρῆγμα εἶναι ὑπὸ ἀπειρίης
καὶ θαυμασιότητος ὅτι οὐδὲν ἔοικεν ἑτέροισι.

that happens is found to happen because of some thing (*dia ti*), and, with this cause, the spontaneous reveals itself not to possess any reality and to be merely a name. But medicine, with its causes and prognoses, reveals itself, and always will reveal itself, to possess reality.

T17 (≠ DK) Hippocrates, *Ancient Medicine*

It is surely necessary to consider that the causes of each phenomenon are those factors whose presence necessarily produces a condition of this sort [scil. a flux of the throat], whereas it ceases when they change so as to create a different mixture. So all the conditions that are produced by pure heat or cold and have no share in any other power will cease in this way, when a change occurs from hot to cold and from cold to hot.

The Natural Origin of Diseases (T18)

T18 (≠ DK) Hippocrates, *On the Sacred Disease*

a

Regarding the so-called 'sacred' disease [cf. **T5**], this is how it is: it does not seem to me to be at all more divine than other diseases nor more sacred, but just as the other diseases have a nature from which they arise, so too this disease has a nature and a cause (*prophasis*). But people thought that it is something divine on account of their inexperience and their astonishment at the fact that it does not at all resemble the other ones.

b [2.1–2, c. 5 Jones]

τὸ δὲ νόσημα τοῦτο οὐδέν τί μοι δοκεῖ θειότερον εἶναι
τῶν λοιπῶν, ἀλλὰ φύσιν μὲν ἔχειν καὶ τἆλλα νοσήματα ὅθεν ἕκαστα γίνεται, φύσιν δὲ τοῦτο καὶ πρόφασιν, καὶ ἀπὸ ταὐτοῦ θεῖον γίνεσθαι ἀφ᾿ ὅτευ καὶ
τἆλλα πάντα, καὶ ἰητὸν εἶναι καὶ οὐδὲν ἧσσον ἑτέρων
ὅ τι ἂν μὴ ἤδη ὑπὸ χρόνου πολλοῦ καταβεβιασμένον
ᾖ ὥστε ἤδη ἰσχυρότερον εἶναι τῶν φαρμάκων τῶν
προσφερομένων. [2] ἄρχεται δὲ ὥσπερ καὶ τἆλλα νοσήματα κατὰ γένος.

c [18, c. 21 Jones]

αὕτη δὲ ἡ νοῦσος ἡ ἱερὴ καλεομένη ἀπὸ τῶν αὐτῶν
προφασίων γίνεται ἀφ᾿ ὧν καὶ αἱ λοιπαί, ἀπὸ τῶν
προσιόντων καὶ ἀπιόντων, καὶ ψύχεος καὶ ἡλίου καὶ
πνευμάτων μεταβαλλομένων τε καὶ οὐδέποτε ἀτρεμι-
ζόντων. ταῦτα δ᾿ ἐστὶ θεῖα ὥστε μὴ δεῖν[1] ἀποκρίνοντα
τὸ νόσημα θειότερον τῶν λοιπῶν νομίζειν, ἀλλὰ
πάντα θεῖα καὶ πάντα ἀνθρώπινα· φύσιν δὲ ἕκαστον
ἔχει καὶ δύναμιν ἐφ᾿ ἑωυτοῦ, καὶ οὐδὲν ἄπορόν ἐστιν
οὐδ᾿ ἀμήχανον.

---

[1] μηδὲν mss., corr. Ermerins

b

It seems to me that this disease is not in any regard more divine than the others, but just as the other diseases have a nature from which each one arises, this one has a nature and a cause, and it is divine for the same reason as all the others, and it can be treated not less than the others, unless it has acquired such force by the passage of much time that it is already stronger than the remedies that are applied to it. But it has its origin, like the other diseases, from within the family.

c

This disease, which is called 'sacred,' comes from the same causes as all the other ones come from, viz. what penetrates in and what goes out [scil. from the body], the cold, the sun, and the winds that change and are never at rest. These things are divine, so that we should not separate off this disease and consider it to be more divine than the other ones: instead, all of them are divine and all of them are human. Each one has a nature and a power of its own, and none is without a way of escape or a means of salvation.

The Multiplicity of Relevant Factors (T19–T22)

T19 (≠ DK) Hipp. *Nat. hom.* 2

τῶν δὲ ἰητρῶν οἱ μέν τινες λέγουσιν ὡς ὥνθρωπος
αἷμά ἐστιν, οἱ δὲ αὐτῶν χολήν φασιν εἶναι τὸν ἄνθρωπον, ἔνιοι δέ τινες φλέγμα· ἐπίλογον δὲ ποιέονται
καὶ οὗτοι πάντες τὸν αὐτόν· ἐν γὰρ εἶναί φασιν, ὅ τι
ἕκαστος αὐτῶν βούλεται ὀνομάσας, καὶ τοῦτο μεταλ-
λάσσειν τὴν ἰδέην καὶ τὴν δύναμιν, ἀναγκαζόμενον
ὑπό τε τοῦ θερμοῦ καὶ τοῦ ψυχροῦ, καὶ γίνεσθαι
γλυκὺ καὶ πικρὸν καὶ λευκὸν καὶ μέλαν καὶ παντοῖον.
ἐμοὶ δὲ οὐδέν τι δοκεῖ ταῦτα οὕτως ἔχειν. οἱ μὲν οὖν
πλεῖστοι τοιαῦτά τινα ἢ ὅτι ἐγγύτατα τούτων ἀποφαί-
νονται, ἐγὼ δέ φημι, εἰ ἓν ἦν ὥνθρωπος, οὐδέποτ᾽ ἂν
ἤλγει· οὐδὲ γὰρ ἂν ἦν ὑπ᾽ ὅτευ ἀλγήσειεν ἓν ἐόν· εἰ
δ᾽ οὖν καὶ ἀλγήσειεν, ἀνάγκη καὶ τὸ ἰώμενον ἓν εἶναι·
νῦν δὲ πολλά· πολλὰ γάρ ἐστιν ἐν τῷ σώματι ἐνε-
όντα, ἅ, ὅταν ὑπ᾽ ἀλλήλων παρὰ φύσιν θερμαίνηταί
τε καὶ ψύχηται, καὶ ξηραίνηται καὶ ὑγραίνηται, νούσους τίκτει· ὥστε πολλαὶ μὲν ἰδέαι τῶν νοσημάτων,
πολλὴ δὲ ἡ ἴησίς ἐστιν.

T20 (≠ DK) Hipp. *Vet. med.* 15

ἀπορέω δ᾽ ἔγωγε οἱ [. . .] ἄγοντες ἐκ ταύτης τῆς ὁδοῦ
ἐπὶ ὑπόθεσιν τὴν τέχνην, τίνα ποτὲ τρόπον θερα-
πεύουσι τοὺς ἀνθρώπους ὥσπερ ὑποτίθενται· οὐ γάρ
ἐστιν αὐτοῖσιν, οἶμαι, ἐξευρημένον αὐτό τι ἐφ᾽ ἑωυτοῦ

The Multiplicity of Relevant Factors (T19–T22)

T19 (≠ DK) Hippocrates, *On the Nature of Man*

Among doctors, some say that a human is blood, others say that a human is bile, and some say phlegm. These too [scil. like the natural philosophers; cf. **T6**] all draw the same conclusion. For they say that he is one thing, whatever name each of them wants to give it, and that this thing undergoes a change in form and power when it is constrained by the hot and cold, and that it becomes sweet and bitter, white and black, and of all sorts. But it does not seem to me that this is how things are in any case. Well, most of them make assertions of this kind or very similar to these. But I myself say that if a human were one he would never suffer, for there would never be anything because of which he could suffer, being one; and even if he did suffer, the remedy too would necessarily have to be one. But as it is there are many of them: for there exist many things in the body which generate diseases when against nature they are heated and cooled by each other, and are dried and moistened; so that there exist many forms of diseases, and many ways of treating them.

T20 (≠ DK) Hippocrates, *Ancient Medicine*

I myself cannot understand: in what way do those people [. . .] who lead our art away from this method [scil. that of ancient medicine; cf. **T7**] toward a postulate (*hupothesis*) treat men in conformity with what they postulate? For I do not think that they have discovered something that is

353

θερμὸν ἢ ψυχρὸν ἢ ξηρὸν ἢ ὑγρὸν μηδενὶ ἄλλῳ εἴδει
κοινωνέον. ἀλλ᾽ οἶμαι ἔγωγε ταῦτα βρώματα καὶ
πόματα αὐτοῖσιν ὑπάρχειν οἷσι πάντες χρεώμεθα·
προστιθέασι δὲ τῷ μὲν εἶναι θερμῷ, τῷ δὲ ψυχρῷ, τῷ
δὲ ξηρῷ, τῷ δὲ ὑγρῷ· ἐπεὶ ἐκεῖνό γε ἄπορον προσ-
τάξαι τῷ κάμνοντι θερμόν τι προσενέγκασθαι· εὐθὺς
γὰρ ἐρωτήσει· τί; ὥστε ληρεῖν ἀνάγκη ἢ ἐς τούτων τι
τῶν γινωσκομένων καταφεύγειν.

T21 (≠ DK) Hipp. *Loc. Hom.* 41.1–2

[1] ἰητρικὴν οὐ δυνατόν ἐστι ταχὺ μαθεῖν διὰ τόδε,
ὅτι ἀδύνατόν ἐστι καθεστηκός τι ἐν αὐτῇ σόφισμα
γενέσθαι, οἷον ὁ τὸ γράφειν ἕνα τρόπον μαθὼν ὃν
διδάσκουσι, πάντα ἐπίσταται· καὶ οἱ ἐπιστάμενοι
πάντες ὁμοίως[1] διὰ τόδε, ὅτι τὸ αὐτὸ καὶ ὁμοίως ποι-
εύμενον νῦν τε καὶ οὐ νῦν οὐκ ἂν τὸ ὑπεναντίον γένοιτο, ἀλλ᾽ αἰεὶ ἐνδυκέως ὅμοιόν ἐστι, καὶ οὐ δεῖ και-
ροῦ. [2] ἡ δὲ ἰητρικὴ νῦν τε καὶ αὐτίκα οὐ τὸ αὐτὸ
ποιεῖ, καὶ πρὸς τὸν αὐτὸν ὑπεναντία ποιεῖ, καὶ ταῦτα
ὑπεναντία σφίσιν ἑωυτοῖσι.

---

[1] ὁμοίως ‹γράφουσι› Ermerins

T22 (≠ DK) Hipp. *Epid.* 1.23

τὰ δὲ περὶ τὰ νοσήματα, ἐξ ὧν διεγινώσκομεν, μαθόν-
τες ἐκ τῆς κοινῆς φύσιος ἁπάντων καὶ τῆς ἰδίης ἑκάστου, ἐκ τοῦ νοσήματος, ἐκ τοῦ νοσέοντος, ἐκ τῶν

hot in itself or cold, or dry or moist, without participating in any other form. But I myself think that they have available the same food and drinks as the ones we all use; but they add that this one is hot, that other one cold, that other one dry, that other one wet, since it would be impossible to prescribe to a patient that he consume something hot—for at once he will ask, "What?" So that either they must be speaking nonsense or else they must have recourse to one of these substances that are known.

T21 (≠ DK) Hippocrates, *On Places in Man*

[1] The reason why it is not possible to learn medicine quickly is that it is impossible for it to produce an established routine (*sophisma*), as someone who is learning how to write in the one way that they have for teaching it knows everything [scil. one must know]; and all those who know [scil. do it] in the same way for the reason that what is done in the same way now and at another time would not become the opposite, but it is always consistently similar and does not depend upon the particular circumstance (*kairos*). [2] But medicine does not proceed in the same way at present and afterward, and it does things that are opposite with regard to the same person, and the same things that are opposite to themselves.

T22 (≠ DK) Hippocrates, *Epidemics*

As for the circumstances concerning diseases from which we establish a diagnosis, we derive our knowledge from the following sources: from the nature that is in common to all people and the individual nature of each person,

προσφερομένων, ἐκ τοῦ προσφέροντος—ἐπὶ τὸ ῥᾷον
γὰρ καὶ χαλεπώτερον ἐκ τούτων –, ἐκ τῆς καταστά-
σιος ὅλης καὶ κατὰ μέρεα τῶν οὐρανίων καὶ χώρης
ἑκάστης, ἐκ τοῦ ἔθεος, ἐκ τῆς διαίτης, ἐκ τῶν ἐπιτη-
δευμάτων, ἐκ τῆς ἡλικίης ἑκάστου, λόγοισι, τρόποισι,
σιγῇ, διανοήμασιν, ὕπνοισιν, οὐχ ὕπνοισιν, ἐνυπνί-
οισι, οἵοισι καὶ ὅτε, τιλμοῖσι, κνησμοῖσι, δάκρυσιν,
ἐκ τῶν παροξυσμῶν, διαχωρήμασιν, οὔροισιν, πτυ-
άλοισιν, ἐμέτοισι, καὶ ὅσαι ἐξ οἵων ἐς οἷα διαδοχαὶ
νοσημάτων καὶ ἀποστάσιες ἐπὶ τὸ ὀλέθριον καὶ κρί-
σιμον, ἱδρώς, ῥῖγος, ψύξις, βήξ, πταρμοί, λυγμοί,
πνεύματα, ἐρεύξιες, φῦσαι, σιγῶσαι, ψοφώδεες,
αἱμορραγίαι, αἱμορροΐδες. ἐκ τούτων καὶ ὅσα διὰ τούτων σκεπτέον.

Human Physiology (T23–T31)
The Brain (T23)

T23 (> 24 A11, 64 C3a) Hipp. *Morb. sacr.* 3, 14, 16–17

[3.1, c. 6 Jones] ἀλλὰ γὰρ αἴτιος ὁ ἐγκέφαλος τούτου
τοῦ πάθεος ὥσπερ τῶν ἄλλων νοσημάτων τῶν μεγί-
στων. [. . .]
[14.1–4, c. 17 Jones] εἰδέναι δὲ χρὴ τοὺς ἀνθρώπους ὅτι
ἐξ οὐδενὸς ἡμῖν καὶ ἡδοναὶ γίνονται καὶ εὐφροσύναι
καὶ γέλωτες καὶ παιδιαὶ ἢ ἐντεῦθεν, ὅθεν καὶ λῦπαι
καὶ ἀνίαι καὶ δυσφροσύναι καὶ κλαυθμοί. καὶ τούτῳ
φρονέομεν μάλιστα καὶ νοέομεν καὶ βλέπομεν καὶ

from the disease, from the patient, from the prescriptions, from the prescriber—for an easier or more difficult [course of illness] depends upon that –, from the general and particular condition of the celestial phenomena and of each country, from the custom, from the way of life, from the activities, from the age of each one, in terms of discourses, personalities, silence, thoughts, sleep, lack of sleep, dreams (of what sort and when), plucking, scratching, weeping, from paroxysms, defecations, urines, sputa, regurgitations, and all the sequences of diseases (from which [scil. phases] to which ones) and the deviations toward fatal conditions and crises, sweat, shivering, cold, cough, sneezes, hiccups, kinds of breaths, eructations, flatulence (silent, noisy), hemorrhages, hemorrhoids. The examination must be performed on the basis of these phenomena and of everything that occurs because of them.

Human Physiology (T23–T31)
The Brain (T23)

T23 (⟩ 24 A11, 64 C3a) Hippocrates, *On the Sacred Disease*

[3.1] The cause of this affection [i.e. the 'sacred' disease, cf. **T5, T18**], as of the other diseases that are most severe, is the brain. [. . .] [cf. **ALCM. D19**]

[14.1–4] People ought to know that it is from no other part [scil. than from the brain] that our pleasures, joys, laughter, and amusements come, and our distress, pains, sorrow, and weeping. And it is by this that we think most of all, reflect, see, hear, distinguish the ugly from the beautiful,

ἀκούομεν καὶ διαγινώσκομεν τά τε αἰσχρὰ καὶ τὰ
καλὰ καὶ τὰ κακὰ καὶ τἀγαθὰ καὶ ἡδέα καὶ ἀηδέα, τὰ
μὲν νόμῳ διακρίνοντες, τὰ δὲ τῷ συμφέροντι αἰσθα-
νόμενοι, τοτὲ δὲ καὶ τὰς ἡδονὰς καὶ τὰς ἀηδίας τοῖσι
καιροῖσι διαγινώσκοντες· καὶ οὐ ταὐτὰ ἀρέσκει ἡμῖν.
τῷ δ᾽ αὐτῷ τούτῳ καὶ μαινόμεθα καὶ παραφρονέομεν,
καὶ δείματα καὶ φόβοι παρίστανται ἡμῖν τὰ μὲν
νύκτωρ, τὰ δὲ καὶ μεθ᾽ ἡμέρην, καὶ ἐνύπνια καὶ πλά-
νοι ἄκαιροι, καὶ φροντίδες οὐχ ἱκνεύμεναι, καὶ ἀγνω-
σίαι τῶν καθεστεώτων καὶ ἀηθίαι. καὶ ταῦτα πάσχο-
μεν ἀπὸ τοῦ ἐγκεφάλου πάντα, ὅταν οὗτος μὴ ὑγιαίνῃ,
ἀλλ᾽ ἢ θερμότερος τῆς φύσιος γένηται ἢ ψυχρότερος
ἢ ὑγρότερος ἢ ξηρότερος, ἤ τι ἄλλο πεπόνθῃ πάθος
παρὰ τὴν φύσιν ὃ μὴ ἐώθει. [. . .]
[16–17, c. 19–20 Jones] κατὰ ταῦτα νομίζω τὸν ἐγκέφαλον δύναμιν πλείστην ἔχειν ἐν τῷ ἀνθρώπῳ· οὗτος
γὰρ ἡμῖν ἐστι τῶν ἀπὸ τοῦ ἠέρος γινομένων ἑρμη-
νεύς, ἢν ὑγιαίνων τυγχάνῃ· τὴν δὲ φρόνησιν αὐτῷ ὁ
ἀὴρ παρέχεται. οἱ δ᾽ ὀφθαλμοὶ καὶ τὰ ὦτα καὶ ἡ
γλῶσσα καὶ αἱ χεῖρες καὶ οἱ πόδες οἷα ἂν ὁ ἐγκέφαλος γινώσκῃ, τοιαῦτα ὑπηρετέουσι. γίνεται γὰρ ἐν
ἅπαντι τῷ σώματι τῆς †φρονήσιος†,[1] τέως ἂν μετέχῃ
τοῦ ἠέρος. ἐς δὲ τὴν σύνεσιν ὁ ἐγκέφαλός ἐστιν ὁ
διαγγέλλων· ὅταν γὰρ σπάσῃ τὸ πνεῦμα ὤνθρωπος
ἐς ἑωυτόν, ἐς τὸν ἐγκέφαλον πρῶτον ἀφικνεῖται καὶ
οὕτως ἐς τὸ λοιπὸν σῶμα σκίδναται ὁ ἀὴρ καταλελοι-

[1] κινήσιος Jouanna

the bad from the good, and the pleasant from the unpleasant, when we discriminate the ones in terms of our custom, perceive others in terms of their utility, and sometimes discern pleasures and displeasures in terms of the circumstances; and the same things are not pleasing to us. And it is by the same [scil. organ] that we go mad and become delirious, that terrors and fears seize us, some at night, some during the day, as well as dreams and somnambulism, pointless anxieties, failure to recognize objects that are present, and uncharacteristic behavior. And all these sufferings have their origin in the brain when it is not healthy but has become either warmer or colder or moister or dryer than its nature, or has undergone some other affection contrary to its nature to which it was not accustomed. [. . .]

[16–17] It is for these reasons that I think that the brain is that part in a human being that possesses the greatest power. For when it is healthy, it is this that is the interpreter for us of what comes from the air. Now, air supplies it with thought; by contrast, the eyes, ears, tongue, hands, and feet merely perform what the brain conceives. For there exists everywhere in the body †thought† to the degree that it has a share in air.[1] But with regard to understanding, the brain is the messenger. For when a human draws breath into himself, the air reaches his brain first, and in this way the air is diffused throughout the rest of

[1] Jouanna suggests that "motion" should be read instead of "thought."

πῶς· ἐν τῷ ἐγκεφάλῳ ἑωυτοῦ τὴν ἀκμὴν καὶ ὅ τι ἂν ᾖ
φρόνιμόν τε καὶ γνώμην ἔχον. εἰ γὰρ ἐς τὸ σῶμα
πρῶτον ἀφικνεῖτο καὶ ὕστερον ἐς τὸν ἐγκέφαλον, ἐν
τῇσι σαρξὶ καὶ ἐν τῇσι φλεψὶ καταλελοιπὼς τὴν διά-
γνωσιν, ἐς τὸν ἐγκέφαλον ἂν ᾔει θερμὸς ἐὼν καὶ οὐκ
ἀκραιφνής, ἀλλὰ ἐπιμεμιγμένος τῇ ἰκμάδι τῇ ἀπό τε
τῶν σαρκῶν καὶ τοῦ αἵματος, ὥστε μηκέτι εἶναι ἀκρι-
βής. [c. 20 Jones] διότι φημὶ τὸν ἐγκέφαλον εἶναι τὸν
ἑρμηνεύοντα τὴν ξύνεσιν. [. . .] ὥσπερ οὖν καὶ τῆς
φρονήσιος² τοῦ ἠέρος πρῶτος αἰσθάνεται τῶν ἐν τῷ
σώματι ἐόντων, οὕτω καὶ ἤν τις μεταβολὴ ἰσχυρὴ
γένηται ἐν τῷ ἠέρι ὑπὸ τῶν ὡρέων καὶ αὐτὸς ἑωυτοῦ
διάφορος γένηται, ὁ ἐγκέφαλος πρῶτος αἰσθάνεται.
διότι καὶ τὰ νοσήματα ἐς αὐτὸν ἐμπίπτειν φημὶ
ὀξύτατα καὶ μέγιστα καὶ θανατωδέστατα καὶ δυσκρι-
τώτατα τοῖσιν ἀπείροισιν.

² τῆς φρονήσιος secl. Jouanna

The Vessels (T24)

T24 (≠ DK) Hipp. *Nat. hom.* 11

αἱ παχύταται δὲ τῶν φλεβῶν ὧδε πεφύκασιν· τέσ-
σερα ζεύγεά ἐστιν ἐν τῷ σώματι, καὶ ἐν μὲν αὐτῶν
ἀπὸ τῆς κεφαλῆς ὄπισθεν, διὰ τοῦ αὐχένος [. . .] ἐς
τοὺς πόδας ἀφήκει. [. . .] αἱ δ' ἕτεραι φλέβες ἐκ τῆς
κεφαλῆς παρὰ τὰ ὦτα διὰ τοῦ αὐχένος [. . .] ἐς τοὺς
ὄρχιας καὶ τοὺς μηροὺς [. . .] καὶ τοὺς πόδας. [. . .] αἱ
δὲ τρίται φλέβες ἐκ τῶν κροτάφων [. . .] ἔπειτα συμ-

the body, after having left behind in the brain the best part of itself, i.e. what thinks and possesses intelligence. For if the air reached the body first and the brain afterward, it would be after having left behind discernment in the flesh and vessels that it would arrive at the brain, in a hot and impure condition, mixed with the moisture coming from both the flesh and the blood, so that it would no longer be precise. That is why I say that the brain is the interpreter of understanding. [. . .] So just as the brain is the first of all the things in the body to perceive the thought that comes from the air, so too if some powerful change occurs in the air by the effect of the seasons and this becomes different from itself, the brain is the first thing to perceive this. That is why I say that the diseases that are the most acute, the most severe, the most deadly, and the most difficult to judge for the inexperienced are the ones that befall it.

The Vessels (T24)

T24 (≠ DK) Hippocrates, *On the Nature of Man*

The largest vessels are arranged by nature in the following way. There are four pairs in the body: the first pair from the back of the head, through the neck [. . .] arrives at the feet. [. . .] The second vessels from the head, along the ears, through the neck [. . .] to the testicles and thighs [. . .] to the feet. [. . .] The third vessels from the temples [. . .]

φέρονται ἐς τὸν πλεύμονα [. . .] καὶ ἡ μὲν [. . .] καὶ ἐς
τὸν σπλῆνα καὶ ἐς τὸν νεφρόν, ἡ δὲ [. . .] καὶ ἐς τὸ
ἧπαρ καὶ ἐς τὸν νεφρόν, τελευτῶσι δὲ ἐς τὸν ἀρχὸν
αὗται ἑκάτεραι. αἱ δὲ τέταρται ἀπὸ τοῦ ἔμπροσθεν τῆς
κεφαλῆς καὶ τῶν ὀφθαλμῶν ὑπὸ τὸν αὐχένα καὶ τὰς
κληῖδας, ἔπειτα δὲ [. . .] ἐς [. . .] τοὺς δακτύλους, ἔπειτα
ἀπὸ τῶν δακτύλων πάλιν [. . .] ἄνω ἐς τὰς συγκαμπάς,
καὶ [. . .] ἡ μὲν ἐς τὸν σπλῆνα ἀφικνεῖται, ἡ δὲ ἐς τὸ
ἧπαρ, ἔπειτα [. . .] ἐς τὸ αἰδοῖον τελευτῶσιν ἀμφότε-
ραι.

Reproduction (T25–T31)
An Argument Against Monism in General (T25)

T25 (≠ DK) Hipp. *Nat. hom.* 3

πρῶτον μὲν οὖν ἀνάγκη τὴν γένεσιν γενέσθαι μὴ ἀφ᾽
ἑνός· πῶς γὰρ ἂν ἔν γ᾽ ἐόν τι γεννήσειεν, εἰ μή τινι
μιχθείη; εἶτ᾽ οὐδὲ ἢν[1] μὴ ὁμόφυλα ἐόντα μίσγηται καὶ
τὴν αὐτὴν ἔχοντα δύναμιν γέννα[2] οὐδ᾽ ἂν μία[3] συν-
τελέοιτο. καὶ πάλιν, εἰ μὴ τὸ θερμὸν τῷ ψυχρῷ καὶ τὸ
ξηρὸν τῷ ὑγρῷ μετρίως πρὸς ἄλληλα ἕξει καὶ ἴσως,
ἀλλὰ τὸ ἕτερον τοῦ ἑτέρου πολλὸν προέξει καὶ τὸ
ἰσχυρότερον τοῦ ἀσθενεστέρου, ἡ γένεσις οὐκ ἂν γένοιτο. ὥστε πῶς εἰκὸς ἀπὸ ἑνός τι γεννηθῆναι, ὅτε γε
οὐδ᾽ ἀπὸ τῶν πλειόνων γίνεται, ἢν μὴ τύχῃ καλῶς
ἔχοντα τῆς κρήσιος τῆς πρὸς ἄλληλα; [. . . = **T8**]

varias corruptelas in mss. sanarunt edd.   [1] εἶτ᾽ οὐδὲ ἢν
Jouanna   [2] γέννα Ermerins   [3] μία Wilamowitz

then converge toward the lung [. . .] and the one [. . .] arrives at the spleen and kidney, the other [. . .] at the liver and kidney; both of them end at the anus. The fourth from the front of the head and the eyes, under the neck and the collarbones, then [. . .] to the fingers, then from the fingers back [. . .] up to the armpits; and [. . .] the one arrives at the spleen, the other at the liver; then [. . .] they both end at the genital organ [cf. **DIOG. D27**].

Reproduction (T25–T31)
An Argument Against Monism in General (T25)

T25 (≠ DK) Hippocrates, *On the Nature of Man*

First of all, therefore, it is necessary that birth not occur from only one thing: for how could something that is only one engender something without mixing with something? And then, even if, without being akin, things mix together that have the same power (*dunamis*), they cannot engender and could not be united in one.[1] Again, if the hot and the cold, the dry and the moist are not in a relation that is proportionate and equal to each other, but rather the one is much greater than the other and the stronger than the weaker, then birth will not occur. So how is it plausible that something be engendered from only one thing, when nothing is born even from a plurality of things when they do not happen to be in a condition to mix properly with each other?

[1] This sentence has been considered obscure since Galen, and the text is suspect.

The Doctrine Called 'Pangenesis' (T26–T27)

T26 (≠ DK) Hipp. *Genit.*

a

[1.1] νόμος μὲν πάντα κρατύνει· ἡ δὲ γονὴ τοῦ ἀνδρὸς
ἔρχεται ἀπὸ παντὸς τοῦ ὑγροῦ τοῦ ἐν τῷ σώματι ἐόν-
τος τὸ ἰσχυρότατον ἀποκριθέν· τούτου δὲ ἱστόριον
τόδε, ὅτι ἀποκρίνεται τὸ ἰσχυρότατον, ὅτι ἐπὴν λα-
γνεύσωμεν σμικρὸν οὕτω μεθέντες, ἀσθενεῖς γινό-
μεθα.

b

[2.2] χωρεῖ γὰρ τὸ πλεῖστον ἀπὸ τῆς κεφαλῆς παρὰ
τὰ οὔατα ἐς τὸν νωτιαῖον μυελόν.

T27 (≠ DK) Hipp. *Aer.* 14.5

[. . . = **T31**] ὁ γὰρ γόνος πανταχόθεν ἔρχεται τοῦ
σώματος, ἀπό τε τῶν ὑγιηρῶν ὑγιηρὸς ἀπό τε τῶν
νοσερῶν νοσερός.

The Development of the Embryo (T28–T29)

T28 (≠ DK) Hipp. *Carn.* 6.3

τὸ δὲ παιδίον ἐν τῇ γαστρὶ συνέχον τὰ χείλεα μύζει
ἐκ τῶν μητρέων τῆς μητρὸς καὶ ἕλκει τήν τε τροφὴν
καὶ τὸ πνεῦμα τῇ καρδίῃ ἔσω· τοῦτο γὰρ θερμότατόν

The Doctrine Called 'Pangenesis' (T26–T27)

T26 (≠ DK) Hippocrates, *On Generation*

a

Law dominates all things; but as for the sperm of a man, it proceeds from all the moisture that exists in the body, the strongest part of it having separated out. There is evidence for the fact that it is the strongest part that separates out: after we have had sexual intercourse, even though what we have ejaculated is so little, we become weak.

b

The greatest part [scil. of the sperm] proceeds from the head along the ears into the spinal marrow.

T27 (≠ DK) Hippocrates, *Airs, Waters, Places*

[. . .] For the sperm comes from the whole body, what is healthy from the healthy places, what is sick from the sick ones.

The Development of the Embryo (T28–T29)

T28 (≠ DK) Hippocrates, *Fleshes*

The fetus in the womb, applying its lips, sucks and draws from its mother's uterus nourishment and breath (*pneuma*) to its heart inside. For it is this [i.e. its heart, or perhaps:

ἐστιν ἐν τῷ παιδίῳ, ὅταν περ ἡ μήτηρ ἀναπνέῃ·
τούτῳ[1] δὲ καὶ τῷ ἄλλῳ σώματι τὴν κίνησιν παρέχει
τὸ θερμὸν καὶ τοῖσιν ἄλλοισι πᾶσιν.

[1] τούτῳ Littré: τοῦτο V

T29 (≠ DK) Hipp. *Nat. puer.*

a

[17.1] ἡ δὲ σὰρξ αὐξομένη ὑπὸ τοῦ πνεύματος ἀρ-
θροῦται, καὶ ἔρχεται ἐν αὐτῇ ἕκαστον τὸ ὅμοιον ὡς τὸ
ὅμοιον, τὸ πυκνὸν ὡς τὸ πυκνόν, τὸ ἀραιὸν ὡς τὸ
ἀραιόν, τὸ ὑγρὸν ὡς τὸ ὑγρόν· καὶ ἕκαστον ἔρχεται
ἐς χώρην ἰδίην κατὰ τὸ συγγενές, ἀφ᾽ οὗ καὶ ἐγένετο,
καὶ ἅσσα ἀπὸ πυκνῶν ἐγένετο πυκνά ἐστι, καὶ ἅσσα
ἀπὸ ὑγρῶν ὑγρά.

b

[18.1] καὶ γέγονεν ἤδη παιδίον καὶ ἐς τοῦτο ἀφικνεῖται, τὸ μὲν θῆλυ ἐν τεσσεράκοντα ἡμέρῃσι καὶ δύο
τὸ μακρότατον, τὸ δὲ ἄρσεν ἐν τριήκοντα ἡμέρῃσι τὸ
μακρότατον.

c

[27.1] φημὶ γὰρ τὰ ἐν τῇ γῇ φυόμενα πάντα ζῆν ἀπὸ
τῆς γῆς τῆς ἰκμάδος, καὶ ὅκως ἂν ἡ γῆ ἔχῃ ἰκμάδος
ἐν ἑωυτῇ, οὕτω καὶ τὰ φυόμενα ἔχειν· οὕτω καὶ τὸ

the air] that is what is hottest in the fetus when the mother breathes in; and it is the heat that provides motion to it, as well as to the rest of the body and all other things.

T29 (≠ DK) Hippocrates, *Nature of the Child*

a

The flesh, growing under the effect of breath (*pneuma*), becomes articulated, and within it what is similar goes to what is similar, the dense to the dense, the rarefied to the rarefied, the moist to the moist; and each thing goes to its proper place in accordance with what is akin to it from which it arose, and everything that comes from dense things is dense, and everything that comes from moist things is moist [. . .].[1]

  [1] There follows a detailed enumeration of the articulation of the parts: bones, head, arms, legs, muscles, nose, ears, eyes, viscera.

b

And a fetus has already been formed and has arrived at this point, the female in forty-two days at most, the male in thirty days at most.

c

For I assert that everything that grows (*phuomena*) in the earth lives from the moisture (*ikmas*) that comes from the earth, and that the condition of what grows depends on

παιδίον ζῇ ἀπὸ τῆς μητρὸς ἐν τῇσι μήτρῃσι, καὶ
ὅκως ἂν ἡ μήτηρ ὑγιείης ἔχῃ, οὕτω καὶ τὸ παιδίον
ἔχει. ἢν δέ τις βούληται ἐννοεῖν τὰ ῥηθέντα ἀμφὶ τούτων ἐξ ἀρχῆς ἐς τέλος, εὑρήσει τὴν φύσιν πᾶσαν
παραπλησίην ἐοῦσαν τῶν τε ἐκ τῆς γῆς φυομένων
καὶ τὴν ἀνθρωπίνην.

Viability of the Fetus (T30)

T30 (≠ DK) Hipp. *Oct.* 9.2–3

αἱ μὲν οὖν ἡμέραι ⟨αἱ⟩[1] ἐπισημόταταί εἰσιν ἐν τοῖσι
πλείστοισιν αἵ τε πρῶται καὶ αἱ ἕβδομαι, πολλαὶ μὲν
περὶ νούσους, πολλαὶ δὲ καὶ τοῖσιν ἐμβρύοισι. [. . .]
ἐν δὲ τοῖσι μησὶ ταυτά τε καὶ ἐν τῇσιν ἡμέρῃσι γινόμενα ἔνεστι κατὰ λόγον [. . .]. ἐξ ὧν δὴ καὶ οἱ ἕβδο-
μοι μῆνες τῇσιν ἐν γαστρὶ ἐχούσῃσι τὰ ἔμβρυα ἐς
τὴν ἀρχὴν καθιστᾶσι τῆς τελειώσιος, τοῖσι δὲ παι-
δίοισιν ἑπταμήνοισιν ἐοῦσι καὶ ἄλλα διαφερόμενα
γίνονται ἐν τοῖσι σώμασι· καὶ οἱ ὀδόντες φαίνεσθαι
ἄρχονται ἐν τούτῳ τῷ χρόνῳ.

[1] ⟨αἱ⟩ Diller

Transmission of Acquired Characteristics (T31)

T31 (≠ DK) Hipp. *Aer.* 14.2–4

τούτων γὰρ οὐκ ἔστιν ἄλλο ἔθνος ὁμοίας τὰς κεφαλὰς
ἔχον οὐδέν· τὴν μὲν γὰρ ἀρχὴν ὁ νόμος αἰτιώτατος

that of the moisture that the earth contains within itself. In the same way, the fetus too lives from the mother in her uterus, and the condition of the fetus' health depends on the mother's. And if someone wishes to reflect from beginning to end about what I have said about these matters, he will find that the nature of everything [scil. that grows, *phusis*], both what grows from the earth and that of humans, is extremely similar.

Viability of the Fetus (T30)

T30 (≠ DK) Hippocrates, *On the Eight-Month Fetus*

The most significant days, in most cases, are the first and the seventh, in many cases regarding diseases, and in many regarding embryos. [. . .] The same thing applies to the months as to the days, proportionately [. . .]. It is for this reason that the seventh months, for pregnant women, bring the embryos to the beginning of their completion, and that significant changes occur in the bodies of seventh-month embryos, including the teeth, which begin to appear at this time.

Transmission of Acquired Characteristics (T31)

T31 (≠ DK) Hippocrates, *Airs, Waters, Places*

There is no other people [scil. than the Macrocephali] that have heads like theirs. For in the beginning it was a custom

369

ἐγένετο τοῦ μήκεος τῆς κεφαλῆς, νῦν δὲ καὶ ἡ φύσις ξυμβάλλεται τῷ νόμῳ· τοὺς γὰρ μακροτάτην ἔχοντας τὴν κεφαλὴν γενναιοτάτους ἡγεῦνται. [. . .] τοῦ δὲ χρόνου προϊόντος, ἐν φύσει ἐγένετο, ὥστε τὸν νόμον ‹μοῦνον›[1] μηκέτι ἀναγκάζειν. [. . . = **T27**].

[1] ‹μοῦνον› Jacoby

that was the principal cause for the length of their head, but now nature too collaborates with the custom. For they think that those who have the longest heads are the most noble, and their custom is the following: [. . .].[1] But as time went by, it became part of their nature, so that it is no longer the custom that constrains them.

[1] There follows a description of a procedure whereby the heads of newborn children are elongated.

30. THE DERVENI
PAPYRUS [DERV.]

The Derveni Papyrus, discovered in 1962 at Derveni, near Thessaloniki in Macedonia, and finally published in an authorized edition in 2006 (KPT, see Bibliography below), is one of the most extraordinary discoveries of the twentieth century regarding ancient Greek philosophy and religion. Unlike most of the texts presented in our collection, it needs some specific clarifications in order to be understood.

The bottom half of the papyrus roll was completely destroyed when it was burned, presumably at the time of the funeral of the man at whose burial site it was found; of the approximately twenty-six columns that remain, the top parts of most of them are quite legible, but others, especially at the beginning, have been reduced to numerous tiny fragments that are extremely difficult to combine and decipher. The papyrus itself is dated, on the basis of its writing style and especially of the archaeological context, to ca. 340/20 BC.

Most of the portion of the book that has survived consists of a series of quotations from an apparently mythical cosmogonic poem attributed to Orpheus (cf. **COSM. T12** and the following texts), followed each time by allegorical interpretations of these passages in terms of natural philosophy presenting striking resemblances to the several

known doctrines, especially those of Anaxagoras and of Diogenes of Apollonia. There are also etymological explanations, especially of the names of gods, and a passage from Heraclitus about the sun is cited and discussed. The first columns, which are very fragmentary, refer to sacrificial practices and beliefs about the Underworld. The author and title of the text are not known; the original allegorical commentary (reproduced on the papyrus) dates most probably from the beginning of the fourth century or indeed the end of the fifth BC; in this case not only the Orphic cosmogonic poem, but also its allegorical commentary, can be assigned with full legitimacy to the Pre-Platonic period.

For the text up to and including Col. VI, we rely upon the edition currently being finished by Valeria Piano (see Bibliography), for columns VII–XXVI upon that of K. Tsantsanoglou and G. M. Parássoglou in KTP.

Starting with Col. III, the top portions of the Derveni Papyrus can be reconstructed, at least partially, with great uncertainty but with varying degrees of confidence. But with regard to the initial columns, at the time of the preparation of this edition (2015), the small size and poor condition of the fragments that can be assigned to these do not permit collocations secure enough to allow a responsible reconstruction of the text preceding Col. III. Furthermore, on the basis of the preserved fragments, it is certain that before the column now numbered III there were originally more than two columns of text, and it cannot be excluded that between what are now Cols. III and IV there was a column referring to sacrifice that, depending on which papyrological hypothesis is adopted, is to be collocated either among the very first columns of text or

else between what are now Cols. III and IV. For papyrological and textual reasons, for Cols. III and IV we have
chosen to maintain the arrangement of the fragments proposed by the editors of the *editio princeps* (except for a
new join proposed by Piano in Col. IV and adopted by us).
But as for the portion of the papyrus roll preceding what
is now Col. III, we have decided, given the high degree of
uncertainty regarding its reconstruction, to refrain from
attempting to assign each of the surviving fragments from
this part of the papyrus to one or another of these first
columns, and instead we simply provide a list, arranged by
fragments, of the significant terms that can be read on the
papyrus fragments that can be identified as belonging to
this portion of the roll. The topics that can be discerned
on the basis of the full or partial words on these exiguous
scraps include justice (or Justice), the Erinyes, various
sacrificial practices, prayers, signs, water and fire, something that is natural, and human; these subjects are all
ones that recur in the later columns, and we provide cross-
references to signal the specific connections. For further
hypotheses of reconstruction for the beginning of the papyrus roll, see the papyrological chapter in the edition of
V. Piano.

In this chapter, as elsewhere, we make use of the following signs:

⟨xx⟩: editorial supplements to lacunae in the papyrus
(xx): transcription, in the translation, of Greek words in
   the papyrus
[xx]: editorial explanations
(?): readings in the papyrus or translations of the Greek
   that are uncertain

But in certain regards our editorial policy in this chapter differs from that used in our treatment of other texts transmitted on papyri:

1. We have decided in this case to maintain the arrangement in columns found in the papyrus (cf. volume 1, Note on.Editorial Principles and Translations) and to keep the iota adscripts (but not the spellings that result from assimilation, e.g. when *nu* becomes *gamma* before *kappa, gamma,* or *chi* in the papyrus).

2. We use double quotation marks ("xxx") for citations from the Orphic poem, for passages from other authors cited by the commentator, and for what people say or could have said, even if they did not actually say it; single quotation marks ('xxx') are used for all citations of a metalinguistic sort, including names that are the object of an explanation provided by the commentator himself.

3. We use three horizontal dashes (— — —) at the top or bottom of the Greek text of a column to indicate that the top or bottom edge of the papyrus as well as at least one line of text are lacking for that column; this is the case for the tops of all the columns up to and including Col. III and for the bottoms of all the columns.

BIBLIOGRAPHY

*Editions and Commentaries on the
Derveni Papyrus*

G. Betegh. *The Derveni Papyrus. Cosmology, Theology and Interpretation* (Cambridge, 2004).

T. Kouremenos, G. M. Parássoglou, and K. Tsantsanoglou. *The Derveni Papyrus. Edited with Introduction and*

Commentary, Studi e Testi per il Corpus dei Papiri Filosofici Greci e Latini 13 (Florence, 2006) (= KPT).

V. Piano. *L'inizio del papiro di Derveni: il rotolo e il testo* (provisional title), in preparation for Studi e Testi per il *Corpus dei Papiri Filosofici Greci e Latini,* 17 (Florence).

Edition of the Orphic Poem

A. Bernabé. In *Poetae Epici Graeci: Testimonia et Fragmenta. Pars II Orphicorum and orphicis similium: Testimonia et Fragmenta, Fasciculus I* (Munich-Leipzig, 2004), pp. 2–32; *Fasciculus III* (Berlin, 2007), pp. 183–269.

Collections of Studies

A. Laks and G. W. Most, eds. *Studies on the Derveni Papyrus* (Oxford, 1997; 2nd ed. 2001).

I. Papadopoulou and L. Muellner, eds. *Poetry as Initiation. The Center for Hellenic Studies Symposium on the Derveni Papyrus* (Cambridge, MA-London, 2014).

THE DERVENI
PAPYRUS [≠ DK][1]

[1] Text up to and including Col. VI ed. Piano; Cols. VII–XXVI ed. KPT; nos = Laks and Most

FRAGMENTS FROM THE COLS.
PRECEDING COL. III

Fr. G5

l. 3:]ε θεῖον τι
l. 4: δίκηι (vel Δίκηι, cf. Cols. III, IV)

Frr. G15+G6 (cf. Col. VI)

G15.2: Ἐριν[
G15.3: τιμῶσιν
G15.4+G6.1: χ]οαὶ σταγόσιν
G15.5+G6.2: τιμάς
G15.6+G6.3: ἑκαστο[.]ς

Fr. G7

l. 5: ἐπέθηκε[

THE DERVENI
PAPYRUS

FRAGMENTS FROM THE COLS.
PRECEDING COL. III

A list of the legible significant terms on the fragments belonging to the part of the papyrus preceding Col. III (the designation of the papyrus fragments is that of the editions of reference).

Frag. G5

line 3: **something divine** [or: some brimstone]
line 4: **to** [or: with] **justice** [or: Justice] (cf. cols. III, IV)

Frags. G15+G6 (cf. Col. VI)

G15.2: **Erinyes**
G15.3: **they honor**
G15.4+G6.1: **libations in drops**
G15.5+G6.2: **honors**
G15.6+G6.3: **each** [or: to each]

Frag. G7

line 5: **he added** [or: imposed]

l. 6:].τα σημαι[

Fr. F10

l. 4: τὰ σημε[ι- (cf. fr. F18+H45; etiam fr. G7.6)

Fr. F14

l. 1:].περ φυσικ[
l. 2: εὐχα[
l. 3: ανημμε[ν-

Frr. F18+H45

l. 2: π]υρὸς ὕδατος δ.[
l. 3: ἕκαστα σημει.[(cf. fr. F10; etiam fr. G7.6)
l. 4: καὶ τἆλλ’ ὅσα

Fr. F19

l. 1:]ιερ
l. 3: ἀνθρω[π

Col. III

— — —

3   ]... αιωc[. . . .]σι κατω[
δαίμ]ων γίνετα[ι ἑκά]στωι ἵλε[ως] ηαλ[ca. 9 litt.]ρ. ἡ
5 γὰρ Δί]κη ἐξώλεας [οὐ μ]έτεισι ἑκ[ὰς] Ἐρινύῳ[ν· καὶ
οἱ] δὲ

3 μυσ]τικαὶ ὡς .[Tsantsanoglou potius quam θυ]ηλαί, ὡς

line 6: **the things signified** (?)

Frag. F10

line 4: **the signs** (?) (cf. Frags. F18+H45; also Frag. G7.6)

Frag. F14

line 1: **natural** (?)
line 2: **prayer** (?)
line 3: **kindled** [or: fastened]

Frags. F18+H45

line 2: **of fire** (?) **of water**
line 3: **each sign** (?) (cf. Frag. F10; also Frag. G7.6)
line 4: **and all the other things that**

Frag. F19

line 1: **holy** (?)
line 3: **human** (?)

Col. III

. . . **below** . . . ⟨a personal de⟩**ity** (*daimôn*) **becomes for each person benevolent or** ⟨otherwise vindictive?⟩. ⟨**For Jus**⟩**tice does not pursue malefactors far from** [i.e. independently of?] **the Erinyes; and the deities**

.[Janko   fin. ὁ δὲ ἴδιος e.g. nos   4 ἴλε[ως Tsantsanoglou   ]ηᾳλ[Piano, ἢ ἄλ[λως ἀλάστω]ρ nos
     4–5 ἡ | [γὰρ Δί]κη KPT   5 ἐξώλεας Tsantsanoglou
[οὐ nos   μ]έτεισι Piano, νουθ]ετεῖ δι᾽ KPT   ἐκ[ὰς]
nos   Ἐρινύω[ν Tsantsanoglou   καὶ οἱ] δὲ Piano mon.
Battezzato qui οἱ] δὲ coni.

δ]αίμονες οἱ κατὰ [γῆς ο]ὐδέκοτ[(ε) . . . .]ρουσι [?
θεῶν ὑπηρέται δ̣[2–3 litt.]ι̣ πάντας υ[ca. 16 litt.]ι
εἰσὶν ὅπωσπερ ἀ[νδρὸς] ἀδίκου θ . . [ca. 17 litt.]νοι
αἰτίην [. ἔ]χουσι[

10   οἴους γ.[. .] . [

. .]υcτ[

— — —

6 ὑστε]ρο̣ῦσι vel ἐκχω]ρο̣ῦσι Piano, τ]ηροῦσι KPT

7 Δ[ίκη]ι̣ vel δ[ίκη]ι̣ coni. Piano, δ'[εἰσ]ὶ̣ KPT   8 ἀ[νδρὸς]
ἀδίκου Piano, ἄ[νδρες] ἄ̣δικοι ceteri   θ . . [Piano, an
θρά[σο- ?   9 [δ' ἔ]χουσι[Burkert fort. recte, [τ' ἔ]χουσι[
Tsantsanoglou

Col. IV

1   [.]ου ε.[   ]εων

ὁ κείμ[ενα] μεταθ̣[εὶς ca. 14 litt. ἐ]κδοῦναι

μᾶλλ[ον ἃ] σίνεται [ca. 17 litt.]τὰ τῆς τύχης
     γὰ̣[ρ]

οὐκ εἴ̣[α λα]μβάνειν. ἆρ' οὐ τα̣[κτὸς ὁ διὰ
     τό]νδε κόσμος;

5   κατὰ [ταῦτ]α Ἡράκλειτος μα[ρτυρόμενος] τ̣ὰ
     κοινὰ

κατ[αστρέ]φει τὰ ἴδ[ι]α, ὅσπερ ἴκελα̣ [ἱερῶι]
     λόγωι λέγων [ἔφη·]

"ἥλιο[ς ...]μου κατὰ φύσιν "ἀνθρω[πηΐου]
     ε̣ὖρος ποδός [ἐστι"],

τὸ μ[έγεθο]ς οὐχ ὑπερβάλλων. εἰ γά[ρ τι
     οὔ]ρους ἑ[ωυτοῦ]

(*daimones*) **under the earth never** ⟨delay? [or: with-draw]⟩ . . . **servants of the gods** ⟨for Justice? [or: justly]⟩ . . . **they all** . . . **they are like an unjust man's** . . . **they have the guilt** [or: responsibility] . . . **such as** (masculine plural) . . .

Col. IV

. . . **he** [i.e. the god? a name-giver?] **having displaced what lay** [scil. inert, or: what was established] . . . **to hand over rather what causes damage** . . . **for he did not allow it** [i.e. probably the world] **to admit the workings of chance. Is not the world** ⟨[scil. that is created] by him [i.e. probably the god]⟩ **ordered? In conformity with this, Heraclitus,** ⟨invoking the testimony of⟩ **what is shared in common** [scil. by all men], **overturns what belongs to each individual** [cf. HER. D2], **he who, saying things similar to a** ⟨holy⟩ **discourse, said, "The sun"** in accordance with the nature of the [perhaps: ⟨world?⟩] **"is of the breadth of a human foot,"** not **exceeding that size. For if it** ⟨exceeds⟩ **at all** ⟨its own

---

1 θ]εῶν KPT   4 οὐ τα[κτὸς ὁ διὰ τό]νδε Piano

5 [ταῦτ]α Tsantsanoglou-Parássoglou, [ταῦτ]ὰ ceteri

6 [ἱερῶι] Tsantsanoglou-Parássoglou, [ἀστρο]λόγωι KPT

7 ἥλιο[ς leg. Piano, ἥλι[ος ceteri   κόσ]μου Piano   an [ἔχει"],?

8 τὸ μ[έγεθο]ς KPT, τοὺ[ς οὔρου]ς Tsantsanoglou

ὑπερβαλε]ῖ, "Ἐρινύε[ς] νιν ἐξευρήσου[σι]·
τὰ δὲ] ὑπελάμ[βανε]

10 ὅπως μὴ εὖρος ὑπερ]βατὸν ποῆι κ[6–7 litt.]ạ
Δίκης[

].ι̣ θυο.[
]α Δίκης[
] μηνὶ τακ[τῶι
]....[.]ι̣ζ.[

— — —

9 ὑπερβαλε]ῖ Tsantsanoglou-Parássoglou   τὰ δὲ] nos
9–10 ὑπελάμ[βανε et Δίκης[Piano ex fr. F17
10 κ[ατὰ μέτρ]ạ tempt. Piano
13]. . . . [.]ι̣ζ.[Piano,] . . ι̣π̣αι̣ϲ̣ε[KPT

Col. V

1]δ̣[.]υ̣δ̣ει.[
χρη[στη]ριαζομ[   ].ọι.ε[
χρησ̣[τ]ηριάζον[ται   ] . [.] ..... [..]ι
αὐτοῖς πάριμεν [εἰς τὸ μα]ντεῖον ἐπερ[ω]τ̣ήσọντ[ες]
5 τῶμ μαντευομέν[ων ἕν]εκεν εἰ θέμι[ς προσ]δ̣ọκ̣ậν
ἐν Ἅιδου δεινά. τί ἀ[πισ]τοῦσι; οὐ γινώσ[κο]ν̣τ̣ε̣ς̣
ἐνύπνια
οὐδὲ τῶν ἄλλων πρ[α]γμάτων ἕκαστ[ον], διὰ ποίων
ἂν
παραδειγμάτων π[ι]στεύοιεν; ὑπό τ[ε γὰρ] ἁμαρ-
τ̓ί̓ης
καὶ [τ]ῆς ἄλλης ἡδον[ῆ]ς νενικημέν̣[οι, οὐ]
μ̣α̣ν̣θ[άνο]υσιν

384

limits,⟩ **"the Erinyes will find it out."** [cf. **HER. D89**]
He made ⟨this⟩ **supposition** ⟨in order that it not⟩ **make**
⟨its breadth⟩ **excessive . . . of Justice . . .** ⟨sacrifice⟩ **. . .**
of Justice . . . at the established month . . .

Col. V

. . . consulting [or: we consult] **an oracle . . . they con-**
sult an oracle . . . for [?] **them we enter into the**
oracular shrine (*manteion*) **in order to ask, for the**
sake of those who are consulting the oracle, if it
is licit to expect terrors in Hades. Why do they dis-
believe? Not understanding dreams or each of the
other real things, how could they believe on the ba-
sis of other examples? For, overcome by error and
by something else, pleasure [or: by the other pleasure],

---

1 Piano mon. Janko qui . . . . Ἄι]δου δειν[ὰ suppl. fort. recte,
]ηδε.[Tsantsanoglou   3 (προσ)τε]ταγμέ[νο]ι Tsantsanoglou

4 ἐπερ[ω]τήσοντ[ες Piano mon. Tsantsanoglou (qui ἐπερ[ω]-
τήσοντες leg.), ἐπερ[ω]τήσ[οντες KPT   5 μαντευομέν[ων
Janko, μαντευομένων Tsantsanoglou   εἰ θέμι[ς προσ]-
δοκᾶν Piano, εἰ θέμι[ς ἀπ]ιστῆσαι Ferrari, εἰ θέμι[ς ταῦτ]α
δρᾶν Tsantsanoglou, θεμι[. . .] . . ηδα[KPT   6 ἐν leg. Piano
mon. West, ἆρ' KPT, ἐξ Ferrari   γινώσ[κο]ντες ἐνύπνια
leg. Piano mon. Tsantsanoglou qui γινώσ[κοντες ἐ]νύπνια suppl.

7 πραγμάτων Tsantsanoglou   ἕκαστ[α Janko
8 ὑπὸ τ[ῆς] Janko   9–11 Tsantsanoglou

10 οὐδὲ] πιστεύουσι. ἀπ[ι]στίη δὲ κἀμα[θίη ταὐτόν· ἢν
         γὰρ]
     μὴ μα]νθάνωσι μη[δ]ὲ γινώ[σ]κωσ[ιν, οὐκ ἔστιν
         ὅπως]
     πιστεύσου]σιν καὶ ορ[
              ]ην ἀπιστί[ην
              ]φαίνεται [

— — —

12 πιστεύσου]σιν Tsantsanoglou   ὁρ[ῶντες Tsantsanoglou, ὁρ[ῶντες ἐνύπνια coni. Janko   13]ην ἀπιστί[ην KPT

Col. VI

ca. 8 litt. εὐ]χαὶ καὶ θυσ[ί]αι μ[ειλ]ίσσουσι τὰ[ς ψυ-
         χάς,]
ἐπ[αοιδὴ δ]ὲ μάγων δύν[α]ται δαίμονας ἐμ[ποδὼν]
γι[νομένο]υς μεθιστάναι. δαίμονες ἐμπο[δίζουσι ὡς]
ψ[υχαὶ τιμω]ροί. τὴν θυσ[ία]ν τούτου ἕνεκεν π[ο(ι)-
         οῦσ]ι[ν]
5 οἱ μά[γο]ι ὡσπερεὶ ποινὴν ἀποδιδόντες, τοῖ(ς) δὲ
   ἱεροῖ[ς] ἐπισπένδουσιν ὕ[δ]ωρ καὶ γάλα, ἐξ ὧνπερ
         καὶ τὰς
   χοὰς ποιοῦσι. ἀνάριθμα [κα]ὶ πολυόμφαλα τὰ πό-
         πανα
   θύουσιν, ὅτι καὶ αἱ ψυχα[ὶ ἀν]άριθμοί εἰσι. μύσται
   Εὐμενίσι προθύουσι κ[ατὰ τ]αὐτὰ μάγοις· Εὐμενί-
         δες γὰρ
10 ψυχαί εἰσιν, ὧν ἕνεκ[εν ὁ θέλων ἱ]ερὰ θεοῖς θύειν

‹they do not learn nor› **do they believe. Disbelief and lack of learning** ‹are the same thing. For if they do not› **learn and do not understand,** ‹it is not possible that they will believe› **and . . . disbelief . . . appears . . .**

Col. VI

. . . prayers and sacrifices ‹placate› **the souls, and** ‹the incantation› **of the Magi is capable of transforming the deities** (*daimones*) **when they are a hindrance. They** [i.e. these *daimones*] **are a hindrance** ‹as avenging souls›. **It is for this reason that the Magi perform a sacrifice, as though they were paying a penalty, and upon the sacrificial offerings they pour water and milk, out of which things they also make the libations. Numberless and many-knobbed are the cakes they sacrifice, because the souls too are numberless. The initiates perform a preliminary sacrifice to the Eumenides in the same way as the Magi do, for the Eumenides are souls, because of which** ‹he who wants› **to perform sacrificial offerings for the gods a**

1–9 Tsantsanoglou   2 τ supra litt. μ (μάγων) Piano recte dispexit, sed interpretatio dubia   3 ἐμπο[δίζουσι ὡς Piano mon. Tsantsanoglou qui ἐμπο[δίζουσι τὰς suppl., ἐμπο-[δὼν δ᾽ εἰσὶ KPT   4 ψ[υχαὶ τιμω]ροί Piano, ψ[υχὰς τιμω]ροί Tsantsanoglou, ψ[υχαῖς ἐχθ]ροί KPT   6 ὔ[δ]ωρ leg. Piano, ὔ[δω]ρ ceteri   9 κ[ατὰ τ]αὐτὰ Piano, κ[ατὰ τὰ] αὐτὰ ceteri   μάγοις Janko (mon. Tsantsanoglou) ex fr. I 70

10 ἕνεκ[εν Tsantsanoglou   ὁ θέλων Piano, ὁ μέλλων ἱ]ερὰ Janko ex fr. I 70, τὸν μέλλοντ]α Tsantsanoglou

`ὸ΄⟦ω⟧ρνίθιον πρότερον [ca. 11 litt.].ιςποτε[2–3 litt.]
   ται

κάτ]ω [ὅ]τε καὶ τὸ κ . [   ]ου ... [. .] . ι.

εἰσὶ δὲ [ψυ]χαὶ ... [   ]τουτο.[

ὅσαι δὲ [   ]ων ἀλλ[

15 φοβου[   ]. . .[

— — —

11 `ὸ΄⟦ω⟧ρνίθιον Piano (post o litt. deleta incerta ω con-
gruens), ὸ⟦ρ⟧ρνίθιον Ferrari, ὸ[ρ]νίθ[ε]ιον Tsantsanoglou   ].ιςποτε[. .]ται KPT, αὐτ]αῖς τότ᾽ ἐ[ρχη]ται
Ferrari   12 κάτ]ω Bernabé   ὅτε Ferrari

13 [ψυ]χαὶ Janko   15 φοβου[Piano, φορου[Tsantsanoglou, φοροῦ[σι Janko

Col. VII

[3–4 litt.]οςε[

[..ὔ]μνον [ὑγ]ιῆ καὶ θεμ[ι]τὰ λέγο[ντα· ἱερουργεῖ]το
   γὰρ

[τῆ]ι ποήσει. [κ]αὶ εἰπεῖν οὐχ οἷόν τ[ε τὴν τῶν ὀ]νο-
   μάτων

[θέ]σιν καίτ[οι] ῥηθέντα. ἔστι δὲ ξ[ένη τις ἡ] πόη-
   σις

5 [κ]αὶ ἀνθρώ[ποις] αἰνι[γμ]ατώδης, [κε]ὶ [᾽Ορφεὺ]ς
   αὐτ[ὸ]ς

[ἀό]ριστ᾽ αἰν[ίγμα]τα οὐκ ἤθελε λέγειν, [ἐν αἰν]ί-
   γμασ[ι]ν δὲ

[μεγ]άλα. ἱερ[ολογ]εῖται μὲν οὖν καὶ ἀ[πὸ το]ῦ
   πρώτου

388

small bird first . . . ⟨down⟩, when the . . . too . . . **But
souls are** [or: . . . are souls] . . . **this** [?] . . . **But all those
⟨souls?⟩ that** . . . **but** [or : others ?] . . . **fear** [?] . . .

Col. VII

. . . **a hymn that says sound and lawful things. For** ⟨he
was performing a sacred rite⟩ **by means of his poem.
And it is not possible to state the meaning imposed**
(*thesis*) **on the words even though they are uttered;
but the poem is an alien one and, for human beings,
riddling, even if Orpheus himself intended by means
of it to say not undeterminable riddles, but rather
great things in the form of riddles. Indeed, he is
making a holy discourse, and from the first word**

---

versum compos. viri docti e comm. e.g. φθέγξομαι οἷς θέμις
ἐστι· θύρας δ' ἐπίθεσθε βέβηλοι = Frag. 3 Bernabé   1 ἱε-
ρουργεῖ]το Tsantsanoglou, ἱερολογεῖ]το Janko   4 [θέ]σιν
Janko, [λύ]σιν vel [φύ]σιν Tsantsanoglou   5 [κε]ὶ KPT,
[κα]ὶ Ferrari   6 [ἀό]ριστ' Ferrari, [ἐ]ρίστ' Tsantsanoglou

[ἀεὶ] μέχρι οὗ [τελε]υταίου ῥήματος, ᾡ[ς δηλοῖ] καὶ
ἐν τῶι

[εὐκ]ρινήτῳ[ι ἔπει· "θ]ύρας" γὰρ "ἐπίθεσ[θε" ὁ
κελ]εύσας τοῖ[ς]

10   ["ὠσὶ]ν" αὐτ[οὺς οὔτι νομο]θετεῖν φη[σιν τοῖς] πολλοῖς

τὴ]ν ἀκοὴν [ἀγνεύο]ντας κατ[ὰ]
]ςειτ[..].

]ωι τ[..]εγ.[...]..[

ἐν δ]ὲ τῶι ἐχομ[έ]ρωι πα[

15   ]ἔτλη ἔργ᾽ ο[ὐ]κ ἀτ[έλεστα

— — —

8 οὗ vel ⟨τ⟩οῦ Tsantsanoglou   9 ἐπίθεσ[θ]ε ὁ [κε]λεύ-
σας Janko ex frr. I 7 et I 55, ἐπιθέ[σθαι κελ]εύσας Tsantsanoglou
11 ἀλλὰ διδάσκειν τοὺς τὴ]ν ἀκοὴν [καθαρεύ]οντας κατ[ὰ]
Janko   15 Janko,].τ . . ειγ.[.]κατ[KPT

Col. VIII

[ca. 10 litt.] ἐδήλω[σεν ἐν τῶι]δε τῶι ἔπ[ει·]

⟨_⟩   ["ο]ἳ Διὸς ἐξεγένοντο [μεγασθεν]έος βασι-
λῆος."

[_]   ὅπως δ᾽ ἄρχεται ἐν τῶ[ιδε δη]λοῖ·
"Ζεὺς μὲν ἐπεὶ δὴ πα[τρὸς ἑο]ῦ πάρα
θέ[σ]φατον ἀρχὴν

5   [_]   [ἀ]λκήν τ᾽ ἐν χείρεσσι ἔ[λ]αβ[εν κ]α[ὶ]
δαίμον[α] κυδρόν."

⟨continuously⟩ **until his last one, as he makes clear in this well-chosen verse too: for he who has ordered them, "put doors to your ears," says that he is** ⟨not legislating⟩ **for the many** . . . ⟨who are pure⟩ **in their hearing according to . . . and in the following verse** . . . **"dared deeds that were not** ⟨unfulfilled⟩**"** . . . [1]

[1] On the basis of the Derveni author's commentary, scholars reconstruct *exempli gratia* a verse from the Orphic theogony: "I shall proclaim to those for whom it is licit; you who are profane, shut your doors."

Col. VIII

. . . **he has made it clear in this verse:**

"who were born from Zeus the mighty king."

And how he begins he makes clear in this one:

"Zeus, when from his father the prophesied rule
  (*arkhên*)
And strength (*alkên*) in his hands he received
  and the glorious divinity (*daimona*)."

---

1 ὥς] Janko   2 [μεγασθεν]έος Sider, [ὑπερμεν]έος ZPE

[τ]αῦτα τὰ ἔπη ὑπερβατὰ ἐό[ν]τα λανθά-
ν[ει·]
[ἔσ]τιν δ' ὧδ' ἔχοντα· 'Ζεὺς μὲν ἐπεὶ τὴ[ν
ἀλ]κὴν
[πα]ρὰ πατρὸς ἑοῦ ἔλαβεν καὶ δαίμονα
[κυδρ]όν.'
[χρὴ ὧ]δ' ἔχοντα οὐκ ἀκούειν τὸν Ζᾶ[να ὡς
κρα]τεῖ
10   [τοῦ πατρ]ὸς ἀλλὰ τὴν ἀλκὴν λαμβά[νει
παρ' αὐτο]ῦ.
[ἄλλως δ' ἔ]χοντα παρὰ θέσφατα δ[όξειεν
ἂν λαβεῖ]ν
[τὴν ἀρχήν· ἔο]ικεν γὰρ τούτωι μα[
[κατ' ἀ]νάγκην νομίζοιτ' [ἂν
[ca. 9 litt.] καὶ μαθὼν το.[.]..[

— — —

9 [χρὴ ὧ]δ' ΖΡΕ, [οὕτω] δ' Tsantsanoglou   ὡς κρα]τεῖ
Piano, mon. Tortorelli, ὅπως κρα]τεῖ Janko, ἐπικρα]τεῖ Tsantsanoglou, ἀμφισβη]τεῖ Betegh

10 λαμβά[νει Bernabé-Piano mon. Janko, λαμβά[νειν ΚΡΤ
mon. Rusten   12 [τὴν ἀρχήν Bernabé-Piano, [τὴν ἀλκήν
Tsantsanoglou   μα[θόντι Janko   13 [ἂν Tsantsanoglou

Col. IX

εἶναι· τὴ[ν ἀρ]χὴν οὖν τοῦ ἰσχυρ[ο]τάτου ἐπόη[σεν]
εἶναι ὥσ[περ]εὶ παῖδα πατρός. οἱ δὲ οὐ γινώσκον-
[τες]
τὰ λεγό[μεν]α δοκοῦσι τὸν Ζᾶνα παρὰ τοῦ αὐτο[ῦ]

People do not notice that these words are transposed; but they are as follows: "Zeus on the one hand when he received from his father the strength and the glorious divinity." If this is so, it is necessary to understand not that Zeus ⟨overpowers his⟩ **father, but rather that he receives the strength** ⟨from hi⟩**m; but if it were otherwise,** ⟨he would seem to receive the rule [or: the strength]⟩ **in violation of the prophecies. For it seems that for him . . . and one would think necessarily . . . and knowing . . .**

Col. IX

. . . to be. Therefore he made the rule [or: the strength] **belong to what is the strongest, just as a son** [scil. belongs] **to his father. But those who do not understand what is said think that Zeus received from his**

---

1 ἀρ]χὴν Tsantsanoglou, ἀλ]κὴν Betegh

πατρὸς [τὴν] ἀλκήν τε κα[ὶ] τὸν δαίμονα λαμβά[-
νειν.]

5 γινώσκ[ω]ν οὖν τὸ πῦρ ἀναμεμειγμένον τοῖς
ἄλλοις ὅτι ταράσσοι καὶ κ[ωλ]ύοι τὰ ὄντα συν-
ίστασθαι
διὰ τὴν θάλψιν ἐξαλλάσ[σει ὅσ]ον τε ἱκανόν ἐστιν
ἐξαλλαχθὲν μὴ κωλύ[ειν τὰ] ὄντα συμπαγῆναι.
ὅσα δ' ἂ[ν] ἀφθῆι ἐπικρα[τεῖται, ἐπικ]ρατηθὲν δὲ
μίσγεται
10 τοῖς ἄλ[λ]οις. ὅτι δ' "ἐν χείρ[εσσιν ἔλαβ]εν" ἠινί-
ζετο
ὥσπε[ρ τ]ἆλλα τὰ π[ρὶν μὲν ἄδηλα φαι]νόμεν[α,
ἀλλ]ὰ
[β]εβαιότατα νοηθ[έντα. αἰνιζόμενος ο]ὖν ἰσχυρῶς
ἔφη τὸν Ζᾶνα τὴ[ν ἀλκὴν λαβεῖν καὶ τὸ]ν δαίμονα
[ὥ]σπερεὶ ε[   ]οῦ ἰσχυροῦ

— — —

Col. X

καὶ λέγειν [οὐδὲ γ]ὰρ λέ[γ]ειν οἷόν τε μὴ
φωνοῦντ[α·]
ἐνόμιζε δὲ τὸ αὐτὸν εἶναι τὸ 'λέγειν' τε καὶ
'φωνεῖν.'
'λέγειν' δὲ καὶ 'διδάσκειν' τὸ αὐτὸ δύναται·
οὐ γὰρ
οἷόν τε δι[δ]άσκειν ἄνευ τοῦ λέγειν ὅσα διὰ
λόγων
5 διδάσκετα[ι.] νομίζεται δὲ τὸ διδάσκειν ἐν
τῶι

own father the strength and the divinity (*daimôn*). Therefore, knowing that fire, if it is mixed with the other things, disturbs the things that exist and prevents them from becoming constituted (*sunistasthai*) on account of its heating, he sets it at a distance far enough that, once it has been set at a distance, it does not prevent the things that exist from solidifying; but whatever is kindled is dominated [scil. by fire], **and, being dominated, it is mixed with the other things. As for "he received in his hands," he expressed this in a riddling way, just like the other ones** [scil. expressions], **which at first seem** ⟨obscure but⟩ **seem quite certain once they have been thought about. Therefore,** ⟨expressing himself in a riddling way,⟩ **he said that Zeus forcefully** ⟨received the strength [or: the rule] and the⟩ **divinity** (*daimôn*) **just as . . . of forceful . . .**

Col. X

. . . and to say. For to say (*legein*) **without uttering** (*phônein*) **is not possible either; and he thought that 'to say' and 'to utter' were the same thing; but 'to say' and 'to teach' have the same meaning, for it is not possible to teach without saying whatever is taught by means of words, and teaching is thought to consist in saying. Therefore teaching is not separated from saying, nor saying from uttering, but**

---

versum compos. Tsantsanoglou e comm. et e fr. 112 Bernabé e.g. ἦστο πανομφεύουσα θεῶν τροφὸς ἀμβροσίη Νύξ   5 ἐν Anonymus in ZPE, ἐν KPT

λέγειν εἶν̣[αι.] οὐ τοίνυν τὸ μὲν διδάσκειν ἐκ
    τοῦ
λέγειν ἐχ̣[ωρί]σθη τὸ δὲ λέγειν ἐκ τοῦ φω-
    νεῖν,
τὸ δ' αὐτὸ̣ [δύνα]ται 'φωνεῖν' καὶ 'λέγειν'
    καὶ 'διδάσ̣[κειν.']
οὕτως [οὐδὲν κωλ]ύει "πανομφεύουσαν" καὶ
    'πάν̣[τα
10   διδά̣[σκουσαν' τὸ αὐ]τὸ̣ εἶναι.
"τροφ[ὸν" δὲ λέγων αὐ]τὴ̣ν̣ α̣ἰ̣ν̣ί̣[ζε]ται ὅτι
    [ἄ]σσα
ὁ ἥλι̣[ος θερμαίνει καὶ δι]α̣λύει ταῦτα ἡ νὺξ
    ψύ̣[χουσα]
συ[νίστησι   ....] ἄσ̣σα ὁ ἥλιος
    ἐθ̣έρ̣[μαινε
                                    ]τα[

        — — —

12 θερμαίνει καὶ δι̣α̣λύει Piano, θερμαίνων δι̣α̣λύει Tsantsanoglou   13 ἐ̣θ̣έ̣ρ̣[μαινε Janko

Col. XI

[τ]ῆ̣ς Νυκτός. "ἐξ ἀ̣[δύτοι]ο" δ' αὐτὴν [λέγει]
    "χρῆσαι"
γνώμην ποιού[με]νος ἄδυτον εἶναι τὸ βάθος
τῆς νυκτός· οὐ γ̣[ὰρ] δύνει ὥσπερ τὸ φῶς,
    ἀλλά νιν
ἐν τῶι αὐτῶι μέ[νο]ν̣ αὐγὴ κατ̣α̣[λ]αμβάνει.
5   'χρῆσαι' δὲ καὶ 'ἀρκέσαι' ταὐτὸ [δύ]ναται.

396

'to utter,' 'to say,' and 'to teach' have the same meaning. Thus ⟨nothing pre⟩vents "all-pronouncing" and 'teach⟨ing all things⟩' from being the same thing.

And ⟨in calling it [i.e. the night]⟩ "nurse," he shows in a riddling way that everything that the sun ⟨heats and dis⟩solves, the night re⟨unites by cool⟩ing . . . everything that the sun was heating . . . [1]

---

[1] On the basis of the Derveni author's commentary and a separately transmitted fragment, Tsantsanoglou reconstructs *exempli gratia* a verse from the Orphic theogony: "She was seated, the all-pronouncing nurse of the gods, ambrosial Night."

Col. XI

. . . of Night. ⟨He says⟩ that "she proclaims the oracle out of the ⟨innermost shrine⟩," his view being that the innermost shrine (*adyton*) is the depth of night; for it [i.e. the night] does not set (*ou . . . dynei*) as the light does, but the daylight seizes it while it remains in the same place. And 'to proclaim an oracle' and 'to prevent harm' have the same meaning; and we must

σκέψασθαι δὲ χρὴ ἐφ᾿ ὧι κεῖτα̣[ι τὸ] ʻἀρκέ-
σαι᾿

_ κα̣ὶ τὸ ʻχρῆσαι.᾿

χρᾶν τόνδε τὸν θεὸν νομίζο̣ν̣τ̣[ες ἔρ]χονται

[_] πευσόμενοι ἄσσα ποῶσι. τάδ᾿ [ἐπὶ τούτ]ωι
λέγει·

10 [_] [ʻʻΝὺξ] ἔχρησεν ἅπαντα τά οἱ θέ[μις ἦν
ἀνύσασ]θαι.ᾇᾇ

[....]θ̣εὶς ἐδήλωσεν ὅτι ο.[   ]ε̣

[......]ι παρὰ τ̣ὰ̣ ἐ̣όντα .[

[......]αι οἷόν τ[ε

[.....] . . σθαι συ.[

— — —

9 τάδ᾿ Janko, τὰ δ᾿ Tsantsanoglou   10 [Νὺξ] Santamaría,
[ἡ δὲ] ZPE, [ἤ οἱ] West   ἀνύσασ]θαι Tsantsanoglou, ἐκτε-
λέεσ]θαι Sider

Col. XII

καὶ ἀφα̣[ιρεῖ]ν· τὸ δ᾿ ἐχόμε[νον ἔ]π̣ος ὧδ᾿
ἔχει·

_ ʻʻὡς ἂ̣ν̣ ἔ̣[χοι κά]τα καλὸν ἕδος νιφόεντος
Ὀλύμπου.ᾇᾇ

ʻὌλυμπ[ος᾿ καὶ ʻχ]ρόνος᾿ τὸ αὐτόν. οἱ δὲ
δοκοῦντες

ʻὌλυμπ[ον᾿ καὶ] ʻοὐρανὸν᾿ [τ]αὐτὸ εἶναι
ἐξαμαρ-

5 τάν[ουσ]ι̣[ν, οὐ γ]ι̣νώσκον̣τ̣ες ὅτι οὐρανὸν
οὐχ οἷόν τ̣ε

398

consider what 'to prevent harm' and 'to proclaim an oracle' refer to.

It is in the belief that this god proclaims oracles that they come to find out what they should do. This is what he says ⟨after this [scil. verse]⟩:

> ⟨"Night⟩ **proclaimed an oracle about all that was**
> **ri**⟨ght for him to perform."⟩

. . . **he made clear that** . . . **next to the things that exist** . . . **as** . . .

Col. XII

. . . **and to re**⟨move⟩ [probably: the power]. **The next verse goes like this:**

> **"That he might reign on the lovely seat of snow-**
> **capped Olympus."**

'Olympus' and 'time' are the same thing. Those who think that 'Olympus' and 'heaven' are the same thing are completely wrong, for they do not understand that heaven cannot be long rather than wide,

μακ[ρό]τερον ἢ εὐρύτε[ρο]ν εἶναι, χρόνον δὲ
  'μακρὸν'
εἴ τις [ὀνομ]άζο[ι] οὐκ ἂν [ἐξα]μαρτάνοι. ὁ
  δὲ ὅπου μὲν
"οὐρανὸν" θέ[λοι λέγειν, τὴν] προσθήκην
  "εὐρὺν"
ἐποιεῖτο, ὅπου [δ' "Ὄλυμπον," το]ὐναντίον
  "εὐρὺν" μὲν
 οὐδέποτε, "μα[κρὸν" δέ. "νιφό]εντα" δὲ φή-
  σας εἶναι
τῆι [δ]υνάμει ε[ἴκαζε τὸν χρόνον ὄρε]ι νιφε-
  τώδει.
[τὸ δὲ νιφετῶ[δες ψυχρόν τε καὶ λ]ευκόν
  ἐ[στι.]
[....] λαμπ[ρ   ] πολιὸν δ'
  ἀ[έρ]α
                         ].ια καὶ τα.[
                         ]...τοδε[

— — —

1 ἀφα[ιρεῖ]ν Janko qui τὴν ἀρχὴν ante 1 suppl.
  9 [δὲ χρόνον Colabella, Parsons   11 ε[ἴκαζε τὸν χρόνον ὄρε]ι Bernabé-Piano, ε[ἰκάζει χρόνον τῶ]ι vel αὐτὸν ὄρε]ι
Tsantsanoglou

whereas if someone were to call time 'long,' he would not be wrong at all. Whenever he wanted ‹to say› "heaven," he added ‹the› epithet "wide," but whenever [scil. he wanted to say] ‹"Olympus"› on the contrary, he never [scil. added] "wide," but "long." And in saying that it is "snow-clad" ‹he was comparing time› in its property with a snowy ‹mount›ain. ‹What is› snowy ‹is cold and› white . . . ; gleaming . . . gray air . . . and . . . this . . .

Col. XIII

"Ζεὺς μὲν ἐπεὶ δὴ πατρὸς ἑοῦ πάρα [θ]έ-
σφατ' ἀκούσα[ς·"]

οὔτε γὰρ τότε ἤκουσεν, ἀλλὰ δεδήλωται
ὅπως

_ ἤκουσεν, οὔτε ἡ νὺξ κελεύει. ἀλλὰ δηλοῖ
ὧδε λέγων·

_ "αἰδοῖον κατέπινεν, ὃς αἰθέρα ἔκθορε
πρῶτος."

5   ὅτι μὲν πᾶσαν τὴν πόησιν περὶ τῶν πραγμάτων

_ αἰνίζεται κ[α]θ' ἔπος ἕκαστον ἀνάγκη λέγειν.

ἐν τοῖς α[ἰδοίο]ις ὁρῶν τὴν γένεσιν τοὺς
ἀνθρώπου[ς]

νομίζον[τας ε]ἶναι τούτωι ἐχρήσατο, ἄνευ
δὲ τῶν

αἰδοίων [οὐ γίν]εσθαι, αἰδοίωι εἰκάσας τὸν
ἥλιο[ν·]

10 ἄνευ [γὰρ τοῦ ἡ]λ[ίο]υ τὰ ὄντα τοιαῦτα οὐχ
οἷόν [τε]

γίν[εσθαι ....]ένων τῶν ἐόντων [

ἠρε[μεῖν .... διὰ] τὸν ἥλιο[ν] πάντα ὁμ[οίως
  ]οὐδ' ἐοῦσ[ιν] ου.[
  ] περιέχειν [

15]. . . . . . .[

— — —

Col. XIII

"When Zeus, having heard the prophecies from his father."

For neither was it at that time that he heard—but it has been made clear in what sense he heard—nor does Night command. But he makes [scil. this] clear saying as follows:

"he swallowed down the *aidoion* [i.e. either 'the reverend one' or the phallus[1]], **the first to have expelled/ejaculated** [or: to leap forth in] **the aether.**"

Because he speaks in a riddling way about real things during the whole poem, it is necessary to speak about each word in turn. Since he saw that men consider generation to be dependent upon the ‹genital›s (*aidoia*) and that this does not happen without the genitals, he used this [i.e. the word '*aidoion*'], comparing the sun to the *aidoion*. ‹For› without the sun, it would not have been possible for the things that exist to be generated . . . of the things that exist . . . to be at rest . . . ‹because of› the sun all things in the same way . . . nor being . . . to encompass . . .

---

[1] The Greek word can have both meanings, and scholars disagree about which one is meant here.

---

2 τότε Betegh, τόδε Tsantsanoglou
4 οὖ emend. Ferrari

Col. XIV

[ἐ]κθόρηι τὸ λαμπρότατόν τε [καὶ θε]ρμό-
[τ]ατον

χωρισθὲν ἀφ᾽ ἑωυτοῦ. τοῦτον οὖν τὸν Κρό-
νον

γενέσθαι φησὶν ἐκ τοῦ Ἡλίου τῆι Γῆι, ὅτι
αἰτίαν ἔσχε

διὰ τὸν ἥλιον κρούεσθαι πρὸς ἄλληλα.

5   διὰ τοῦτο λέγει "ὃς μέγ᾽ ἔρεξεν." τὸ δ᾽ ἐπὶ
τούτωι,

   "Οὐρανὸς Εὐφρονίδης, ὃς πρώτιστος βα-
σίλευσεν"

κρούοντα τὸν Νοῦν πρὸς ἄλληλ[α] ῾Κρόνον᾽
ὀνομάσας

"μέγα ῥέξαι" φησὶ τὸν Οὐρανόν. ἀφ[αι]-
ρεθῆναι γὰρ

τὴν βασιλείαν αὐτόν. ῾Κρόνον᾽ δὲ ὠνόμασεν ἀπὸ τοῦ

10   ἔ[ρ]γου αὐτὸν καὶ τἆλλα κατὰ τ[ὸν αὐτὸν
λ]όγον.

[τῶν ἐ]όντων γὰρ ἀπάντ[ω]ν [οὔπω κρουο-
μέ]νων

[ὁ Νοῦ]ς ὡς ὁρ[ίζω]ν φύσιν [τὴν ἐπωνυμίαν
ἔσχε]ν

Col. XIV

. . . **it** [i.e. the fire?] **expelled/ejaculated** [or: leaped forth,] **what is brightest and hottest** [i.e. the aether], **separated from itself** [i.e. the fire?]. **Therefore he says that this Cronus was born to Earth from the sun because he was the cause via the sun that they** [i.e. the things] **strike** (*krouesthai*) **against one another. That is why he says,**

> **"He who did a great deed."** [= COSM. T12a.1][1]

And the verse after this,

> **"Ouranos, son of Euphronê** [i.e. Night]**, who was the first of all to rule."** [= COSM. T12a.2]

Having called 'Cronus' Mind (*Nous*) **that makes things strike** (*krouonta*) **against each other, he says that he** [i.e. Cronus] **did a great deed to Ouranos; for** [scil. he says that] **he** [i.e. Ouranos] **was deprived of his kingship. And he called him 'Cronus' from his action, and all the others** [scil. things] **according to the same principle. For when all the things that exist** ‹were not yet striking against one another, Mind,› **since it delimits** (*horizôn*) **nature,** ‹received the name

---

[1] Here Janko suggests that a line has been lost, e.g. "And to him from Gaea was born Cronus, who did a great deed" (see the textual note on line 6).

---

1 [ἐ]κ{χ}θόρηι Janko   τὸ{ν} Rusten   2 χωρισθέν‹τα› Janko si τὸν l. 1 conservandum esset   6 ante hanc lineam versum compos. e comm. Janko e.g. τῶι δ᾽ αὖτ᾽ ἐκ Γαίης γένετο Κρόνος ὃς μέγ᾽ ἔρεξεν

[Ὀυρανό]ς.’ “ἀφαιρ[εῖ]σθαι” δ’ αὐ[τόν φησι
  “τὴν βασιλ]είαν”
[κρουο]μένων τ[ῶν] ἐ[ό]ντ[ων
  ].ντα   — — —

14 τὰ ἐό]ντα vel τὰ ὄ]ντα Janko

Col. XV

κρούε‹ι›ν αὐτὰ πρὸ[ς ἄλ]ληλα κά[ν] ποήσηι
  τὸ[ν ἥλι]ον
χωρισθέντα διαστῆναι δίχ’ ἀλλήλων τὰ
  ἐόντα·
χωρ[ι]ζομένου γὰρ τοῦ ἡλίου καὶ ἀπολαμ-
  βανομένου
ἐν μέσωι πήξας ἴσχει καὶ τἄνωθε τοῦ ἡλίου
5 _ καὶ τὰ κάτωθεν. ἐχόμενον δὲ ἔπος,
  _   “ἐκ τοῦ δὴ Κρόνος αὖτις, ἔπειτα δὲ
      μητίετα Ζεύς”.
λέγει ὄτι ἐκ τοῦδε [ἀ]ρχή ἐστιν, ἐξ ὅσου
  βασιλεύει. ἡ δὲ
ἀρχή· διηγεῖται, ὄ[τι τὰ] ἐόντα κρούων πρὸς
  ἄλληλα
διαστήσας τ’ ἐ[πόει τὴ]ν νῦν μετάστασιν
  οὐκ ἐξ ἑτέρ[ων]
10 _ ἔτερ’ ἀλλ’ ἔτε[ρα ἐκ τῶν αὐτῶν.]
  τὸ δ’ “ἔπειτα [δὲ μητίετα Ζε]ύς”. ὅτι μὲν
    οὐχ ἔτερ[ος]

'Oura›nos.' And ‹he says› that he "was deprived of his kingship" while the things that exist were striking against one another . . .

Col. XV

. . . to strike against one another, even if he [i.e. Orpheus] made the ‹sun›, having been separated, hold the things that exist at a distance from one another; for when the sun is separated and is confined in the middle, he [i.e. Mind] fastens and maintains both what is above the sun and what is below it. And the next verse,

"from him in turn came Cronus and then prudent Zeus" [= COSM. T12a.3]:

he [i.e. Orpheus] says that the beginning (archê) dates from the time when he [i.e. Zeus] is king. And the beginning [scil. of the verse]: he explains that he [i.e. Mind], by making the things that exist strike against one another and by holding them apart, ‹made› the current reconfiguration, [scil. making] not different things out of different ones but diff‹erent things out of the same ones.› As for ‹"then prudent Zeus":› it is

---

1 κἀ[ν] Betegh, κα[ὶ] Tsantsanoglou   τὸ[ν ἥλι]ον Betegh, τὸ [πρῶτ]ον Tsantsanoglou   7 ὅτι legit Piano, ‹ὅ›τι ZPE, τι KPT   ἡ δὲ Burkert, ἥδε KPT   7–8 ita dist. nos, post βασιλεύει Rusten, post ἀρχή Tsantsanoglou   8 ὅ[τι τὰ] ἐόντα Rusten, Ν[οῦς τ]ὰ̣ ὄντα KPT   9 τ᾽ ἐ[πόει τὴ]ν Bernabé-Piano mon. Burkert, τ᾽ ἐ[πόησε τὴ]ν Janko, τε [πρὸς τὴ]ν Tsantsanoglou   10 Janko

407

_ ἀλλὰ ὁ αὐ[τὸς δῆλον σημαίν]ει δὲ [τ]όδε·
"μῆτιν κα.[ca. 13 litt.]ων βασιληίδα τιμ[ήν."]
εϲ.[   ].αι ἶνας ἀπ.[
15   ει[

— — —

13 καὶ [μακάρων κατέχ]ων coni. West,]εν βασιληίδα KPT

Col. XVI

[αἰδοῖ]ον τὸν ἥλιον ἔφ[η]σεν εἶναι δε[δήλ]-
    ωται· ὅτι δὲ
_ ἐκ τῶν ὑπαρχόντων τὰ νῦν ὄντα γίνεται
    λέγει.
    "πρωτογόνου βασιλέως αἰδοίου· τῶι δ'
        ἄρα πάντες
    ἀθάνατοι προσέφυν μάκαρες θεοὶ ἠδὲ
        θέαιναι
5   καὶ ποταμοὶ καὶ κρῆναι ἐπήρατοι ἄλλα τε
        πάντα,
_   ἄσσα τότ' ἦν γεγαῶτ', αὐτὸς δ' ἄρα μοῦ-
        νος ἔγεντο."
    [ἐ]ν τούτοις σημαίνει ὅτι τὰ ὄντα ὑπῆ[ρ]χεν
        ἀεί, τὰ δὲ
    νῦν ἐόντα ἐκ τῶν ὑπαρχόντων γίν[ε]ται. τὸ
        δὲ
    "[αὐ]τὸς δὲ ἄρα μοῦνος ἔγεντο"· τοῦτο δὲ
        [λ]έγων δηλοῖ

408

⟨clear⟩ **that this is not a different one, but the same one. He ⟨indicat⟩es this:**

"**Metis . . . royal honor.**"

. . . sinews . . .

Col. XVI

. . . **it has been made clear** [scil. that] **he said that the sun is** *aidoion* (i.e. 'reverend' or 'phallus'). **And he says that the things that are now come to be from the things that exist:**

"**Of the firstborn king, the reverend one. And upon him all**
The immortals grew, blessed gods and goddesses
And rivers and lovely springs and everything else
That was born then; and he himself was alone."
[= **COSM. T12b**]

In these [scil. verses] **he indicates that the things that are have always existed and that the things that are now come to be out of the things that exist.**

As for "and he himself was alone": in saying this

---

3 Πρωτογόνου West

10   [ἀεὶ] τὸν Νοῦν πάντων ἄξιον εἶναι μόν[ο]ν
ἐόντα,

[ὥσπερ]εἰ μηδὲν τἆλλα εἴη· οὐ γὰρ [οἷόν τε
δι' α]ὐτὰ εἶναι

[τὰ νῦν] ἐόντα ἄν[ε]υ τοῦ Νοῦ. [καὶ ἐν τῶι
ἐχ]ομένωι

[—]   [ἔπει τούτ]ου ἄξιον πάντων [τὸν Νοῦν ἔφησεν ε]ἶναι·

[—]   ["νῦν δ' ἐστὶ]ν βασιλεὺς πάντ[ων καί τ'
ἔσσετ' ἔπ]ειτα."

15   [δῆλον ὅτι] Νοῦς καὶ π[άντων βασιλεύς ἐστι
τα]ὐτόν.

— — —

12 [τὰ νῦν] ἐόντα KPT, τὰ ὑπάρχ]οντα Janko

Col. XVII

π[ρ]ότερον ἦν πρ[ὶν ὀν]ομασθῆναι, ἔπ[ει]τα
ὠνομάσθη·

ἦν γὰρ καὶ πρόσθεν `[ἐ]ὼν´ ἢ τὰ νῦν ἐόντα
συσταθῆναι

ἀὴρ καὶ ἔσται ἀεί· οὐ γὰρ ἐγένετο, ἀλλὰ
ἦν. δι' ὅ τι δὲ

'ἀὴρ' ἐκλήθη δεδήλωται ἐν τοῖς προτέροις.
γενέσθαι δὲ

5   ἐνομίσθη ἐπείτ' ὠνομάσθη 'Ζεύς,' ὥσπερεὶ
πρότερον

μὴ ἐών. καὶ "ὕστατον" ἔφησεν ἔσεσθαι
τοῦτον, ἐπείτ'

410

he makes clear that Mind itself, being alone, is ⟨always⟩ worth everything, ⟨as if⟩ everything else were nothing. For ⟨it is not possible⟩ for the things that are ⟨now⟩ to exist ⟨by⟩ themselves without Mind.
⟨And in the verse foll⟩**owing** ⟨this one⟩, ⟨he has said that Mind⟩ is worth everything:

   "⟨He is now⟩ **the king of** ⟨all things and will be⟩ later."

⟨It is clear that⟩ **Mind and** ⟨the king of all things are the sa⟩me thing.

Col. XVII

. . . it existed before it was named; and it was named later. For air existed both before the things that are now were assembled, and it will always exist. For it was not born, but it existed. The reason why it was called 'air' (*aêr*) was made clear in what preceded. But it was thought that it was born, because it was named 'Zeus,' as if it did not exist previously. And he said that this one would be "the last" [cf. COSM.

---

2 ⟨ἐ⟩ὼν´ Janko, ⟨ὼν´ Tsantsanoglou

ὠνομάσθη 'Ζεὺς' καὶ τοῦτο αὐτῶι διατελεῖ
ὄνομα ὄν,
μέχρι εἰς τὸ αὐτὸ εἶδος τὰ νῦν ἐόντα συνεστάθη
ἐν ὧιπερ πρόσθεν ἐόντα ἠιωρεῖτο. τὰ δ'
ἐόντα δ[ηλοῖ]

10   γενέσθαι τοιαῦτ[α] διὰ τοῦτον καὶ γενόμενα
π[άλιν]

_   ἐν τούτωι [ca. 5 litt. .ση]μαίνει δ' ἐν τοῖς
ἔπεσι το[ῖσδε·]

_   "Ζεὺς κεφα[λή, Ζεὺς μέσ]σα, Διὸς δ' ἐκ
[π]άντα τέτ[υκται."]

κεφαλὴν [ο]ντ' αἰν[ί]ζεται .[
κεφαληι[   ] ἀρχὴ γίνεται συ[στά-
σεως]

15   δ[συστ]αθῆναι ν[

— — —

10 π[άλιν dub. Tsantsanoglou, ε[ἶναι Janko
11 post τούτωι π[άντα. leg. et coni. Janko, [μένειν. vel [κεῖ-
σθαι. West, [ἐνεῖναι. Tsantsanoglou
13 [φήσας ἔχειν τὰ ἐό]ντ' Janko   fin. ὅ[τι] coni. Janko

Col. XVIII

καὶ τὰ κάτω [φερό]μενα. `[τὴν δὲ "Μοῖρα]ν" φάμε-
νος [δηλοῖ]´
τήνδ[ε γῆν] καὶ τἆλλα πάν[τ]ᾳ εἶναι
ἐν τῶι ἀέρι [πνε]ῦμα ἐόν. τοῦτ' οὖν τὸ πνεῦμα
Ὀρφεὺς

**T12c.1] because it was named 'Zeus,' and this will
continue to be its name until the things that are now
have been assembled into the same form in which
they were floating** (*êiôreito*) **when they existed previously. And he s⟨hows⟩ that the things that exist become such** [scil. as they are] **because of him and that,
once they have come about, they** [scil. are] ⟨all?⟩ **once
again in him. He indicates it in the following verses**
[or: words]:

> **"Zeus** [scil. is] **the head, Zeus the middle, and by
> Zeus all things are made."** [= COSM. T12c.2]

**. . . head . . . he indicates the things that exist in a
riddling way . . . head . . . the beginning of the organization takes place . . . to be assembled . . .**

Col. XVIII

**. . . and the things that move downward. And by
saying** ⟨**"Destiny"** (*Moira*)⟩ [cf. COSM. T12c.3], ⟨he
shows⟩ **that this earth and all the other things are in
the air, which is** (?) **breath** (*pneuma*)**. This breath,
therefore, Orpheus named it 'Moira'; but all other**

---

unum versum compos. West e comm. et e frag. 31.1 et 243.1
Bernabé e.g. Ζεὺς πρῶτος γένετο, Ζεὺς ὕστατος ἀργικέραυνος, alterum Merkelbach e.g. Ζεὺς πνοίη πάντων, Ζεὺς πάντων
ἔπλετο μοῖρα   1 τὴν δ[ίνην] Burkert

ὠνόμασεν 'Μοῖραν,' οἱ δ' ἄλλοι ἄνθρωποι κατὰ
    φάτιν "Μοῖραν
ἐπικλῶσαι" φασὶ[ν] "σφίσιν" καὶ "ἔσεσθαι ταῦθ'
    ἄσσα Μοῖρα
5   ἐπέκλωσεν," λέγοντες μὲν ὀρθῶς, οὐκ εἰδότες δὲ
οὔτε τὴν 'Μοῖραν' ὅ τι ἐστὶν οὔτε τὸ 'ἐπικλῶσαι.'
    Ὀρφεὺς γὰ ρ'
τὴν φρόνησ[ι]ν 'Μοῖραν' ἐκάλεσεν· ἐφαίνετο γὰρ
    αὐτῶι
τοῦτο προσφερέστατον ε[ῖ]ναι ἐξ ὧν ἅπαντες
    ἄνθρωποι
ὠνόμασαν· πρὶν μὲν γὰρ κληθῆναι 'Ζῆνα,' ἦν
    Μοῖρα
10 φρόνησις τοῦ θεοῦ ἀεί τε καὶ [δ]ιὰ παντός· ἐπεὶ δ'
    ἐκλήθη
'Ζεύς,' γενέσθαι αὐτὸν ἐ[νομ]ί[σθ]η, ὄντα μὲν καὶ
    πρόσθεν
[ὀ]νομαζόμ[ε]νον δ' ο[ὔ. διὰ τοῦτο λέ]γει "Ζεὺς
    πρῶτος
[γέν]ετο"· πρ[ῶ]τον γὰ[ρ ἦν Μοῖρα φρόνησις], ἔπει-
    τ[α δ'] ἱερεύθη
[Ζεὺ]ς ὤν. οἱ δ' ἄνθρω[ποι οὐ γινώσκοντ]ες τὰ λε-
    γόμενα
15 [ὡς π]ρωτόγονο[ν] ὄντα [θεὸν νομίζουσι] τὸν Ζῆνα [
      ]...[..]...[   ]..[

— — —

men, according to common usage, say, "Moira has spun for them" and "these things will be whatever Moira has spun"—speaking correctly, but not knowing either what 'Moira' is or what 'spinning' is. For it is wisdom that Orpheus called 'Moira': for this seemed to him to be the most suitable out of the names that all men have given. For before he [i.e. Zeus] was called 'Zeus,' Moira was the wisdom of the god, always and everywhere. But since he has been called 'Zeus,' they think that he was born, although he existed before but did not have a name. ⟨This is why he sa⟩ys, "Zeus was born first." For at first ⟨Moira was wisdom⟩, but then she became consecrated (?) as being ⟨Zeus⟩. But people, ⟨not understanding⟩ what is said, ⟨think⟩ that ⟨Zeus⟩ is the firstborn god . . . [1]

---

[1] On the basis of the Derveni author's commentary and separately transmitted fragments, West reconstructs *exempli gratia* one verse from the Orphic theogony, "Zeus was born first, Zeus the last, god of the bright bolt," and Merkelbach another, "Zeus, the breath of all, Zeus is the fate of all."

---

13 ἱερεύθη KPT leg. at vestigia valde dubia
15 ὄντα KPT qui an huc collocandum recte dub.

Col. XIX

ἐκ [τοῦ δ]ὲ̣ [τ]ὰ̣ ἐ̣ό̣ντα, ἓν [ἕκ]αστον κέκ[λη-
τ]αι ἀπὸ τοῦ
ἐπικρατοῦντος, Ζεὺ[ς] πάντα κατὰ τὸν αὐτὸν
λόγον ἐκλήθη· πάντων γὰρ ὁ ἀὴρ ἐπικρατεῖ
τοσοῦτον ὅσον βούλε̣ται. "Μοῖραν̣" δ' "ἐπικλῶσαι"
5   λέγοντες τοῦ Διὸς τὴν φρόνησιν ἐπικυρῶ-
σαι
λέγουσιν τὰ ἐόντα καὶ τὰ γινόμενα καὶ τὰ
μέλλοντα,
ὅπως χρὴ γενέσθαι τε καὶ εἶναι κα[ὶ] παύ-
σασθαι.
βασιλεῖ δὲ αὐτὸν εἰκάζει (τοῦτο γάρ οἱ
προσφέρειν
_   ἐφα[ί]νετο ἐκ τῶν λεγομένων ὀνομάτων) λέγων ὧδε·
10 [—] "Ζεὺς βασιλεύς, Ζεὺς δ' ἀρχὸς ἁπάντων
ἀργικέραυνος."
[βασιλέ]α ἔφη εἶναι ὅτι πολλῷ[ν τῶν ἀρ]-
χῶν μία
[πασῶν κ]ρατεῖ καὶ πάντα τελεῖ [ἄπερ θνη]
τῶν οὐδενὶ
[ἄλλωι ἔξεσ]τιν τε[λ]έσαι· ..[   ].ν.[.]ευ.[
[.] ἀρχὸν δὲ [ἁπάντων ἔφη εἶναι
α]ὐτὸν
15   [ὅτι πάντα ἄρ]χεται δια̣[   ].δε

— — —

Col. XIX

. . . ⟨ever since?⟩ **each single thing that exists has received its name from what dominates, all things have been called Zeus according to the same principle. For the air dominates all things as much as it wishes. And when they say, "Moira has spun," they are saying that the wisdom of Zeus ratifies how the things that are, the things that become, and the things that will be must come to be, exist, and cease. And he compares him to a king (for out of the names that are said, this one seemed to him to be suitable), when he says as follows:**

> **"Zeus the king, Zeus the ruler of all, god of the bright bolt."** [= COSM. T12c.4]

He said that he is ⟨king⟩ because, although there are **man**⟨y magistra⟩**cies, there is one that governs** ⟨all of them⟩ **and accomplishes everything** ⟨that it is⟩ **not per**⟨mitted⟩ **to any** ⟨other mort⟩**al to accomplish**. . . . ⟨he said that⟩ **he** ⟨was the⟩ **ruler** ⟨of all because all things are ru⟩**led by** . . .

417

Col. XX

ἀνθρώπω[ν ἐν] πόλεσιν ἐπιτελέσαντες [τὰ
  ἱ]ερὰ εἶδον,
ἔλασσόν σφας θαυμάζω μὴ γινώσκειν· οὐ
  γὰρ οἷόν τε
ἀκοῦσαι ὁμοῦ καὶ μαθεῖν τὰ λεγόμενα· ὅσοι
  δὲ παρὰ τοῦ
τέχνην ποιουμένου τὰ ἱερά, οὗτοι ἄξιοι
  θαυμάζεσθαι
5 καὶ οἰκτε[ί]ρεσθαι· θαυμάζεσθαι μὲν ὅτι δοκοῦντες
πρότερον ἢ ἐπιτελέσαι εἰδήσειν ἀπέρχονται
  ἐπι-
τελέσαντες πρὶν εἰδέναι οὐδ' ἐπανερόμενοι
  ὥσπερ
ὡς εἰδότες τι ὧν εἶδον ἢ ἤκουσαν ἢ ἔμα-
  θον· [οἰ]κτε‹ί›ρεσθαι δὲ
ὅτι οὐκ ἀρκεῖ σφιν τὴν δαπάνην προανηλῶ-
  σθαι, ἀλλὰ
10 _ καὶ τῆς γνώμης στερόμενοι πρὸς ἀπέρχονται,
πρὶν μὲν τὰ [ἱ]ερὰ ἐπιτελέσαι ἐλπίζον[τε]ς
  εἰδήσειν,
ἐπ[ιτελέσ]αντ[ες] δὲ στερηθέντες κα̣[ὶ τῆς]
  ἐλπί[δος] ἀπέρχονται.
 _ τω[ca. 10 litt.].νοντ[...] λόγος ..[...]ται.[..].να
.[   ].ι τῆι ἑαυτοῦ ο..[μ]ητρὶ μὲν
15   ]δ̣' ἀδελφη[   ]ωσειδε
                     ].·[

— — —

Col. XX

... ⟨those⟩ **men who, having performed holy rites in the cities, have seen them** [i.e. the sacred objects]— **I am less astonished that they do not understand: for it is not possible to hear and at the same time to understand what is being said. But all those** [scil. who hope to acquire knowledge] **from an expert in holy rites—they deserve that people feel astonishment and pity for them: astonishment because, thinking, before they perform the rites, that they will know, they go away after having performed them, before they know and without asking further questions, as though they knew something of what they had seen or heard or learned; and pity because it is not enough that they have spent their money in advance, but also they go off thwarted of their intention as well, since, hoping before they perform the holy rites that they will know, they go away after they have performed them, having been thwarted of this hope too** ... **discourse** ... **to his own** ... **mother** ... **sister** ...

---

ante 1 ὅσοι μὲν coni. Burkert

8 τι ὧν Tsantsanoglou, τέων KPT

14 Δήμ]ητρι coni. Janko

Col. XXI

οὔτε τὸ ψυχ[ρὸν] τῶι ψυχρῶι. "θορνηι" δὲ λέγ[ων]
δηλοῖ
ὅτι ἐν τῶι ἀέρι κατὰ μικρὰ μεμερισμένα ἐκινεῖτο
καὶ ἐθόρνυτο, θορνύμενα δ' ἕκα<σ>τα συνεστάθη
πρὸς ἄλληλα. μέχρι δὲ τούτου ἐθόρνυτο, μέχρι
5 ἕκαστον ἦλθεν εἰς τὸ σύνηθες. Ἀφροδίτη
Οὐρανία'
καὶ 'Ζεὺς' καὶ 'ἀφροδισιάζειν' καὶ 'θόρνυσθαι' καὶ
'Πειθὼ'
καὶ 'Ἁρμονία' τῶι αὐτῶι θεῶι ὄνομα κεῖται. ἀνὴρ
γυναικὶ μισγόμενος 'ἀφροδισιάζειν' λέγεται κατὰ
φάτιν. τῶν γὰρ νῦν ἐόντων μιχθέντων ἀλλ[ή]λοις
10 'Ἀφροδίτη' ὠνομάσθη· 'Πειθὼ' δ' ὅτι εἶξεν τὰ
ἐ[ό]ντα
ἀλλήλο[ι]σιν· 'ε[ἴ]κειν' δὲ καὶ 'πείθειν' τὸ αὐτόν·
'[Ἁ]ρμονί'α' δὲ
ὅτι πο[λλὰ ....ἡ]ρμοσε τῶν ἐόντων ἑκάστω[ι.]
ἦν μὲν γ[ὰρ καὶ π]ρόσθεν, ὠνομάσθη δὲ γενέ-
σθ[αι] ἐπεὶ

versum compos. Tsantsanoglou e comm. e.g. Πειθώ θ' Ἁρμονίην τε (vel Ἁρμονίην Πειθώ τε) καὶ Οὐρανίην Ἀφροδίτην
1 θόρνηι (dativum) Kapsomenos, θορνῆι West, θορῆι vel θορ-
ν<ύ>ηι Janko, θόρηι (verbum) Tsantsanoglou   12 πο[λλὰ
συνή]ρμοσε Kapsomenos

Col. XXI

. . . nor the cold to the cold. And when he says "by leaping" (?) (*thornei*[1]), he shows that, divided into little pieces, they [scil. the particles or the things that are] were moving in the air and were leaping, and by leaping each of them was put into mutual relation with the other ones. And they went on leaping until each one came to its fellow. 'Heavenly Aphrodite' and 'Zeus,' 'to engage in the works of Aphrodite' (*aphrodisiazein*) and 'to leap,' and 'Persuasion' and 'Harmony' are names established for the same god. A man who mixes [scil. sexually] with a woman is said by common usage 'to engage in the works of Aphrodite.' For she [i.e. Aphrodite] received the name 'Aphrodite' when the things that exist now were mixed with one another. And 'Persuasion' [scil. received her name], because the things that exist yielded to one another; and 'yield' and 'persuade' are the same. And 'Harmony' [scil. received her name], because she fitted together (*hêrmose*) many of the things that exist to each one [scil. among them]. For they existed before too, but the term 'being born' was used for them after they had been separated. And he shows that

---

1 The form and meaning of this word are very uncertain.

διεκρίθ[η· ...... δι]ακριθῆναι δηλοῖ οτ[.].[.....]τε̣ι̣ς

15   κ]ρατεῖ ὥστε δι... [   ]

        ].[   ]ν̣.[   ]νῦν

— — —

14 δι]ακριθῆναι δηλοῖ ὅτ[ι] τ[ὰς γενέ]σε̣ι̣ς Piano

Col. XXII

πάν[τ' οὗ]ν ὁμοίω[ς ὠ]νόμασεν ὡς κάλλιστα
    ἠ[δύ]νατο,

γινώσκων τῶν ἀνθρώπων τὴν φύσιν, ὅτι οὐ
    πάντες

ὁμοίαν ἔχουσιν οὐδὲ θέλουσιν πάντες
    ταὐτά·

κρατιστεύοντες λέγουσι ὅ τι ἂν αὐτῶν
    ἑκάστωι

5 ἐπὶ θυμὸν ἔλθηι, ἅπερ ἂν θέλοντες τυγ-
    χάνωσι,

οὐδαμὰ ταὐτά, ὑπὸ πλεονεξίας, τὰ δὲ καὶ
    ὑπ' ἀμαθίας.

Γῆ δὲ καὶ Μήτηρ καὶ Ῥέα καὶ Ἥρη ἡ
    αὐτή. ἐκλήθη δὲ

'Γῆ' μὲν νόμωι, 'Μήτηρ' δ' ὅτι ἐκ ταύτης
    πάντα γ[ίν]εται,

'Γῆ' καὶ 'Γαῖα' κατὰ [γ]λῶσσαν ἑκάστοις.
    'Δημήτηρ' [δὲ]

10 ὠνομάσθη ὥσπερ ἡ 'Γῆ Μήτηρ,' ἐξ ἀμφο-
    τέρων ἓ[ν] ὄνομα·

they have been separated . . . they [or: it] **dominate** [or: dominates]² **so that . . . now . . .** ³

² The subject of the verb is uncertain.   ³ On the basis of the Derveni author's commentary, Tsantsanoglou reconstructs *exempli gratia* a verse from the Orphic theogony: "Peitho, Harmonia, and Heavenly Aphrodite."

Col. XXII

So he named all things in the same way, as best as he could, knowing the nature of men, viz. that not all of them have a similar one [scil. nature] **nor do all want the same things. When they have power, they say anything that occurs to each one's mind, whatever they happen to want, never the same things, through greed, sometimes also through ignorance. Earth and Mother and Rhea and Hera are one and the same. 'Earth'** (*Gê*) **was given as a name by convention; 'Mother,' because all things are born from her; 'Gê' and 'Gaia,' according to each one's dialect. She was named 'Demeter' just like 'Gê-meter'** [i.e. 'Earth-Mother']: **one name made out of both of them,**

versum compos. e comm. West e.g. μήσατο δ' αὖ Γαῖάν τε καὶ Οὐρανὸν εὐρὺν ὕπερθεν

τὸ αὐτὸ γὰρ ἦν.—ἔστι δὲ καὶ ἐν τοῖς
Ὕμνοις εἰρ[η]μένον·
"Δημήτηρ [ʿΡ]έα Γῆ Μήτηρ Ἑστία
Δηιώι." καλε[ῖτ]αι γὰ[ρ]
καὶ ʿΔηιὼʾ ὅτι ἐδηϊ[ώθ]η ἐν τῆι μείξει· δη-
λώσει δὲ [ὅτ]αν
κατὰ τὰ ἔπη γέν[ηται.] ʿΡέαʾ δʾ ὅτι πολλὰ
καὶ παν[τοῖα]
ζῷα ἔφυ [ἐκρεύσαντα] ἐξ αὐτῆς, ʿΡέαʾ καὶ
ʿ[ʿΡείη]ʾ
κατ[ὰ γλῶσσαν ἑκάστοις. ʿΉ]ρη᾿ δʾ ἐκ[λήθη
ὅτι

— — —

12 cf. Frag. 398 Bernabé   13 [ὅτ]αν Janko, [λί]αν Tsantsanoglou   14 γέν[ητα]ι Janko, γεν[νᾶν] Tsantsanoglou
παν[τοῖα] Tsantsanoglou, πο[ι]κ[ίλα] KPT

Col. XXIII

τοῦτο τὸ ἔπος πα[ρα]γωγὸν πεπόηται καὶ
το[ῖς] μὲν
πολλοῖς ἄδηλόν ἐστιν, τοῖς δὲ ὀρθῶς γινώσκουσιν
εὔδηλον ὅτι Ὠκεανός ἐστιν ὁ ἀήρ, ἀὴρ δὲ
Ζεύς.
οὔκουν "ἐμήσατο" τὸν Ζᾶνα ἕτερος Ζεύς,
ἀλλ᾿ αὐτὸς
αὐτῶι "σθένος μέγα." οἱ δ᾿ οὐ γινώσκοντες
τὸν

for they were the same. And it is said in the *Hymns* too:

"Dêmêtêr Rhêa Gê Mêtêr Hestia Dêiô."[1]

For she is called '*Dêiô*' too, because she was split apart (*edêiôthê*) during the mixture [i.e. the episode mentioned at the beginning of Col. XXI?]. He will show this when in his verses she is born. [Scil. she is called] 'Rhea' because many animals of all kinds were born ⟨by flowing out⟩ of her, 'Rhea' and ⟨'Rheiê'⟩, according to ⟨each one's dialect⟩. And ⟨she was called⟩ 'Hêrê' because . . . [2]

[1] A collection of eighty-seven hymns ascribed to Orpheus and focusing on Dionysus survives; this line is not found in any of them, but the same line is attributed to the Orphic hymns by Philochorus *FGrHist* 328 F185 = Philodemus, *Piet.* P. Herc. 1428 fr. 3 + 248 fr. 2.   [2] On the basis of the Derveni author's commentary, West reconstructs *exempli gratia* a verse from the Orphic theogony: "And he devised in turn Earth and broad Sky on high."

Col. XXIII

This verse has been composed in such a way as to be misleading, and it is unclear to the many, but to those who understand correctly it is quite clear that Ocean is the air and that the air is Zeus. It is not the case that one Zeus "devised" another Zeus, but instead the same one [scil. devised] for himself "great strength" [cf. COSM. T12d.1–2]. But those who do

versum compos. West e comm. e.g. μήσατο δ' Ὠκεανοῖο μέγα σθένος εὐρὺ ῥέοντος, Burkert μήσατο δ' Ὠκεανὸν βαθυδίνην εὐρὺ ῥέοντα

Ὠκεανὸν ποταμὸν δοκοῦσιν εἶναι ὅτι "εὐρὺ
ῥέοντα"

— προσέθηκεν.—ὁ δὲ σημαίνει τὴν αὑτοῦ
γνώμην

ἐν τοῖς λεγομέν[ο]ις καὶ νομιζομένοις
ῥήμασι.

καὶ γὰρ τῶν ἀν[θ]ρώπων τοὺς μέγα δυνα-
τ[οῦ]ντας

10 — "μεγάλους" φασὶ "ῥυῆναι." τὸ δ' ἐχόμενον,

— "ἶνας δ' ἐκατ[έλε]ξ' Ἀχελωΐου ἀργυ[ρ]-
οδίνε[ω."]

τῶ[ι] ὕδα[τι] ὅλ[ως τίθη]σι 'Ἀχελῶιον' ὄνο-
μ[α. ὅ]τι δὲ

τά[σ]δ' ἶνα[ς ἐγκαταλ]έξαι ἐστ[ὶ τάσ]δε
ἐγκατῶ[σ]αι·

τὴν [γ]ὰρ [ca. 10 litt.]των αυ[τ   ]...

15 ἑκασ[τ   ]δε βουλ[

ε.ν[   ]οντε[

——   ——

13 τά[σ]δ' potius quam τά[σ]δε Kouremenos

Col. XXIV

ἴσα ἐστὶν ἐκ τοῦ [μέ]σου μετρούμενα· ὅσα
δ[ὲ μ]ὴ

— κυκλοειδέα οὐχ οἷόν τε ἰσομελῆ εἶναι. δηλοῖ δὲ τόδε·

— "ἢ πολλοῖς φαίνει μερόπεσσι ἐπ'
ἀπείρονα γαῖαν."

not understand think that Ocean is a river because
he added "broadly flowing" [cf. **COSM. T12d.1–2**].
But he indicates his thought in current and custom-
ary expressions. For they say that those who are very
powerful among men "have flowed great." And the
next [scil. verse],

> "He placed in it the sinews of silver-eddying
>   Achelous." [= **COSM. T12d.3**]

He ⟨attribu⟩tes the name 'Achelous' to water in general. And his placing these sinews in it is his having
pushed these down . . . for the . . . each . . . [1]

[1] On the basis of the Derveni author's commentary, West reconstructs *exempli gratia* a verse from the Orphic theogony: "he
devised the great strength of broadly flowing Ocean"; Burkert reconstructs the verse as "he devised Ocean, deep-eddying, broadly
flowing."

Col. XXIV

. . . **they** [i.e. either things that have a circular shape
or those that are "equal-limbed"] **are equal, measured
from the center; but it is not possible that all those
that are not circular be "equal-limbed"** [cf. **COSM.
T12e.1**]. **This is what this** [scil. verse] **shows:**

> "She who shines for many mortals upon the
>   boundless earth." [= **COSM. T12e.2**]

τοῦτο τὸ ἔπος δόξειεν ἄν τις ἄλλως ἐ<ἰ>ρῆ-
σθαι, ὅτι,

5 ἢν ὑπερβάληι, μᾶλλον τὰ ἐόντα φαίνεται ἢ
πρὶν

ὑπερβάλλειν. ὁ δὲ οὐ τοῦτο λέγει, φαίνειν
αὐτήν·

εἰ γὰρ τοῦτο ἔλεγε, οὐκ ἂν "πολλοῖς" ἔφη
φαίνειν αὐτήν,

ἀλλὰ "πᾶσιν" ἅμα τοῖς τε τὴν γῆν ἐργαζο-
μένοις

καὶ τοῖς ναυτιλλομένοις, ὁπότε χρὴ πλεῖν
τούτοις

10 τὴν ὥραν. εἰ γὰρ μὴ ἦν σελήνη, οὐκ ἂν
ἐξηύρ[ι]σκον

οἱ ἄνθρωποι τὸν ἀριθμὸν οὔτε τῶν ὠρέων
οὔτε τῶν

ἀνέμω[ν ca. 8 litt.] καὶ τἆλλα πάντα [ca. 7
litt.]ην

εκ[   ]σα εν[   ]ει
              ].θατω.[   ]ι
15   ]νητουτ.[   ]
              ] ἄλλα ἐόν[τα   ]ς
              ]φηϲ[   ]

— — —

4 ἐ<ἰ>ρῆσθαι Bernabé-Piano mon. Kapsomenos, ἐρῆσθαι
KPT

428

Someone might think that this verse is said in a different sense, namely that if she is at her maximum, the things that exist come to appear more than before she is at her maximum. But he does not say this, namely that she shines; for if this were what he was saying, he would have said that she shines not "for many" but rather "for all," both for those who work the land and for those who sail, when it is necessary that they sail at the right season. For if there were no moon, men would not have discovered the number either of the seasons or of the winds . . . and all the other things . . . other things that exist . . .

Col. XXV

καὶ λαμπρό[τ]ητα· τὰ δ’ ἐξ ὧν ἡ σελήνη
[λ]ευκότατα μὲν
τῶν ἄλλων κατὰ τὸν αὐτὸν λόγον μεμερισμένα,
θερμὰ δ’ οὐκ ἔστι. ἔστι δὲ καὶ ἄλλα νῦν ἐν
τῶι ἀέρι ἑκὰς
ἀλλήλων α[ἰ]ωρούμεν’, ἀλλὰ τῆς μὲν
ἡμέρης ἄδηλ’ ἐστὶν
5   ὑ[π]ὸ τοῦ ἡλίου ἐπικρατούμενα, τῆς δὲ
νυκτὸς ἐόντα
δῆλά ἐστιν, ἐπικρατεῖται δὲ διὰ σμικ[ρ]-
ότητα.
αἰωρεῖται δ’ αὐτῶν ἕκαστα ἐν ἀνάγκηι, ὡς
ἂν μὴ συνίηι
πρὸς ἄλληλα· εἰ γὰρ μή, συνέλθοι ἀλέα
ὅσα τὴν αὐτὴν
δύναμιν ἔχει, ἐξ ὧν ὁ ἥλιος συνεστάθη. τὰ
νῦν ἐόντα
10 ὁ θεὸς εἰ μὴ ἤθελεν εἶναι, οὐκ ἂν ἐπόησεν
ἥλιον. ἐποίησε δὲ
τοιοῦτον καὶ τ[ο]σοῦτον γινόμενον οἷος ἐν
ἀρχῆι τοῦ λόγου
διηγεῖται. τὰ δ’ ἐπὶ τούτοις ἐπίπροσθε
π[ο]ιεῖται
[οὐ β]ου[λό]μενο[ς] πάντας γιν[ώ]σκε[ι]ν. ἐν
δὲ [τ]ῶιδε σημαί[ν]ε[ι·]

Col. XXV

. . . and brightness; but the things out of which the moon is composed, being divided according to the same principle, are the most luminous [or: white] of all, but they are not hot. And there are now too other things floating in the air far from one another; but during the day they are invisible, since they are dominated by the sun, but during the night it is visible that they exist. They are dominated because of their smallness. Each of them floats by necessity, so as not to be united with one another; for otherwise there would have been united in a single mass all the things that have the same property, and of which the sun is composed. If the god had not wished the things that exist now to exist, he would not have made the sun. But he made it of such a sort and of such a size as he [i.e. Orpheus] explains in the beginning of his account. The ones [i.e. verses] that follow these he puts forward [scil. as a screen], since he does not wish all men to understand. He indicates [scil. that] in this one:

---

8 συνέλθοι ⟨ἂν⟩ Burkert

"[αὐτ]ὰρ [ἐ]πεὶ δ[ὴ πάν]τα Διὸ[ς νοῦς μή]σα-
τ[ο ἔ]ργα."

15   ]. φρονησ[
        ]μπηγι̣.[
        ]ων.[

— — —

14 νοῦς Sider, φρὴν Tsantsanoglou
15]. φρονησ[Piano   16]μπηγι̣.[Bernabé-Piano leg.

Col. XXVI

"μη[τρ]ὸς" μὲν ὅτι μήτηρ ὁ Νοῦς ἐστιν τῶν
    ἄλλων,
"ἐᾶς" δὲ ὅτι ἀγαθῆς. δηλοῖ δὲ καὶ ἐν
    τοῖσδε τοῖς ἔπεσιν
ὅτι 'ἀγαθὴν' σημαίνει·
    "Ἑρμῆ Μαιάδος υἱὲ διάκτορε δῶτορ
    ἐάων."
5   δηλοῖ δὲ καὶ ἐν τ[ῶ]ιδε·
    "δοιοὶ γάρ τε πίθοι κατακήαται ἐν Διὸς
    οὔδει
    δώρων, οἷα διδοῦσι, κακῶν, ἕτερος δέ τ'
    ἐάων."
οἱ δὲ τὸ ῥῆμα οὐ γινώσκοντες δοκοῦσιν εἶ-
    ναι
'μητρὸς ἑαυτοῦ.' ὁ δ' εἴπερ ἤθελεν ἑαυτοῦ
    μητρὸς
10 ἐν φιλότητι ἀποδεῖξαι θέλοντα μιχθῆναι
    τὸν

432

"But when Zeus' mind conceived all the deeds"

... thought (?) ...

Col. XXVI

**... "of mother" because Mind is the mother of all
other things; and "of his own"** (*heas,* i.e. also "good")
**because she is good. And he also shows in the follow-
ing words that it** [i.e. the word] **means 'good':**

> **"Hermes Diaktoros, son of Maia, giver of goods
> (*eaôn*)."** [cf. Homer, *Od.* 8.335]

And he also shows it in this one:

> **"For two urns are placed on Zeus' threshold,
> Of gifts such as he gives: of evils** [scil. in the one],
> **and the other one of goods (*eaôn*)."** [Homer, *Il.*
> 24. 527–28, cf. **MOR. T10**]

**Those who do not understand the term think that
it is 'of his own mother.' But if he had wished to
show the god "wishing to unite in love with his own**

---

versum compos. Burkert e comm. e.g. μητρὸς ἑᾶς ἐθέλων
μιχθήμεναι ἐν φιλότητι, West ἤθελε μητρὸς ἑᾶς μιχθήμεναι
ἐν φιλότητι

θεόν, ἐξῆν αὐτῶι γράμματα παρακλίναντα
"μητρὸς ἑοῖο" εἰπε[ῖ]ν. οὕτω γ[ὰ]ρ ἂν ʻἑαυ-
τοῦʼ γίνοιτο,
[υἱὸς δʼ] αὐτῆς ἂν ε[ἴη.....δ]ῆλον ὅτι .[.....]..[ ]
[.....] ἐν τῆι συγ[γ........].ἀμφοτερ[
[......] ἀγαθη.[   ].a..[
[......].ενα. [

— — —

11 παρακλίναντι emend. Janko   textus desinit in Col.
XXVI, nam *agraphon* sequitur

mother," he could have altered the letters and said "of his own (*heoio*) mother." For thus it would have been 'of himself,' and he would be ‹her son› . . . it is clear that . . . in the . . . both . . . good . . . [1]

---

[1] On the basis of the Derveni author's commentary, Burkert and West reconstruct *exempli gratia* a verse from the Orphic theogony: "he wished to be mixed in the love of his mother." At the end of this column, the written text on this papyrus roll ends.